KB105466

무송
김태길 전집

윤리학 개설

Naturalism and Emotivism

보운 김태길 전집

윤리학 개설

Naturalism and Emotivism

철학과 현실사

1970년대 불국사에서

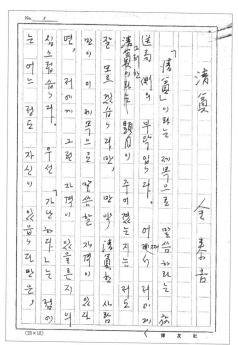

자필 원고

차례

윤리학 개설

Naturalism and Emotivism

윤리학 개설

序

道義의 昂揚을 외치는 사람은 많다. 社會의 頹廢相을 憂慮하는 사람은 더욱 많다. 그러나 오늘날 새로운 世代의 生理에 適合한 處方이 果然 이 땅에 提示되고 있는가는 疑問이다. 외침이나 憂慮가 좀 더 親切하였거나, 참을 수 없어 터져 나온 그것이었다면, 問題의 根本的인 探索이 先行하였음직한 일이요 時代의 變易과 呼吸을 같이하였음직한 일이언마는, 우리에게 있어서 지금 가장 要求되면서도 敬遠되어 있는 것이 다름아닌 倫理의 學的 研究요 疎忽히 되어 있는 것이 이에 關한 새로운 面의 開拓이다. 時急한 만큼 于先 政策이나 信仰의 힘을 빌려 解決을 꾀하는 것도 無妨함직 하되, 知性에 依한 核心의 把握이 缺如되어서는 是非 正邪를 批判할 수 있는 基本的 土臺가 서지 못할 것이요 昏迷의 狀態를 벗어나기 힘들 것이다.

著者는 내가 알기에 多年間 이에 潛心致思하여 오는 少壯學究다. 일찍이 東京大學에서 哲學을 工夫하였고 다시 서울大學 哲學科에서 倫理를 專攻한 俊聰으로서 그 後 꾸준한 研究와 아울러 各 大學에서 젊은 學徒들을 相對로 講義하여 온 오랜 經驗의 結晶이 이제 이 『倫理學槪說』을 낳게 한 것이다.

이 著書에서 著者는 于先 倫理學을 社會相과 關聯시켜 倫理學 自體의 反省

을 促求하였고 다시 그의 根本目標를 追窮하면서 새로운 課題를 提起한다. 그러나 問題를 愼重히 다루기 爲하여 倫理學說의 史的 管見과 道德現象의 本質을 論하여 倫理學의 全貌를 簡明하고 要領있게 敍述한다. 그리고 나서 새로 構想되어야 할 倫理學의 方向을 示唆하며 人間性과 行爲의 世界를 分析하면서 卑近한 具體的 問題를 銳利한 觀察로써 밝히고 있다.

　이러한 意味에서 이 著書는 倫理學槪說의 包括的인 任務를 다하는 同時에 淸新 明快한 論調와 究竟을 剔扶하여 마지 않는 氣魄이 讀者를 이끌어 거듭 생각하게 하고야 말 것이다.

　우리나라가 이제 이러한 新進學究의 좋은 著述을 가지게 된 것을 나는 무엇보다 기뻐하는 同時에 뜻있는 人士, 特히 將來 有爲한 靑年學徒層이 이 著書를 通하여 새로운 힘을 얻기 바라는 바이다.

一九五五年 九月

朴鍾鴻

自序

倫理學이 새로운 方向과 새로운 構想을 가져야 할 것이라고 느낀 것은 이미 오래다. 그러나 새로운 倫理學이 果然 어떠한 方向과 構想을 가져야 한다는 分明한 見解를 얻지 못한 채 近十年이 흘렀다. 社會的 混亂과 個人的 困窮에 責任을 轉嫁하면서 헛되이 歲月을 보냈던 것이다

焦燥한 마음에서 머리 위를 스쳐 가는 漠然한 생각이나마 一旦 종이 위에 記錄해 보고 싶었다. 내가 무엇을 생각하고 있는지 내 自身이 똑똑히 알고 싶었으며 변변치 않은 생각이나마 恩師와 先輩 앞에 펼쳐 놓고 忌憚 없는 鞭撻을 받고 싶었던 것이다. 이리하여 내 自身과 몇몇 분 앞에 個人的으로 내놓기 爲하여 조그마한 試論을 엮어 본 것은 昨年 初春의 일이었다.

그 試論을 읽어 보신 尊敬하는 恩師 한 분이 많은 激勵와 더불어 여러 가지 貴重한 教示를 주었다. 論文展開의 順序를 바꾸어 보라는 것과 初學者도 理解하기 좋도록 '歷史的 考察'을 添加해 보라는 것이 그 中에서도 特히 重要한 暗示였다. 처음에는 엄두가 안 나서 버려 두었다가 數個月 前에 또다시 刺戟받는 바 있어 버려 두었던 것을 다시 뜯어 고쳐 볼 뜻을 세웠다. 이제 質量으로 若干 보탠 바 있다고 생각되는 草稿를 얻고 보니 慾心은 늘어서 이를 世

上에 보내어 初學 여러분께 紹介하는 同時에 널리 先輩와 同學 一般의 批判을 얻고 싶은 생각까지 난 것이다.

序章에서는 오늘날 實踐의 學인 倫理學과 實踐의 世界인 現實社會가 遊離된 듯한 矛盾을 痛感하는 바 있어, 倫理學은 本是 남의 일이 아닌 우리 自身의 問題를 問題 삼는 學問이라는 것, 따라서 우리 時代와 우리 社會의 特殊性을 無視하거나 現實的인 '人間性'을 考慮하지 않은 倫理學은 現代 우리의 倫理學이 될 수 없다는 것을 말하고 싶었다.

第一章에서는 人間이 '絕對'나 '永遠'을 念願하는 것은, 人間性 自體 안에 깊은 뿌리를 둔 現象이라는 것을 指摘함으로써, 近來 往往 들리는 道德의 否定과 倫理學의 無用說에 對抗하고자 하였다. 現代는 過去의 道德과 從來의 倫理學을 否定한다. 그러나 이 否定 自體가 새로운 道德에 對한 要求를 意味하는 것이며, 새로운 倫理學의 課題를 示唆하는 것이다.

第二章에서는 倫理學의 歷史를 一瞥하되, 無數한 學者를 均等하게 다루기보다는 各時代의 一般思潮와 關聯시키면서 各時代에 있어 代表的인 學說을 重點的으로 살피고 싶었다. 그리고 各學說에 對하여 未熟하나마 現代의 立場에서 본 簡略한 批判을 꾀하고, 第四章에서 새로운 倫理學의 方向을 模索하는 伏線을 準備하고자 하였다.

第三章에서는 道德現象이 多樣性과 變遷性을 갖는다는 經驗論의 主張을 肯定하면서, 이 肯定을 心理學的으로 正當化하고자 試圖하였다.

第四章에서는 設令 道德現象이 變遷한다 하더라도 그것이 道德을 無意味하게 하지 않으며 倫理學을 不可能하게 하지 않을 것을 論하고, 道德現象의 主觀性을 肯定하는 새로운 倫理學의 方向과 構想에 關한 試論을 꾀하였다.

처음에는 以上으로 이 小著를 끝마치려고 하였다. 그러나 主로 初學者를 讀者로서 豫想하는 이 槪說이 倫理學의 學的 性格을 論究하는 일에만 힘을 기울이고 倫理學이 問題 삼는 行爲의 主體인 '人間'에 關하여 좀 實質的인 面

을 敍述하는 바가 全혀 없을 수 없다고 생각되어서 끝으로 第五章을 追加하게 되었다.

第五章에서는 먼저 人間을 個人 單位로 다루는 一般心理學이 '人間性'의 形成을 어떻게 記述 乃至 說明하는가를 要略하고 다음에 人間을 集團單位로 다루는 社會科學이 '人間'의 構造를 어떻게 보고 있는가를 簡單히 紹介하고 싶었다. 따라서 여기에서는 獨自性 있는 敍述은 거의 없이 普通들 하는 말을 整理한 데 不過하다. 그러나 '人間存在'라는 宏大한 問題를 좁은 紙面 위에서 섣불리 다루어 보려는 것은 無理한 試圖였으며 淺學과 菲才를 여기서 같이 切實히 느껴 본 적이 없다.

勿論 全卷을 通하여서 著者의 獨自的 創意라고는 別로 없다. 先哲들이 이미 示唆한 바를 著者 스스로가 肯定할 수 있는 路線을 따라 더듬어 본 데 不過하다. 그나마 先哲들의 깊은 哲理에 對한 理解의 淺薄함과 讀書範圍의 狹少함으로 말미암아 誤謬를 犯한 바 적지 않으리라고 두려워한다. 叱正을 바라 마지 않는다.

이 변변치 못한 册 한 卷이 나오는데도 著者는 世上에서 많은 恩惠를 입었다. 特히 公私 多忙하신 가운데 草稿 全篇을 通讀하시고 많은 是正과 깊은 示唆를 베푸신 恩師 朴鍾鴻 敎授와 心理學 方面에 關한 좋은 忠告를 주신 高麗大學校 成百善 敎授께 깊은 謝意를 表한다. 끝으로 未熟한 著作의 出版을 맡아 주신 民衆書館의 여러분을 비롯하여 이 書籍의 刊行을 爲하여 陰陽으로 後援해 주신 여러 先輩와 同僚에게 感謝한다.

檀紀 四二八八年 九月

著者

차례

序章
現代와 倫理學

序章 現代와 倫理學

1. 哲學의 一部門으로서의 倫理學

人生이 '問題'를 包含한 過程이라는 見解에 對하여서 아무도 異見이 없다. 人生이 內包한 問題를, 사람에 따라, 或은 깊이 느끼고 或은 얕이 느끼는 程度의 差異는 있다. 人生의 問題를, 性格에 따라, 或은 正面에서 부딪치고 或은 슬슬 回避하는 態度의 差異는 있다. 그러나 깊건 얕건 間에 問題는 萬人에게 있으며, 잘하든 못하든 間에 萬人은 自己의 問題에 對應하고 있다.

人生이 當하는 問題의 解決을 超越한 他者에게 依賴하는 感性的 態度에서 宗敎가 생겼다면, 自己의 問題를 自己의 힘으로 풀어 보리라는 知性的 態度에서는 科學이 생겼다고 할 것이다. 그러므로 모든 感性的인 사람이 宗敎와 多少間에 因緣을 가졌듯이 모든 知性的인 사람은 깊건 얕건 間에 科學과 關聯을 가졌다. 萬若에 人間이 完全히 感性的이거나 完全히 知性的일 수가 없다면, 卽 人間은 比率의 差異는 있더라도 感性的인 同時에 知性的인 生物이라면, 모든 사람은 宗敎와 科學의 兩者에 多少間 因緣이 있다는 結論이 된다.

英國이 낳은 現代의 偉大한 哲學者 버트런드 러셀(Bertrand Russel)은 그의 著書『西洋哲學史(*A History of Western Philosophy*)』序章 첫머리에 다음과 같이 말하였다. "우리가 '哲學的(philosophical)'이라고 부르는 人生과 世界의 諸概念은 두 가지 要素의 産物이다. 그 要素의 하나는 옛날부터 내려오는 宗敎的 倫理的 觀念이요, 또 하나는 가장 넓은 意味에서 '科學的(scientific)'이라고 부를 수 있는 部類의 探究이다. … 哲學이란 내가 理解하기에는 神學과 科學과의 中間에 位置하는 무엇이다."

러셀이 말하듯이 宗敎와 科學과의 中間에서 哲學이 생겼다면, 그리고 앞서 우리가 말했듯이 모든 사람이 相反하는 두 個의 傾向인 宗敎와 科學에 아울러 關聯이 있다면, 모든 사람은 가장 넓은 意味의 '哲學'과 多少間의 因緣이 있으리라는 推理에 到達한다.

哲學은 人間性 안에 뿌리를 가졌다. 우리 마음속에 일어나는 問題와 苦憫, 우리가 이를 解決하고자 하는 사람다운 態度는, 우리가 그것을 '哲學的'이라고 意識하고 안 하고에 關係없이, 그 自體는, 가장 넓은 意味로 '哲學的'인 것이다. 近來 哲學의 語義가 무척 좁은 意味로 쓰이고, 衒學의 氣質 있는 專門家들이 어려운 術語를 愛用하는 弊風의 影響도 있거니와 大體로 物質主義的인 現代의 思潮는 哲學과 一般大衆과의 間隔을 멀리 떨어뜨렸다. 그러나 오늘날 物質主義는 드디어 自己의 限界를 自學하기 始作한다. 그리고 男女老少 아무하고나 아무데서나 哲學을 對話하던 소크라테스(Socrates)나, 쉬운 말로 깊은 哲理를 敍述한 플라톤(Platon), 아리스토텔레스(Aristoteles)의 態度에 새로운 關心이 깊어 간다. 哲學은 一部 專門家들만의 職業이 아니다. 人生을 하나의 問題라고 생각하는 사람이라면 哲學은 樵童牧夫에게도 남의 일이 아니다

紀元前 六百年頃 希臘에 發生한 以來 오늘날까지 내려오고 있는 哲學의

흐름을, 우리는 크게 두 갈래로 나누어 볼 수가 있다. 그 하나는 存在하는 事實을 있는 그대로 밝히는 知, 卽 '知識(knowledge)'을 目標로 삼는 存在의 學 또는 '理論哲學'이요, 또 하나는 앞으로 實現되어야 할 理想을 價値論의 立場에서 밝히는 知, 卽 '知慧(wisdom)'를 目標로 삼는 當爲의 學 또는 '實踐哲學'이다. 그리고 앞으로 우리가 問題 삼고자 하는 倫理學(ethics)이, 이를 哲學의 一部分으로 본다면, 위에 말한 둘째 方向인 實踐哲學에 該當함은 두말할 것도 없다.

勿論 哲學의 理論的 方面과 實踐的 方面은 相互關聯하여 發達되었으며, 모든 時代 모든 哲學者들은 大槪 이 두 가지 方面을 아울러 살폈다. 그러나 時代에 따라서 哲學의 中心이 理論問題로 기울어진 時代도 있고, 反對로 實踐問題로 기울어진 時代도 있다. 大體로 平和가 持續되어 生活이 安穩하던 時代에는 理論哲學이 盛行하고, 戰亂이 거듭하여 社會相이 險難하던 時代에는 實踐哲學이 發達한 傾向이 있다. 民心이 騷亂하고 道義가 무너진 時代에 도리어 倫理學의 硏究는 깊어 갔던 것이다.

2. 現代의 不安性

現代가 問題 많은 時代, 이를테면 '亂世'라는 見解에 現代人의 意見은 一致하고 있다. 勿論 各 時代人은 大槪 自己네의 時代를 問題 많은 時代라고 느낀다. 各 時代人의 主觀的 見地에서 본다면, 모든 時代는 '危機'에 處해 있고 歷史는 '轉換期'의 連續일는지도 모른다. 그러나 現代人이 現代를 '危機'라고 規定할 때 그것은 單純한 自己中心的 判斷은 아닌 듯하다.

現代는 後世의 史家도 이를 '多難한 時代'로서 規定함에 反對하지 않을 것이다. 現代는 東西洋을 莫論하고 地球上을 통틀어서 無數한 難問題에 逢着하고 있다. 時代가 짊어진 難問題란 國際紛爭이라든지 國內政變 같은 大

書特筆할 '事件'에만 나타나는 것이 아니다. 時代의 問題는 山間僻地에까지 滲透하며 우리네의 하찮은 日常生活 속에서도 그 片鱗은 엿보인다.

오늘날 우리의 日常生活은 確實한 軌道를 잃었다. 오늘날 自己가 하는 일에 對해서 정말 '옳다'는 評價를 내리면서 마음 놓고 處事하는 境遇는 드물다. 入學試驗期에, 또는 兵役問題에 關聯하여 돈을 쓰면서, 그 돈을 쓰는 사람 自身도 世上을 恨嘆하는 것이다. 國家에게 바칠 金錢의 半額을 稅吏에게 주면서 脫稅하는 사람은, '이래서야 나라 꼴이 될 수 있나!' 하고 속으로 自笑한다. 또 自己가 積極的으로 '옳다'고 생각하는 일이 있더라도, 우리는 좀처럼 그 생각을 實踐에까지 옮기지 못한다. '奢侈를 버려야 한다'고 생각한다. '國産品을 愛用함이 옳다'고 생각한다. 그러나 우리는 外來品을 排斥하는 示威運動에 如前히 外來品을 입고 나가는 것이다.

簡單히 말하자면 우리의 生活은 딜레마(dilemma)에 빠져 있다. 우리는 自己가 하는 行爲에 自信이 없다. 우리는 自己가 하는 行爲를 좋지 못하다고 생각한다. 그러나 이 '좋지 못하다'는 생각은 '絕對로 不當하다'는 信念에까지는 到達하지 않았다. 우리는 自己의 行爲에 絕對로 옳다고 自信하지도 못하며 그러나 絕對로 不當하다는 斷定도 내리지 못하는 것이다. 可否間에 徹底한 信念이 없기 때문에 우리의 行爲는 '그저 適當히'를 標語로 삼는 曖昧한 路線을 彷徨한다. 우리에게는 '이 길은 옳고 저 길은 그르다'는 確固한 信念이 없기 때문에, 그때그때의 氣分에 左右되고, 어제 한 行爲와 오늘 하는 行爲 사이에 一貫性이 없으며, 理論과 實踐 사이에 矛盾이 생긴다. 이리하여 우리의 生活에는 躊躇와 後悔 그리고 不安이 떠나지 않는다.

個人의 日常生活에 나타난 이와 같은 不安은 勿論 世界史的 全體의 不安의 局所的인 反映이다. 1914年 以來 우리가 經驗한 것은 戰爭의 反復이었다. 間或 있는 平和는 暫定的이었고 皮相的이었다. 二十世紀에 들어와서의 우리나라의 事情은 唯獨 不幸하였다. 日本에게 合邦을 當한 것은 1910年

이었고 三十八度線을 境界로 南北이 兩斷된 것은 1945年의 일이었다.

　萬若 現代가 不安과 動亂의 世紀라면, 그리고 動亂時代의 哲學이 實踐方面으로 關心을 集中시키는 것이 通則이라면 現代는 倫理學이 매우 널리 論議되어야 할 時代이다. 그러면 오늘날의 倫理學은 果然 現代思想界에서 中樞的 活動을 하고 있는가. 現代는 混亂된 精神生活의 再建을 倫理學에 期待하고 있는가.

3. 現代社會와 倫理學과의 遊離

　倫理學은 實踐問題에 關한 가장 根本的인 原理의 解明을 目標로 삼는다. 實踐의 學으로서의 倫理學은, 現實 속에서 그 問題를 發見해야 할 것이며, 現實 속에서 그 解決의 端緒를 探求해야 할 것이다. 問題의 深刻性이 根源的 解決을 要請하는 現代에 있어서, 倫理學은 가장 좋은 意味로 '現實的'이어야 할 것이며, 實踐의 世界인 現實社會와 가장 密接히 連結되어 있어야 할 것이다. 그러나 實際에 있어서는 오늘날 우리 社會에서 倫理學보다 더 時代와 遊離되고 社會에서 忘却된 學問이 드물다. 倫理學者는 象牙塔 속의 深遠한 哲理에는 밝으나 京鄕의 俗事에는 大體로 어둡다. 常識은 倫理學을 '高等修身'의 同義語로 생각하고, 巷間에서는 倫理學者를 僧侶의 族屬이 아니면 陳腐한 道學者로서 敬遠한다. 巷間에서의 이와 같은 見解는 이를테면 認識의 不足으로 돌리고 默過할 수도 있다. 그러나 識者層이나 一般學界에서까지도 倫理學에 對하여 否定的인 態度를 取하는 傾向이 있음에 이르러서는, 깊이 省察할 問題가 있다고 생각된다. 오늘날 科學者들의 倫理學에 對한 見解는 크게 두 種類로 나누어진다. 하나는 倫理學이 '學 (science)'으로서 成立할 수 없다는 理論的인 否定이요, 또 하나는 倫理學이 現實社會를 움직일 만한 力量이 없으니 無用하다는 實踐的인 攻擊이다.

우리는 前者의 例를 흔히 自然科學者의 입에서 듣고 後者의 例를 흔히 社會科學者의 意見에서 본다. 倫理學에 對하여 가장 理解가 깊다고 생각되는 狹義의 哲學者들까지도 倫理學을 名譽롭지 못한 庶子처럼 보는 傾向이 있다. 慘憺한 現實에 直面하고 世界史的인 危機를 呼吸하면서 자라나는 現代의 哲學은, 內實에 있어서 純粹한 理論問題보다도 切迫한 實踐問題에 對하여 더욱 關心이 깊다. 그러나 現代의 哲學者들은 자기네의 研究에 '生의 哲學', '歷史哲學' 等의 이름을 붙여서 從來의 倫理學과는 區別되기를 願한다.

한편 倫理學者 側에서는 自身이 받는 冷待의 責任을 社會一般의 道義心의 低落과 '深遠한 哲理'에 對한 大衆의 無知에 돌리고, 스스로는 超然히 慨嘆함으로써 自足한다. 이와 같은 獨善的 態度는 倫理學과 社會一般과의 離間을 더욱 助長할 뿐이다. 하나의 惡循環이 倫理學과 現實社會와의 間隔을 漸漸 넓히고 倫理學者는 後堂으로 물러앉아 實踐性 없는 實踐의 學을 獨白으로 消日한다.

實踐의 學인 倫理學과 實踐의 世界인 現實社會가 이토록 遊離됨에는 반드시 여러 가지 事情이 關聯되고 있을 것이다. 倫理學을 非難하는 側의 理解의 不足도 있을 것이요, 倫理學에 從事하는 專門家들의 責任도 있을 것이다. 우리는 오늘날 倫理學을 에워싸고 展開되는 論難의 代表的인 것을 두어 가지 檢討해 보기로 한다.

4. 倫理學의 反省

倫理學이 學으로서 成立할 수 없다는 純理論的 問題에 對해서는 後章에서 좀 더 詳細히 考察하기로 하고 여기서는 主로 實踐的인 論難에 對해서 次例로 살펴보기로 한다.

倫理學의 無用을 主張하는 見解에 于先 다음과 같은 것이 있다. 現代가 가진 精神生活의 混亂의 根本原因은 物質生活의 不安定에 있다. 따라서 現代의 不安은 그 不安의 根源인 經濟事態를 改善함으로써만 根本的 解消를 볼 수 있을 것이요, 精神의 秩序를 云謂하는 倫理學等屬은 無用한 閑事이다. 이 見解에는 半分의 正當性이 있다. 論者가 主張하듯이 精神生活이 物質生活의 制約을 받는다는 것, 따라서 精神生活의 安定을 爲하여서 物質生活의 安定이 要求된다는 것은 오늘날 도리어 平凡한 常識이다. 孟子도 이미 "無恒産者는 無恒心"이라 하였고, 管子도 "倉廩이 實則 知禮節"이라고 하였다. 精神生活을 偏重했던 옛 時代도 이같이 말했거늘, 하물며 物質의 意義가 一層 深刻하게 느껴지는 現代에 있어서랴. 오늘날 아무도 經濟生活 改善의 時急性을 否認하지 않을 것이다.

그러나 現代의 不幸이 오로지 '物質'에만 基因하는 것일까? 萬若 人間의 幸不幸이 오로지 物質로만 決定되는 것이라면, 그리고 現代가 世人이 말하듯이 '가장 不幸한 世紀'라면, 現代는 歷史上에서 가장 物質이 缺乏한 時代라는 結論이 된다. 그러나 事實은 도리어 그 反對에 가깝다. 人間이 物質을 左右하는 能力이 오늘같이 强大한 時代는 過去에 없었다. 現代는 有史以來로 物資가 가장 豊富한 時代이다. 科學을 驅使하는 人間의 生産力은 人口의 增加보다도 빠른 速度로 增進되고 있다.

러셀도 指摘한 바와 같이, 現代의 不幸은 物質 自體의 缺乏에서 오는 것이 아니라, 物質을 使用하는 人間 自身의 精神的 貧困에서 오는 것이다. 自然을 征服하는 人間의 知力은 놀라운 發展을 이루었으나, 欲望과 感情에 움직이는 人間의 心情은 太古적 狀態를 멀리 벗어나지 못하고 있다. 오늘도 우리는 原始人처럼 이웃사람을 미워하고 샘내고 두려워한다. 깊은 敎養이 있다는 사람들까지도 남의 어깨를 밟고 올라서려고 하며, 남의 成功이 나의 失敗를 意味하는 듯한 錯覺에 사로잡힌다. 憎惡, 嫉妬와 恐怖, 그리고

勢力 다툼은 個人에게만 있는 것이 아니라 團體가 커갈수록 더욱 甚해진다. 오늘날 國內的으로는 政黨 싸움보다 더 活潑한 것이 없으며, 國際的으로는 戰爭보다 더 큰 關心事가 없다. 世界의 어떠한 個人도 戰爭을 願한다는 사람은 없음에도 不拘하고, 여러 强大國은 生産力의 大部分을 武器生産에 기울이고 歲入의 大部分을 國防費로서 支出하지 않으면 아니 될 矛盾에 빠지고 있다.

이 時代의 問題에는, 政策變更, 法律改正, 經濟機構의 改革 또는 國際條約의 更新 等 技術的 改革만으로는 미처 解決할 수 없는 根源性이 있다. 人類가 이 危機에 自滅하지 않기 爲하여서는 物質面의 改革뿐만 아니라 物資를 生産, 分配, 使用하는 人間의 心情 自體에도 새로운 秩序를 가질 必要가 있다. 마음의 새로운 秩序는 一時的인 氣分이나 興奮으로 이루어지지는 않을 것이다. 거기에는 깊은 原理와 不動하는 信念 그리고 整然한 論理가 있어야 한다. 이 같은 原理와 信念과 論理를 우리는 哲學에 求하는 것이며 實踐에 關한 哲學을 우리는 '倫理學'으로서 理解하는 것이다.

倫理學에 對한 더 一般的인 論難은, 倫理學이 가리키는 바는 理想으로서는 좋으나 現實生活을 이끌어 나갈 만한 力量이 없다는 것이다. 이 非難에 對하여서는 倫理學 自身이 많이 反省해야 할 點이 있다. 從來의 倫理說은 或은 人間의 理想을 '幸福', '完全', '自我의 實現' 等으로 規定하고, 또는 行爲가 依據할 普遍的인 法則을 '神意', '良心', '實踐理性' 等의 이름으로 밝혔다. 그러나 이와 같이 漠然한 槪念들을 原理로 삼는 倫理說들은, 抽象的으로 생각할 때에는 정말 그럴듯하나 막상 이를 우리 現實生活에 適用하여 어떤 具體的인 目標를 定하고자 한다든지 또는 定한 目標를 實現하기 爲한 現實的인 方案을 發見하고자 할 때에는 恒常 그 無力이 暴露되는 것이다. 아리스토텔레스의 幸福說, 플라톤의 解脫說, 中世紀의 基督教的 倫理觀, 칸트(I. Kant)의 形式說, 벤담(J. Bentham)의 功利說, 其他 어떠한

有名한 倫理說을 가지고 오더라도, 戰爭과 貧困과 그리고 虛無感에 시달리고 있는 現代人에 對하여 무슨 實質的으로 신통한 解決의 端緒를 示唆해 줄 것 같지는 않다. 倫理學者들은 듣기에 아름다운 '行爲의 法則'을 많이 세웠다. 그러나 그 法則이 지나치게 아름다웠던 關係로, 社會 全體를 輔導하는 力量은 姑捨하고 自己 個人도 實踐 못할 空論이 되곤 하였다.

傳統的 倫理說의 이 같은 實踐的 缺陷은 勿論 그 理論的 缺陷의 反映이다. 長久한 歷史를 通하여 形形色色으로 發展한 諸倫理說의 理論的 弱點을 一括하여 論하기는 困難한 일이다. 그러나 우리는 하나의 共通的인 根本缺陷을 指摘할 수가 있다. 그것은 傳統的인 倫理說이 現代 우리 自身의 切實한 要求에 立脚하지 못했다는 事實이다.

傳統的 倫理說이 가장 腐心한 것은 行爲規範에 있어서의 '普遍性'의 發見이다. 學者들은 倫理學의 基本課題는 東西古今을 通하여 普遍的으로 妥當한 絶對的 道德을 提示함이라고 믿었다. 그들은 自己네의 道德律에 普遍性과 絶對性을 賦與하기 爲하여 絶對普遍的인 意志의 存在가 必要하였다. 그러나 經驗의 世界는 좀처럼 이 必要한 것을 提供하지 않는다. 이에 남은 길은 오직 超經驗的 學問 卽 形而上學(Metaphysics)을 動員하는 길뿐이다. 이리하여 그들은 普遍意志의 主體를 或은 神, 佛, 天 等 外在하는 超越者에 求하고, 或은 先天的 良心, 純粹實踐理性 等 人間 內部에 求하였다. 論證의 對象이 될 수 없는바 이들 形而上學的 諸槪念의 是非를 論究하는 것은 이 자리에서의 우리의 課題가 아니다. 오직 한 가지 決定的인 事實을 指摘함으로써 煩瑣한 論議에 代身하기로 한다. 그 事實이란 神, 天, 佛 같은 超越者는 말할 것도 없거니와, 人間에 內在한다는 先天的 良心 또는 純粹實踐理性의 命令에 依據했다는 道德律도 오늘날 우리 自身의 가장 內面的인 要求와 符合되지 않는 點이 있다는 것이다. 現代 우리 良心의 要求는 孔孟時代 中國人의 良心의 要求와 반드시 一致하는 것은 아니다. 우리 自

身의 理性의 命令은 十八世紀 歐洲人의 理想을 反映한 칸트의 純粹理性의 命令과 어긋나는 바 없지 않다. 孔孟이나 칸트의 倫理思想에 現代人의 生活을 實質的으로 輔導할 力量이 없다면, 그것은 그들의 敎示하는 바가 우리의 皮相的인 衝動과, 그뿐만 아니라 우리들의 가장 深奧한 要求와도 背馳되는 點이 있다는 證左이다.

그러나 過去의 倫理學이 現代에 있어서 實踐力이 薄弱하다는 事實은 반드시 그 倫理說이 過去에도 無力했다는 것을 意味하지 아니하며, 將次 새로이 構想될 어떠한 種類의 倫理學도 必然的으로 '非實踐的'이 될 수밖에 없다는 것을 意味하지도 않는다. 그것은 오직 現代의 倫理學이 現代의 立場에서 다시 檢討되어야 할 것을 要求할 뿐이다.

우리의 實踐規範은 우리 自身의 切實한 要求에 立脚해야 할 것이다. 神佛이 아닌 人間의 道德律은 거짓 없는 人間性의 要求에 忠實하기를 要請한다. 人間의 道德律에는 人間의 '靈'만이 아니라 그 '肉'도 反映되어야 한다. 現代의 倫理學에는 現代의 時代精神이 反映되어야 하며, 우리나라의 倫理說에는 우리나라의 特殊事情이 考慮되어야 한다. 우리 時代, 우리 國家, 그리고 우리 自身의 切實한 要求를 離脫한 道德은 우리들에게는 他律的이요, 따라서 實踐을 强要할 根據를 갖지 않는다. 現代는 現代의 立場에서 본 自律의 道德을 要望한다. 自律의 道德만이 오직 '實踐的'이다.

倫理學의 無用을 主張하는 좀 色다른 것으로서 '絶望'이 있다. 世上은 이미 末世에 達하였고 人心은 벌써 極度로 腐敗했는데, 이제 '倫理'니 '道德'이니 하고 외쳐 본들 무슨 所用이 있느냐는 것이다. 오늘의 現實은 너무나 絶望的이기 때문에, 아무리 훌륭한 哲理도 이를 돌이켜 세울 才幹이 없다는 斷念이다. 이와 같은 自暴自棄는 自己네의 無軌道한 生活에 對한 辨明이기도 하다.

그러나 人生은 于先 살고 보아야 할 것이다. '絶望' 自體가 人生에 對한

愛着의 反動이요 '斷念' 自體가 一種의 選擇이다. 現在 우리가 이렇게 살고 있다는 事態 自體가 生物로서의 愛着과 價値判斷으로서의 選擇을 包含하는 것이다. 愛着과 選擇이 已往에 生의 制約이라면 우리는 좀 더 勇敢하게 愛着하고 좀 더 合理的으로 選擇하는 것이 마땅할 것이다.

니체(F. Nietzsche)의 눈물겨운 말 "네 運命을 사랑하라(Amor fati)."는 우리에게 恒常 새로운 敎訓이다. 주어진 運命에 順應하면서 스스로 가장 아름답다고 믿는 길로 살아가 보자는 생각 — 이것은 現代의 知性에게 許諾된 마지막 信仰일는지도 모른다.

우리는 우리 自身의 '生'에 無關心할 수가 없다. 우리는 우리 時代와 우리 國家를 對岸火視할 수는 없다. 우리는 우리의 生이 確乎한 信念 위에서 展開되기를 念願한다. 우리는 우리 時代와 우리 國家에 合理的인 指導原理가 支配하기를 希望한다. 오늘날 倫理學은 確乎한 信念과 指導原理를 現實 속에서 찾아 보려는 人間的인 努力이다. 倫理學은 一部 專門家의 職業이 아니라 나의 問題를 問題 삼는 내 自身의 일이다.

一章
倫理學의 課題

一章 倫理學의 課題

1. 倫理學의 目標

倫理學은 行爲의 價値를 그 根源에 있어 硏究하는 '規範의 學'이다. 알기 쉽게 말하자면 '우리는 어떻게 行爲할 것인가' 또는 '우리는 어떻게 살 것인가' 이러한 問題를 바닥까지 파고들어 解明하고자 하는 것이 倫理學을 하는 사람의 基本的인 動機라고 하겠다. 그러므로 人間의 지킬바 道德을 說敎하는 道學者나 宗敎家의 事業과 倫理學은 密接한 關聯性을 갖는다. 그러나 倫理學은 道學者나 宗敎家가 가리키는 바를 無批判하게 받아들이지는 않는다. 도리어 道學者나 宗敎家가 主張하는 바에 疑惑을 품고, 그 主張의 妥當根據를 追窮한다. 여기에 倫理學이 修身이나 公民과 正反對되는 方向이 있다. 또 倫理學은 道學者나 宗敎家가 말하는 좁은 意味의 '道德', 卽 '義務로서의 道德'만을 硏究對象으로 삼는 것이 아니라, 藝術, 經濟 等까지도 包含한 實踐問題 全般에 걸쳐서 그 原則을 究明하고자 한다. 이 點에 있어서도 '正直'이니 '博愛'니 하고 德目의 解說을 일삼는 修身과는 많이 다른 것이 있다.

倫理學은 '착한 行爲' 또는 '옳은 行爲' 等의 準則을 發見하고자 한다. 一定한 行爲가 現實社會 안에서 받는 評價에는 區區한 矛盾이 內包되고 있다. 다시 말하면 同一한 行爲에 對하여서도 그것을 評價하는 主觀的 立場의 差異에 따라서 여러 가지로 서로 다른 判斷이 내려지는 것이 現實로서의 道德現象이다. 倫理學은 이와 같이 雜多한 道德現象을 批判하고 行爲評價에 있어 絶對로 妥當한 原理를 發見함으로써 그 根本使命으로 삼는다. 倫理學이 이와 같이 行爲評價에 關한 絶對的 原理를 發見하고자 하는 그 根柢에는 하나의 前提가 있다. 그것은 人間의 行爲에는 반드시 '善惡' 또는 '是非'의 絶對的인 區別이 嚴然히 있다는 信念이다. 다시 말하면 一定한 事態에 處한 사람의 行爲는, 이래도 좋고 저래도 좋은 것이 아니라, 반드시 이래야 하고 저래서는 안 된다는 區別이 있다는 信念이다. 是非善惡의 絶對性에 對한 이 信念은 어떤 經驗的 事實에 依하여 科學的으로 論證된 原理는 아니다. 是非善惡이 絶對性을 갖는가 안 갖는가 하는 問題는 追後에 論及하기로 하고, 여기서는 行爲의 世界에 있어서 絶對性 있는 價値의 規準을 얻고자 하는 것은 人間性 自體 안에 깊이 뿌리 박은 必然的 要求라는 事實을 論及함으로써, 倫理學의 課題의 性質을 밝히는 도움으로 삼고자 한다.

2. '絶對'에 對한 念願

人間性은 習慣을 通하여 形成된다. 그리고 習慣은 그 本質에 있어서 現狀을 維持하려는 傾向性이다. 그러므로 人間性의 根柢에는 現狀을 維持하고자 하는 强한 欲求가 支配하고 있다. 現狀維持에 對한 欲求를 基盤으로 삼는 人間性에 있어서, 가장 굳센 것은 生命에 對한 愛着이요, 가장 切實한 것은 永生에 對한 念願이다.

사람은 누구나 自己의 生命을 아끼고 自己의 生命이 永遠할 것을 願한다. 微賤하고 貧困한 사람들까지도 生에 愛着함은 一般的 傾向이거니와, 特히 不幸의 고비를 넘어 現世를 背反한 사람들이 來世 안에 永生의 樂土를 建設하려 한 宗敎的 態度도, 亦是 現狀持續을 念願하는 基本欲求의 變態的 發露에 不過하다. 더욱이 富貴와 榮華를 누린 사람들에 있어서는, 生에 對한 愛着이 더 正常的으로 더 率直하게 發現될 理由가 있었다.

勿論, 現狀의 持續을 希求하는 基本欲求가 作用하는 反面에, 現狀의 打破를 指向하는 正反對의 欲求가 恒常 머리를 들고 있다는 事實을 看過할 수는 없다. 그러나 묵은 現狀을 打破하고 새로운 것을 얻고자 하는 改新의 欲求도 그 根本을 캐어 보면 現狀을 維持하고자 하는 基本欲求에 歸一함을 본다. 自然界에 流轉이 멈추지 않고 人間界에 變動이 그칠 사이 없으므로, 옛 慣習 또는 옛 制度가, 그리고 모든 옛 狀態가, 恒常 發展하는 새로운 事態에 언제까지나 適合할 수는 없다. 過去에는 '生存'이라는 基本欲求를 滿足시키기 爲하여 必要하였던 옛 慣習 또는 옛 制度가, 時日이 가면 生存에 不利한 妨害物이 되기도 한다. 이때 生存이라는 基本狀態를 지키기 爲하여서 過去에는 아끼고 지켜 오던 옛것에 對한 改革이 스스로 要求되지 않을 수 없다. 옛것을 무너뜨리고자 하는 運動은, 一見 現狀을 持續하려는 欲求와 矛盾되는 別個의 欲求에 基因되는 듯하나, 그 根本은 自我의 生命을 維持하려는 基本欲求에 있으니, 亦是 現狀을 持續하고자 하는 根本原理에 一致하는 것이다.

옛것을 지키고자 하는 欲求와 옛것을 깨뜨리고자 하는 欲求와의 對立은 經濟, 政治, 法律 等을 둘러싸는 一般社會問題에 있어서 매우 뚜렷하게 나타난다. 옛 慣習이나 옛 制度에 關聯되는 利害關係는 各界各層에 一率的으로 均等하지가 않다. 一部 人士들에게는 時急한 革新이 要請되는 어떤 制度나 慣習이, 다른 一部 人士들에게는 如前히 利益을 意味하는 것이 普通

이다. 이리하여 各各 그 利害關係에 따라서, 또는 利害關係에서 派生되는 觀念的 象徵에 따라서, 또는 利害關係를 둘러싸는 群衆心理에 따라서, 어떤 이는 保守의 陣營에 서고 다른 어떤 이는 急進의 立場으로 기울어지는 暗鬪와 決戰이, 歷史上에 許多한 不幸을 招來했고 또 한편 文化發展에 不朽의 功獻을 남겼다.

그러나 비록 男女老少, 富貴貧賤 等의 社會的 立場의 差異에 따라, 다시 말하면 利害關係의 差異에 따라서, 社會問題를 둘러싸고 或은 더 保守로 기울어지고 或은 더 改新으로 기울지는 程度의 差異는 있을지라도, 이것은 自我生命의 持續을 꾀하는 方法에 關한 態度의 差異에 不過한 것이요, 萬人은 모두가 自我生命의 永續을 願한다는 根本欲求에 있어서 一致하였다. 그리고 萬人은, 永生의 宿願에도 不抱하고 다 같이 죽음을 免치 못했다는 點에 있어서, 또는 親愛하는 家族이나 同僚들과 離別하지 않을 수 없었다는 點에 있어서, 大體로는 共通된 運命下에 사는 '有限者'였다. 그러므로 卑賤한 사람은 卑賤한 사람대로, 더 나은 生을 彼岸에 憧憬할 理由가 있었으며, 高貴한 사람은 高貴한 사람대로, 永生과 常住의 新天地를 來世에 希求하지 않을 수 없는 動機가 있었다. 來世를 約束하는 宗敎가 東洋에서도 西洋에서도 數千年의 歷史를 이어서 繁昌한 것은 決코 偶然한 事實이 아니다.

永生의 念願은 無限한 自己同一性에 對한 欲望이다. 生命에 있어서 無限한 自己同一性을 欲望하는 人間의 心情은, 事物一般에 關하여서도 無限한 自己同一性을 希求한다. 卽 모든 것에 있어서 '絕對(absolutness)'를 念願한다. 自我生命의 永劫持續을 願한 같은 마음이, 永遠히 變節 없는 사랑을 求했으며, 또 같은 마음이 變化無常한 現象背後에 變化 없는 絕對的 存在 — '原質(arche)' 또는 '實體(substance)' — 를 探求하였다. 萬事에 있어서 絕對를 希求하는 마음은 自我生命의 永劫持續, 卽 永生을 念願하는 마

음의 延長이다.

　永遠 乃至 絶對를 人間 밖에 있는 超越者에게 求했을 때, '宗敎'가 成立
하였다. 이와 反對로 人間 內部에 그것을 求했을 때, '道德'이 人生의 中心
問題가 되었다. 人格 內部에 絶對를 實現하려면 그것은 '絶對로 옳게 行爲
함'을 通하여서만 可能할 것이기 때문이다. 宗敎와 道德은 人間이 永遠을
希求해 온 두 갈래의 重要한 通路이다. 人間이 絶對를 希求해 온 또 하나의
通路, 即 '藝術'은, 人間이 理想으로 삼는바 善美한 것을 假像의 世界 안에
實現시켜 본 것이다. 眞正한 藝術은 넓은 意味로 道德的이요, 참된 道德은
넓은 意味로 藝術的이다.

3. 道德과 '絶對에 對한 念願'

　絶對를 念願하는 人間理性의 一般的 傾向은, 特히 道德問題에 關하여서
一層 顯著하게 나타난다. 道德的 行爲란 가장 善하고 가장 正當하다고 認
定된 行爲다. 自身에 있어서 가장 善하고 가장 正當하다고 認定되는 行爲
를, 他人에 있어서도 가장 善하고 正當하다고 믿으려는 傾向은, 絶對 乃至
普遍을 希求하는 人間理性의 一般的 傾向의 片貌이다. 同一한 傾向은, 現
在에 妥當한 行爲가 먼 將來에까지도 永遠히 妥當하기를 願한다.

　絶對를 念願하는 人間의 一般的 傾向이, 特히 道德에 關하여 顯著하게
나타나게 된 하나의 契機는, 原始人의 思辨이 行爲의 價値와 後日의 果報
와를 神秘롭게 連結시키는 宗敎的 傾向, 即 因果應報의 思想에 찾아볼 수
가 있을 것이다. 行爲와 現世에서 當하는 禍福과의 사이에 烏飛梨落格의
因果關係를 想定하고, 여러 가지 禁制(taboo)를 案出한 原始部族의 慣習
에는 이미 超越者를 前提하는 宗敎思想의 萌芽가 깃들여 있다. 그것은 禁
制가 어떤 魔力에 對한 迷信을 基盤으로 하는 것이며, 이 魔力에 對한 迷信

은 將次 超越者에 對한 信仰으로 發展할 可能性을 숨기고 있기 때문이다.

苛酷한 現實에 시달린 人間이, 人間의 힘으로는 現世 안에서 極樂을 實現할 可能性이 없다고 斷念하게 되자, 그들은 人間의 無力과 有限性을 自認한 나머지 全知全能한 超越者 乃至 絶對者에게 歸依하지 않을 수 없었으며, 來世의 至福에 期待하지 않을 수 없었다. 그러나 絶對者의 救援은 無條件하고 萬人에게 고루 施與될 理가 없다. 現世에서의 善美한 行爲만이 來世에 있어서 善美한 果報를 招來하는 原因이 될 것이다. 그러나 그 善美한 行爲라는 것은 絶對者의 眼目이 善美하다고 認定하는 行爲, 따라서 人間의 主觀的 意見에 달린 相對的 善行이 아니라 客觀的 標準에 依한 絶對的 善行이 아니면 아니 된다. 歷史上에 長久한 生命을 維持한 宗敎의 大部分이 絶對善을 標榜하는 道德的 戒銘을 崇尙하고 있다는 事實은 決코 偶然한 일이 아니다.

現實社會에서 主導權을 掌握한 政治勢力도 道德의 絶對化에 寄與한 契機의 하나이다. 政權은 恒常 그 本質에 있어서 保守的이다. 그리고 秩序維持는 그 內政에 關한 主要 使命이다. 모든 社會에 있어서 主潮를 이룬 道德思想은, 恒常 그 社會를 다스리는 政權이 秩序維持의 根幹으로 삼는바 '法律'의 基盤이 되었으며, 또 法律만으로는 다하지 못하는 分野를 補充擔當하는 任務를 맡아 왔다. 政權이, 不斷히 展開되는 新事態에 適應하기 爲하여, 慣習이나 制度의 一部를 自進하여 改革하는 境遇도 적지 않다. 그러나 政權이 自進하여 行하는 改革運動은 스스로 限界가 있으며, 그 社會의 秩序와 治安의 基盤이 되는 根本的 道德觀念에까지 미칠 수는 없다. 그것은 改革이라기보다는 바로 '革命'을 意味하기 때문이다. 또 비록 傳統的 道德觀念의 全面的 破棄를 主張하던 革命勢力일지라도, 一旦 革命이 成事된 다음에는 自己네의 뜻에 맞는 새로운 制度와 秩序를 反映하는 '新道德'을 絶對化하는 方向으로 기울어지기는 每樣 一般이다.

認識을 指向하는 人間의 意欲도 決코 相對的 知識에 滿足하지 않는다. 哲學이란 元來 絕對知의 探求를 試圖하는 모든 努力의 總稱이었다. 이 絕對知에 對한 要求는 일찍부터 哲學의 中心問題가 된 道德問題에 關하여서도 當然히 發露되었으니, 大體로 道德을 絕對視하는 一般的 傾向을 理論을 부쳐 正當化하는 任務를 맡아 보았다. 이리하여 道德律을 絕對化하고자 하는 傾向은, 永生을 渴望하는 宗敎에 依해서도, 現實社會의 方向을 左右하는 政治에 依해서도, 그리고 絕對知를 探求하는 學問에 依해서도 다같이 擁護되고 助長되어 왔다.

4. 道德에 對한 懷疑와 새로운 倫理學의 課題

그러나 現代에 있어서 한 가지 注目할 現象은, 從來 우리 生活感情 속에 깊이 滲透했던 이 '道德의 絕對性'에 對하여, 매우 深刻한 懷疑가 擡頭하고 있다는 事實이다. 바야흐로 道德을 相對視하는 見解가 새로운 常識으로서 登場하고 있다. 勿論 道德相對論은 近來 처음 생긴 思想은 아니다. 이것은 멀리 프로타고라스(Protagoras, 480-411 B.C.)에 淵源을 가졌으며, 近世初에 있어서도 英國 經驗論의 影響 아래 活氣를 띤 일이 있다. 그러나 이 思想이 現代에 있어서와 같이 우리 生活感情 속에 깊이 滲透한 일은 일찍이 없었다. 더욱이 오늘날의 道德相對論에는 民俗學, 社會學, 心理學, 生物學 等 人間을 對象으로 삼는 自然科學들이 經驗的 根據를 提供하고 있는 것이다. 道德相對論은 現代思潮의 重要한 一側面이다.

道德相對論의 立論根據나 그 是非에 關한 考察은 後章으로 미루기로 한다. 여기서 우리가 論及해 두고자 하는 바는, 設令 從來의 形而上學的 倫理說의 絕對論이 그 威信을 잃고 從來의 宗敎나 哲學이 提示한바 永遠 乃至 絕對의 原理를 하나의 偶像으로서 打倒함에 모든 사람이 一致한다 치더라도 永遠이나 絶對를 希求하는 人間의 本性 自體는 抹殺되지 않으리라는 것이다. 永遠이나 絶對를 希求함은, 習慣을 通하여 形成된 人間性의 本質이다. 過去의 歷史가 남긴 絶對나 永遠의 原理에 不合理한 點이 發見되어 그 原理가 廢棄되는 바로 그 瞬間부터, 人間은 새로운 絶對, 새로운 永遠을 찾아서 헤매기 始作한다. 現代의 知性이 道德의 變遷을 主張하고 傳統的 道德律의 絶對性을 否認한다 하더라도, 그것으로써 生活의 規準 即 行爲가 絶對로 安心하고 依據할 수 있는 標尺을 希求하는 人間의 基本要求를 抹殺할 수는 없다. 묵은 것의 否定은 이미 새로운 것의 肯定을 豫想한다.

永遠과 絶對를 念願함은 人間性에 있어서 本質的인 것에 屬한다. 行爲에 있어서도 絶對的으로 善美한 것을 希求함은 옛날이나 오늘이나 다를 바가 없다. 行爲評價에 關한 絶對的 規準을 發見하고자 하는 基本動機에 있어서, 倫理學의 課題는 恒常 如一하다. 다만, 무엇에 부쳐서 絶對나 永遠을 求하는가는 時代에 따라서 變遷이 있다. 이 時代的 變遷에 따라서 倫理學의 課題에도 스스로 方向의 變遷이 생긴다. 現代倫理學의 課題는 現代人의 知性이 肯定하는바 行爲評價의 準尺을 發見하는 일이다. 다시 말하면 우리의 生命이 納得할 수 있는바 生活의 不動하는 中心을 發見하는 일이다. 우리의 이 問題를 直接 다루기 前에, 文化의 歷史가 絶對나 永遠을 把握하고자 하는 人類의 宿題를 둘러싸고 어떻게 模索해 왔는가, 그 足跡을 簡略하게 더듬어 보는 것이 좋을 것이다.

二章
倫理學說에 關한 史的 管見

二章 倫理學說에 關한 史的管見

1. 古代 希臘의 倫理學說

1) 소크라테스 以前

古代 希臘에 있어서, 絕對探求의 方向은 于先 自然界로 向하였다. 創始期의 哲人들은, 形形色色으로 雜多한 萬物 中에서, 그 本原으로서의 一物素 卽 '原質(arche)'을 發見하고자 하였다. 그들은 森羅萬象이 時時刻刻으로 變化流轉하는 가운데도, 그 背後에는 絕對不變하는 恒存의 世界가 存在할 것을 想定하였다. 或은 '물'을 原質이라고 보고(Thales), 或은 '空氣'를 原質이라고 생각하고(Anaximenes), 또는 '불'을 原質로 보는 等(Herakleitos), 各各 見解의 差異는 있었으나, 그들은 모두 自然界의 雜多한 가운데서의 '一者'를, 變化하는 가운데서의 '不變者'를, 卽 '絕對者'를 求한 點에 있어서 一致하였다.

自然을 說明하는 原理를 發見함으로써 根本課題로 삼은 創始期의 哲人들이 探求한 '絕對'는, 自然界의 存在와 生成의 原理로서의 絕對이며, 그

것은 多分히 唯物論的인 絕對였다. 따라서 行爲의 世界에 있어서의 絕對者, 卽 實踐의 原理로서의 絕對者를 探求하는 問題는, 비록 全然 度外視當한 것은 아니라 할지라도, 哲學의 中心問題는 아니었다. 倫理學이 直接對象으로 삼는바 實踐의 原理로서의 絕對探求에 關心의 主力을 기울이는 端初를 이룬 것은, 精神과 自然과의 差異를 明確히 理解하고 自然에 對한 精神의 優位를 認識하기 始作하는 同時에 混亂한 社會相을 反映하여 理論의 問題보다도 實踐의 問題를 더욱 切實한 것으로서 느끼게 된 소피스트 (Sophist)들이었다. 그러나 소피스트들의 活動은, 絕對探求의 肯定的인 方向보다도 否定的인 方向으로 기울어졌다. "人間은 萬物의 尺度이다. 있는 것에 關하여서는 있는 것의, 없는 것에 關하여서는 없는 것의"라는 프로타고라스의 命題가 明示하는바 主觀性의 原理를 發達시킨 功勞는 컸으나, 그 主觀性을 各 個人의 經驗的 主觀性 以上의 것으로 생각할 수 없었던 소피스트들은, 理論認識에 關하여서도 眞理의 客觀性을 否認하고 行爲의 世界에 있어서도 絕對善의 存在를 斷念했던 것이다.

2) 소크라테스

소피스트들과 마찬가지로 自然보다도 人生의 問題가 眞正한 哲學이 關與할 바라고 믿고, 또 主觀性의 原理를 高調하면서, 그러나 그 主觀性을 個個人의 經驗的 主觀性이 아니라, 普遍者의 絕對的 主觀性으로서 定立하는 새로운 課題를 擔當하고 나온 사람이 소크라테스(Socrates, 470-399 B.C.)였다. 소크라테스는 萬物의 眞正한 尺度는 各 個人의 私的인 意見이나 意欲이 아니라, 모든 人間에게 經驗에 앞서서 遍在하는 理性者라고 믿는다. 眞, 正, 善, 義務 等을 決定하는 것은 나의 思惟이기는 하나, 나의 思惟는 나에게 特有한 것이 아니라, 모든 理性的 存在에 있어서 共通된 것이다. 따라서 認識은 主觀性에 依하여 決定되는 것이기는 하나 그 主觀이 普遍性을 가진 絕對的 主觀性인 까닭에 眞理는 絕對普遍性을 갖는다. '人間'은 萬物의 尺度이기는 하나, 그 尺度가 되는 人間은 소피스트들이 생각하는 差別相의 個人이 아니라, 普遍的 理性的 存在로서의 人間이라는 것 — 이것이 소크라테스의 思想의 根本이요, 이 根本思想에 依하여서 소피스트들의 相對論을 克服하고자 한다.

소크라테스는 絕對眞理가 普遍的 理性의 認識에 있다는 것을 原理로서 主張하고 槪念的 認識의 必要性을 力說하였으나, 그의 哲學은 아직 하나의 體系를 이루지는 못하였다. 그의 功績은 眞正한 哲學의 方法을 提示한 데서 그친다. 이 方法을 柱礎로 하여 綜合的인 體系를 樹立한 것은 完全 소크라테스 學徒로서의 플라톤이었다.

3) 플라톤

플라톤(Platon, 427-347 B.C.)은 經驗世界에 關한 限 프로타고라스의 相對論을 肯定한다. 卽 認識의 主體와 客體가 經驗의 範圍內에서는 恒時 生滅流轉한다는 것, 따라서 絕對 不變의 眞理라는 것이 없다는 것을, 經驗界에 關한 限 認定한다. 그러나 플라톤은 經驗的 現象이 相對的임에도 不拘하고 絕對的 認識은 可能하다는 소크라테스의 信念을 따른다. 여기서 絕對的 認識이 可能하기 爲하여서 플라톤에게 要請된 것은, 經驗界를 超越하는 認識의 主體와 生滅流轉함이 없는 認識의 對象이다. 다시 말하면 經驗界에 있어서 絕對眞理가 不可能한 以上, 絕對眞理를 可能하게 해줄 또 하나의 世界가 經驗界를 떠나서 別途로 存在할 必要가 있었던 것이다. 소크라테스를 따라서 絕對眞理의 可能性을 確信한 플라톤은, 이 또 하나의 世界가 存在한다는 것을 疑心하지 않았다. 이 또 하나의 世界를, 플라톤은 이데아(Idea)의 世界라고 불렀다. 이데아는 個物에 共通된 普遍者요, 變轉하는 現象 背後에서 恒久不變한 實體이다. 主觀的 側面으로 보면 이데아는 經驗을 超越한 認識의 原理 卽 認識作用의 先天的 主體요, 客觀的 側面으로 보면 現象的 自然界의 背後에서 그 不變의 原理가 되는 非空間的 非物質的 實體이다.

플라톤은 그의 이데아論을 前提로 하고 元來 哲學의 根本問題인 倫理에 關한 學說을 이끌어 낸다. 그의 이데아論에 依하면 經驗的 感性의 世界는 不完全과 惡의 世界이다. 따라서 人間의 最高의 使命은, 不完全과 惡의 原理인 이 感性의 世界를 超脫함이다. 人間의 靈魂은, 本來 이데아界에 屬해 있었으나 墮落하여, 生滅界(經驗界)로 떨어진 中間的 存在이다. 人間의 靈魂이, 肉體的인 모든 欲求를 克復하고 感性的인 모든 不純을 벗어나서, 그 本來의 世界 卽 眞實과 永遠만이 사는 고요한 思惟的 認識의 世界로 復歸함— 이것이 人間에게 完全한 幸福을 가져오는 唯一한 길이다.

한便 플라톤은, 善의 이데아와 一致하는 解脫의 理想이 現實에 있어서 到達하기 至難함을 考慮하고, 現世에 있어서 實現할 수 있는 善, 卽 人間의 努力으로 捕捉할 수 있는 善은 善의 이데아 그 自體가 아니라 善의 現象的인 表現으로서의 學, 眞理, 美, 德 等이라는 것— 우리들의 使命은 神과 同等하게 되는 것이 아니라 神에 가까워지는 것이라는 緩和論을 表明하고 있다.

이와 같은 絶對善 또는 現世的인 善을 實現하고자 하는 人間의 理想은, 貧弱한 人間이 個人的 努力으로 達成하기는 困難하다. 大多數의 凡人을 爲하여서는 國法의 他律的인 道德規範이 必要하다. 國家의 目的은, 倫理的 原理를 普遍的 永續的으로 實現함으로써, 各 個人을 有德한 人間으로 만드는 同時에, 德으로 하여금 共同社會를 支配하는 永續的 權力이 되게 하는 일이다.

따라서 플라톤의 理想國家에 있어서는, 各 個人은 自己의 一切를 普遍的 인 것을 爲하여 바치지 않으면 아니 된다. 人間이 精神生活을 完成하는 것은, 孤立한 個人生活을 通하여서가 아니라, 有機的으로 組織된 國家生活을 通하여서만 可能하다고 믿었던 그는, 各 個人의 特殊意志는 國家 全體의 普遍意志를 爲하여 犧牲되어야 한다고 主張하였다.

個人의 特殊性을 無視하고 全體의 普遍性을 强調하는 플라톤의 理想國家는 必然的으로 專制主義的이다. 마치 個人에 있어서 感性的 諸機能이 個人의 最高機能인 理性에게 絶對 服從해야 하듯이, 國家에 있어서도 全國民은 國家의 最高機能인 統治者에게 絶對 服從하여 各自의 任務를 다하지 않으면 아니 된다. 理想國家는 全體가 完全히 調和된 統一體이며, 마치 個人의 倫理生活과 같은 有機性을 갖지 않으면 아니 된다. 이와 같은 理想國家에서 最高의 指示를 내릴 수 있는 것은, 이데아의 世界를 가장 깊이 認識하고 있는 哲人이 아니면 아니 된다.

플라톤은 이데아의 世界에 '絶對'를 求하였다. 그러나 플라톤의 이데아란 그리 分明한 槪念이 아니다. 特히 우리가 實際로 經驗하는 現象界와의 關係가 매우 模糊하다. 플라톤은 個個의 現象이 이데아를 分有하느니, 이데아는 原型이요 現象은 그 影像이니 하는 說明을 꾀하고 있으나, 이러한 表現은 일찍이 아리스토텔레스도 非難한 바와 같이, 한갓 空虛한 詩的 比喩에 不過한 것으로서 자못 不明確하다. 經驗界에 살고 있는 우리 人間의 立場에서 볼 때에, 플라톤의 이데아가 都大體 무엇을 意味하는 것인가를 차근차근 따지고 본다면, 그것은 오직 漠然한 希望 以上의 것이 될 수 없다. 플라톤이 본 이데아의 세계는 바로 華麗한 樓閣이기는 하나, 그 現象界와의 關係가 分明하지 않은 限 結局 沙上의 樓閣이다.

플라톤과 마찬가지로 絶對者의 存在를 確信하면서 그러나 그 絶對者가 우리의 經驗界와 遊離됨이 없도록 現象世界 內部에 있어서 이를 定立하려

한 것은 플라톤 第一의 弟子로서의 아리스토텔레스였다.

4) 아리스토텔레스

아리스토텔레스(Aristoteles, 385-322 B.C.)는 經驗的인 現象界 그 自體의 內部에 있어서 絕對的인 것, 永遠한 것을 求한다. 모든 現象, 모든 個物을 完全히 現實化된 絕對者라고 보지는 않았으나, 經驗에 나타난 모든 事物은 絕對者 또는 永遠한 것을 指向하는 生成體, 다시 말하면 '可能態(dunamis)'에 있는 絕對者라고 아리스토텔레스는 믿는다.

아리스토텔레스에 依하면, 모든 現實的 存在는 그 事物의 素材로서의 '質科(hule)'와 事物의 目的으로서의 '形相(eidos)'과의 合成體이다. 그러나 質科와 形相과의 對立은 固定的인 것이 아니다. 甲에 對해서 質科인 것이 乙에 對해서는 形相이 될 수 있다. 例컨대 材木은 家屋에 對하여는 質科이나 山野에 서 있는 生木에 對하여는 形相이요, 生木은 材木에 對해서는 質科이나 種子에 對해서는 形相이듯이. 이와 같은 見地에서 볼 때에 存在全體는 形相을 조금도 包含하지 않은 '第一質科'를 最下段으로 하고, 조금도 質科를 包含하지 않은 純粹한 形相 卽 '絕對形相'을 絕頂으로 삼는바 하나의 커다란 段階的 組織을 이루고 있을 것이다. 그 兩端의 中間에 있는 모든 것은, 그 위의 것에 對하여는 質科고 그 아래 것에 對하여서는 形相이니, 한마디로 말하면 質科에서 形相으로 指向하는 生動體이다.

아리스토텔레스에 依하면, 全自然은 質科에서 形相으로 發展하는 生動的 存在로서, 各各 最高의 存在를 指向하여 더 높은 段階를 追求하고 있다. 自然界의 모든 生成은 目的, 卽 形相을 가지고 있으며, 그 最高의 形相은 純粹한 精神(Nous)으로서의 '神'이다. 地上에 있어서는 모든 自然物의 目的은 實現된 形相으로서의 人間, 特히 人間의 男性이다.

人間은 모든 地上的 自然의 目的이요 모든 發展段階의 最高峰이다. 그것은 人間이 最高의 形相인바 精神, 即 理性을 그 機能 안에 內包하고 있기 때문이다. 人間도 植物과 마찬가지로 榮養의 機能을 가졌으며, 一般動物과 같이 感覺과 運動의 機能을 가졌다. 그러나 人間이 特히 高貴한 것은, 다른 生物에 없는 理性의 機能을 保有하기 때문이다. 理性은 人間이 保有한 絕對와 永遠의 原理이다. 따라서 理性의 機能을 遺憾 없이 發揮함은 人間 各者에게 賦課된 最高의 使命이요, 이 使命의 達成이 곧 人間行爲의 窮極目的으로서의 '幸福'이다.[1] 여기서 人間은 어떻게 살 것인가, 또는 어떻게 行爲할 것인가 하는 倫理學의 窮極問題에 對한 아리스토텔레스의 解答이 演繹된다. 그것은 "理性의 機能을 遺憾 없이 發揮하라."는 一言으로 表現할 수 있는 格率이다.

勿論 自然을 尊重하는 아리스토텔레스는, 人間性의 底面을 形成하는 生理的 欲求를 無視하지 않는다. 行動의 基本은 理性이기보다도 오히려 自然에 依하여 規定되는 '衝動' 即 '欲求'라는 事實을 그는 看過하지 않는다. 따라서 아리스토텔레스는 感性的 欲求의 原理에 對한 正當한 權利를 認定하고, 有德한 行爲가 感性的 欲求와 理性的 叡智와의 調和에서 實現된다고 主張한다. 그에 依하면 '德'은 곧 感性과 理性이 조화된 '中庸'의 行爲가 習慣化한 것이다. 이와 같이 中庸을 高調함으로써, 人間에 있어서의 肉體的인 것에 正當한 地位를 認定하려고는 했다 할지라도, 그러나 그 中庸은 어디까지나 精神的 要素가 優位에 서는 中庸이요 肉體와 精神이 同列에 서는

---

1 아리스토텔레스는 모든 行爲의 窮極目的이 '幸福(Eudaimonia)'이라고 보았다. '幸福'이란 '잘 사는 것'을 意味한다. 그리고 '잘 산다' 함은 '自己의 機能을 잘 發揮함'이다. 그런데 人間의 本質的 機能은 그 '理性'에 있다. 따라서 人間의 本質的인 幸福은 '理性'의 機能을 잘 發揮하는 것이라고 그는 推理한다.

中庸은 아니다. 오직 現實에 있어서 肉體的인 것을 否認할 수 없다는 것뿐이요, 畢竟에 가서는 理性一色으로써 神에 到達함을 人間의 理想으로 삼는 것이 아리스토텔레스 自身의 形而上學에 整合的인 倫理說이라 하겠다.

아리스토텔레스의 倫理說은 그의 形而上學 및 自然哲學의 系論이다. 따라서 그의 形而上學 또는 自然哲學의 難點은, 그대로 그의 倫理說에 있어서도 難點의 根源이 된다. 플라톤의 二元論을 反對한 아리스토텔레스가, 現象 內部에 實體를 發見하려 한 것과 世界를 靜止한 것으로서가 아니라 生成하는 것으로서 把握하려 한 것은, 그의 卓見이라 아니 할 수 없다. 그러나 그의 目的論的 世界觀에는 이를 正當化할 만한 根據가 없는 것이다. 아리스토텔레스에 依하면, 모든 個物은 더 높은 것을 爲한 素材요, 그 '더 높은 것'은 또다시 더 높은 目的 卽 形相을 爲한 質料이다. 이리하여 모든 存在는 神的 存在로서의 理性을 그 窮極의 目的으로 삼는다. 그러나 이와 같은 段階的 目的論에는 何等의 客觀的 妥當性이 없는 것이다. 生木은 材木이 되기 爲하여 있는 것이 아니며, 材木은 册床이 되기 爲하여 있는 것이 아니다. 生木은 오직 그 自身의 法則에 따라 生木으로 있을 뿐이요, 이를 材木으로 加工하는 것은 人間이 人間을 爲하여서 하는 主觀的 造作에 不過하다. 人間의 立場에서 본다면 材木은 册床을 만들기 爲한 素材도 될 수 있을 것이나, 그 材木 自體의 立場에서 본다면 材木은 何等의 目的을 가진 바 없는 無心한 存在이다. 이리하여 萬物이 理性을 最高의 目的으로 삼는다는 아리스토텔레스의 自然哲學에는, 이를 正當化할 根據가 없다.

아리스토텔레스는 理性 또는 理性의 完成으로서의 神에게 絶對와 永遠을 求하고 있다. 그러나 '理性(Nous)'이라는 槪念 自體가 模糊한 抽象에 不過하다는 事實은 姑捨하고라도 무엇 때문에 理性이 宇宙 안에서 最高의 地位를 차지하는 것인지, 무엇 때문에 萬物이 理性을 窮極의 目標로 삼고 努力해야 할 것인지 그 理由가 分明치 않다. 아리스토텔레스는, 榮養이나

感覺의 機能은 植物 或은 動物에도 있으나 理性은 人間에게만 特有한 것인 까닭에, 理性은 人間의 本質이요, 이 理性을 遺憾 없이 發揮하는 것은 人間으로서 잘 사는 것, 卽 人間의 幸福이라고 推論하고 있다. 그러나 設令 理性이 人間에게만 特有하다는 것을 認定한다 하더라도, 그 '特有'하다는 事實은 그것이 바로 人間의 '本質'이라는 事由가 될 수는 없다. '特有'하다는 것과 '本質'이라는 것과는 元來 別것이다. 혹(癌)은 혹 달린 사람에게 特有한 것이나, 그의 本質은 아니다. 理性의 感性에 對한 優位를 主張하려면 兩者를 比較하는 價值의 尺度가 따로 準備되지 않으면 아니 될 것이다.

人間性을 基礎로 하고 人間의 善을 規定하고자 한 아리스토텔레스는, 그 以前의 누구보다도 着實한 倫理說을 提唱하였다. 그러나 그 人間性의 把握이 充分히 正確하지 못하였던 關係로, 아리스토텔레스 亦是 倫理學에 있어서 가장 基本的인 問題를 後世의 課題로서 남기지 않으면 아니 되었다.

5) 倫理時代의 思想

아리스토텔레스 以後에 希臘의 哲學界는 새로운 傾向에 依하여 支配되었다. 그때까지는 哲學의 中心은 理論問題에 있었으며 참된 認識에 最高의 價值를 認定하는 主知主義(intellectualism)가 支配하였다. 그러나 이제 理論的 認識은 오직 正當한 行爲를 爲한 手段으로 보이게 되있으며 實踐的 關心이 哲學의 中心을 차지하게 되었다.

哲學에 있어서의 이 같은 變遷은 希臘 國家社會相의 變遷의 反映이었다. 아테네(Athenai)와 스파르타(Sparta)의 反目을 爲始한 內紛에 依하여 漸次 衰退의 길을 밟아 가던 希臘의 國勢는, 알렉산더(Alexthander) 大王의 東征을 契機로 急激한 崩壞에 當面하였다. 政治的 自由와 獨立을 잃은 希臘은 經濟生活에 混亂을 免치 못하였으며, 한때 極度로 華麗하던 國民文化

도 거의 水泡로 돌아갔다. 社會의 安寧과 秩序는 무너져, 共同의 生活도 共同의 精神도 消失되었다. 이제 밖으로 公共生活에 對한 期待를 잃고 人生의 虛無함을 痛感하게 된 사람들이 갈 길이라곤, 오직 안으로 安心立命의 땅을 찾아 헤매는 일뿐이었다. 學者의 關心도 國家社會의 公共事業이 아니라 個人의 幸福問題에 集中되었다. 貧困과 不安에 시달리는 學界는, 超然한 理論問題에 消日할 餘暇도 없이, 目前에 當面한 實踐問題에 오로지 勞心하였다. 한마디로 말하면 이 時代의 哲學은 個人的 處世에 關한 敎訓이다. 哲學史上에서 '倫理時代(ethische Periode)'라고 불리는 이 時代의 哲學의 代表的인 것은, 에피쿠로스學派(Epicureans)의 快樂主義와 스토아學派(Stoics)의 禁欲主義다.

快樂主義(hedonism)는 일찍이 소크라테스 學徒의 一派인 키레네派(Cyrenai)에 依하여 主張되었다. 키레네 學徒가 人生의 目標로 삼았던 '快樂(hedonê)'은 元來 肉體的이요 瞬間的인 快樂이었다. 그러나 에피쿠로스學派의 開祖인 에피쿠로스(Epikuros, 314-270 B.C.)가 理想으로 삼은 快樂은, 精神的이요 永續的인 것으로 修正된다. 勿論 快樂이라면, 그 原初에 있어서는, 肉體的인 것, 官能的인 것을 意味하였을 것이다. 그러나 官能的 快樂의 끊임없는 追求는 決코 그 所期의 目的을 達成하지 못한다. 欲望은 元來 限量이 없는 것이며, 欲望充足의 手段인 物質이나 肉體는 有限한 것이다. 無限한 것을 有限한 것으로 채우려는 無理한 努力은 畢竟 不滿과 苦痛을 招來함으로써 그친다. 이른바 '快樂主義의 逆理(paradox of hedonism)'이다. 이리하여 元來 官能的인 것을 意味하던 快樂主義가 스스로 '修正'의 必要를 느낄 날은 早晩間 찾아온다.

頹廢期에 一般的인 現象인 精神的 墮落과 物質的 缺乏은, '快樂主義의 逆理'의 體驗을 促進하는 好適한 條件이다. 亂世의 哲人 에피쿠로스도, 元來 "快樂 以外에 善이 없고 苦痛 以外에 惡이 없다."는 見解로부터 出發하

였으나, 드디어 快樂이라고 반드시 追求할 것이 아니며 苦痛이라고 반드시 回避할 것이 못 된다는 反省에 達하였다. 欲望을 채움으로써 느끼는 積極的 快樂이 아니라, 欲望에 依하여 흔들림이 없이 安靜된 마음에서 오는 消極的 快樂에 永遠한 價值로서의 '幸福'이 認定된다. 眞正한 幸福은 永遠한 快樂을 意味하는 것이며 永遠한 快樂이란 欲望도 없고 不滿도 없이 '安靜된 마음의 狀態(ataraxia)'를 이루기 때문이다. 幸福은 肉體의 快樂에 있는 것이 아니라 精神의 快樂에 있다. 精神의 快樂을 爲하여 肉體의 快樂은 犧牲되지 않으면 아니 된다. 이리하여 快樂을 唯一한 善으로 보는 信念에서 出發한 에피쿠로스의 倫理學은, 도리어 肉體의 欲望, 따라서 肉體의 快樂을 否認하는 結論에 達하고 말았다.

스토아學派도 '幸福'을 窮極의 目的으로 삼은 點은 에피쿠로스學派와 다를 바가 없으며, 亦是 希臘 倫理思想의 傳統을 벗어나지 않았다. 다만 그 幸福에 到達하는 方途에 있어서 스토아 學徒들은[2] 에피쿠로스와 正反對의 極에서 出發한다. 스토아 學徒들은 바로 에피쿠로스의 到達點인 저 厭世觀에서부터 出發하는 것이다.

스토아 哲學의 理想은 '賢者'의 生活이다. 賢者란 世上의 轉變에 依하여 左右됨이 없고, 人間의 感動과 情欲을 벗어난 者를 意味한다. 賢者의 生活은 스토아 學說에 依하면 '自然'을 따르는 生活이다. '自然과 一致하게 生活함', 이것은 스토아學派의 道德原理였다. 그러나 스토아學派의 '自然'은 常識的인 自然現象을 意味하지 않는다. 自然의 本質은 宇宙의 가득 찬 '道

---

2 스토아學派의 哲學은 한 사람 또는 한 時代가 지어낸 思想이 아니라 여러 사람이 여러 時代를 두고 建設한 것이다. 學派의 創始者는 제논(Zenon, 336-264 B.C.)이라는 사람이다.

(Logos)', 即 普遍的인 世界의 法則이다. 로고스는 人間 안에도 깃들어 있으니, 이는 곧 人間의 理性이다. 理性은 人間 內部에 있는 自然이니, 理性을 따르는 生活이 賢者의 生活 即 人間的 努力의 最高目標이다.

스토아學派에 依하면, 感性的 欲望은 人性의 自然이 아니라 人性의 自然인 理性을 妨害하는 疾病이다. 따라서 感性的 欲望은 理性에 依하여 制御되지 않으면 아니 된다. 感性的 欲望이 理性에 依하여 制御되고 모든 煩惱를 解脫한 境地(apatheia) — 이것이 스토아學派의 理想이다.

初期의 스토아學派는, 그 禁欲主義에 徹底하여 絕對善 絕對賢의 理想을 實現할 것을 指向하였다. 그러나 人間에 있어서 感性的인 欲求를 全的으로 抹殺한다는 것은 實際에 있을 수 없다는 것을 깨닫게 되자, 後日의 스토아學徒들은 그 嚴格한 理性主義를 次次 緩和시켜 간다. 感性의 極端에서 出發한 快樂主義가 漸次 理性의 重要性을 强調하게 된 것과 反對로, 理性의 極端에서 出發한 스토아學派는 漸漸 感性과의 調和를 꾀하였던 것이다. 兩極에서 出發한 快樂主義와 禁欲主義가 畢竟 이와 같이 接近하게 되는 推移에 있어서, 우리는 '中庸'의 思想이 東洋에서도 西洋에서도 崇尙을 받은 事由의 一端을 본다.

에피쿠로스學派는 個人의 快樂에 人生의 窮極目的을 보았다. 이 快樂主義의 基盤이 되는 것은, 모든 人間은 恒常 快樂을 追求하고 있다는 心理說이다. 그러나 이 素朴한 心理說에는 科學的 妥當性이 없다. 人間이 直接 追求하는 것은 快樂 그 自體가 아니라 食欲, 性欲, 休息欲 等 生理的 欲求 또는 名譽欲, 權勢欲 같은 社會的 欲求를 充足시키는 일이다. 快樂이란 이러한 欲望이 充足되었을 때 自動的으로 同伴하는 情緒의 屬性에 不過하다. 欲望充足에 附隨的으로 따르는 情緖를 欲望의 目標 自體인양 認定하는 點에 快樂主義의 그릇된 出發點이 있다. 快樂은 우리의 自然的인 欲求를 自然스럽게 充足시킬 때에 스스로 오는 것이요, 快樂 自體를 目標로 삼고 行

動할 때는 도리어 快樂은 얻어지지 않는다. 그러므로 快樂 自體에 行爲의 目標를 두는 快樂主義는 結局 快樂이 人力으로 얻을 수 없는 것이라는 覺醒에 達한다. 快樂이 唯一한 善이라는 信念에서 出發한 快樂主義가 도리어 快樂의 否認에 가까운 制欲主義로 기울어진 것은 不可避한 歸結이었다.

한편 스토아學派가 그 典型을 보여준 禁欲主義는 元來 快樂主義의 反動이다. 그들의 出發點은 겉으로 快樂을 否認하면서 속으로는 快樂을 耽求하는 矛盾이다. 出發點에 矛盾을 內包한 이 哲學에는 全體系를 通하여 이 矛盾이 貫流한다. 禁欲主義는, 感性的 欲望이 禁止 當해야 할 惡이라고 主張한다. 그 理由는, 感性的 欲望이 人性의 自然이 아니라 人性의 自然 卽 理性을 妨害하는 疾病이라는 것이다. 이 主張이 根據 없는 獨斷임은 두말 할 것도 없거니와, 欲望의 禁止라는 것 自體가 無理한 試圖이다. 欲望을 禁止하려는 것 自體도 하나의 '欲望'이거늘, 生命이 持續하는 동안 欲望은 가실 날이 없다. 欲望을 解決하는 것은, 그 欲望을 直接 或은 間接으로 充足시키는 외에 길이 없다. 抑制하면 抑制할수록 도리어 일어서는 것이 欲望의 本性이다. 抑制로써 欲望을 다스리려고 한 禁欲主義가 人生問題를 끝내 解決 짓지 못한 것은 오히려 當然하다 하겠다.

그러나 快樂主義와 禁欲主義의 意義는 그 理論的 缺陷을 넘어서서 重大하다. 그것은, 이 두 개의 對立하는 倫理觀은 모든 時代와 모든 地域을 通하여 그것이, 理論的으로는 否定을 當하는 瞬間에 있어서까지도, 우리들 生活感情 속에 끈덕지게 作用하는 事實이기 때문이다. 快樂主義와 禁欲主義는, 그 後 中世와 近代를 通하여 가지가지 形態로 살아왔으며, 現代에 있어서도, 하나의 理論體系로서는 거의 無視를 當하고 있는 形便이면서도, 하나의 常識과도 같은 無意識的 傾向으로서 우리의 行動을 制約하고 있다. 이 두 가지 傾向의 對立은 人間性에 全面的인 改革이 이루어지지 않는 限 永遠한 딜레마로서 우리의 生活을 흔드는지도 모른다.

6) 宗敎時代로의 移行

에피쿠로스는 快樂에 永遠한 價値를 求하였다. 그러나 快樂은 人力으로 애써서 얻을 수 있는 것이 아니다. 快樂을 求하면 도리어 苦痛이 結果되는 逆理조차 있다. 苦痛은 有限한 人間의 힘으로는 어찌 할 수 없는 必然이다. 한편 스토아 學徒들은 情欲을 抹殺하는 理性的 生活에 絶對를 求하였다. 그러나 生命이 存續하는 限, 人間은 情欲을 떠날 수가 없다. 情欲도 理性과 一般으로 人間의 本性에 屬한다. 理性的 生活도 有限한 人間의 힘으로는 實現할 수 없는 彼岸의 夢想이다. 이와 같이 快樂主義와 禁欲主義가 모두 失敗하는 根本原因은 人間의 有限性에 있다. 人間의 救濟는 人間의 힘만으로는 不可能할 것 같다. '無限者'의 保護와 助力이 必要하다. 이리하여 倫理時代의 뒤를 이어서 全知全能한 無限者, 卽 '神'에게 依支하여 人間의 幸福을 이룩하려는 새로운 傾向의 哲學이 나타나게 된다. 이른바 '宗敎詩代(religiöse Periode)'의 哲學이다.

希臘 末期의 思想界를 代表하는 宗敎詩代의 哲學은, 그 時代의 有識層을 背景으로 삼은 宗敎思想이다. 새로운 獨創性을 가진 것이 아니라 피타고라스(Pythagoras), 플라톤 같은 옛 哲人의 思想을 若干 變形한 데 지나지 않는 이 時代의 哲學은, 플로티노스(Plotinus, 204-270)의 華麗한 體系를 보기는 하였으나, 그 後 크게 發展할 餘地도 없이 希臘哲學의 終幕을 내렸다. 다 같이 宗敎思想이면서도 오랜 傳統을 지니고 世界文化에 큰 影響을 미친 것은, 도리어 그 時代의 下層階級을 土臺로 삼고 일어선 基督敎(christianism)의 思想이다.

2. 中世 基督敎의 倫理思想

1) 基督敎의 起源과 原始基督敎의 基本思想

基督敎는, 元來 그보다 時代的으로 앞선 希臘의 哲學을 繼承하고 出發한 것이 아니라, 또 하나의 다른 起源, 卽 이스라엘(Israel) 民族 內에 옛날부터 傳해 내려오던 猶太敎에서 出發하고 있다. 世上萬物을 創造한 것은 唯一한 神이며 神은 全知全能한 絶對者라는 이스라엘 民族의 信仰은 그대로 예수(Jesus) 自身의 信仰이기도 하다. 그리고 이 絶對者 神의 뜻을 따르는 것이 被創造者로서의 人間의 正義라는 道德思想에 있어서도, 또 未久에 天國이 到來하리라는 終末觀에 있어서도, 基督敎는 猶太敎의 遺産을 그대로 繼承한 點이 적지 않다. 그러나 基督敎는 猶太敎의 單純한 延長은 아니다. 첫째로, 예수는 神을 오로지 두렵고 嚴肅한 審判者로만 보는 猶太敎의 觀念을 버리고, 神은 無限한 사랑을 베푸는 아버지라는 思想으로 고쳤다. 猶太敎의 神(Jahweh)은, 오직 義로운 사람만을 救濟하고 義롭지 못한 사람에게는 容恕 없이 罰을 내리는 差別의 神이다. 그러나 基督敎의 神은 神을 背反한 罪人까지도 버리지 않는 無限한 사랑의 神이다. 그뿐 아니라 罪를 지은 者는, 悔悟를 通하여 神의 사랑을 느끼고 神을 理解함이 더욱 깊은 까닭에, 義로운 者보다도 오히려 神에게 더 가깝고 神의 사랑을 더 두텁게 받는다. 다음에 예수는 猶太敎의 形式主義的인 律法主義에 反對하였다. 外面的 形式的인 義務履行의 問題는 神의 앞에서 그리 重大한 意義를 갖는 것이 아니다. 오직 마음속의 靈魂만이 깊은 뜻을 갖는다. 예수의 說敎에 있어 또 하나 새로운 點은 民族的 偏狹性을 超越하고 있다는 事實이다. 猶太民族의 選民의 思想은 救濟를 오직 猶太民族에게만 約束하는 것이었으나, 예수는 全人類에게 天國의 福音을 豫告하였다.

苛酷한 律法主義에 反對하고 萬人에게 無差別한 救濟를 約束하는 예수의 說敎는, 于先 下層階級 사람들의 熱狂的인 歡迎을 받았다. 예수가 十字架에 犧牲된 後 그의 敎는 一時 挫折되었으나, '復活'을 믿는 그의 熱烈한 使徒들에 依하여 다시 蘇生되었다. 그 後 特히 바울(Paulos)의 卓越한 傳導에 依하여 基督敎는 로마 帝國 全域으로 傳播되고 世界宗敎로서의 地盤을 닦았다. 勿論 基督敎가 完全한 世界宗敎로서 脫皮할 때까지의 經路는 平坦한 것이 아니었다. 그것은 四百餘年의 長久한 歲月에 걸친 迫害와 忍從, 그리고 無數한 犧牲 끝에 이루어진 多難한 事業이었다.

다른 모든 信仰도 그렇거니와 以上에 簡單히 言及한 바와 같은 基督敎의 敎理도 어떤 自明한 事實로부터 演繹的으로나 또는 歸納的으로 推理된 眞理, 다시 말하면 論證된 眞理는 아니다. 基督敎의 眞理는 元來는 論證의 對象이 아니라 오직 啓示로서 把握된 眞理이다. 外在하는 絕對者에 對한 信仰의 出發點이 되는 것은, 人間 自身의 有限性, 卽 人間의 無力과 無知에 對한 自覺이다. 神의 存在를 疑心한다거나 그 性格을 究明하려고 꾀한다면, 그 自體가 無知하고 無力한 人間으로서는 分을 헤아리지 못한 不遜이다. 被造造者 人間이 할 바는 오직 神을 믿고 神을 사랑하며 神의 뜻에 服從하는 일이다. 알고서야 비로소 믿을 수 있다는 것은 純粹한 信仰의 態度는 아니다. 于先 믿어야 하며, 믿음으로써 비로소 알 수도 있는 것이다. 特히 基督敎는, 그 始初에 있어 學識을 일삼지 않는 下流大衆을 地盤으로 삼고 일어난 것인 만큼 그 原始期에 있어서는 理論이라는 것이 問題되지 않았다. 그것은 批判을 超越한바 純眞한 信仰이었다. 簡單히 말하면 基督敎는 神秘와 感動에 가득 찬 헤브라이(Hebrai) 精神을 母胎로 삼고 일어난 것이다.

따라서 原始基督敎의 倫理觀은 古代 希臘의 그것과는 正反對의 價値尺度를 信奉한다. 希臘의 倫理는 大體로 人間과 自然을 肯定하는 土臺 위에

자라나 現世主義的이었다. 그러나 基督教의 倫理는 人間과 自然을 否定하는 來世主義를 그 地盤으로 삼는다. 希臘의 倫理는 自己의 發揚을 目標로 삼는 데 反하여, 基督教의 倫理는 自己의 克服을 目標로 삼는다. 希臘의 倫理는 自然 안에 善美의 極致를 보았으나, 基督教의 倫理는 自然 속에 도리어 醜惡의 根源을 보았다. 基督教는 自然의 죽음을 通한 人間의 再生을 꿈꾼다.

希臘의 倫理가 '德'으로서 讚揚한 諸價値는, 基督教 倫理에 있어서는 全的으로 否認을 當하거나, 그렇지 않으면 적어도 修正을 받는다. 希臘에 있어서는 知識이 가장 崇尙되는 德이었다. 그러나 原始基督教에 있어서는, '마음이 가난한 者'에게 도리어 多幸이 있다. 希臘에 있어서 實踐에 關한 最高의 德은 '正義'였다. 그러나 基督教의 倫理는 "남이 萬若 네 오른쪽 뺨을 치거든 왼뺨마저 내밀라."고 가르친다. 希臘의 '勇氣' 代身에 '忍從'이 讚美되고, 希臘의 '節制' 代身 '禁欲'이 鼓吹된다.

2) 信仰과 知識과의 對立

元來는 理論이나 知識을 度外視하고 일어난 基督教도, 後日에 世界國家로서의 로마 帝國에 適切한 背景을 얻어 民族宗教의 地境을 벗어나 世界宗教로 發展하며 上流 知識層까지 그 信徒로서 包攝하게 되자, 이들 知識層까지 納得시킬 수 있는 宗教가 되기 爲하여서는, 信仰에 關한 理論, 卽 神學을 必要로 하게 되었다. 斷片的 信條를 綜合하여 秩序整然한 敎義의 體系를 세우는 急先務를 完遂한 것이, 基督教 初期의 學者들인 敎父(fathers)들이며, 이 敎父들이 把握한바 敎義를 正當化하고 說明하는 任務를 맡아 본 것이, 基督教 理論家의 中樞를 이룬 스콜라(Schola) 哲學者들이다.

모든 宗教에 있어서 그러하듯이, 基督教에 있어서도 그 思想의 根本이 되는 것은 '神'의 槪念이다. 絶對者 神이 存在한다는 것, 神은 全知全能한 宇宙의 創造者이며 人間은 無力한 被創造者라는 것, 그리고 神은 萬民을 어버이처럼 사랑하는 이며 人間은 깊이 罪지은 者라는 것 等은, 基督敎에 있어서 根本前提요 自明한 眞理이다. 人間이 할 바는 오로지 絶對者 神에게 歸依하는 일이다. 禍福 萬事를 神의 뜻에 맡김으로써 濟度의 可能性도 열린다. 人間이 神에 對하여 批判的이거나 또는 評價의 態度를 取해서는 아니 되며, 人間 스스로의 運命을 自力으로 開拓하고자 하는 積極的 態度도 宗敎 本來의 思想에서는 距離가 있다. 人間이 努力은 自己의 自由意志의 命令을 좇아 할 것이 아니라, 神의 뜻을 따라서 神에게 가까이 가도록 애쓰는 他律的 努力이 아니면 아니 된다. 人間이 할 바는 오직 神을 믿고 神이 사랑하듯이 隣人을 사랑하고 神의 恩寵에 依하여 天國이 到來할 것을 冀望하는 일뿐이다.

따라서 神을 知識으로써 理解한다거나 信仰을 理論으로써 合理化하려는 그 意圖 自體에, 基督敎 信仰의 原初的 思想과 背馳되는 要因이 있다. 純粹한 信仰에서 出發한 基督敎가 理論的 認識의 問題를 들고 나선 것은, 異質的인 두 가지 精神의 混線을 意味하였다. 그것은 파토스(pathos)를 原理로 삼는 헤브라이즘(Hebraism)에 움돋은 原始基督敎 思想 위에 그와 反對되는 또 하나의 思想, 卽 로고스(logos)를 原理로 삼는 헬레니즘(Hellenism)을 土臺로 한 希臘哲學의 主知主義的 思想을 接木하고자 하는 試圖라고 볼 수 있다. 大體로 中世紀의 哲學이란 異質的인 두 개의 思想, 卽 猶太的인 파토스와 希臘的인 로고스와의 妥協과 對立을 되풀이하는 交涉의 展開로서 理解된다.

勿論 中世紀의 思想家들은 信仰을 根幹으로 삼고 認識은 오직 枝葉的 要素로서 添加할 것을 꾀하였다. 다시 말하면 基督敎 諸信條에 對하여 完全히 知的인 態度 卽 批判的 態度를 取한 것이 아니라, 基督敎 信條의 絶對眞

理性을 前提하고 이 前提에 理論的 根據를 賦與함을 그 元來의 使命으로
삼았던 것이다. 그러나 一旦 食道를 通過한 知識의 열매는 自己 本來의 屬
性을 따라 作用하였다. 파토스의 言語로 엮어진 信仰의 書를 로고스의 言
語로써 飜譯하고자 한 試圖에는, 파토스와 로고스와의 根本的 異質性에 因
한 難關이 있었다. 飜譯者가 아무리 原著者의 意思에 忠實하기를 期한다
하더라도 飜譯書에는 亦是 譯者의 個性이 反映되는 法이다. 中世의 學者들
은 極力 그 信仰에 忠實할 것을 꾀하였다. 그러나 學者로서의 知的 要求와
宗敎家로서의 情的 要求와는 畢竟 調和될 수 없는 葛藤을 內包하였다. 이
러한 葛藤이 個人 위에 나타나서는 同一한 思想家의 體系的 不整合을 招來
했으며, 派別로서 나타나서는 唯名論(Nominalism)과 實念論(Realism)의
對立에서 보는 바와 같은 學說의 對立을 惹起하였다.

3) 敎權과 政權의 對立

信仰과 知識의 對立에 倂行하여 또 하나의 커다란 對立이 中世紀를 通하
여 顯著하니, 이는 精神에 領域을 가진 敎權과 物質界에 領域을 가진 政權
과의 對立이다. 本來 原始基督敎의 根本思想은 俗世의 榮華를 無常한 것으
로서 輕視하며, 神의 恩寵과 天國의 永遠한 幸福에 憧憬하는바 彼岸的이요
超世俗的인 世界觀이다. 가톨릭 敎會(Catholic church)가 設立되던 當時
에 있어서 基督敎의 指導者들이 關心을 기울인 바는 人間의 靈魂에 關한
方面이었다. 敎會가 그 理念에 있어서 使命으로 삼은 바는 人間의 精神을
다스림이요, 經濟나 政治 같은 俗世의 權力은 本來 그 眼中에 없었다. "皇
帝의 것은 皇帝에게로, 神의 것은 神에게로"의 原則을 따라서, 物質과 肉
體에 關한 社會秩序를 維持하는 最高의 指導者로서는 로마 皇帝가 있었으
며, 敎會 最高의 指導者인 로마 法皇은 오직 精神界를 그 支配의 領域으로

삼았던 것이다. 이와 같이, 精神界를 領域으로 삼는 가톨릭 敎會의 敎權과 物質界를 領域으로 삼는 로마 帝國의 政權은 적어도 形式上으로는 確然히 分立되어 있었다.

그러나 精神界와 物質界를 分離하여 各其 分業的으로 統治한다는 것은, 오직 觀念的으로만 可能한 일이요, 實際에 있어서는 根本的인 無理를 包含한 抽象論이다. 都大體 肉體를 떠나서 精神이 獨立해 있다거나, 政治나 經濟의 勢力을 超脫하여 宗敎가 따로 自立할 수 있다는 見解는 啓蒙 以前의 形而上學的 思辨을 土臺로 한 空想이었다. 精神은 肉體와 表裏의 緊密性을 가졌으며, 宗敎는 政治, 經濟와 不可分의 關聯性을 가졌다. 가톨릭 敎會의 理想은, 觀念的으로는 精神界에 關한 것이 있으나, 막상 그 理想을 實現하고자 하는 現實的 努力이 이루어질 段階에서는, 恒常 物質世界와의 相互聯關을 免할 수 없었다. 때로는 俗世의 支配者가 敎會의 彈壓者로서 妨害하였으며, 또 때로는 敎會發展의 積極的인 援助者로서 協力하였다. 마치 中世紀의 思想史가 信仰과 知識과의 對立 乃至의 妥協의 過程을 中心으로 展開되었듯이, 中世紀의 政治史는 敎權과 政權과의 抗爭 乃至 提携를 樞軸으로 삼고 發展했다고 하여도 過言이 아니다.

主知主義的 態度와 主情主義的 態度는 人生觀에 있어서 對立되는 두 갈래의 커다란 潮流이다. 스콜라 哲學者들은 이 두 가지 潮流 속에 包含된 本質的인 矛盾性을 無視하고, 이 兩者를 無條件 結合시킴으로써 그 根本任務로 삼았다. 中世紀 思想界를 貫流하는 信仰과 知識의 對立은 스콜라 哲學의 出發點에 內包된 矛盾의 必然的인 發露였다. 信仰과 知識과의 對立이 不可避한 것이었듯이, 政權과 敎權과의 對立도 亦是 中世紀에 있어서 必然的인 現象이었다. 그것은 獨立한 精神의 王國을 樹立하려 한 敎會의 理想 속에 包含된 不合理에 起因한다. 敎會의 理想은 靈魂이 肉體로부터 分離될 수 있으며, 物質을 無視한 精神生活이 可能한 듯이 보는 臆見에서 出發하

고 있다. 그러나 靈魂은 肉體와 表裏一體의 關係에 있으며, 精神生活은 物質生活의 土臺 위에서 이루어진다. 人間에 있어서 靈魂과 肉體, 精神生活과 物質生活이 不可分의 關係에 있는 以上, 그 人間을 두고 두 개의 支配權, 卽 그의 靈魂 乃至 精神生活을 支配하는 敎權과 肉體 乃至 物質生活을 支配하는 政權이 無難히 兩立할 수는 없다. 敎會가 그 理想을 實現하는 것은, 그 理想이 아무리 超世俗的인 것이라 할지라도, 經濟와 政治가 作用하는 現實社會 안에 있어서의 敎會는 그 理想을 實現하는 過程에 있어서, 世俗的 勢力 또는 異敎的 勢力과 衝突한다. 따라서 元來 武力을 갖추지 않은 敎會가 障碍를 克服하고 進出하기 爲하여서는, 武力을 準備하고 있는 政權과 結托하거나 또는 可能하면 政權을 敎權의 支配下에 둘 必要가 있었다. 元來 基督敎의 理想은 物質을 度外視하고 財産을 貪내지 아니함이었다. 그러나 全혀 非生産的인 敎會가 그 巨大한 組織體를 維持發展시키기 爲하여서는, 莫大한 經濟力이 要求되었다. 여기서 敎會는 宏大한 法皇領을 占有하고 또는 信徒들에게 寄進金을 强要하는 自己矛盾에 빠진다. 俗世를 超越함으로써 元來의 念願으로 삼았던 敎會가, 政權에 干涉하고 財産에 關心을 갖게 된 矛盾은 超世俗的 理想 自體에 內包된 矛盾에 由來한다.

世俗을 超脫한 敎權의 樹立을 指向한 敎會의 理想은, 肉體를 떠나서 靈魂을 생각하는 原始基督敎의 禁欲主義的 傾向에 根源을 두었다. 그리고 禁欲主義的 傾向의 母胎가 되는 것은, 缺乏과 苦痛에 가득 찬 生活條件이다. 原始基督敎가 發祥한 社會的 背景은, 迫害와 生活苦에 시달리던 弱少民族의 微賤한 階級이었다. 따라서 原始基督敎에 있어서 禁欲主義的 人生觀이 支配한 것은 怪異치 않은 일이었다. 그러나 基督敎가 異端을 물리치고 政權의 彈壓을 벗어나 堂堂한 國敎로서 進出하게 되었을 때, 그리고 敎會의 指導者들이 社會的으로 優勢한 地位를 차지하게 되었을 때, 그들의 處地는 이미 禁欲主義的 人生觀의 溫床은 아니었다. 人間에 있어서 가장 自然스러운 權勢欲, 名譽欲, 그리고 여러 官能的 欲望이 抑制의 重壓을 떠들치고 일어설 刺戟이 있었다. 現世의 否定에서 出發한 基督教가 政權이나 經濟權에 關心을 갖게 되어 俗化의 길을 더듬은 것은, 靈肉의 葛藤을 免하지 못한 '人間性'으로 보아도 不可避한 일이었다.

4) 스콜라 哲學의 崩壞

中世史를 通하여 顯著한바 信仰과 知識의 對立, 教權과 政權의 軋轢, 그리고 來世主義와 現世主義, 意志決定論과 意志自由論 等의 對立은 모두 同一한 根源에서 由來한 것이다. 그것은 二大 根本思潮의 對立 卽, 헤브라이즘과 헬레니즘과의 對立의 여러 가지로 角度를 달리한 表現에 不過하다. 元來 希臘哲學은, 自然과 現實에 忠實하고 自律과 自由를 崇尙하며 經驗主義와 主知主義의 傾向이 濃厚한 헬레니즘의 精華였으며, 原始基督教의 思想은, 自然을 超越하고 未來에 憧憬하며 他律과 服從을 崇尙하고 超經驗主義와 主情主義를 特色으로 삼은 헤브라이즘의 地盤 위에 움돋은 것이었다. 그리고 中世의 學界를 代表하는 스콜라 哲學은, 헤브라이즘의 神과 헬레니즘의 人間과를 媒介하려는 努力, 卽 헤브라이즘의 信仰을 헬레니즘의 學의 立場에서 正當化하고자 하는 努力이었다. 그러나 根本的으로 對立하는 이두 潮流는 좀처럼 圓滿히 調和되지 않았다. 二大 潮流는 到處에서 一進一退의 相衝과 妥協을 거듭하였으나, 全體의 形勢는 헬레니즘이 漸次 헤브라이즘을 壓倒해 가는 方向으로 기울어졌다. 知識이 隱然中에 信仰의 領域을 蠶食해 갔으며, 政權이 次次로 教權을 制壓하고 得勢하였다. 이리하여 스콜라 哲學은 바로 그 發達의 絶頂에 있어서 衰退의 길을 밟기 始作하였던 것이다. 스콜라 哲學體系의 崩壞는 가톨릭 教會 勢力의 崩壞를 象徵하는 것이었다. 스콜라 哲學의 消長은 가톨릭 教會의 消長의 反映이었다. 스콜라 哲學의 全盛期인 十三世紀는, 敎會의 黃金時代에 該當하며 同時에 敎會가 衰退의 徵兆를 보이기 始作하던 時代이기도 하다.

가톨릭 敎會가 衰退하게 된 第一의 因子는, 敎會 自體의 內部的 崩壞에 있었다. 敎權의 政權 乃至 經濟權에 對한 關心이 助長됨에 따라서, 敎會의 俗化가 不可避하게 되었으며, 敎會의 指導層이 眞摯한 敎徒들의 信任을 喪失하게 된 事實 等은 敎會의 內部的 崩壞의 端緖가 아닐 수 없었다.

敎會의 俗化가 基督敎에 對한 信仰을 動搖시킨 內的 因子라면, 商人階級의 得勢와 自然科學的 思潮의 發達은 그 外的 因子라고 하겠다. 中世의 經濟生活은 元來 農業을 根本으로 하는 自然經濟의 生活이었다. 十世紀頃까지는, 工業은 小規模로 運營되었으며 商業은 地方的 性質을 벗어나지 못하였다. 그러나 封建制度가 高潮에 達함에 이르러, 社會狀態가 安定되고 交通도 漸次 發達을 보게 되었다. 古代의 大交通路도 復活되고 이에 沿하여 都市들이 形成되었다. 이러한 形勢는 十字軍에 依하여 더욱 促進되고, 東方貿易의 進展과 더불어 伊太利와 南獨逸에 諸都市의 勃興을 보게 되었다.

市民階級의 擡頭는 僧侶 以外에도 學問에 從事하는 사람들의 出現을 보게 하였으며, 東方思潮의 傳來에서 온 刺戟과 아울러 實用의 學으로서의 自然科學的 硏究의 盛行을 招來하였다.

本來 基督敎의 敎義는 啓蒙 以前의 知識에 立脚한 것이니만큼, 그 自然觀은 多分히 神秘主義的인 것이었다. 모든 自然現象은 神의 原理로 說明되었다. 그러나 十四, 十五世紀부터 漸次 고개를 든 自然硏究의 傾向은, 自然 自身의 原理에서 卽 經驗과 理性에 依據하여 自然現象을 說明하고자 하였다. 自然을 自然의 立場에서 보려는 이 새로운 傾向이 神學的 自然觀의 거짓을 冷酷하게 드러냈을 때, 基督敎的 世界觀 中 그 自然에 關한 部分뿐만 아니라, 基督敎 思想體系 全般에 걸쳐서 致命的인 動搖를 招來하지 않을 수 없었다.

教權에 對한 政權의 優位, 現世的 物質生活에 中心을 두는 商工人의 擡頭, 그리고 神學的 宇宙觀을 打破하는 自然科學的 思潮의 胎動 等等 一連의 諸史實은, 密接히 相互關係하는 것이며 모두가 헤브라이즘에 對한 헬레니즘의 勝利를 意味하는 것이었다. 現世的 光明과 人間的 進步를 希求하는 새로운 時代精神은, 于先 古代 希臘의 밝은 文化를 憧憬하는 復興運動의 形態로서 表現되었다. 이른바 '文藝復興(Renaissance)'의 精神的 革命運動이다. '文藝復興'을 轉換期로 삼고 世界의 歷史는 中世로부터 近代로 넘어간다.

3. 近代의 倫理學說

1) 文藝復興期[3]의 一般思潮

르네상스는, 神 앞에 自己의 存在를 喪失한 人間이, 敢히 對하여 反旗를 들고, 다시 自我를 回復하려는 精神運動이다. 基督敎的 世界觀에 依하면 被創造者 人間은 至極히 微弱하고 罪 많은 存在이다. 人間이 할 바는 오직 神을 信仰하고 神에게 服從하는 일뿐이다. 人間에게는 스스로 自己의 行爲를 調整할 意志의 自由가 없으며, 人間의 禍福은 오로지 全能한 神의 恩寵에 달려 있다. 人間이 스스로의 意思를 따라서 行動한다거나, 人間이 自力으로 運命을 開拓한다는 것은 있을 수 없는 일이다. 基督敎의 敎義는, 絶對를 外在하는 神에게 求하고 超越者 神에게 依持함으로써 人間의 救濟가 可

---

3 大體로 新時代의 氣運은 十四世紀에 擡頭하여 十五世紀에 크게 發展하고 十六世紀에 그 絶頂에 達하였다. 但 이것은 伊太利를 標準으로 한 것이요, 佛, 獨, 英 等 北方諸國에서는 約 一世紀 늦게 展開되었다.

能하다고 믿었던 것이다. 그러나 스콜라 哲學의 絶頂에 있어서 이미 中世紀的 神學의 體系는 崩壞의 路程을 밟기 始作하였다. 現世를 肯定하는 헬레니즘이 蘇生하고, 人間이 自律과 自由에 生活의 原理를 發見하고자 하는 新時代의 氣運이 胎動하였다. 이와 같은 時代精神의 發現으로서 일어난 르네상스 運動은, 外在하는 絶對者 神을 물리치고 人間 스스로를 宇宙의 王座에 앉히고, 人間의 힘으로 人間의 길을 열어 보려는 革新運動이다. 이제는 人間 自身에게, 卽 人間 안에 內在하는 '理性'에게, 絶對者의 地位가 認定된다. 神의 抑壓을 벗어난 自由人間이 歷史를 創造하는 主人公이 되려는 것이다.

新時代의 精神은 情熱的 氣風이 있는 南方에서는 于先 伊太利를 中心으로 한 文藝運動으로서 展開되고, 氣質이 剛健한 北方에서는 獨逸을 中心으로 한 '宗敎改革(Reformation)'으로 發現되고, 現實的인 民族性을 가진 英國에서는 近代的인 國民國家를 率先 形成시킴으로써 그 特色을 나타냈다. 이와 같이 地域에 따라서 그 表現의 形態에는 各各 差異가 있었으나, 그 根本精神은 近代的인 人間發見과 近代的인 自然發見에 있었다는 點으로 共通되었다.

哲學方面에 있어서는 르네상스의 精神은 于先 플라톤, 아리스토텔레스를 爲始한 古代 希臘哲學에 對한 새로운 硏究로서 나타나고, 이어서 伊太利의 自然哲學(Giordano Bruno, Telesius, Campanella)으로서 發揮되었다. 그러나 이 過渡期의 哲學者들은 그 情熱과 意氣는 衝天의 氣勢를 보였으나, 그 思想體系의 內容에 들어서는 永續的인 結實을 保障할 程度로 充實한 것이 못 되었다. 이들은 新時代의 創造者라기보다는 先驅者에 該當하였던 것이다. 近代的인 哲學 乃至 倫理學이 제법 體系가 서게 되는 것은 十七, 十八世紀에 들어선 다음의 일이다.

2) 合理論과 經驗論

러셀이 말하듯이 哲學을 宗敎的 要素와 科學的 要素의 綜合이라는 見地에서 볼 때에, 中世의 哲學은 그 宗敎的 要素가 가장 優勢하고 그 科學的 要素가 가장 劣勢한 哲學이라고 말할 수 있으며, 르네상스의 精神은, 哲學的 側面에서 볼 때에, 元來 哲學을 構成하는 重要한 要素이면서도 宗敎的 勢力에 抑壓 當하고 있던 '科學的' 精神이 擡頭하면서, 잃었던 均衡을 回復하려는 運動이라고도 할 수가 있다. '科學的'이라는 말은 '經驗主義的'이라는 말과 서로 通한다. 르네상스의 過渡期를 지난 十七, 十八世紀 哲學界에 있어서, 이 '科學的'인 精神, 卽 '經驗主義的'인 傾向을 남보다 앞서 가장 徹底히 發揮한 것은 英國이었다. 英國은 그 民族의 氣質과 歷史的 傳統이 元來 '現實的'이었을 뿐만 아니라, 이 時代의 英國의 政治的 經濟的 事情이 經驗主義(empiricism)의 哲學을 일으키기에 매우 좋은 條件에 있었기 때문이다. 近代的 國民國家를 남보다 앞서 建設한 先進國家로서의 英國에 있어서, 抽象的인 理想보다도 具體的인 現實에 關心이 集中되었다는 事實은, 學問이 一般大衆에게 普及되었다는 또 하나의 事實과 함께 當時 英國의 哲學을 經驗論의 方向으로 推進시켰던 것이다.

한편 이 時代의 大陸에 있어서는, 宗敎界의 新舊의 軋轢과 政治界의 覇權을 둘러싼 紛爭이 서로 엉켜서 多年間 混亂을 겪어 伊, 獨, 佛 모두 近代的 國民國家의 統一이 遲延되었으며, 哲學이나 倫理學에 있어서도 中世紀的 傳統을 좀처럼 벗어나지 못하고, 形而上學的인 合理論(rationalism)의 盛行을 보게 되었다.

[大陸의 合理論]

데카르트(R. Descartes, 1596-1650), 스피노자(Spinoza, 1632-1677),

라이프니츠(Leibnitz, 1646-1716)가 代表하는 大陸 合理論에 內包되는 倫理說들은, 基督敎 乃至 敎會로부터 離脫한 點에 있어서는 ‘近代的’이다. 그러나 道德의 根本을 依然히 ‘神’에게 結付시키고 있는 點에 있어서는, 亦是 宗敎的이요 中世的인 色彩를 完全히 脫却하지 못하고 있다. 이 時代의 大陸의 倫理說은, 基督敎的 人格神은 이를 물리쳤으나, 그 代身 汎神論的인 神을 이끌어 들임으로써, 全體를 形而上學的 基調 위에 두었다. 따라서 近代의 特色인 自然科學的인 思考方式은 充分한 滲透를 이루지 못하였다. 自己의 哲學體系를 敍述한 主要著作에 『倫理學(Ethica)』이라는 書名을 붙인 스피노자의 思想에 있어서, 우리는 이 時代 大陸의 倫理說의 典型을 볼 수가 있다.

스피노자의 哲學體系(Ethica)는 세 部分으로 나누어진다. 첫째로 宇宙의 實體를 論究하는 形而上學으로부터 出發하여, 다음에 情熱과 意志를 中心問題로 한 人性論을 거쳐서, 마침내 그의 形而上學과 人性論을 基礎로 한 倫理說에 到達하고 있다. 그의 形而上學은 데카르트 形而上學의 變形이었고, 그의 人性論은 홉스(T. Hobbes)를 繼承한 것이었으나, 이 土臺 위에선 그의 倫理說은 많은 獨創性을 보이고 있다. 스피노자의 倫理說은 그의 全 哲學 中에서 가장 重要한 部門이다.

스피노자에 依하면 ‘實體(Substantia)’는 오직 한 가지 ‘神’ 또는 ‘自然’이 있을 뿐이다. 데카르트가 實體로서 認定한 ‘思惟’와 ‘廷長’은, 그 自體實體가 아니라 實體인 神의 無數한 ‘屬性(Attrbutum)’ 中에서 人間에게 알려진 두 가지에 不過하다. 그리고 精神과 物質은 이 두 가지 屬性의 單純한 ‘樣態(Mobus)’로서, 그 自體 어떤 實在性을 가진 事物은 아니다. 모든 個物은, 精神이거나 物質이거나 神의 屬性의 樣態이므로, 宇宙萬物은 모두가 神의 表現이다. 스피노자의 形而上學은 徹底한 汎神論(pantheism)이다.

精神과 物質은 서로 全혀 다른 屬性의 樣態이므로, 相互間에 因果關係는 없다. 다시 말하면 精神界와 物質界는 各各 獨立한 두 갈래의 因果의 連鎖를 가졌다. 그러나 思惟와 延長은 그 根本에 있어서는 同一한 實體인 '神'의 두 屬性이므로, 各各 그 樣態인 精神과 物質은 實體上으로 본다면 同一存在의 두 方面이다. 延長의 側面에서 物體로서 나타난 것은, 思惟의 側面에서는 精神으로서 나타난다. 그러므로 精神界와 物質界를 支配하는 두 갈래의 因果의 連鎖는, 畢竟은 같은 因果關係의 兩面이 된다. "觀念의 順序와 連絡은 物體의 順序와 連絡과 同一하다." 이것은 스피노자의 有名한 말이다.

스피노자에 依하면 萬物은 絕對的인 必然性에 依하여 支配되고 있다. 精神界에 自由意志라는 것이 있을 수 없으며, 物質界에 偶然이라는 것이 있을 수 없다. 萬物은 例外 없이 헤아릴 수 없는 神의 性質의 表現이다. 따라서 이 世上에 '善'이니 '惡'이니 하는 區別이, 事物 그 自體로 말하면, 있을 수가 없다. 善이니 惡이니 하는 區別은 人間의 情緒에 基因한 主觀的인 解釋이다. 그리고 情緒의 起源은 萬物에 共通된 自己保存의 本性에 있다.

萬物은 可能한 限 自己를 保存하려고 힘쓴다. 自己保存의 努力은 萬物의 本性이다. 이 基本的 努力이 精神에 意識되었을 때, 이를 '欲求'라고 부른다. 이 欲求에 滿足을 주는 것을 우리는 善이라 하고, 障碍가 되는 것을 惡이라고 부른다. 欲求가 充足된다고 느낄 때에 '기쁨'의 情緖가 생기고, 그와 反對의 境遇에 '슬픔'의 情緖가 생긴다. 스피노자는 欲求, 喜悅, 悲哀를 基本的인 情緖로 보고, 其他의 모든 情緖는 이로부터 派生된다고 생각하였다.

欲求는 自然스러운 것이며 情緖도 元來는 나쁠 것이 없다. 그러나 情緖가 不充分한 觀念과 結合된 것, 例컨대 憤怒, 嫉妬, 恐怖, 憂愁 等의 '情念'은 마음의 平和를 깨뜨리는 不幸의 根本이다. 그러나 이러한 情念은 事物을 自己中心的으로 考察하는 狹量과, 事物의 本質을 洞察하지 못하는 無知

에서 오는 것이다. 宇宙의 萬物은 神의 自己原因에 依하여 必然的으로 存在한다는 것, 各自가 '自己'라고 생각하는 것은 獨立한 存在가 아니라 實은 全體의 一部로서 다른 事物과 必然的으로 連結되어 있다는 것, 小我의 立場에서 본다면 不幸으로 느껴지는 것일지라도 大我의 立場에서 본다면 淡淡한 平凡事에 不過하다는 것, 이와 같은 眞相을 完全히 認識한다면, 그러한 情念에 사로잡힐 理가 없다. 煩惱란 事物을 部分的으로 考察하는 偏見에서 오는 것이다. 事物을 '그 永遠한 眞相'에 있어서 把握한다면, 人生의 煩惱는 消滅되고 말 것이다.

事物을 그 永遠한 眞相에 있어서 把握함은, 思惟를 本質로 삼는 人間이 그 本性을 充分히 發揮함, 다시 말하면 人間의 참된 自由를 意味하는 것이니, 至上의 幸福이 그 中에 있다 할 것이다. 그리고 眞正한 認識이란 事物을 神과의 關聯下에서, 卽 神의 部分的 表現으로서 理解함을 意味한다. 따라서 眞正한 認識은 神에 對한 認識을 意味하고, 마침내는 神에 對한 사랑에까지 到達한다. 이 神에 對한 사랑이란 恩寵이나 報酬를 期待하는 感性的 情緒가 아니라, 神 卽 天地自然의 理法 속에 自我를 沒却하는 理知的인 사랑이다. '스피노자'는, 모든 利己心을 버리고 神明과 合一하는 理知的인 靜觀 속에, 人間의 至福을 發見한 것이다.

우리는 以上에 略述한바 스피노자의 倫理觀의 基調에 '스토이시즘(Stoicism)'이 흐르고 있음을 본다. 스토아의 思想은, 그 厭世的 傾向에 있어서, 現世를 超越하고자 하는 宗敎的 思想에 隣接한다. 이 隣接性으로 말미암아, 스토아의 思想은 中世紀 十餘世紀를 通하여 꾸준히 살아남았던 것이다. 스피노자의 倫理說이 스토아의 人生觀을 基調에 두고 있는 限, 그는 中世紀를 象徵하는 宗敎的 人物이며, 近世로의 脫皮를 完成하지 못한 思想家라 아니 할 수 없다.

스피노자는 哲人다운 達觀과 解脫을 通하여, 自己가 生存한 時代의 不安

과 自己가 타고난 個人的 不運을 解決하고자 하였다. 이와 같은 問題의 解決은, 問題를 正面에서 부딪쳐 뚫고 나아가는 解決이 아니라, 實은 問題로부터의 回避를 意味하는 解決이다. 이도 一種의 解決임에는 틀림이 없으나, 積極的인 意味의 解決은 못 된다. 萬若 回避도 眞正한 解決이라고 말할 수 있다면, 人生에는 恒常 完全한 解決策이 準備되어 있다. — '自殺'이라는 解決策이. 그러나 眞義의 解決이란, 于先 살고 나서 問題를 뚫고 나아가는 積極性을 意味할 것이다. 中世紀的인 宗敎의 目標는 '잘 죽는 것'이었을지도 모르나, 近代的인 倫理學의 目標는 '잘 사는 것'이 아니면 아니 된다. 스피노자는 自殺을 讚美하는 代身, 達觀 乃至 諦念을 勸告한다. 그러나 아무리 修辭를 戱弄한다 하더라도, '諦念'은 結局 '斷念'에 相通하는 것이며, 斷念은 一種의 精神的 自殺을 暗示하는 것이다. 그뿐 아니라 達觀이니 解脫이니 하는 것은, 聖者에도 가까운 스피노자 같은 哲人에 있어서 비로소 現實性이 있다. 凡人이 함부로 이를 꾀한다면 도리어 變態的 精神을 招來할 뿐이다. 이 點으로 보더라도, 스피노자의 倫理說은 眞理의 大衆化를 標榜하는 近代의 것으로서는 不足하다. 스피노자의 倫理觀에 包含된 高潔한 精神과 深遠한 洞察을 過少評價해서는 안 된다. 그러나 그의 倫理說이, 近代 乃至 現代의 立場에서 볼 때, 滿足스러운 體系가 아니라는 것을 否認할 수는 없다.

[英國의 經驗論]

十七, 十八世紀의 英國의 倫理說은 처음부터 宗敎와의 袂別을 明確히 하고 있다. 따라서 結局에 가서는 모든 것을 神에게 歸着시켜 버리는 形而上學으로 歸結하지도 않았으며, 神과 人間과의 關係를 倫理學의 中心問題로 삼지도 않았다. 이 時代의 英國의 倫理學이 中心問題로 삼은 것은 '人間'이다. 이 人間을 把握하되 때로는 先天的인 槪念에 呼訴한 바도 (例컨대 '良

心(conscience)', '道德感(moral sense)' 等을 先天的인 機能으로 認定한 바와 같이) 없지 않으나, 大體로는 人間을 心理學的으로 把握하려는 經驗論的 見地가 主潮를 이루었다. 그것이 形而上學的으로 把握되었든, 心理學的으로 把握되었든 間에, 神이 아닌 '人間'이 人間行爲의 善惡을 評價하는 規準이 되고 있는 點에 있어서, 우리는 이 時代 英國 倫理學의 完全한 近代性을 엿볼 수가 있다.

英國 經驗論의 基礎를 確立한 것은 베이컨(F. Bacon, 1564-1626)이었으며, 베이컨의 뒤를 이어서 그의 見解를 道德, 社會 等 實踐 方面에 徹底히 發展시켜 獨創性 있는 體系를 세운 것은, "萬人의 萬人에 對한 戰爭"을 調停하기 爲하여서 各 個人의 契約으로 社會를 構成했다고 主張한 홉스(T. Hobbes, 1588-1679)였다. 홉스의 說은, 淸新한 맛이 있었으나 좀 極端으로 흘렀기 때문에, 많은 反對者를 招來하였다. 홉스의 說을 穩健한 方向으로 調和 있게 發展시켜, 이 時代의 英國 經驗論을 大成한 것은 로크(J. Locke, 1632-1704)였다.

로크는 그의 哲學의 中樞部門인 認識論的 研究에 있어서, 特히 認識의 起源에 關한 論設에 있어서, 經驗論的 立場을 闡明하고 있다. 로크의 認識論은 두 개의 基本命題를 中心으로 展開된다. 그 하나는 "生得觀念(innate ideas)은 없다."는 것이요, 또 하나는 "우리의 認識은 모두 經驗에 由來한다."는 것이다. 前者는 그의 認識論의 消極的 方面의 基本이요, 後者는 그 積極的 方面의 基本이다.

傳統的인 合理論이 信奉하는바 絶對眞理의 基礎가 되는 것은, 모든 사람에게 普遍妥當하는 生得觀念(angeborene Ideen)이라는 것이 있다는 信念이다. 로크는 基本信念을 否認함으로써 그 認識論의 出發點을 삼는다. 論者들이 生得觀念이 있다고 主張하는 論據로 삼는 것은, 萬人에게 普遍된 觀念이 現實에 있다는 것이다. 그러나 設令 그와 같은 普遍的인 觀念이 實

際 있다고 前提하더라도, 그 普遍性이 그 觀念의 生得性을 證明하지는 않을 것이라고 로크는 反駁한다. 그 普遍的 一致가 다른 어떤 原因에 起因할지도 모르기 때문이다. 그뿐 아니라, 로크에 依하면, 그와 같은 普遍性을 가진 觀念은, 理論의 領域에 있어서나 實踐의 領域에 있어서나, 實際로 存在하지 않는다. 理論的 領域에 있어서 例를 들어 말하자면, 思考의 基本原理로 되어 있는 同一律이나 矛盾律 같은 것도 決코 普遍的으로 承認된 觀念이 아니다. 兒童이나 無敎育한 사람들은 그런 抽象的 命題를 理解하지 못한다. 또 實踐의 領域으로 말하더라도, 모든 地域과 모든 時代의 國民들이 例外 없이 承認하는 그러한 道德律은 없다는 것이다. 그리고 普遍的 觀念이 元來 內在해 있으나 다만 意識되지 않았을 뿐이라고 主張한대도, 別로 辨明이 되지 않는다. 그것은 '悟性 안에 있다' 함은 '알려져 있다'는 뜻이 아니면 아니 되기 때문이다. 萬若에 同一律이나 矛盾律 같은 普遍的 原理가 生得的인 것이라면, 幼兒들은 個別的 觀念보다도 먼저 이러한 普遍原理를 알고 있어야 할 것임에도 不拘하고, 事實은 普遍原理에 앞서서 個別的 觀念을 먼저 갖게 된다. 矛盾律을 理解하기보다 훨씬 앞서서, 어린이들은 '단 것'은 '쓴 것'이 아니라는 것을 알고 있다. 以上에 論한 바로 生得觀念이 없다는 것은 分明하다. 로크는 人間의 悟性을 元來 空虛한 暗室 또는 아무것도 쓰이지 않은 白紙와 같다고 比喩하였다.

그러면 觀念은 어디서부터 오는 것인가? 로크에 依하면 모든 觀念은 經驗에 由來한다. 經驗에 두 가지 種類가 있다. 하나는 外部의 知覺, 感官을 媒介로 하는 것으로서 感覺(sensation)이라고 부른다. 또 하나는 우리 自身의 悟性의 作用에 關한 知覺으로서 內官(inner sense) 또는 反省(reflextion)이라고 부른다. 感覺과 反省은 悟性에게 모든 觀念을 提供한다. 그것은 마치 悟性이라는 元來 暗黑한 室內에 光線을 들이는 두 개의 窓門과 같다. 感覺은 外部의 諸對象에 對한 觀念을 주고, 反省은 自己 內部의

諸作用에 對한 觀念을 준다. 이와 같이 直接 주어진 觀念을 '單純觀念(simple ideas)'이라고 한다. 悟性은 單純觀念을 材料로 이를 여러 가지로 結合하여, 마치 文字를 結合하여 單語를 構成하듯이, '複合觀念(complex ideas)'을 만든다. 道德上의 諸觀念은 行爲를 法則과 比較함으로써 생기는 複合觀念으로서, '關係(relations)'의 觀念에 屬한다.

로크는, 그 倫理說에 있어서도 그가 認識論에 있어서 取한 바와 같은 經驗主義에 立脚하고자 한다. 그러나 그는 倫理說에 있어서 經驗主義를 貫徹하지는 않았다. 그가 道德의 分析에서 心理를 論하지 않고 오히려 心理의 分析에서 道德論을 이끌어 내려고 한 데까지는 經驗論者였다. 그러나 道德的 命題의 論證的 妥當性을 主張한 것과, 그의 心理說이 結果하는 利己的 快樂主義와 그의 人格이 要求하는 社會的 公益을 調和시키기 爲하여, 絶對的인 '神의 法則(law of God)'을 前提한 點에 있어서, 로크는 도리어 合理論에 接近하고 있다.

로크의 倫理說은, 모든 사람은 오직 自己自身의 幸福 또는 快樂을 爲한 欲望에서 行動한다는 心理說에서 出發하고 있다. "事物은 오직 快樂이나 苦痛과의 關聯下에서만 善惡이 있다. 우리가 善이라고 하는 것은, 우리에 있어서 快樂을 惹起 或은 增加하는 깃 또는 苦痛을 減少하는 것이다."[4] "充分한 意味의 幸福이란 可能한 限 最大의 快樂을 얻음을 意味한다." 萬若에 이러한 見解만을 오로지 貫徹시킨다면, 利己的 快樂說 以外의 것이 나올 수가 없었을 것이다. 그러나 實際에 있어서 로크는 그와 反對의 結論에 到達하고 있다. "美德보다도 惡德을 行하는 것은 判斷이 그릇되었음을 表明하는 것이다." "우리의 情念을 統禦함은 眞正한 自由의 增進을 意味한

---

4 J. Locke, *Essay Concerning Human Understanding*, Book Ⅱ, ch. ⅩⅩ.

다."[5]고 그는 말하고 있다.

勿論 快樂이 行動의 目標라는 心理說만을 前提로 하고서는, 他人의 利益을 尊重하는 德論이 나올 수가 없다. 로크는 또 하나의 前提를 導入한 것이다. 그것은 人間이 지켜야 할 道德의 法則이 神에 依하여 作定되었다는 것과, 이 法을 따르는 사람은 來世에서 福을 받고 이 法을 어기는 사람은 罰을 받는다는 信條이다. 當面한 利害만을 眼中에 둔다면, 사람은 利己的으로 行動해야 할 것이다. 그러나 來世까지의 長久한 利害를 考慮한다면, 도리어 神의 法을 따라서 公益에 이바지하도록 行爲함이 自己自身에게도 有利할 것이다. 따라서 로크가 가장 尊重한 德目은 '愼重(purdence)'이었다.

로크는, 倫理學의 命題는 유클리드(Euclid)의 幾何學과 一般으로 '論證할 수 있는(capable of demonstration) 認識'이라고 主張한다. "所有가 없는 곳에 不正이 없다."든지, "어떤 政治도 無制限한 自由를 許容하지 않는다."는 것은 "三角形의 內角이 二直角과 같다."는 命題와 마찬가지로 確實하다.[6]

그러나 로크는 倫理學의 命題가 論證될 수 있다는 것을 充分히 論證하지 못하고 있다. 위에 例를 든 바와 같은 命題의 妥當性은, '不正(injustice)'이라든지 '政治(government)'라는 槪念을 分析함으로써 그 妥當性이 認定된다고 볼 수 있으나 이와 같은 分析的인 判斷은 어디까지나 하나의 '存在判斷'이요 그것만으로는 當爲에 關한 어떠한 絶對法則도 推理되지 않는다. 그러므로 義務나 道德律의 絶對性을 論證하기 爲하여서, 로크는 絶對的인 '神의 法則'을 前提하는 것이다. 그러나 神의 法則의 存在라는 것은,

5 Ibid., Book Ⅱ, ch. XX.
6 Ibid., Book Ⅳ, ch. Ⅲ.

自明한 原理도 아니요 論證된 事實도 아니다. 이와 같이 不確實한 前提 밑에 推理된 論證은 決코 正當한 論證이 아니다. 로크가 神의 法則이라고 認定하는 道德律이, 神이 아닌 '人間'의 法則이 아니라는 것을 로크는 論證한 바가 없다.

로크의 倫理說은 그 心理學的 基礎에 있어서도 難點이 있다. 그는 萬人이 快樂만을 欲求한다고 하나, 이것은 말 앞에 馬車를 매는 格의 先後倒錯이다. '快樂'이라는 價値가 먼저 있어서 欲求가 그것을 따르는 것이 아니라, 欲求라는 現象이 먼저 있어서 그것이 充足되는 곳에 快樂이라는 情緒가 따르는 것이다.

로크의 倫理說은 두 개의 命題를 基礎로 한 것이었다. 하나는 "人間은 快樂을 爲하여 行爲한다."는 것이며, 또 하나는 "神이 定한 道德을 어기면 不幸이 結果한다."는 것이었다. 이 두 개의 命題는 各各 不充分한 證據 위에 서 있을 뿐만 아니라, 相互間에 排斥하는 두 개의 異質的 原理 위에 地盤을 두고 있다. 卽 前者는 經驗論의 地盤 위에, 後者는 合理論의 地盤 위에. 로크가 이와 같이 對立하는 두 개의 原理를 折衷하려고 꾀한 事實은 두 가지로 考察할 수가 있을 것이다. 그 하나는 當時의 英國의 時代思潮이다. 十七世紀의 英國은, 絶對君主의 專制主義와 個人의 利益을 爲主하는 民權主義를 棄揚하여, '統制'와 '自由'를 折衷하는 自由主義(liberalism)의[7] 方向으로 發展하는 過程에 있었으며, 로크 自身도 立憲君主制를 理想으로 삼은 바, 典型的인 自由主義者였던 것이다. 社會理論에 있어서 折衷主義를 擇한

---

7 '自由主義'는 個人的으로는 '放任主義'와 同義로 쓰이기도 하나, 社會的으로는 '保守主義'와 '急進主義'와의 折衷으로서의 '進取主義'를 意味하는 것이 普通이다. 러셀은 自由主義를 "近代의 狂的 主觀主義에 對한 反動"이라고 말하고, "政府와 個人과의 權限을 配定하려는 折衷主義의 哲學"이라고 規定하면서, 이 思想의 近代的 先驅者를 로크라고 主張하였다. B. Russel, *A History of Western Philosophy*, xxii.

그는, 그 哲學的 背景을 經驗論과 合理論과의 折衷에서 求했다고 볼 수 있을 것이다.

또 하나의 考察할 點은, 經驗에 忠實하고자 하는 科學的 精神과 絶對를 希求하는 宗教的 心情을 아울러 가진 人間性 一般의 反映이다. 로크의 銳利한 批判精神은 經驗論으로 달려갔으나 그의 溫和한 性品은 그의 經驗論이 終局까지 貫徹될 때에 必然的으로 到達한 懷疑論(scepticism)에 견디지 못했던 것이다. 英國이 經驗論을 貫徹하여, 實際로 懷疑論의 종점까지 到達한 것은 흄(D. Hume)이었거니와, 英國의 經驗論과 大陸의 合理論을 로크보다도 더욱 深遠한 角度에서 綜合하여, 近代 倫理學을 完成한 것은 다름 아닌 칸트(I. Kant, 1724-1840)다.

3) 칸트

以上에 略述한 것처럼 古代 希臘 以來의 여러 倫理說은, 프로타고라스 以下 極少數의 例外를 除外한다면, 모두 共通된 基本前提에서 出發하고 있음이 注目된다. 그 基本前提란, 人生에는 時代와 地域을 超越하여 모든 사람이 指向해야 할 絶對目標 또는 모든 사람이 遵守해야 할 行爲의 絶對法則이 있다는 것과, 우리는 누구나 自己가 하고자 하면 그 絶對目標 乃至 絶對法則에 따라서 行爲할 수 있는 '意志의 自由'를 가졌다는 것이다. 이 基本前提는 歷代 學者들에게만 共通된 것이 아니라, 實로 一般大衆의 無意識的인 道德觀念에까지 滲透하여 常識化된 基本信條이기도 하다. 칸트 以前의 正統的인 思想家들은, 이 常識化된 基本信條를 無反省하게 받아들이고, 그 前提 위에서 各自의 倫理說을 體系 세웠던 것이다. 그러나 칸트는, 이러한 基本信條를 常識的인 道德觀念이 하듯이, 無反省하게 前提함으로써 出發하지는 않았다. 批判哲學家로서의 칸트가, '普遍的 實踐法則', '意志의

自由'等 形而上學的 概念을 아무런 根據 없이 받아들일 수는 없었던 것이다. 그러나 그렇다고 해서 칸트는 보편적 實踐法則이 果然 存在할 수 있을까, 또는 人間의 意志는 自由로울까. 하는 懷疑的 態度에서 出發하지도 않았다. "내 머리 위에 빛나는 별과 내 가슴속의 道德律"[8]에 對한 感歎과 崇敬을 禁치 못한 敬虔한 道德家 칸트에게는, 그와 같은 虛無觀에 가까운 懷疑도 容納되기 어려웠던 것이다. 實로 絕對普遍的인 實踐法則의 存在, 純粹理性(reine Vernunft)의 實踐的 使用의 可能性 및 意志의 自由(Willens Freiheit)를 굳게 믿고, 그러나 그것을 無條件 前提하는 代身, 그 信念의 妥當根據를 可能한 限 明白히 해보려고 한 것이, 칸트가 그 倫理學에서 取한 根本態度였다.

칸트가 倫理學을 세움에 즈음하여 于先 當面한 課題는, 上述한 바와 같이 傳統的인 道德觀念이 그것을 믿어 왔고 칸트 自身도 믿고 있던바, 道德上의 基本信條의 客觀的 妥當性을 어떤 根據 위에서 밝히는 일이었다. 칸트가 根據 주어야 할 道德上의 基本信條를 우리는 다음과 같은 세 개의 命題로 表現할 수가 있을 것이다.

(1) 時間과 空間의 制約을 받음이 없이 모든 人類에게 普遍妥當한 實踐의 法則이 있다.

(2) 사람은 그 普遍的인 實踐의 法則을 認識할 수가 있다.

(3) 사람은 그가 認識한 實踐의 法則을 언제나 實踐할 수 있는 '意志의 自由'를 가졌다.

지금 便宜上 세 개의 命題로 나누어 본 이 基本信條는, 元來 따로따로 떨어져 있는 것, 다시 말하면 各各 別個의 根據에서 立證되어야 할 問題들은

---

8 I. Kant, *Kritik der Praktischen Vernunft*, S.161.

아니다. 萬若에 普遍的 實踐法則이 存在한다는 것이 밝혀지려면, 그것은 理性의 實踐的 使用을 通하여서만 可能할 것이니, 그 法則의 內容이 어떠한 것인가가 밝혀지는 同時에 그 存在한다는 것도 밝혀질 수가 있다. 따라서 (1)과 (2)는 相互關聯하여 釋明될 問題이다. 그리고 普遍的 實踐法則의 存在는 必然的으로 意志의 自由를 要請하므로, (1)이 밝혀짐에 따라서 (3)도 間接的으로 演繹된다. 또 이와 反對로, 意志의 自由가 먼저 밝혀진다면, 그것은 모든 經驗的 動機에 制約되지 않는 先天的인 人間의 意志 또는 純粹意志(Reiner Wille)가 自己의 固有한 法則을 가지고 있음을 意味하는 것이니, '意志의 自由'라는 槪念 自體의 分析에서, 普遍的 實踐法則의 存在는 저절로 論證될 것이다. 이 點은 칸트의 다음 句節에서 明示되고 있다.

"지금 내가 自由를 道德法則의 制約(Bedingung des Moralischen Gesetzes)이라고 말했고, 나중에 이 論述에 있어서 道德法則은 무엇보다도 먼저 그것에 依하여서 우리가 自由를 意識할 수 있는 制約이라는 것을 主張할 때에, 여기에 矛盾이 있는 것처럼 사람들이 誤解하지 않도록, 나는 自由는 分明히 道德法則의 存在根據(Ratio essendi)이나, 그러나 道德法則은 自由의 認識根據(Ratio cognoscendi)라는 것만을 注意할까 한다. 그 것은, 萬若 道德法則이 우리 理性에 依하여 미리 分明하게 생각되지 않았다면, 自由라는 것이 (設令 自由가 自己矛盾이 아닐지라도)있다는 것을 想定할 權利를 우리는 생각할 理가 없기 때문이다. 그러나 萬若 自由가 없었다면, 우리들은 決코 道德法則을 發見할 수가 없었을 것이다."[9]

그러면 칸트는 이 '相互的으로 關係하는' 自由와 '無制約的 實踐法則 (unbedingtes praktisches Gesetz)'의 難關을 어느 便으로부터 究明하기

9　Ibid., S.4.

始作하는가? 萬若에 '叡知的 直觀(intellectuelle Anschaung)'이 人間에게 許容되어 있다면, 칸트는 應當 '自由'로부터 出發했을 것이다. 自由가 直觀으로 把握될 수만 있다면, 實踐法則은, 先天的 綜合判斷을 기다릴 必要 없이, 自由의 分析에서 스스로 導出될 수가 있을 것이기 때문이다. 그러나 칸트는 自由로부터 出發하지는 않았다. 人間에게는 自由를 直觀할 能力이 賦與되지 않았기 때문에, 이 點을 칸트는 다음과 같이 밝히고 있다.

"無制約的으로 實踐的인 것의 認識(Erkentnis des Unbedingt-Praktischen)은 어디로부터 始作되는가? — 그것이 自由에서부터인가, 實踐的 法則에서부터인가? … 그런데 이 認識은 自由로부터 出發될 수는 없다. 우리는 自由를 直接 意識할 수는 없기 때문이다. 왜 그런가 하면 自由에 關하여 우리가 얻은 最初의 概念은 消極的이기 때문이다."[10]

이제 칸트에게 남은 길은 '實踐法則'으로부터 出發하는 길뿐이다. 더 具體的으로는 우리의 行爲가 지켜야 할 實踐的 法則을 于先 發見하고, 그것이 先天的 普遍性을 가진 法則임을 밝힘으로써, 우리는 이 法則을 無條件 實踐에 옮겨야 하며 또 實踐에 옮길 수 있다는 것을 밝히는 길이다. 이리하여 칸트 '實踐理性批判(Kritik der Praktische Vernunft)'의 最高의 課題는, 普遍的 實踐法則에 對한 先天的 綜合判斷으로서의 實踐的 認識, 그 中에서도 特히 그 基本的인 것으로서의 '純粹實踐理性의 原則(Grundsätzen der Reinen Praktischen Vernunft)'을 發見하는 일이다.

칸트가 그 最初의 課題인 純粹實踐理性의 原則을 發見함에 있어 成功하는가, 失敗하는가는, 칸트의 倫理說 全體의 成功 與否를 左右하는 關鍵이다. 實踐理性의 原則이 適確한 事實을 土臺로 하여 發見만 된다면, 그 原則

10　Ibid., S.29.

의 客觀的 妥當性은 따로 論證할 必要 없이, 그것이 實踐理性의 事實임으로써 自明하게 되며, 또 實踐理性의 原則의 確立은 곧장 自由의 認識根據가 되기 때문이다. 그러면 칸트는 무엇에 依據하여 實踐理性의 原則을 發見하는가.

앞서도 言及했거니와 칸트는 無制約的 實踐法則이 果然 可能할까 하는 懷疑에서 出發한 것이 아니라, 그 可能性을 確信하면서 그것을 獨斷 아닌 事實의 土臺 위에서, 卽 우리의 體驗의 背景 앞에서 發見하려 한 것이다. 그러므로 實踐理性의 原則을 發見함에 있어 칸트가 依據한 것은, 다름 아닌 '道德의 事實'이다. 그는 現象界 안에 雜多한 形態로 나타난 道德의 事實을 資料 삼아, 그로부터 純粹한 道德의 法則을 抽出하고자 한다. 칸트는 이 點을 다음과 같이 敍述하고 있다. "그러나 어찌하여 저 道德法則의 意識이 可能한가. 우리가 純粹實踐法則을 意識할 수 있는 것은, 純粹理論的 原理를 意識하는 것과 같은 方式을 따라서이다. 다시 말하면 理性에 依據하여 우리에게 그 法則을 주는 必然性과, 理性이 우리에게 敎示하는바 모든 經驗的 制約을 捨象함에 注意함으로써 可能하다."[11]

그러나 칸트에 있어 實踐的 法則 發見의 出發點이 되는 것은 '實踐法則(praktisches Gesetz)'이라는 槪念 自體의 分析이다. 無制約的으로 妥當한 實踐法則은, 첫째로 普遍性(Allgemeinheit) 卽 모든 理性的 存在에 對한 無制約的 妥當性을 가져야 하며, 둘째로 必然性(Notwendigkeit) 卽 義務로서 命令(gebieten)하는 叡知的인 强制力(ein intellektueller Zwang)을 가져야 한다. 그런데 後天的 經驗的인 것은 普遍性을 가질 수가 없다. 따라서 實踐法則은 첫째로 모든 經驗的 要素의 捨象을 要求한다. 다음에

---

11 Ibid., S.30.

어떤 目的의 達成을 爲한 命令, 卽 어떤 實質的 內容(感性的 欲求의 對象)의 制約을 받는바 假言命法(hypothetischer Imperativ)은, 義務로서 强要하는 必然性이 없다. 그러므로 實踐法則은 둘째로 感性的 欲求의 對象이 되는 모든 實質的 內容의 捨象을 要求한다. 이에 칸트는, 普遍性과 必然性을 具備한 實踐法則은 先天的 立法의 形式만의 制約을 받고 成立되지 않으면 아니 된다는 結論에 到達한다.

實踐法則은 于先 單純히 主觀的 意志의 規定根據인 '格率(Maximen)'과 區別되어야 하며 다음에 條件附로 妥當하는 '假言命法'과 區別되지 않으면 아니 된다. 이와 같이 普遍性과 必然性을 具備한 實踐法則을 實踐法則으로서 妥當하게 하는 原理를, 칸트는 '實踐理性의 根本法則(Grundgesetz der reinen praktischen Vernunft)'이라고 부르고 이 根本法則을 다음과 같은 形言으로 表現하였다.

"네 意志의 格率이 恒常 同時에 普遍的 立法의 原理로서 妥當하도록 行爲하라."

萬若에 無制約的 實踐法則이 眞正으로 可能하다면, 그것은 上述한 根本法則을 滿足시켜야 할 것이며, 따라서 이 根本法則이 實踐法則의 規定原理라는 것은 分明할 것이다. 그러나 이 根本法則이 純粹實踐理性의 根本法則이라는 것은 別途로 論證되어야 할 問題다. 卽 이것이 '實踐理性의 根本原理'라는 權威가 認定되기 前에, 純粹實踐法則이 정말 可能하다는 것이 따로 밝혀지지 않으면 아니 된다. 그러면 칸트는 이 難關을 무엇으로써 突破하는가? 實로 칸트로 하여금 이 難關을 突破하게 하는 것은 '純粹理性의 事實(Faktum der reinen Vernunft)'이라는 概念이다. 칸트에 依하면, "네 意志의 格率이 恒常 同時에 普遍的 立法의 原理로서 妥當하도록 行爲하라."는 根本法則이 '理性의 事實' 또는 '純粹理性의 唯一한 事實'인 것이다. 칸트는 이 點을 다음과 같이 論述하고 있다.

"우리들은 이 根本法則의 意識을 理性의 事實이라고 부를 수가 있다. 왜 그런가 하면 우리는 이것을 理性에 先行하는 所與에서, 例컨대 自由의 意識에서, 推理함으로써 이끌어 내지는 못하나, (自由의 意識이란 우리에게 미리 所與된 것이 아니기 때문에) 그러나 이 根本法則의 意識은 그 自體로서 어떠한 — 純粹하거나 經驗的이거나 — 直觀(Anschaung)에도 依據하지 않는 先天的 綜合命題(synthetischer Satz a priori)로서 肉迫해 오기 때문이다. … 이 法則은, 經驗的 事實이 아니라, 이 法則을 通하여 自身을 本來 立法的(나는 이같이 하고자 한다. 나는 이같이 命令한다)인 것으로서 明示하는 純粹理性의 唯一한 事實이다."[12] 이 根本法則의 意識은 純粹理法의 事實인 까닭에, 이것은 純粹理性의 根本法則이며, 따라서 모든 無制約的 實踐法則의 根本原理가 된다는 것이 칸트의 論理다.

칸트는 그 根本法則의 安當性을 論證한 것은 아니다. 칸트에 依하면 이論證은 不可能할 뿐 아니라 必要하지도 않다. 칸트는, 이 根本法則이 우리가 實踐을 通하여 把握하는 純粹理性의 事實이기 때문에, 特別한 證明을 기다림이 없이도 그대로 實踐法則의 原則으로서 安當하다고 믿는다.

칸트의 純粹實踐理性의 法則은 오직 '形式(Form)'의 原理일 뿐이요 如何한 內容規定도 包含하지 않았다. 그것은 純粹理性의 原則으로서, 어디까지나 純粹한 것이요, 應當 叡知界(intelligible Welt)에 屬한다. 그러나 實踐法則의 實踐은 行爲를 通하여만 卽 感性界(Sinnenwelt) 안에서만 可能하다. 形式으로서의 純粹實踐理性의 根本法則은 內容을 具備한 그 對象을 決定하지 않으면 아니 된다. 바꾸어 말하면, 根本法則에 있어서 抽象的으로(in abstrakto) 指示된 바가, 實際行爲를 通하여 具體的으로(in concreto)

---

12 Ibid., S.31.

實現되어야 한다. 여기서 칸트는 또 하나의 難關에 逢着한다. 그것은 叡知界에 屬하는 純粹한 自由의 法則이, 어찌 能히 感性界에 屬하는 經驗的 行爲의 是非를 決定할 수 있느냐는 問題다. 實踐的 判斷力이 個個 行爲의 普遍的 原則에 對한 適否를 判定할 수 있으려면, 全혀 異質的인 두 개의 世界, 卽 叡知界와 感性界를 連結하는 어떤 媒介가 있어야 할 것이다. 여기서 이 媒介의 任務를 擔當하는 것이 칸트의 '典型(Typus)'이라는 槪念이다. 實踐的 判斷力은, 個個의 行爲가 實踐理性의 根本法則에 合致하는가, 또는 違反되는가를 直觀的으로 判定할 能力은 없다. 그러나 自然의 法則(Naturgesetz)에 비추어 이를 判定할 수는 있다는 것이다. 自然의 法則도, 그것이 普遍妥當性을 갖는다는 形式의 側面에 있어서는, 叡知界의 法則과 一般이다. 따라서 自然의 法則은, 實踐的 判斷力이 그것에 비추어 어떤 行爲의 格率이 道德의 原理에 合當한가, 合當하지 않은가를 判定하는 標識이 될 수 있다는 것이다. "自然의 法則은 ― 그러나 그 形式에 關하여서만 (aber nur sein Form nach) ― 判斷力(Urteilskraft)을 爲한 法則을 삼을 수가 있다. 따라서 우리는 이 自然의 法則을 道德法則의 典型(Typus des Sittengesetzes)이라고 부를 수가 있다."[13] 이와 같이 칸트는 말하고 있다.

그러면 自然의 法則을 '典型'으로서 使用한다면 實踐的 判斷力은 具體的으로 어떠한 規準을 얻는가. 칸트에 依하면, 典型을 媒介로 삼을 때 純粹實踐理性의 法則에 立脚한 判斷力의 規則은 다음과 같다. "萬若 네가 하고자 하는 行爲가, 네 自身을 그 一部로 삼는 自然의 法則을 따라 일어난다면, 너는 그 行爲를 네 意志로써 可能하다고 認定할 수 있는가 없는가를 自問하라."[14]

----

13 Ibid., S.69.

例컨대 連續的인 不運에 困難을 겪는 사람은, 그 苦痛을 免하고자 차라리 自殺하는 것이 善인가 惡인가를 判定하려면, 다음과 같은 格率이 自然의 法則으로서 可能하다고 認定할 수 있는가 없는가를 살펴보면 된다는 것이다. "萬若 生命을 더 延長시켜도 그것이 快樂을 約束하기보다는 오히려 禍害로써 威脅한다면, 나는 自愛之情에서 自己의 生命을 短縮함을 나의 原理로 삼는다."[15] 칸트에 依하면 이 格率은 自然의 法則으로서 不可能하다는 것이다. 그 理由는, "感情의 職分은 生命의 進陟을 促求하는 것인데 도리어 그 感情이 生命 自體를 破壞하는 것이 自然의 法則이라면, 그러한 自然은 自己矛盾에 빠짐으로써 自然으로서 存立할 수 없다."[16]라고 說明한다.

以上에 略述한 바에 依하여, 우리는 "무엇을 나는 行해야 할 것인가."라는 칸트 第二의 問題를, 칸트 自身이 그 批判哲學의 方法으로 究明해 가는 過程을, 그 根幹의 線을 따라 더듬어 본 셈이다. 이리하여 이 實踐哲學의 基本問題는 칸트로서는 一旦 그 解決을 본 것으로 되어 있다. 即 ① 實踐法則의 根本原則이 發見되었고, ② 自然法則을 典型으로 媒介삼음으로써 個個의 行爲가 이 原則에 맞는가 어긋나는가를 判定할 수 있으며, ③ 自由가 可能한 人間의 意志는 이 判定이 指示하는 대로 行爲할 수 있으니, 우리에게는 恒常 옳고 착한 行爲를 할 수 있는 길이 열려 있다는 것이 哲學的으로 밝혀졌다고 칸트는 믿었다.

칸트는 그 實踐哲學에 있어서도 놀랍게 緻密한 論理와 整然한 體系로써 一貫하였다. 그러나 칸트 實踐哲學의 體系에는 一見 整然한 論理에도 不抱

---

14 Ibid., S.69.
15 I. Kant, *Grundlegung Zur Metaphysik der Sitten*, S.57.
16 Ibid., S.57.

하고, 몇몇 弱한 고리가 있다. 이 弱한 고리들의 位置는 칸트의 實踐哲學에 있어서, 그의 理論哲學에서 埋葬된 形而上學이 다시금 蘇生되고 있는 部分과 大體로 符合된다. 그리고 이 弱한 고리들은 칸트의 實踐哲學의 가장 重大한 要所 要所를 連結하는 고리인 까닭에, 이 弱點은 或 칸트의 實踐哲學 全體에 致命傷을 招來할는지도 모르는 性質의 것이다.

弱한 고리의 첫째는, 칸트가 말하는 純粹實踐理性의 根本法則이 '純粹理性의 事實'이라는 主張이다. 우리가 '正義'니 '公正'이니 불리는 立場에 서서 判斷할 때는, 우리 意志의 格率이 同時에 普遍妥當한 立法의 原則이 될 수 있도록 行爲해야 한다는 것은, 누구나 認定할 것이다. 그러나 '正義' 乃至 '公正'의 立場에 선다는 것은 先天的인 必要性이 要求하는 것일까? "네 意志의 格率이 恒常 同時에 普遍的 立法의 原理로서 妥當하도록 行爲하라."는 根本法則의 意識이, 經驗的 意志의 事實이 아니라, '純粹理性의 事實'이라는 論據가 어디 있을까? 칸트는 "이 根本法則의 意識은, 그 自體로서 어떠한 … 直觀에도 依據하지 않는 先天的 綜合命題로서, 肉迫해 온다."고 말하였다. 그러나 이 根本法則의 意識이 先天的 綜合命題라는 것은 아직 自明한 事實은 아니다. 칸트가 말하는 '純粹理性의 事實'이라는 것은, 常識的인 用語로는 '良心의 事實'이라고 바꾸어 말할 수도 있을 것이다. 그런데 이 '良心(Gewissin, conscience)'이라는 것을 先天的 精神機能처럼 생각하는 從來의 見解에 對하여서는, 오늘날 人間을 對象으로 삼는 여러 가지 科學에 依하여 적지 않은 疑心이 提起되고 있다. 良心이 先天的이라는 從來의 信念이 어떤 科學的 探求 아래 허물어지는 날, 칸트의 倫理說은 그 根柢에 있어서 龜裂을 免치 못할 憂慮가 있다.

우리 經驗 안에 具體的으로 顯示되는 '純粹理性의 事實'의 例로서, 칸트 自身은 다음과 같은 境遇를 들고 있다. "萬若 어떤 사람이 自己의 情慾에 關"하여 그 愛好의 對象과 그 對象을 獲得할 機會가 나타났을 때, 그는 이

것에 對하여 全혀 抵抗할 수 없다고 明言한다고 하자. 萬若 그가 이러한 機會를 주는 그집 門前에, 그가 快樂의 滿足을 채운 다음에 卽時 그를 絞殺하기 爲하여 絞首臺가 設置되어 있다고 하면, 그는 果然 그때도 그 情慾을 抑制할 수 없는지 물어보라. 그가 어떠한 對答을 할 것인가는 오랫동안 推測할 必要도 없다. 그러나 그의 君主가 上述한 바와 같은 卽席死刑이라는 威脅으로, 虛僞의 口實下에 죽이려 하는 어떤 正直한 사람에 對하여 僞證을 서라고 命令한다면, 이때 그의 生命에 對한 愛着이 아무리 强하다 할지라도, 그것을 克服할 수 없는가를 그에게 물어보라. 그가 實際로 克服할지 안할지는 아마 그도 敢히 確言하지 않을 것이다. 그러나 이 克服이 可能하다는 것은 그가 躊躇 없이 容認할 것이다. 따라서 그는 어떤 일을 해야 한다고(dass er es soll) 意識하기 때문에, 그것을 할 수 있다고(dass er es kann) 判斷한다. 이리하여 그는 道德法則이 아니라면 決코 알지 못하였을 自由를, 自己 안에 意識한다."[17] 여기서 그 僞證을 設令 實際로는 拒否하지 못했다 하더라도, 그 拒否의 可能性을 自己 안에 體驗했다는 事實이, '純粹理性의 事實'을 證明한다는 것이다. 그러나 이 주장에는 若干 疑心스러운 點이 없지 않다.

칸트 또는 그와 同類의 人生觀을 가진 嚴正한 人物이라면, 누구나 칸트의 主張대로 情慾의 滿足을 爲하여서는 決코 生命을 걸 수 없으나 僞證을 拒否하기 爲하여서는 生命을 바칠 수도 있다고 느낄 것이다. 그러나 이와 같은 느낌을 萬人에게 共通된 體驗, 卽 人類의 普遍的인 體驗이라고 主張하는 것은 速斷이라고 보아야 할 것이다. 칸트와는 反對로, 一時的 情慾의 滿足을 爲하여서는 生命을 걸 수도 있으나, (世上에는 그러한 性質의 情死

---

17 I. Kant, *Kritik der Praktischen Vernunft*, S.30.

가 있다) 僞證을 拒否하기 爲하여서는 손가락 하나 자를 수 없다고 느끼는 사람도 없지 않을 것이다. 勿論 칸트는 僞證을 拒否하고자 하는 意欲은 純粹理性의 事實이요, 情慾의 滿足을 爲하여서 生命을 아끼지 않겠다는 衝動은 經驗的 感性의 事實이라고 主張하여, 이 두 가지 意欲을 異質的인 것으로서 確然히 區別할는지도 모른다. 그러나 이 區別을 正當化하는 確實한 徵表가 어디 있을까? 果然 情慾의 誘惑을 克服하지 못하는 사람과 生命을 걸고 僞證을 拒否할 수 있는 사람과의 사이에는, 懸隔한 人格의 差異가 있다. 그러나 人格은 그 個人의 遺傳과 環境이 決定한 것, 다시 말하면 그 個人의 生得的 素質과 그 個人이 成長한 社會의 慣習 또는 政治的, 經濟的 生活條件, 그리고 그가 그 社會 안에서 차지한 地位나 特有한 立場 等이 相互作用하여 形成한 歷史的 所産이다. 遺傳과 環境이 다른 까닭에 그 人格이 달랐으며, 人格이 다른 關係로 하나는 快樂의 길을 擇하고 또 하나는 正直의 길을 擇하였을 뿐이다. 여기에 있어서 前者를 純粹理性의 事實이라하고, 後者를 經驗的 感性의 事實이라고 區別할 만한 別다른 根據가 없다. 生命을 걸고 快樂을 좇을 수 있다는 意識도, 목숨을 바쳐 僞證을 拒否할 수 있다는 意識도, 다 같이 歷史 안에서 일어난 經驗的 事實이다. 그리고 이 經驗的 事實을 歷史 안에 일으킨 것은, '理性'이나 '感性'의 이름 아래 抽象할 수 있는 部分的 精神機能이 아니라, '人格'이라는 말로 表現되는 全體로서의 具體的 人間 自體라고 보는 것이 더 理解하기 쉬운 考察이다. 칸트가 말하는 '純粹理性의 事實'이 眞實로 純粹理性의 事實이요, 秋毫도 經驗的 要素를 包含하지 않았다는 것이 疑心 없는 命題가 되기 爲하여서는, 칸트는 좀 더 確實한 根據를 提示해야 했을 것이다.

칸트 倫理說의 第二의 弱한 고리는 意志自由에 關한 論說이다. 칸트에 依하면, 우리는 自由를 直觀할 수는 없다. 그러나 道德法則의 事實이 自由의 必然性을 保證한다. 道德의 法則은 '自由에 依한 原因性의 法則'이다.

따라서 自由를 前提하지 않는다면, 道德法則 自體가 不可能하다. 그러므로 道德法則의 嚴然한 事實은 '自由의 認識根據'가 된다는 것이다. 이 點을 밝힌 칸트의 論述은 다음과 같다. "그 自體 論證을 必要로 하지 않는 道德法則은, 非單 自由의 可能性을 證明할 뿐만 아니라, 그 現實性까지도, 이 法則을 自身에 對한 拘束力을 갖는 것으로서 認識하는 存在者에 關하여, 證明한다. 道德法則은 自由에 依한 原因性의 法則이요, 따라서 超感覺的 自然을 可能하게 하는 法則이다."[18]

어떤 感性的 利欲으로 기울어질 때, 그 心事를 道德法則에 비추어 反省한다면, 現實에 있어서는 그 道德法則대로 行爲하지 못하더라도 마음으로나마 感性的 誘惑을 물리치고 道德法則의 命令대로 實踐할 수도 있었다고 느끼는 그 自覺, 그리고 道德法則에 어긋나는 行爲를 한 뒤에 느끼는 自責과 自己輕蔑의 心情, 이것은 칸트에 依하면 意志의 自由를 立證하는 確乎한 事實이다. 여기에 있어 칸트의 論理는 "너는 해야 하는 까닭에 너는 할 수 있다(Du kannst, denn du sollst)."라고 推理한다.

그러나 以上의 論述은, 意志自由의 演繹으로서는 매우 不充分한 點이 있다. 于先, 칸트의 意志自由論은 '道德法則은 純粹理性의 事實'이라는 前提에서 出發하고 있다. 그리고 이 前提가 不確實한 命題라는 것은 앞서 論及한 바와 같다. 그뿐만 아니라, 지금 "道德法則은 果然 純粹理性의 事實인가?" 하는 難問을 提起하지 않더라도, 칸트의 意志自由의 演繹이 不充分함을 指摘할 수가 있다. 첫째로 사람은 自己가 信奉하는 實踐法則에 關하여서는, 그 規則대로 實踐할 수도 있었다고 反省할 것이다. 그러나 萬人이 信奉하는 實踐의 法則은 決코 同一하지 않다. 칸트와 人生觀이 다르고 따라

---

18 Ibid., S.47.

서 칸트와는 다른 行爲의 格率을 가진 사람들은, 칸트가 普遍的이요 必然的이라고 믿는 그 實踐法則대로 行爲할 수 있는 自由를 意識하는 代身, 아마 自己自身이 正當하다고 믿는 다른 路線을 따라 行爲할 수 있는 自由를 意識할 것이다.[19] 다음에 '그렇게 할 수도 있었다'는 意識과 實際로 그렇게 했다는 것, 다시 말하면 마음속에서 可能하다고 생각한 것과 外部行爲에 있어서 實現한 것과는 混同할 수 없는 두 가지 事實이다. 칸트가 '할 수 있었다'고 心中에서 느끼는 自覺을, 바로 行動으로써 外部에 實踐할 수 있는 自由의 論據로 삼은 點에는, 首肯하기 어려운 無理가 있다.[20] 셋째로, '해야 하겠다'는 義務의 意識은 '할 수 있다'는 自由의 保證은 아니다. 'Du sollst'라는 前提에서 'Du kannst'라는 歸結을 이끌어 내는 것은, 어떤 飛躍에 依하여서만 可能하다.[21]

칸트 自身도 그가 意志의 自由를 幾何學이 그 定理를 論證하듯이 論證했다고는 생각하지 않는다. 無制約的 實踐法則의 論證이 不可能했듯이, 自由의 論證도 嚴密하게는 不可能하다는 것을, 칸트 自身도 認定하고 있다. 칸트 倫理學에 있어서 根源的인 것은 理論的인 論證의 問題가 아니라, 實踐

---

19 例컨대 結婚 前의 男女交際를 罪惡이라고 믿으면서도 그런 關係에 빠진 少女는, 後日에 그 일을 後悔하고, '그렇게 안할 수도 있었다'고 느낄 것이다. 그러나 結婚 前의 男女交際를 正當하다고는 믿었으나 周圍의 事情으로 靑春時節을 無意味하게 보낸 黃昏期의 男子는, 後日에 그것을 後悔하고, 좀 더 靑春을 즐길 수도 있었다고 느낄 것이다.

20 設令 觀念上으로는 '할 수 있다'고 느꼈더라도, 現實에 안 했으면 結局은 안 한 것이다. 여기에 自由가 있다면, 안 한 自由와 後悔하는 自由가 있을 뿐이다.

21 '해야 한다'는 義務感 가운데는 이미 '할 수 있다'는 自由意識이 包含되고 있다. 自己의 힘으로는 到底히 不可能한 일이라고 생각되는 일이라면, '해야 한다'는 느낌조차도 일어나지 않는다. '해야 한다'고 믿기 때문에 '할 수 있다'고 느끼는 것이 아니라, 反對로 '할 수 있다'고 느끼기 때문에 '해야 한다'고 믿는 것이다. 그러나 할 수 있다는 느낌은 實際로 할 수 있는 自由의 完全한 保障은 아니다. 우리에게 問題가 되는 自由는 意識 內에 局限된 自由가 아니라, 外部行動을 包含한 行爲 全體의 自由이다.

的인 信念의 問題다. 칸트의 倫理說을 그 根柢에 있어서 떠받들고 있는 것은, 칸트의 人生觀이요 또 그의 人格이다. 가장 形式的인 外觀을 가지고 있는 칸트의 倫理說 안에 豊富한 內容을 感觸할 수 있는 것도, 그 全篇을 通하여 그의 生動하는 人格性이 滲透되어 있기 때문이다. 우리는 그 倫理說을 通하여 엿보이는 칸트의 人格과 個性에 對하여는 尊敬의 뜻을 禁치 못한다. 그러나 칸트의 個性이 表現되었고 十八世紀의 啓蒙思潮가 反映되어 있는 칸트의 倫理說을, 個性과 時代性을 超越한바 完全히 客觀的이요 普遍的인 純粹理性者의 體系로서 認定하기에는 躊躇를 느끼는 것이다. 學으로서의 倫理說이, 主觀的 信念이나 時代의 精神을 地盤으로 삼고 體系 설 수는 있을 것이다. 그러나 信念이나 時代精神을 土臺로 삼는 倫理學은, 칸트의 倫理學이 自認하듯이, 時間과 空間을 超越하는 無制約的 妥當性을 主張할 수는 없을 것이다. 主觀的 信念이나 時代의 精神을 地盤으로 삼는 倫理學의 任務와 方向은, 칸트의 倫理說이 擇한 그것과는 相當한 距離가 있어야 할 것이다.

類似한 弱點은 先天的인 實踐法則의 原理를 經驗的인 日常生活에 어떻게 適用시키느냐 하는 問題, 卽 實踐的 判斷力이 個個의 行爲가 純粹實踐理性의 根本法則에 合致하는가, 背馳되는가를 判別하는 手法에 關한 問題에 있어서도 나타나고 있다. 自然法則을 典型으로 使用하여 善惡을 判別하는 實例가 칸트의 著書『道德形而上學의 基礎(*Grundlegung zur Metaphysik der Sitten*)』안에 詳細히 들어 있다. 그 中의 하나로서 自殺이 惡임을 論證한 例는 앞서 言及한 바가 있다. 칸트는 感情의 職分은 生命의 進陟을 促求시키는 것임에도 不抱하고, 도리어 그 感情이 生命 自體를 破壞하는 것은 自己矛盾인 까닭에 自殺은 惡이라고 推論한다. 그러나 '感情의 職分은 生命의 進陟을 促求시키는 것'이라는 前提는 아직 科學的으로 根據 주어져 있지 않다. 現實에 있어서는 生命을 助長하는 感情도 있고, 生命을

破壞하는 感情도 있다. 感情이 生命의 進陟을 促求해야 한다는 것은, 오직 우리의 所望으로서 또는 우리의 人生觀의 一部로서만 肯定될 수 있는 主張이다. 感情 그 自體로 말하면, 오히려 精力의 消耗에 가까운 것이다.[22] 다음에 富裕한 環境에 있는 사람이 素質을 硏磨하지 않고 享樂을 일삼는 것이 道德的으로 어떠한가 하는 問題에 關한 推理에 있어서는, 論者 칸트의 主觀的 態度가 더욱 露骨的으로 表現되고 있다.[23] 칸트는, "素質의 硏磨를 게으리하고 享樂을 일삼으라."는 格率은 普遍的 自然法으로서 思惟(denken)할 수는 있으나 意欲(wollen)할 수는 없기 때문에, 이것은 道德法則으로서 妥當하지 않다고 言明한다. 그러나 사람이 무엇을 意欲하는가는 個性이 反映되는 人生觀의 問題요, 時代와 社會의 影響을 받는 世界觀의 問題다.[24]

칸트의 倫理說 各處에 發見되는 以上과 같은 弱點은 모두 同一한 源泉, 卽 칸트 倫理說의 出發點에 뿌리를 두고 있다. 칸트의 倫理說은, 人間의 道

---

22 心理學者들은 '感情(emotion)'도 一種의 行動(behavior)이라고 본다. 感情 또는 情緒의 基礎는, 刺戟에 反應하는 肉體的 變動(呼吸이 빨라지고 心臟의 鼓動이 亢進하며 消化機能이 停止 乃至 減退되는 等)에 있으며, 그 特徵은 反應의 全體性과 快不快 等의 主觀的 느낌(feeling)이 同伴되는 點에 있다고 본다. 情緒 緊張時에는 大體로 呼吸, 循環系統의 活動은 促進되고 消化系統의 機能은 低下된다. 따라서 情緒의 緊張은 大體로 生命의 消耗를 意味하는 것이다.

23 I. Kant, *Grundlegung zur Metaphysik der Sitten*, S.58.

24 '素質의 硏磨를 게으리하고 享樂을 일삼는 것'은 우리로서 意欲할 수 없기 때문에 그것을 우리의 道德法則으로 삼을 수 없다는 見解라면 反對하지 않는다. 人間의 意欲을 떠나서 道德律의 根據가 될 수 있는 것은 없다. 다만 이 意欲 乃至 意志의 어느 것을 特히 '先天的'이요 絶對不變하는 것으로 보는 見解에 對하여 疑心을 갖는 것이다. 칸트는, 人間性의 絶對的인 것에서부터 道德의 絶對性을 推理한 것이 아니라, 反對로 道德의 絶對性을 保證하기 爲하여 人間性의 絶對的인 것을 超經驗界에 求하였다. 그러나 우리는 道德律에서 出發하여 人間性을 想定할 것이 아니라, 人間性에서부터 出發하여 道德律을 決定해야 할 것이다. 그리고 可能하다면 經驗的 歷史의 世界 안에서 生成되는 人間性을 土臺로 하는 道德律 안에 칸트와는 다른 意味의 絶對性을 發見해야 할 것이다.

德意識이 純粹實踐理性의 事實이라는 前提下에, 無制約的으로 妥當한 實踐的 法則을 確立하고자 하는 意圖에서부터 出發하고 있다. 칸트는 그 實踐的 法則을 確立함에 있어 經驗의 具體的 事實로부터 出發하여 窮極의 原理를 把握하는 上昇의 길을 擇하는 代身 根本的 原理로부터 出發하여 具體的 個別事實의 判定에 이르는바 이를테면 下降의 길을 取하였다. 칸트 倫理說의 出發點은, 經驗世界에 나타난 道德現象의 分析 乃至 批判이 아니라, 道德의 先天的 絕對性을 믿는 그의 道德的 信念이다. 嚴密하게 말하자면, 그는 自己가 主張하듯이 道德의 原理를 多樣한 素材 中에서 發見하려 한 것이 아니라, 이미 自己의 人格 안에 端的으로 形成되어 있는 道德原理의 正當性 또는 普遍妥當性을 그의 先驗的 方法(transcendentale Methode)에 依하여 立證하려 한 것이다. 絕對普遍性을 主張하기 爲하여서는, 그 道德의 原理가 經驗的 要素로부터 完全히 獨立된 先天的 原理, 따라서 超現象界 卽 叡知界의 所屬임을 認定하지 않을 수 없었으며, 純粹理論理性에 對하여서는 그 認識의 可能性을 拒否했던 叡知界의 認識을 純粹實踐理性에게 許容하기 爲하여서(이것을 許容하지 않으면 칸트의 倫理說은 成立하지 않는다), 實踐理性의 優位(Primat der praktischen Vernunft)를 認定하는 同時에, 그 理論哲學에서 斷念했던 形而上學을 그 實踐哲學에서 또다시 蘇生시키지 않으면 아니 되었던 것이다. 形而上學을 導入한 칸트의 倫理說에는 '意志自由', '靈魂不滅', '神의 存在' 等을 要請(Postulat)으로서 認定하는 曖昧한 部面이 생겼으며, 그 理論哲學에 있어서와 같은 明白性이 缺如되어 있는 것도 不得已한 結果라고 생각된다.

道德律의 時空을 超越하는 絕對普遍性을 根本前提로 한 칸트의 倫理說은, 必然的으로 形而上學的 倫理說이 되는 同時에 形式倫理說(Formalism)이 되었다. 實質的(materiell) 價值는 모두 經驗的이며, 經驗的인 것에는 絕對普遍性이 없기 때문이다. 倫理說이 '形而上學的'임은 理

論的 難點을 內包한다. 形而上學은 妥當根據를 追究하는 批判的 精神에 對하여 滿足스러운 答辯을 恒常 回避하기 때문이다. 또 倫理說이 '形式的'임은 實踐的 難點을 意味한다. 行爲가 實踐되는 것은 經驗世界에 있어서이며, 經驗世界에 있어서 行爲를 制約하는 力量을 갖는 것이, 法則의 抽象的形式이기보다는, 目的의 王國이 決定하는 實質的 價値이기 때문이다. 칸트는, 그 形式說에 實踐性을 賦與하기 爲하여서, 畢竟은 目的論을 隱密히 許容하지 않으면 아니 되었다. 그러나 칸트의 形式說이 目的論을 容納할 수 있었던 것은, 體系 全體를 通한 '理論의 整合'을 若干 犧牲에 바침으로써만 可能하였다. 人間이 그 안에서 善美한 行爲를 實現할 現實社會는 流轉과 變化의 現象的 世界이다. 形而上學的 形式說이 變化流轉하는 現實社會에 對하여 提示하는 實踐의 準則은, 現實性 없는 空論이거나 多義의 解釋을 容納하는 抽象論임을 免치 못한다.

칸트 倫理說의 基礎가 된 것은 人間의 理性이다. 倫理學의 基礎를 人間性에 求한 것은 正當하였으나, 그 人間性의 把握이 充分히 具體的이 못 된 것은 致命的인 缺陷이었다. 칸트에 依하여 把握된 人間은, '個人'으로서의 人間이요 叡知界에 屬하는 '理性者'로서의 人間이다. 이와 같이 二重의 抽象을 겪은 人間像은, 現實 속에 生動하는 人間으로부터는 먼 距離가 있다. 具體的인 人間은 첫째로, '社會'와 '歷史' 안에서 把握되어야 하며, 둘째로, 經驗界에 사는 現實的 存在로서 把握되어야 할 것이다. 近代의 倫理學이 이와 같은 方向으로 發展하게 되는 것은, 主로 十九世紀에 들어선 다음의 일이다. 여기서는 人間의 共同體로서의 社會 乃至 國家가 倫理學을 決定함에 있어서 重要한 意味를 갖게 된다. 大陸 合理論의 傳統 위에서 크게 이 方面을 開拓한 것은 獨逸理想主義의 大成者 헤겔이었으며, 英國 經驗論의 立場에서 이 方面으로 倫理學을 發展시킨 것은 벤담과 존 스튜어트 밀을 代表로 하는 功利論者(utilitarianist)들이었다.

4) 헤겔

헤겔(G. W. F. Hegel, 1770-1871)에 依하면 世界는 理念(Idee)의 辨證法的 發展過程이다. 理念은 그 自體 精神이나, '他在(Anderssein)'의 形式으로서는 '自然(Natur)'으로서 나타난다. 他在의 形式으로서의 理念, 卽 自然이 自己에게로 回歸하면, 卽 向自(für sich)의 形式을 取하고 나타나면, 이것이 狹義의 '精神(Geist)'이다. 이 狹義의 精神이 發展한 過程을 省察하는 것이 헤겔의 精神哲學이며, 그의 倫理思想이 表明되는 것은 이 精神哲學의 一部分으로서다.

(狹義의) 精神은 ① 主觀的 精神(subjektiver Geist), ② 客觀的 精神(objektiver Geist), ③ 絶對的 精神(absoluter Geist)의 三段階로 展開된다. 主觀的 精神은 넓은 意味의 心理學의 對象이다. 아직 自然의 품을 멀리 떠나지 못한 人間의 精神으로서, 오직 本能과 利己的 情欲을 따라서 盲動하는 精神이다. 精神의 本質은 '自由(Freiheit)'에 있다. 主觀的 精神은, 放縱하다는 意味로는 自由이나, 其實은 奴隷狀態에 있는 것이다. 本能이라는 自然力에 屈從하기 때문이다. 그러나 主觀的 精神은, 그 意識의 發達과 더불어 他人의 存在를 認知히고, 他我도 自我와 同類의 人間임을 認識하는 同時에 自由는 自己에게만 있을 것이 아니라 他人에게도 있어야 할 것을 깨닫게 된다. 여기서 他人의 自由와 權利를 爲하여 自己의 欲望(盲目的 自由)을 制約하게 되며, 自我欲求의 制約을 通하여 主觀的 精神은 참된 自由에로 一步 上昇한다. 참된 自由는 盲目的인 것을 克服하는 理性的 行爲에 있기 때문이다. 이와 같이 主觀的 精神이 自己의 否定을 媒介로 삼고 더 높은 段階로 上昇한 狀態 — 이것이 곧 客觀的 精神이다.

이 第二의 段階, 卽 自由를 實現하는 客觀的 精神은, 넓은 意味의 倫理가 實現되는 곳이요, 넓은 意味의 倫理學이 그 對象을 求할 場面이다. 客觀的

精神이 指向하는 바는 '自由'이다. 그러나 여기서 問題가 되는 自由는, 칸트까지도 包含하는 從來의 倫理學에서와 같이, 個個人의 意志를 核心으로 한 個人主義的 自由는 아니다. 이제 自由는 全體로서의 社會現實에 求하지 않으면 아니 된다. 各個人의 目的은 社會的 承認을 얻어서 비로소 達成될 수 있으며, 個人의 自由는 社會의 法則 안에 客體化한다. 客體化된 自由意志 ― 이것이 곧 '法(Recht)'이다.

法은 客觀的 精神의 첫 段階의 發現이다. 이것은 自由意志의 客觀的이요 抽象的인 實現이다. 法 앞에서 萬人은 平等하고 無差別하다. 平等하고 無差別한 個人을 헤겔은 '人格(Person)'이라고 불렀다. 헤겔이 말하는 人格, 卽 法의 擔持者로서의 人格은, 칸트가 말하는 人格과는 다르다. 칸트의 人格의 本質은 '尊嚴性(Würde)'에 있었으나, 헤겔의 人格의 中心은 '平等性(Gleichheit)'에 있다. 法은, 人格이 物質을 支配하는 '所有'와, 人格과 人格 間에 이루어지는 '契約'과, 法을 侵犯한 人格에 對한 '刑罪'로서 發現된다.

客觀的 精神의 第二의 段階는 '道德(Moralität)'이다. 法은 行爲의 外面的 合法性(Legalität)을 問題 삼는 것이나, 道德에 있어서는 行爲의 內面的 動機가 問題된다. 道德은 法的인 것의 外面性의 否定이다. 道德은 '良心(Gewissen)'으로서 發現한다. 道德은 自由意志의 主觀的이요 內面的인 實現이다. 그러나 良心에만 依存하는 道德은, 元來 主觀的인 까닭에, 恒常 客觀的인 妥當性을 期必할 수는 없다. 良心이 善으로 認定한 行爲일지라도 實際에 있어서는 惡이 되는 境遇도 없지 않다. 따라서 道德은 그 自體만으로서 完全할 수가 없다. 여기서 客觀으로 치우친 法과 主觀으로 치우친 道德이 綜合되어, 다시 '人倫(Sittlichkeit)'으로 發展하지 않으면 아니 된다.

'人倫'은 客觀的 精神의 第三段階이다. 그것은 法과 道德과의 對立을 棄揚(aufheben)하여 最高의 實現段階에 到達한 自由意志다. 人倫은 道德에

있어서와 같이 內面的 自由도 아니며, 法에 있어서와 같이 抽象的 自由도 아니다. 헤겔은 '人倫'에 있어서 가장 現實的이며 具體的인 自由의 實現을 보았다.

人倫의 最初의 段階는 '家族(Familie)'이다. 家族은 人倫의 가장 原始的인 自然形態이며, 人倫의 直接的인 表現이다. 家族을 形成하는 것은, 抽象的으로 平等한 人格이 아니라, 有機的 全體의 部分에 該當하는 '成員(Glied)'이다. 成員은 家族 內에서 各各 特有한 使命을 가지고 있다. 家族 成立의 條件인 '結婚'은 세 가지 契機를 包含하고 있으니, 첫째는 '性的 關係'요, 둘째는 '民事契約'이요, 셋째는 '愛情'이다. 그러나 헤겔은, 結婚에 있어서의 第三의 契機, 卽 主觀的인 感情을 그리 重要視하지 않았다. 相互間의 愛情은 結婚生活을 하는 동안에 必然的으로 생길 것으로 믿었던 것이다. 結婚을 義務라고 생각한 헤겔은, 結婚하고자 하는 決意를 重大視하는 同時에, 個人的인 愛情은 副次的 結果로서 생기는 것이 人倫의 本質에 合當하다고 보았다.

家族은 子女의 成年과 結婚을 契機로 分家한다. 한 家族이 여러 家族으로 分家함으로 말미암아, '市民社會(Bürgerliche Gesellschaft)'가 形成된다. 市民社會는, '人倫' 發現의 第二의 段階에 該當한다. 市民社會를 構成하고 있는 것은 '市民(Bürger)'이다. 市民은 自由와 平等을 原理로 삼는 獨立한 個人들이다. 市民社會를 統一하여, 各者의 生命과 財産의 安全을 圖謀하는 것은 法的 制度와 警察的 秩序이다.

헤겔은 市民社會와 '國家(Staat)'를 本質이 다른 것으로서 區別하였다. 市民社會에 있어서는, 各 市民은 自由獨立的이다. 市民에게는 自己自身만이 目的이며 殘餘는 모두 手段이다. 그러나 國家에 있어서는, 이와 反對로 全體가 目的이요 個人은 그 手段이다. 國家 內에 있어서는, 自己 個人의 幸福만을 追求할 것이 容納되는 獨立한 個人이라는 것이 있을 수 없다고 헤겔은 力說한다.

市民社會에 있어서, 自由와 平等을 原理로 삼는 各 個人이 各自의 欲求를 無限定하고 追求할 때, 홉스의 이른바 "萬人의 萬人에 對한 爭鬪"가 招來된다. 그러므로 各自의 欲求를 中心으로 生活하는 市民의 利己的 結合體인 市民社會는, 人倫의 解體 — 人倫의 否定을 契機로서 內包하고 있다. 家族에 있어서 措定되고, 市民社會에 있어 否定되는 人倫이, 그 對立을 棄揚하여 더 높은 段階로 綜合될 때에, '國家'가 成立한다. 國家는 人倫의 最高 完成된 形態이다.

헤겔은 國家를 人倫的 理念의 現實態라고 보았다. 國家는, 모든 個人이 온갖 理性的 活動과 더불어 그 속으로 吸收되어야 할 運命을 가진바, 完全한 生活共同體라고 보았다. 헤겔은 國家의 歷史的 說明 또는 心理學的 說明에 反對하였으며, 特히 元來 利己的인 個人들이 各自의 安全과 福利를 爲하여서 打算과 約束에 依하여 國家를 造成하였다는 홉스 式의 國家觀에 反對하였다. 헤겔에 依하면, 國家는 歷史的 偶然性에 依하여 構成된 것이 아니라, 內面的 必然性에 依하여 展開된바 民族精神의 理性的 實現이다.

헤겔의 國家觀은, 個人의 權利나 特殊性을 國家의 全體性 속에 解消시켜 버리는, 古代 希臘的인 國家觀念에 매우 接近하고 있다. 헤겔에 있어서는, 國家는 個人이 各自의 利害를 全的으로 그 안에 棄揚해야 할 全能者이다. 헤겔은, 個人이 제멋대로 批判하고 要求하는 近代的인 自由主義에 反對하였다. 헤겔이 最善의 政體라고 생각한 것은 英國式의 世襲的 立憲王政이다. 그는 革命에 反對하고, 漸進的 改良主義를 擇하였던 것이다.

헤겔은, 最初에는 國家에 있어서 人間理性의 最高의 實現이 可能하다고 믿었으나, 그의 思想에 浪漫主義(romanticism)의 傾向이 높아 감에 따라서, 人間的 精神生活에 더 높은 價値를 認定하게 되었다. 그는 近代의 個人에게, 國家의 힘을 超越하는 獨自의 活動力을 認定하고, 國家生活보다도 더 높은 精神的 生命力의 權限을 認定하였다. 여기에 이르러, 客觀的 精神은 國家의 範域을 넘어서, 다시 한 걸음 絶對的 精神으로 展開한다. 絶對的 精神의 發現으로서 藝術과 宗敎와 哲學이 順序로 論議된다.

헤겔에 있어서, 倫理學에 關한 問題는 結局 '國家'로 歸結하고 말았다. 道德的인 行爲란, 結局 國家라는 全體의 小部分으로서의 國民이 各者의 맡은 바 任務를 다하는 生活속에서 實現된다. 倫理學의 問題가, 從來의 道德哲學이 생각해 왔듯이 抽象的인 個人의 主觀的 心情에 局限될 것이 아니라, 도리어 全體로서의 社會共同生活 안에 그 重心을 두어야 할 것을 指摘한 點은 헤겔의 卓見이며, 칸트에 이르러 窮地에 빠져 버린 個人的 道德哲學에 活路를 示唆한 것이라 하겠다. 그러나 헤겔이 '國家'에게 絶對權威를 認定하는 나머지, 國家의 成員이 되고 있는 個人의 地位가 疎忽히 되는 한편, 行爲의 道德的 價値가 오로지 '國家'라는 目的을 爲한 手段價値로 떨어지고 만 것은, 首肯하기 어려운 難點이라 아니 할 수 없다.

헤겔 倫理思想의 基本的인 難點은 그의 國家觀念에 있다. 첫째로, 하나의 '世界國家'를 想定한다면 모르거니와,[25] 數十個의 國家가 倂立하고 있는 形便에 있어서, 國家에게 絶對權威를 認定한다는 것은 理論的 根據가 薄弱할 뿐만 아니라, 實際에 있어서도 危險性 있는 생각이다. 理論的 根據가 薄弱하다는 것은, 于先 같은 地球上에 있어서 絶對權威가 두 個 以上 있

---

25 萬若 헤겔이 自己의 論理에 忠實했다면, 오히려 그의 理想은 世界國家에까지 發展됐어야 할 것이다. 歷史的 現段階에서는 民族國家가 可能한 最高의 共同體라고 主張했다면 좋다. 그러나 理念의 無限한 發展을 論하는 헤겔의 哲學에 있어서, 理想이 民族國家에서 멈추어야 할 何等의 論理的 根據도 없다. 헤겔의 國家論을 制約한 것은 그의 辨證法的 論理뿐만은 아니다. 冷徹한 哲人은 헤겔의 表面이었고, 熱烈한 愛國者는 그의 裏面이었다. 世界國家란, 오늘날에 있어서도 尙今 實現性이 없거늘, 十八世紀에 있어서 그러한 空論을 提唱하지 못한 헤겔을, 우리는 '歷史的 現實'이라는 背景 앞에서 理解할 뿐이다.

을 수 없다는 論理만을 想起하더라도 明白할 것이다. 國家는 絕對權威者인 까닭에, 國家間에 對立抗爭이 생기는 境遇에, 그 對立을 解決할 만한 더 높은 權威는 있을 수 없다. 따라서 國家間의 問題는 結局 武力에 呼訴하는 길밖에 없게 되며, 戰爭은 正當한 手段으로서 合理化된다. 이러한 思考는, 結局 國際間에 있어서 正義를 決定하는 것은 武力의 强弱에 있다는 結論으로 引導한다. 勿論 어떤 歷史的 段階에 있어서 民族國家가 現實的으로 可能한 最高의 共同體라는 主張이라든지, 一定한 境遇에 國際間의 對立은 事實上 戰爭 以外에 解決의 方策이 없다는 主張이라든지, 또는 現實에 있어서 國際間에 正義의 行勢를 하는 것은 武力的 强者라는 主張이라면, 얼마든지 正當할 수가 있다. 그러나 어느 時期에 있어서 戰爭이 事實上 不可避했다는 歷史的 事實은, 決코 戰爭 自體가 祝福 받을 것이라는 價値判斷을 正當化할 수 없으며, 또는 强者가 正義의 行勢를 한다는 現實이, 强者에게 正義를 認定해야 한다는 當爲判斷의 根據가 될 수도 없다. 歷史的 事實이나 當面한 現實을 모조리 있는 그대로 是認하는 것은, 道德的 態度가 아닐 뿐만 아니라, 人間性의 現實에도 背馳된다. 人間性은 一般的으로 現在의 段階에 不滿을 느끼고, 더 높은 狀態를 將來에 意圖한다. 더 높은 것을 爲하여 現在를 밟고 넘어서려는 意欲은, 人間性 自體에 뿌리 깊은 것이며, 이것이 있는 까닭에, '道德'이라는 現象이 人間에게 나타나게도 된 것이다.

헤겔의 國家觀이 實際的 危險性을 가졌다는 것은, 첫째로, 上述한 바와 같이 戰爭侵略者의 攻擊이 이를 理論的 防牌로 삼을 수 있기 때문이며, 둘째로, 無道한 暴君이 그의 殘虐을 爲하여 惡用할 수 있기 때문이다. 헤겔이, 當時 메테르니히(Metternich)가 主宰한 神聖同盟을 反對하고, 칸트가 提唱한 '平和聯盟'을 非難하며, 諸民族이 相爭하는 世界史的 過程에 있어서 支配的인 民族이 現在의 段階에 있어 世界精神의 主人公이요, 殘餘의 諸民族은 이 勝利者의 光榮을 裝飾하기 爲하여 그 王座 周邊에 參列한다고

主張한 것은, 그의 國家觀念으로 보아 當然한 結論이라 하겠으나, 우리는 이 結論을 倫理學의 立場에서 是認할 수는 없다. 또 國內問題에 關하여, 헤겔은 "國家의 人格性은 한 사람의 人格 即 君主로서만 現實的"이라고 말하여 國家의 主權을 君主 一人에게 맡기는 同時에, 世襲的 君主制度를 擁護하였으나, 이러한 政治思想의 不當性을 指摘하기 爲하여, 民主主義가 常識化한 오늘날, 우리가 張皇한 論說을 일삼을 必要는 없을 것이다. 헤겔이 한참 活躍한 것은, 十八世紀 歐羅巴를 휩쓴 急激한 自由主義 即 急進主義(radicalism)가 漸次 그 弊端을 나타내어, 그 反動으로서 保守主義가 歐羅巴의 政界를 支配하던 時代였다.[26] 急進主義의 爆發인 佛蘭西革命이 일어난 1789年은 헤겔이 弱冠 二十時節이었으며, 一時 世界에 君臨했던 나폴레옹(Napoleon)이 沒落한 1851年은 헤겔이 四十六歲의 壯年期였다. 革命의 禍亂과 뒤이은 戰亂이 疲困한 當時 유럽 社會는, 지나친 自由運動에 不安을 느끼고 도리어 反動的 保守思想으로 기울어졌던 것이다. 이와 같은 歷史的 背景을 通해서 볼 때에, 우리는 헤겔의 君主主義 國家論을 理解할 수가 있다. 그러나 헤겔의 國家觀이 永遠한 眞理가 못 된다는 것은 百五十年 後의 現實이 이를 證明하고 있다.

大體로 헤겔의 '國家'에 있어서는 個人의 價値가 지나치게 낮게 評價되고 있다. 個人은 何等의 自己目的을 가진 存在가 아니라, 國家라는 全體를 爲한 一介 手段의 地位를 甘受하지 않으면 아니 된다. 헤겔은 國家와 國民의 關係를 마치 有機體와 有機體를 形成하는 部分으로서의 器官의 關係에 比喩할 수 있다고 생각한다. 身體를 떠나서 '눈'이 그 自體만으로는 아무런 價値도 없듯이, 國家를 떠나서 國民 個人에게는 아무런 價値도 없다고 그

---

26 大類伸, 『西洋史 新講』, 近代史(下), 第四章 參照.

는 믿는다.

그러나 이 比喩는 妥當하지 않다. 國家와 國民의 關係도 一種의 全體와 部分의 關係이기는 하나, 有機體와 器官의 關係와 同一한 意味의 全體와 部分은 아니다. 全體와 部分의 關係라 할지라도 여러 가지가 있다. 甲이라는 全體에 妥當한 見解가 乙이라는 全體에 關하여서도 반드시 妥當할 수는 없다. 벽돌집과 벽돌의 關係에 있어서, 벽돌은 벽돌집을 爲한 手段이라는 見解를 우리는 躊躇 없이 받아들인다. 그러나 이 比喩를 直接 國家와 國民의 關係에 轉用할 수는 없다. 무릇 目的과 手段이 云謂되는 境遇에는 恒常 어떤 것을 目的으로 삼고 어떤 것을 手段으로 삼는 評價의 主體가 있다. 벽돌집의 境遇에는 벽돌집을 所有 乃至 使用하는 人間이 評價의 主體이다. 이것을 目的으로 삼고 저것을 手段으로 삼는 人間이 있는 까닭에, 벽돌과 벽돌집 사이에는 手段과 目的의 關係가 成立할 수 있는 것이다. 萬若 地球 上에 人類가 絶滅되고 벽돌집들만이 남는 날이 온다면, 그때는 이미 벽돌집에 關한 目的과 手段의 關係는 解消되고 말 것이다. 그렇다면 國家와 國民의 關係가 目的과 手段의 關係로서 規定될 수 있으려면, 여기에도 반드시 國家를 目的으로 삼고 國民을 手段으로 삼는 評價의 主體가 있어야 할 것이다. 헤겔의 國家에 있어서 國民이 그 主體가 될 수 없음은 勿論이다. 個個의 國民이 그것이 될 수 없을 뿐만 아니라, 國民의 總和도 그것이 될 수가 없다. 그 主體는 左右間 國民 以外에 있어야 한다. 그러면 國王이 主體가 될 수 있는가? 헤겔은 그렇다고 對答할지 모르나, 우리는 이를 否認한다. 마지막 希望은 人間을 超越한 어떤 絶對者, 例컨대 神에 걸려 있다. 그러나 論理에 窮하여 神을 빌려 올 때, 問題는 恒常 形而上學을 거쳐서 宗敎圈으로 逃避한다.

倫理學은 社會的인 人間構造를 떠나서 解明될 수가 없다. 이 點을 分明히 드러낸 헤겔의 功績은 컸다. 그러나 헤겔은 그 社會的 人間構造, 卽 '人

倫'을 밝힘에 있어서 지나치게 形而上學的이었다. 正-反-合으로 展開되는 그의 辨證法的 論理를 事事件件에 適用하려 한 그의 無理는 그의 人間把握으로 하여금 科學, 特히 社會科學과 등지게 하였다. 다음에 論及하고자 하는 功利主義者(Utilitarianist)들은, 人間構造의 社會性에 注目하면서, 그 社會性을 더 科學的인 見地에서 考察하고자 한 사람들이다.

5) 功利主義

普通 功利主義(Utilitarianism)의 創造者로 認定되는 벤담(J. Bentham, 1748-1832)이 元來 關心의 重心을 둔 것은 法律學이었다. 그가 倫理學과 政治學에 注目하게 된 것도 法律學에 對한 關心에 基因하고 있다.

벤담의 倫理說은, 善(good)은 곧 快樂이라는 元來 利己的이었던 快樂說과, 人間은 自己 個人의 幸福만을 追求할 것이 아니라 社會 全體의 福祉를 圖謀해야 한다는 愛他的 色彩가 있는 公益主義와를 折衷한바, 이를테면 社會的 快樂主義라고 부를 수 있는 特色을 가졌다. 그러나 功利主義의 이름을 가진 思想의 內容이 벤담에 이르러 비로소 새로 생긴 것은 아니다. 로크에 있어서도 實質的으로는 같은 原理가 이미 包含되어 있었다. 벤담의 功績은 이 原理를 여러 現實問題에 適用한 點에 있어서 더욱 컸다.

벤담의 倫理說의 基礎가 되는 것은, "自然은 人類를 苦痛과 快樂이라는 두 君主의 支配下에 두었다. 우리가 해야 할 바를 指摘하고 우리가 하지 아니할 바를 限定하는 것은 오직 이 두 君主에 依存한다."[27]는 心理說이다. 모든 行爲는 快樂과 苦痛에 달려 있다. 따라서 善(good)은 곧 快樂

---

27 J. Bentham, *Introduction to the Principle of Morals and Legislation*, p.1.

(pleasure)과 一致하고, 惡(evil)은 곧 苦痛(pain)과 一致한다.

그러나 벤담은 各 個人의 利己的 快樂追求를 是認하지 않는다. 그의 倫理說은 社會 全體의 快樂, 卽 '最大多數의 最大幸福(the greatest happiness of the greatest number)'이 各 個人의 目標로 삼을 바라고 主張한다. 그러나 그의 心理說이, 各 個人은 모두 自己自身의 快樂을 爲하여 行爲하는 利己的 生物이라고 認定하면서, 도리어 社會 全體의 公益을 爲하여 行爲하라는 倫理說을 提唱하는 것은, 어떠한 事由에 依한 것일까?

벤담의 '最大幸福의 原理(the greatest happiness principle)'는 本來 倫理的 原理로서 라기보다도, 立法의 原理 또는 政治의 原理로서 提唱되었던 것이다. 卽 個人의 行爲가 基準으로 삼을 目標를 發見하기 爲한 原理가 아니라, 國家 全體가 立法 또는 政治의 目標를 發見하기 爲한 原理였다. 快樂主義의 心理說을 個人的 實踐問題에 適用시킨다면, 各自는 自己 個人의 最大幸福을 期하라는 準則을 얻을 것이다. 그러나 立場을 個人으로부터 國家 全體로 옮기고 같은 心理說을 實踐問題에 適用시킨다면, 各國은 自國의 最大幸福을, 卽 最大多數의 最大幸福을 招來하도록 立法하고 政治하라는 原則을 얻을 것이다. 各 個人은 어디까지나 自己自身을 爲하여 行爲하는 心性이 있다. 따라서 이 利己的 心性이 社會 全體의 安寧秩序를 깨뜨림이 없도록 하여, 個人의 利益과 社會의 利益을 調和시키는 것이 바로 立法家의 使命이다. 이것이 벤담의 見解의 要點이다. 어떤 個人으로 하여금 盜賊질을 못하도록 막는 것은 社會 全體의 利益이다. 그러나 效果的인 刑法의 制定이 있는 境遇에, 盜賊질을 않는 것은 그 個人의 利益이기도 하다.

立法과 政治에 關心이 깊은 벤담이, 萬人은 自己의 快樂을 追求하는 利己的 生物이라는 心理說을 믿었을 때, 法學者 또는 政治家의 立場에서 그가 最大幸福의 原理를 探擇하고, 나아가서 이 原理를 넓은 意味의 倫理的 原理로 認定한 經緯는 理解할 수가 있다. 그러나 都大體 벤담이 立法家 乃

至 政治家의 立場, 卽 國家 全體의 立場에서 事物을 考察하는 것은 무엇 때문일까? 벤담이 國家 全體의 立場에서 考察하는 것도 亦是 自己自身에 利己的인 動機에서인가? 벤담의 心理說에 忠實하다면 그렇게밖에 생각할 길이 없다. 그러나 萬若 立法家나 政治家의 立場이 單純히 利己的인 것이라면, 立法이나 政治의 原理는 立法家나 政治家 自身들에게 最大의 幸福을 가져오도록 硏究되어야 할 것이요, 國民 全體의 最大幸福을 目標로 삼을 理由가 없다. 또는 最大幸福의 原理가 實은 立法家나 政治家들의 最大幸福을 爲한 手段으로서 採擇된 것이라면, 이 原理는 立法家나 政治家에 限하여 適合한 原理가 될 뿐이요, 一般國民에게까지 適用될 倫理的 原理가 될 수는 없을 것이다. 이 難點을 克服하기 爲하여, '最大多數의 最大幸福의 原理'는 立法家, 政治家를 비롯하여 모든 國民 各 個人에게 고루 最大量의 幸福을 가져온다고 辨明할 것인가? 그러나 이와 같은 辨明은 分明한 經驗的 事實에 依하여 立證되지 않는 限 한갓 詭辯에 不過하다.

벤담 自身으로 말하면, 그가 立法 乃至 政治에 對한 關心에서 最大幸福의 原理를 提唱했을 때, 이 原理가 自己 一個人의 利益을 圖謀하는 길이라고는 생각하지 않았을 것이다. "假令 어떤 다른 나라에서 벤담에게 法典編纂를 依賴했다면, 그는 亦是 그 나라의 公益을 爲하는 見地에서 編纂했을 것이요, 自己 一個人이나 自己의 階級을 爲하는 마음에서 그 일을 遂行하지는 않았을 것이다."라고 러셀은 말하고 있다.[28] 벤담에게는 自己 一個人의 利益을 떠나서 社會 全體의 福利를 念願하는 마음이 있었다. 벤담은 自己自身의 心理說에 가로막혀 自己 안에 있는 이 事實을 意識하지 못하였던 것이다. 實은 벤담의 心理說이 먼저 修正을 받아야 할 것이었다. 벤담의 心

---

28 B. Russel, *A History of Western Philosophy*, p.778.

理說에 修正을 加하여, 利己的 人間이 公益을 爲하여 行爲할 수 있는 根據를 밝힌 것은, 그의 親舊 제임스 밀(James Mill, 1773-1836)이다.

제임스 밀이 人間의 利己性과 利他的 行爲를 連結시키는 橋梁으로 삼은 것은, 當時 英國에 勢力이 있던 聯想心理說(the association principle)이다. 元來 人間은 自己의 快樂을 追求하는 것이나 觀念聯合의 法則에 依하여서 他人의 快樂도 亦是 自己의 快樂인 양 聯想하게 된다. 이와 같은 聯想이 漸次 强固하게 되면, 마침내 他人의 快樂과 自己의 快樂을 同一視하게 되고, 따라서 利己的인 人間이면서도 利他의 行爲가 可能하게 된다는 것이다.

聯想心理說은 파블로프(Pavlo, 1849-1936)의 偉大한 發見인 條件反應說(conditioned response theory)과 同一한 原理의 素朴한 表現이다. 素朴한 心理說에 依한 것인 만큼 밀의 說明은 充分히 緻密하지는 못하였다. 設令 利己的인 人間이 利他的으로 行爲할 수 있는 心理的 根據가 充分히 說明되었다 하더라도, 그것만으로는 功利主義의 難點이 모두 解決되지 않았을 것이다. 功利主義에는 그 밖에도 根本的인 難點이 있기 때문이다.

벤담이 基礎를 다진 英國의 功利主義는, 제임스 밀을 거쳐 그의 아들인 존 스튜어트 밀(John Stuart Mill, 1806-1873)에게로 繼承된다. 벤담은 快樂의 量的 多少만을 問題 삼고 質的 差異는 認定하지 않았으나, J. S. 밀은 快樂에 質的 差異가 있음을 主張하여 벤담의 功利說에 있어 難點의 하나가 되고 있는 快樂의 量的 計量의 困難性을 常識的으로 緩和시키는 同時에, 利己的인 個人이 公益을 爲하여 行爲할 수 있는 根據에도 補充을 加하였다. 그러나 快樂에 質的 差異를 認定한다는 것은, 이미 快樂 以外에 評價의 標準을 豫想하는 것이다. J. S. 밀은 功利說에 改良을 베풀었으나, 그 改良은 本來의 功利說의 理論的 破綻을 暗示하는 性質의 것이었다.

功利主義가, 倫理學의 問題를 一種의 社會問題로 看做하고, 政治, 法律

과의 協助下에 現實에 있어 社會를 改造하는 力量이 되고자 한 것은, 倫理學 本來의 面目을 새롭게 한 것이었다. 實際에 있어서 英國의 功利說은 十九世紀 中葉의 英國 立法과 政治에 놀라운 影響을 주었다.[29] 實踐面으로 볼 때에는 功績이 莫大한 功利說이었으나, 그 理論的 方面에서 볼 때에는 몇몇 基本的 難點이 있음을 否認할 수가 없다.

功利說이 가진 理論的 難點의 하나는 快樂主義 一般에게 共通된 難點이다. 希臘 倫理時代에 屬하는 에피쿠로스의 快樂說을 紹介했을 때, 이미 言及한 바 있거니와, 모든 人間은 快樂을 追求하고 苦痛을 回避한다고 主張했을 때, 快樂說은 心理的 事實의 先後를 바꾸었다. 快樂이 먼저 있어서 欲求가 그것을 좇는 것이 아니라, 欲求가 滿足되는 곳에 快樂이 느껴지는 것이다. 難點의 둘째는, 元來 利己的인 人間에게 公益을 爲하여 行爲하라는 그 理論根據가 薄弱하다는 點이다. 設令 聯想說이 他人의 利益을 自己의 利益과 同一視하게 되는 心理的 過程을 科學的으로 밝힐 수 있다 하더라도, 難點은 依然히 풀리지 않는다. "觀念聯合에 依하여 우리는 他人의 快樂을 自己의 그것과 同一視하게 된다."는 前提로부터, 우리는 도리어 "他人의 快樂이 自己의 快樂처럼 느껴지는 것은 心理的 虛僞에 依한 것이니, 이에 속지 말고 自己의 快樂을 確保하도록 十分操心하라!"는 格言을 結論으로서 얻을 수도 있기 때문이다.

---

29 벤담은 實際的 政治運動에도 參加하였고 末年에는 過激派로 기울어지기까지 하였다. 初期 社會主義者 로버트 오웬(Robert Owen)은 벤담의 親舊였다. 벤담 以下 哲學的 過激派들(Philosophical Radicals)은 社會主義에는 反對하였다. 그러나 社會改造를 標榜하는 社會主義와 最多數의 最大幸福을 目標로 삼는 功利主義와는 現代에 와서는 和解하기 어려운 對立을 이루고 있으나, 그 發足 當時의 動機로 말하면 分水嶺的 距離에 있었다고 볼 수도 있다. 헤겔의 哲學이 左右 兩派로 分裂되어 天地의 相隔을 結果한 事實과 아울러 興味 깊다.

그 理論的 難點에도 不拘하고, 功利主義의 思想은 오늘도 英國人의 生活 속에 살아 있다. 그것은 英國民의 傳統的인 人生觀에 地盤을 가졌기 때문이다. 自己 나라의 傳統的인 人生觀을 哲學的으로 根據 주려고 한 '功利說'이라는 學說은 失敗하였으나, 그 人生觀 自體는 如前히 生命을 持續하는 것이다. 앵글로 색슨(Anglo-Saxon)의 이 傳統的인 人生觀은 新大陸으로 건너가서는 實用主義(pragmatism)의 哲學을 産出하였다. 功利主義의 基本思想은 現代의 標語인 民主主義(democracy)의 基本思想이기도 하다. 民主主義가 現代의 思想이라면, 功利主義도 아직 現代의 思想이다. 民主主義가 그러하듯이 功利主義는 오늘날 우리에게 理論과 實踐에 關한 여러 가지 難問을 提起하고 있다.

6) 現代의 倫理思潮

우리는 以上에서 古代 希臘으로부터 十九世紀 中葉에 이르기까지의 西洋倫理學說 中 重要하다고 생각되는 것들을, 大體로 時代의 順序에 따라서 그 要旨를 略述하였다. 그리고 各 倫理說에 對하여 現代의 立場에서 느낀 不滿을 表明하였다. 이 不滿은, 筆者의 個人的인 不滿이기보다는 現代의 一般思潮가 過去의 精神에 對하여 느끼는 時代的인 不滿에 가깝다.

過去의 倫理學者들이 누구나 根本課題로 삼은 것은, 行爲의 世界에 있어서 絶對的인 基準을 發見하는 일이었다. 그러나 '絶對'를 希願한 것은 倫理學者만이 아니었다. 人類는 生活 全面에 걸쳐서, 반드시 意識的인 것은 아니었다 할지라도, 大體로 絶對性에 對한 念願을 품어 왔던 것이다. 各 時代에는 各 時代가 信奉하는 絶對者가 있었다. 歷史의 흐름을 따라서, 한 時代는 그 時代의 偶像을 세웠고 다음 時代는 前時代의 偶像을 打倒하고는 새로이 自己自身의 偶像을 세웠다. 時代마다 헌 偶像이 破壞되고 새 偶像

이 樹立되었다.

永遠과 絶對를 希求하는 人間精神이, 그 目標를 于先 自然 안에 探索하고, 다음에 人間 自身 안으로 옮긴 것은 元來 古代 希臘의 옛일이었다. 希臘 末期에 이르러, 永遠과 絶對에 關한 希望은 人間으로부터 人間 밖에 外在하는 '超越者', 卽 神에게로 옮겨졌다. 이리하여 于先 知識層을 中心으로 한 希臘의 宗敎時代가 出現하였고, 다음에 一般 大衆 안에 地盤을 가진 基督敎가, 로마 帝國의 背景 앞에서, 世界宗敎로서 發展하였다. 中世紀 一千數百年은 宗敎가 君臨한 時代였다.

世界史 위에서 確乎한 勢力과 長久한 傳統을 樹立한 諸宗敎는, 各其 敎理의 是非는 如何하든 間에, 모두 人間精神 위에 安靜과 休息을 주었다는 實用的(pragmatic) 功獻이 컸던 것은 事實이다. 科學의 眼目으로 볼 때 矛盾을 指摘할 수 있는 敎理일지라도, 그것이 實際에 있어서 多數 民衆에게 마음의 依支處가 되었다면, 우리는 비록 그 敎理 自體를 全的으로 容認하지는 못할지라도, 그 敎理의 存在價値를 全的으로 否認하지도 않을 것이다. 基督敎의 權威가 民心을 完全히 掌握했던 中世紀의 大部分은, 비록 後世의 史家는 이를 '暗黑時代(the dark ages)'라고 부를지라도, 그 時代人의 立場에서 본다면 一種의 祝福된 時代이기도 하였다.

그러나 文藝復興期에 이르러 全般的 爆發을 보게 된 새 時代의 氣運은, 中世紀 또는 그 以前의 先人들이 애써 建立한 偶像을 破壞하는 作業을 始作하였다. 中世打破의 運動을 意味하는 文藝復興은, 무엇보다도 中世 人間生活의 精神的 中樞를 이루었던 基督敎 敎理에 對한 反旗였으며, 一千數百年의 歷史를 짊어진 巨大한 偶像에 對한 不信任의 表明이었다. 勿論 中世에서 近世로의 轉換은 非連續的 飛躍은 아니었다. "文藝復興은 古代文化의 復興에 汲汲한 感이 있으며, 宗敎改革은 中世 初期의 宗敎理想에 固執한 點이 顯著하다." 이 革新運動은 "徹頭徹尾 革新的이 아니라, 舊傳統을

完全히 離脫하지 못한 運動이었다."[30] 神은 依然히 信仰되었고 敎會는 如前히 存續하였다. 그러나 近世와 現世에 있어서 神과 敎會가 人間生活 안에서 차지하는 地位는, 中世紀에 있어서의 그것과는 本質的으로 다르다. 神은 벌써 萬人이 모든 것을 그의 뜻에 내맡기고 晏然할 수 있는 絕對者가 아니다. 人間은 스스로의 運命을 人間 自身의 힘으로 開拓해야 한다는 自覺에 이르렀다. 敎權은 이미 政權이 그 무릎 아래 屈服해야 할 最高의 主權은 아니다. 도리어 精神界를 다스리는 敎權이 物質界를 다스리는 政權의 支配下에 包攝된다. 오늘날 基督敎를 信奉하는 어떠한 國家도, 基督敎를 背斥하는 다른 國家와 對戰함에 즈음하여, 오직 神을 信仰하고 神의 뜻을 받는 義로운 行爲를 함으로써 最後의 勝利가 찾아올 것을 確信하고, 戰爭의 不安으로부터 完全히 自由로울 수는 없을 것이다. 이것은 基督敎國뿐만 아니라 佛敎, 回敎, 其他 어떠한 國敎를 信奉하는 國家에 있어서도 마찬가지다. 神佛은 이미 全知全能한 絕對者가 아니다.

自然科學의 發達과 人間的 自覺에 나타난 近世의 精神은, 人間 밖에 外在하는 超越者에게 '永生과 絕對'의 救援을 期待하던 묵은 希望을 버렸다. 그러나 超越的 絕對者를 抛棄한 近世人은, 永生과 絕對를 念願하는 人間의 基本的 要求 自體를 抛棄한 것은 아니었다. 絕對者를 人間 밖에 求하기를 斷念한 近世의 精神이, 絕對者를 人間 안에 求한바 오직 方向의 轉換이 있었을 뿐이다. 人間을 敎會와 僧侶의 羈絆으로부터 解放한 近世의 精神은, 한 걸음 더 나아가 人間을 宇宙 上座에 앉히고, 人間으로 하여금 歷史의 主人公에 任하였다. 人間性의 尊重은 近世의 標語이며, 人間主義(humanism)는 近世思潮의 主流였다. 한마디로 말하면 人間 밖에 있던 神을 人間 안으

---

30 大類伸, 『世界史 新講』, p.306.

로 모셨다.

그러나 近世에 있어서 宇宙의 上座를 차지한 '人間'은 動物로서의 人間
은 아니다. 至尊한 것으로서 崇尙을 받은 '人間性'은 肉體와 더불어 生滅하
고 經驗과 더불어 消長하는 生物學的 人間性은 아니었다. 오직 一般動物과
는 宛然히 區別되는 '萬物之靈長'으로서의 人間이 崇尙되었으며, 肉體와
經驗을 超越하는 人間理性(reason, Vernunft)이 絶對視되고 偶像化되었
을 뿐이다. 理性은 人間의 本質이요 人類에게 共通된 普遍者이다. 理性은
絶對知에 到達하는 認識能力을 가졌으며, 絶對善을 實現하는 實踐能力을
가졌다. 이렇게 그들은 믿었다. 마침내 理性은 宇宙의 根柢로서의 目的과
理想의 原理에까지 昇進하여, '絶對理性(absolute Vernunft)' 乃至 '世界
理性(Weltvernunft)'의 槪念을 보기에까지 이르렀다.

그러나 理性에 絶對者를 求하려는 人間의 希望도 또한 暗礁에 올랐다.
理性 自身이 '理性'의 絶對性에 對하여 疑心을 품기 始作했던 것이다. 近
世의 黎明과 함께 人生의 希望이 人間 위에 걸리자, 學者들의 關心과 興味
도 스스로 人間에게로 集中되었다. 人間을 對象으로 하는 學問이, 中世에
있어서 神을 對象으로 삼던 學問에 代身하였다. 勿論 이와 같이 擡頭한 '人
間學'이 哲學的 人間學(philosophische Anthropologie)에 그 分野와 方法
을 局限하였을 동안은, 人間을 絶對視하는 信念은 一路 그 理論的 背景을
튼튼히 해갔을 뿐이다. 그러나 人間學이 自然科學的 方法을 導入하고 生物
學, 特히 動物學의 一分科로서, 卽 人類學(Anthropology)으로서 發展하기
始作하자, 人間性의 '先天性(Apriorität)' 乃至 '普遍性(Allgemeinheit)'
에 對한 懷疑와 批判도 따라서 始作되었다. 原始人으로부터 文化人에 이르
는 發展過程이 物的 資料를 中心으로 追究되었으며, 靈長 人間과 禽獸 動
物이 同列에 있어 比較되었다. 마침내 다윈(Charles Darwin, 1809-
1882)이 代表하는 生物進化論(the theory of organic evolution)의 新說

은, 人間과 其他動物과의 間隔을 發達段階의 差異로서 說明한다. 人間이 牛馬와 더불어 同一한 類 概念下에 包攝되었으며, 아메바와 人間 사이에 한 줄기 連續線이 發見되었다. 그리고 生物學的 基礎 위에 樹立된 '科學으로서의 心理學'은 理性(Vernunft)과 感性(Sinnlichkeit)과를 確然히 區別하던 넘나들 수 없는 境界線을 抹殺해 버렸다. 勿論 人間理性의 先天性을 固執하는 學者들은, 人類學의 對象은 '經驗界에 屬하는 人間'이요, 哲學的 人間學의 對象은 '超經驗界에 屬하는 人間'이므로 兩者는 그 對象의 範圍가 다르다는 立論으로 應酬한다.[31] 그러나 出生도 死亡도 하지 않고 住所도 姓名도 없는 '純粹人間' 乃至 '本體(Nounmenon)'로서의 人間이 果然 어떠한 事實을 意味하는 것인지는 아직 分明히 되지 않았다.

이리하여 轉換은 또 한 번 準備되지 않으면 아니 되었다. 近代의 精神이 絶對者의 地位에까지 끌어 올렸던 理性者 人間을, 現代의 精神이 單番에 禽獸의 系列에까지 끌어 내렸던 것이다. 그리고 이것은 實驗과 觀察을 根本으로 삼는 自然科學的 觀點으로부터 出發한 近世的 精神의 必然的 歸結點이기도 하였다. 勿論 '實存哲學(Existenzphilosophie)'의 이름이 드높은 오늘날, 現代의 思潮를 '科學的(scientific)'이라고만 特色지을 수는 없다. 그러나 人間의 諸般問題를 生物學的 見地에서 살피고자 하는 態度는, 現代精神의 적어도 基本的 特質이라는 것만은 分明하다.

思想家들은 '不安(Angst)'이라는 말로 現代를 形言한다. 經濟의 逼迫,

---

31 이 問題는 앞으로도 繼續 論爭될 것이다. 아마 永遠히 解決을 못 볼 問題의 하나일지도 모른다. 그러나 設令 現象으로서의 人間과 本體로서의 人間의 兩立을 確認한다 하더라도, 우리 自身이 經驗界에 屬하는 人間이요 우리 自身의 當面한 生의 問題가 經驗의 社會生活의 그것이라는 事實을 反省할 때에, 우리 自身의 問題의 解明을 꾀하는 實踐의 學으로서의 倫理學이, 果然 어느 쪽 世界의 人間을 問題 삼아야 할 것인지는, 平凡한 常識으로도 判斷할 수 있는 問題일 것이다.

戰爭의 威脅, 政治의 變動 — 이러한 觀點에서도 우리는 現代의 不安을 理解할 수가 있다. 그러나 人間이 確乎한 信念으로 더불어 그 위를 달릴 수 있는 絶對的 行路가 杜絶되었다는 意味로 볼 때, 우리는 現代의 不安을 더욱 深刻한 角度에서 理解한다. 近世의 精神은 外在하는 偶像을 打倒하였다. 現代의 精神은 內在하는 絶對者를 追放하였다. 人間 밖에도 人間 안에도 모든 絶對者를 拒否한 現代의 知性에게는, 이제 다시 絶對를 求해 볼 場所가 없는 듯하다. 그러나 人間은 아직도 永遠을 渴望한다. 知性은 오늘도 絶對를 希願한다. 永遠과 絶對를 渴願하면서, 스스로 이를 斷念해야 하는 現代의 知性은 不安을 지나서 絶望에 빠진다.

勿論 現代에도 敬虔한 宗敎徒가 있다. 篤實한 道學者도 있다. 그러나 現代의 緊迫한 社會相은, 모든 宗敎人과 道學者에게 그들이 表面上 理想으로 삼는 그 信條대로 實踐할 行動의 實地를 許諾하지 않는다. 牧師는 說敎하면서 政治를 念頭에 두어야 하며, 僧侶는 念佛하면서 經濟를 打算하지 않으면 아니 된다. 勿論 現代的인 基督敎, 現代에 맞는 佛敎를 생각할 수는 있다. 그러나 이 생각 앞에는, 近 二千年 前의 猶太社會 또는 二千四百餘年 前의 印度社會를 地盤으로 삼고 꽃핀 옛 時代 異邦人의 理想을, 어떻게 그 本質을 바꿈이 없이, 文物制度가 바뀐 오늘날, 우리 地域社會에 適合하도록 '現代化'할 수 있는가 하는 根本的 難問題가 가로막고 있다.

宗敎가 絶對性을 갖던 時代에는 聖書, 佛經 또는 其他의 經典이 人間의 갈 길을 明示하였다. 良心이 絶對的이던 時代에는, '道理'가 搖動 없는 善惡의 標準을 提示하였다. 男女老少 누구에게나 安心하고 歸依할 道標가 있었으며, '人道'를 떠나 彷徨한 사람에게도 悔改하면 다시 돌아갈 길이 있었다. 옛 時代의 罪人의 不安은 解決될 수 있는 不安이었다. 그러나 合理性을 要求하는 人間의 精神은, 스스로가 세운 偶像을 自己의 손으로 次例次例 破壞해 버렸다. 同時에, 永遠을 約束하던 希望과 더불어 人間에게 갈 길을

指示하던 道標도 쓰러졌다. 外在하는 神佛도 內在하는 理性도 믿지 못하는 現代의 知性이 自己의 行爲를 安心하고 依托할 確固한 標準이라고는 없다.

上述한 바와 같은 一般思潮를 反映하여 一部에서는 道德의 無用을 主張하고, 따라서 倫理學이 成立할 可能性을 否認하며, 또는 그 無意味함을 論斷하였다. 그러나 오늘도 우리는 行爲가 依據할 道標를 希求한다. 그리고 우리의 道標가 合理的 根據 위에서 發見되기를 念願하며, 發見된 道標를 正當化하는 理論體系를 要求한다. 端的으로 말하자면 現代는 새로운 倫理學을 希求하고 있는 것이다.

三章
道德現象의 本質

1. 道德現象의 起源
2. 道德의 本質

三章 道德現象의 本質

　萬若 現代가 要求하는 倫理學이 構想될 수 있다면, 그것은 可能한 限 形而上學이나 神學의 槪念을 介入시키지 않은 倫理學, 卽 人間構造의 個人的 社會的 現實에 立脚함으로써 實踐性을 갖춘 思想體系가 아니면 아니 될 것이다. 倫理學이 特히 實踐의 學이요, 實踐의 問題가 幾個人의 意思로만 解決될 수 없는 社會共同의 問題라면, 우리의 倫理學은 常識的 判斷으로도 認定할 수 있는 分明한 事實을 土臺로 하고 이루어지지 않으면 아니 될 것이다. 道德에 關하여 손쉽게 接觸할 수 있는 分明한 事實은, 社會生活 안에 具現된 道德現象이다. 行爲의 世界는 經驗의 世界요, 行爲의 問題 中 가장 基本的인 것은 衣食住를 爲始한 日常生活의 그것이다. 우리는 彼岸에 가로 놓인 叡知의 世界를 論하기 前에, 가장 直接的인 現象의 世界를 살펴야 하며, 高達한 至高善(highest good)을 思辨하기 前에, 迫到한 日常生活의 善惡을 헤아리지 않으면 아니 될 것이다.

　過去의 倫理說을 살피면서 우리가 恒常 느끼는 것은, 倫理學者들이 大體로 行爲規範에 關한 '絶對普遍律'을 發見하기에 지나치게 性急했다는 事實이다. 勿論 여기에는 道德의 先天性을 믿는 傳統的 信念이 背景이 되고 있으며, 倫理學의 硏究가 어떤 事實(Sein)의 理論을 밝히기 爲하여서보다도, 人生에 있어 當面한 當爲의 問題에 不動의 指針을 얻고자 하는 實踐的 關心에서 일어났다는 心理的 事實이 動機가 되고 있다. 그들은 倫理, 道德의 當爲 卽 理想을 解明하기에 急한 나머지, 倫理, 道德의 存在, 卽 現實을 分析할 餘暇가 없었고, 또 大槪는 倫理, 道德의 本質이 무엇이라는 것은 自明한 事理처럼 생각해 왔던 것이다. 따라서 그들은 '道德(Moral)', '風習(Sitte)', '良心(Gewissen)' 等이 意味하는 바가 무엇인가, 널리 道德現象의 本質이 무엇인가에 對하여 深刻하게 反問하지 않았던 것이다. 그러나 分明한 事實에 立脚한 倫理學은 모든 先入見 乃至 假設의 破棄를 要求한다. 絶對普遍的인 道德의 原理가 있다든지, 人間의 本性은 理性的이라든지, 甚至於 우리는 善良한 人格者가 되어야 한다는 等의 信條까지도 一旦 括弧에 넣어 두는 것이 必要하다. 우리가 어떠한 道德을 가질 것인가를 묻기 前에, 道德이 本是 무엇인가를 알아보아야 할 것이다. 모든 先入見과 모든 價値觀念을 一旦 括弧 안에 넣고, 自然科學者가 하듯이 現社會 또는 過去 歷史上에 나타난 道德現象을 하나의 現象으로서 把握하고, 그 由來와 本質의 究明을 꾀하는 것은, 倫理學의 새로운 方向을 希求하는 우리에게 貴重한 地盤을 提供하리라고 생각된다. '道德現象의 本質'을 묻는 우리는, 于先 '道德現象의 起源'으로부터 始作한다.

1. 道德現象의 起源

1) H.G. 웰스의 示唆

무릇 現象 發生에 關한 究明이 現象 本質에 關한 究明을 意味하는 것은 아니다. 그러나 道德現象의 起源에 關한 記述 乃至 說明은 그 本質 究明에

根本的 端緒를 提供할 것이다. 理由는, 道德의 起源과 發達이 經驗的으로 밝혀지느냐 않느냐는 道德現象에 關한 가장 本質的인 問題이기 때문이다.

　歷史 全般을 通하여 道德現象의 起源과 發達過程을 밝힘에 있어서는, 民俗學 또는 社會學의 貢獻이 있다. 한便 個人 안에서 道德意識이 어떻게 發生하여 어떻게 發達하는가에 關하여서는, 道德心理學의 課題가 있다. 道德의 歷史學이나 道德의 心理學을 窮極의 目標로 삼지 않는 우리는, 다만 先驅者들의 研究에 依據하여 道德現象 發生의 基本的이요 一般的인 原理만을 略察하되, 먼저 社會的 側面에서 概觀하고 다음에 個人 안에서의 道德意識을 살피는 順序를 밟기로 한다.

　道德現象의 起源을 묻기 前에, 우리는 于先 '道德現象'이라는 넓게도 좁게도 解釋되는 槪念을 輪廓이나마 規定지어 둘 必要가 있다. 좁은 意味의 道德現象은 넓은 意味의 道德現象을 地盤으로 삼고 分化 限定된 것이라고 생각된다. 그러므로 道德現象의 起源을 밝히고자 하는 우리는, 이 槪念을 可及的 넓은 意味로 잡아 두는 것이 目的에 合當할 것이다. '道德現象'을 가장 넓은 意味로 解釋할 때, 그것은 '行爲에 對한 評價現象'을 말한다고 볼 수 있을 것이다. 行爲에 對한 非難, 稱讚, 處罰, 褒賞 等은 그 具體的인 것이다. 勿論 行爲에 關한 모든 種類의 評價를 우리는 '道德現象' 속에 包含시키지 않는다. 例컨대 運動競技, 藝術, 工業 等에 있어서의 卓越한 技術을 讚揚하는 現象을 普通 '道德的'인 現象이라고는 부르지 않는다. 생각건대 '道德'이라 하면, 行爲의 外面이나 結果보다도, 그 內面의 心情 卽 動機에 깊이 關聯시켜 생각하는 것이 우리의 常識이다. 그러나 行爲의 外面的 評價와 內面的 評價가 그 根柢에 있어서 不可分離의 關聯을 가졌을 뿐 아니라, 起源으로 본다면 行爲의 外面的 評價가 오히려 原初的인 것이라고 생각할 理由가 있는 까닭에, 우리는 여기서 道德이라는 말에 拘碍하지 않고, '行爲의 評價'라는 一般的 現象에 關하여 그 起源을 略察하기로 한다.

所謂 有史以前의 人類生活에 關하여서는 分明한 記錄은 없다. 다만 僅少한 地質學的 資料에 對한 考古學的 解釋, 또는 現存하는 原始民族에 對한 觀察을 土臺로 한 民俗學者들의 比論을 通하여 그것을 推定할 뿐이다. 따라서 現在의 우리로서는 이러한 推定的 記錄을 參考로 함에 滿足할 밖에 길이 없다.

現存하는 人類의 祖上이라고 認定되는 最初의 眞人(true men)이, 그 規模의 大小는 如何튼, 一種의 集團生活을 했으리라는 點에 學者들의 見解는 一致한다. 그리고 生活이 集團의 形態를 取했다는 事實이야말로 '道德'이라는 現象을 招來한 重大한 要因의 하나라고 생각된다. 그것은, 道德이라는 現象은 行爲의 社會的 制約을 意味하는 것으로서 人間과 人間과의 社會的 關係를 前提로 하기 때문이다.

原始人의 生活이 集團的이었다면, 그 集團을 構成한 各 個人의 相反하는 利害關係와 對立되는 意見의 差異를 調停하는 어떤 制約이 作用했을 것이다. 그렇지 않다면 原始人의 集團은 恒時 相爭하는 修羅場이었을 것이며, 하나의 社會로서 成立할 수가 없었을 것이다. 勿論 原始人이, 그 利己性과 自我意識에 있어서, 現代 文明人과 同一하다고 보는 것은 아니다. 그러나 人間에 가까운 靈長類의 生活이나 現存하는 原始族屬의 生活로 미루어 볼 때, 原始人에게 利己性이 全혀 缺如되었으리라고 보기는 困難하며, 따라서 各 個人間의 利害對立이 先天的 調和에 依하여 未然防止되었으리라고 보기도 어렵다. 그러면 不可避했으리라고 생각되는 이 利害나 意見의 對立을 生死決斷의 血鬪에 이르지 않도록 解決하게 한 것이 무엇일까? 이 問題의 關鍵을 '先天的 良心'이라든지 '本能的 血族愛'에서 求하는 것은 우리의 出發點과 整合하지 않는다. 오히려 이 問題를 自然科學的 方法으로 追究한 人類學者들의 見解를 參考 삼는 것이 合當할 것이다.

이 原始的 利己性의 克復 問題에 關하여서 特히 깊은 示唆를 주는 것은 웰스(H. G. Wells)의 다음과 같은 敍述이다. "아마 眞正한 人類歷史 始初期에 있어서, 最初의 人間社會는 조그마한 家族團體(family groups)였을 것이다. 마치 初期의 哺乳類들의 무리가 家族에서부터 出發하여 그 集團이 增大해 갔듯이, 最初의 人間部族도 그와 같이 形成되었을 것이다. 그러나 이 部族이 形成될 수 있기 前에 各 個人의 原始的 利己性을 克服할 무슨 制約(restraint)이 이루어졌어야 할 것이다. 父親에 對한 恐怖와 尊敬이 長成 後까지 持續되지 않으면 아니 되었으며, 젊은 男性이 長成해 감에 따라서 自然的으로 일어나는 一族長老(the old man of the group)의 嫉妬를 緩和시키지 않으면 아니 되었다. 人間의 社會生活은, 젊은이들이 長成함에 따라 (父母를) 離脫하여 自己네끼리 結合하고 싶은 野生的 本能과 한편 이러한 離脫의 危險性과 不利함과의 中間에서 일어난 反應(reaction)을 通하여 發達된 것이다. 天才的 人類學者 애킨슨(J. J. Atkinson)은, 그의 『原始法(Primal Law)』에 있어서 原始人의 慣習法, 卽 部族生活에 있어서 너무나 顯著한 事實인 禁制(taboo)가, 發展해 가는 社會生活에 對한 原始人의 欲求에 이러한 心的 對應(adjustment)에 起因하는 바가 얼마나 큰 것인가를 明示하고 있다."[1]

웰스에 依하면, 原始家族團體에 있어서 成人 男子는 오직 長老 한 사람뿐이다. 長老는 그 家族 內의 모든 女性을 獨占한다. 家族 中의 年少한 男子가 嫉妬의 對象이 될 程度로 長成하면, 長老는 그를 追放하거나 殺害한다. 追放을 當하거나 或은 自進하여 그 家族을 離脫한 原始時代의 靑年은, 自己 집 또는 남의 집의 젊은 女性과 野合하여 새로운 家族團體의 長老가 된다. 長老는 迫害를 加하는 暴君일 뿐만 아니라, 對外的 鬪爭에 있어서는 幼年

---

1 H. G. Wells, *A Short History of the World*, p.37.

과 女人을 守護하는 고마운 保護者이기도 하다. 長老에 對한 그 部下의 感情에는 恐怖와 尊敬이 混合된다. 長老의 意思는 그대로 順從하지 않으면 아니 될 法이다. 長老의 所有物을 다쳐서는 안 된다. 特히 長老의 所有인 女人을 다치게 하는 것은 禍害를 招來할 張本이다. 이리하여 여러 가지 禁制, 特히 性에 關한 禁制가 發生하였다. 偉大한 長老는 死後에까지 그 威力을 떨친다. 死亡한 長老가 꿈에 나타나는 現象은, 어리석은 原始人에게 靈魂의 不滅을 確信하게 하기에 充分하다. 꿈에 보인 長老와 現實에 일어난 禍福과의 사이에 因果關係를 想定하는 것은, 原始人의 知性으로서는 너무나 自然스러운 傾向이다. 生存時에 그토록 威力이 있던 長老는 정말 죽은 것이 아니라, 어느 超越한 世界로 姿態를 감추고 그 먼 곳에서 遺家族의 運命을 神秘로운 힘으로 左右하고 있는 것이다. 따라서 死者의 靈은 極盡히 爲하지 않으면 아니 된다. 이에 死者를 慰安하고 感謝하는 許多한 儀式이 생기고 그것이 慣習化한다. 이리하여 이미, 原始家族社會를 背景 삼고, 後世에 法과 道德과 宗敎로 分化할 行動의 制約 乃至 規範이 混然한 形態를 가지고 發生하였다. 이와 같이 보는 것이 웰스의 이 點에 關한 論說의 要旨이다.

'道德의 起源'이라는 局限된 問題를 밝히려 함이 아니요, 原始人의 生態 一般을 推測해 본 것에 不過한 웰스의 論述은, 勿論 "行爲에 對하여 評價하는 現象이 어떠한 起源을 가졌는가?"라는 우리 疑問에 充分한 解答을 주는 文獻은 아니다. 그러나 '長老'라는 强者의 意思나 欲求가 그 所屬家族에 對하여 行爲의 制約이 되고, 나아가서는 是非의 標準을 이루는 諸條件의 하나가 되었다는 點만은 그것을 反證할 만한 다른 事實이 發見되지 않는 限, 적어도 貴重한 假說로서 保存될 價値가 認定될 것이다.

2) 評價에 있어서 '生理的인 것'과 '社會的인 것'

비록 原始社會일지라도 長老의 意思만이 單獨으로 行爲의 規範을 形成했으리라고는 생각되지 않는다. 設或 强者의 意思가 弱者의 行爲에 對하여 一種의 規範을 提示했다 할지라도, 바로 그 '强者의 意思'를 決定한 것이 무엇인가라는 더 基本的인 問題가 남아 있다. 原初期에 있어서는 食欲이나 性欲 같은 生理的 欲求가 强者의 意思뿐만 아니라 弱者의 意思까지도 오로지 決定했을지도 모른다. 그러나 未開 野蠻社會에 있어서도 生理的 欲求 以外의 要素가 行爲의 規範을 決定하는 因子로서 混入되고 있다. 이 '生理的 欲求 以外의 要素'는, 때로는 生理的 欲求와는 矛盾對立하는 것이며, 이 것이야말로 後世에 '道德'이라는 이름 아래 一括되는 諸現象의 母體가 되었을지도 모른다. 이것은, 이른바 道德의 要求가 大體로 生理的 欲求를 制約하는 것이며 甚至於는 否認하는 傾向까지 있다는 注目할 만한 事實이 暗示하는 바이다.

무릇 人間이 自己의 生理的 欲求를 充足시켜 주는 對象에 對하여 愛好를 느끼고 生理的 欲求에 逆行하는 對象에 對하여는 嫌惡를 느끼는 것은, 生物學的 常識에 屬하는 事實이다. 人間行爲에 對하여서도, 그것이 自己의 行爲든 他人의 行爲든, 自身의 生理的 欲求 滿足에 도움이 되는 것에는 愛好를, 그와 反對되는 것에는 嫌惡를 느끼는 것은, 적어도 意識을 가진 모든 動物과 人間에 通有한 '一次的 傾性'이다. 이 一次的 傾性을 우리는 '評價에 있어서의 生理的인 것'이라고 부를 수가 있을 것이다. 評價에 있어서의 또하나의 傾向性, 卽 發達된 社會에 있어서 特히 顯著한바 生理的 欲求와는 直接 關係 없이 甚至於는 生理的 欲求에 逆行하여 行爲의 是非가 評價되는 傾向性은, '二次的 傾性'이라는 말로 區別해 둘 必要가 있는 人間에 特有한 現象이다. 그것은, 이 '二次的 傾性'의 存在야말로 人間에 特有한바

‘道德’이라는 現象을 發生하게 한 根源이라고 생각되기 때문이다. 이 二次 的 傾性을 우리는 ‘評價에 있어서의 社會的인 것’이라고 부를 수가 있을 것 이다.

原始家族團體의 最强者인 長老가, 그 部下 一族의 行爲에 關하여 自己의 欲求 滿足에 貢獻하는 것은 ‘是’라 하고, 이에 妨害되는 것은 ‘非’라 한 것 은, 위에서 말한 一次的 傾性에 該當한다. 長老의 이 完全히 利己的인 一次 的 傾性에는 이른바 ‘道德的(moral)’인 要素는 아직 보이지 않는다. 그러 나 家族 內의 弱者로서의 部下들이 自己네의 生理的 欲求를 抑制하고, 그 長老의 意思를 尊重하여 이에 適應하려는 傾向, 卽 위에서 말한 二次的 傾 性에는 우리가 普通 말하는 ‘道德的’인 要素까지는 없다 할지라도, 그것과 一脈相通하는 心理的 要素가 包含되어 있는 것만은 看取할 수가 있다. 그 러나 우리는 이 二次的 傾性이 道德의 根源인가 아닌가를 論斷하기 前에, 우리가 二次的 傾性이라고 부를 수 있는 現象의 性質을 좀 더 넓은 眼界에 서 考察함이 必要할 것이다.

위에서 ‘一次的’이라고 부른 傾性은 生理的 欲求(physiological needs) 에 直接的으로 對應하는바, 이를테면 生理的 欲求의 直接的 延長이다. 따 라서 生理的 欲求의 諸特徵은 바로 一次的 傾性의 諸特徵이기도 하다. 生 理的 欲求는 生得的이요, 必然的인 欲求이다. 그것은 從來 ‘先天的(a priori)’ 또는 ‘本能(instinct)’의 이름으로 불리던 것이다. 따라서 生理的 欲求의 直接的 延長인바 一次的 傾性도, 從來式으로 말하면, 先天的이요 本能的이라고 부를 수 있는 傾向性이다. 여기서 우리의 關心은 이른바 ‘二 次的 傾性’도 亦是 生得的이요 必然的인가 아닌가에 集中된다.

3) 社會的 評價의 經驗性

우리가 二次的 傾性이라고 부른 것은, 人間이 生理的 基本欲求에 直接 關係 없이 어떤 事物을 愛好하고 또는 嫌厭하는 傾向 全體를 指稱하였다. 그것이 바로 心理學에서 말하는 社會的 欲求(social meeds)[2]에 對應하는 것, 다시 말하면 社會的 欲求의 直接的 延長임이 分明하다. 따라서 二次的 傾性의 諸特徵은 社會的 欲求의 諸特徵에 一致할 것이다.

어떤 社會的 欲求가 生得的인가 또는 習得的인가는, 오래 論爭된 重要한 問題 中의 하나이다. 支配欲, 名譽欲, 所有欲, 父性愛, 孝心, 群居性, 協同性, 慈愛心 等等의 社會的 欲求를, 人間의 本能 또는 先天的 人間性이라고 본 것은, 傳統 있는 見解 中에 屬한다. 그러나 近來 人間을 그 研究對象으로 삼는 여러 科學者들이, 그러한 社會的 欲求를 本能視 乃至 先天視하는 從來의 見解를 反證하는 諸事實을 指摘하고 있다. 例컨대 브리트(S. H. Britt)는, 베네딕트(R. Benedict) 女史의 研究를 引用하여, 從來 '本能的(instinctive)'이라고 생각되던 攻擊性(aggressiveness)과 協同性(co-operativeness)이 社會環境의 所産이라는 示唆를 주고 있다. 卽 베네딕트에 依하면, 뉴멕시코(New Mexico)의 주니族(the Zuni)에게는 攻擊性이나 個人主義는 찾아볼 수가 없다. 間或 利己的인 行爲가 있으면 處罰을 當한다. 競走에 連勝한 選手는 다음 出戰의 資格을 喪失한다. 이와 反對로 뉴기니아(New Guinea)의 도부안스族(the Dobuans)은 萬事에 利己的이요

---

2 社會的 欲求란 直接 生理的 解剖的 基礎가 없는 欲求로서 從來 '社會的 本能(social instincts)'이라 하여, 生得的 固定的인 것으로 생각되었던 諸欲求를 包含한다(南博,『社會 心理學』, p.67). 그것은 셰퍼가 "Motives derived chiefly from emotional tensions"라고 부른 것의 大部分을 指稱한다(F. Shaffer, *The Psychology of Adjustment*, p.101).

競爭的이며, 協同性이라고는 全혀 없다. 도부안스族에 있어서는 反逆, 詐欺, 殘忍性 等 文明社會에서 惡德으로 생각되는 것은 모두 美德이요, 그와 反對로 우리가 善이라고 생각하는 것은 大概 惡으로 看做된다. 그들은 어떠한 두 사람도 眞實로 親密할 수는 없다. 萬人은 모든 이웃사람을 害칠 것을 恒常 勞心하며, 또 이웃사람으로부터 被害를 받지나 않을까 언제나 두려워하고 있다. 모든 災禍가 남의 咀呪에 起因한다고 믿는 도부안스族 中에서, 어떤 男子가 죽었을 때, 그 死亡의 原因으로서의 最初의 容疑者는 바로 그 夫人이다.[3]

미드(Margaret Mead)의 뉴기니아의 세 가지 族屬 — 아라페시族(the Arapesh), 문두구머族(the Mundugumor), 챔블리族(the Tchambuli) — 에 關한 硏究도, 從來 本能的이라고 생각되던 社會的 欲求가 社會環境의 빚어낸 바라는 것을 示唆하는 興味 있는 資料를 提供한다.

(1) 아라페시族은 全혀 攻擊이나 競爭은 모르고 산다. 어린이의 遊戲에도 競爭的 性質은 없다. 거기에서는 男女老少의 階級的 區別이 없으며 모든 사람들은 溫順한 婦女子에 가깝다.

(2) 문두구머族은 아라페시族과는 正反對로 殘忍無雙한 食人種이다. 이 族屬의 모든 男子는 모든 男子의 敵이다. 暴力과 自他의 生命을 輕視하는 殘忍性은 이 部族에서 成功하기 爲한 最高의 德性이다. 문두구머族은 新生兒를 歡迎하지 않을 뿐만 아니라, 一旦 出生된 幼兒에 對하여서도 우리네 社會의 母性愛 또는 父性愛와는 天壤의 距離가 있는 態度를 取한다. 어린이가 젖꼭지를 빨 때 어머니는 冷酷하게 밀어 제친다. 離乳期는 몹시 빠르되 離乳時에는 辱說과 毆打가 甚하다. 이 族屬은 男女가 모두 惡漢의 性格

---

3 S. H. Britt, *Social Phychology of Modern Life*, pp.43-45.

을 갖추고 있다.

(3) 챔블리族은 아라페시族과도 문두구머族과도 判異한 族屬이다. "아라페시族의 理想은 溫順한 男子가 溫順한 女子와 結婚하는 것이요, 문두구머族의 理想은 亂暴한 남자가 亂暴한 女子와 結婚하는 일이다. 이 셋째 族屬 卽 챔블리族에 있어서는 男女의 態度가 우리의 文化와 正反對이다. 卽 女子가 優勢하고 冷靜하며 男便을 指示한다. 男子는 責任感이 적고 依賴心이 많다."[4]

이 밖에도, 性生活에 關聯된 羞恥나 秘密을 모르는 사모아族(the Samoa)의 異習은,[5] 性道德에 關聯되는 人間性이 社會나 文化에 左右됨을 立證하는 것이요, 未開社會에서 볼 수 있는 老親殺害,[6] 高麗葬 等의 慣習은, 父母에 對한 孝心이 타고난 普遍的 人間性이 아님을 指摘하는 事實이다.

以上에 引用된 社會學者 또는 民族學者들의 研究는, 人間의 社會的 欲求와 社會的 欲求의 直接的 廷長으로서의 二次的인 評價傾性 卽 '評價에 있어서 社會的인 것'이 生得的인 것이 아니라, 詩會環境에 影響되는 經驗的 所産이라는 見解를 支持하는 有力한 資料임을 否認할 수 없다. 그러나 一部 哲學者 中에는 다음과 같은 主張으로 反駁하는 사람도 있을 것이다. "人間의 普遍的 本性은 潛勢態로서 儼然히 存在한다. 다만 그것이 어느 程度까지 現勢化하느냐는 것은 社會環境에 달려 있다. 現象界에 나타난 人間性의 差異는 現勢化한 人間性의 差異다. 現勢化한 人間性의 差異를 根據로

---

4 M. Mead, *Sex and Temperament*, p.279.
5 M. Mead, *Coming of Age in Samoa*.
6 W. G. Sumner, *Folkways*, pp.324-327.

하여, 先天的으로 潛在하는 人間의 本性 自體의 普遍性을 否認할 수는 없다." 이와 같은 形而上學的 思辨과 直接 對峙하는 것은 無益한 노릇이다. 오히려 우리는 社會的 評價傾性이 經驗的으로 形成되는 過程을 좀 더 具體的으로 밝힘으로써, 우리의 立場을 더욱 鞏固히 다지는 것이 賢明할 것이다.

設令 우리가 '社會的'이라고 指稱한 動機 또는 評價傾性 — 例컨대 父母에 對한 孝誠, 象徵的 報酬(symbolic rewards)의 尊重, 權勢에 對한 羨望 等等이 先天的인 것이 아니요, 經驗的 所産이라 하더라도, 全혀 無에서 이러한 有가 생겼을 理는 없다. 반드시 生得的으로 所有되는 어떤 素質이 이와 같은 經驗的 傾性의 바탕으로서 있어야 할 것이다. 그리고 어떤 傾性이 經驗的으로 생긴다면, 그것이 突發的으로 即 無原則하게보다는 어떤 過程의 順序를 따라서 形成된다고 보는 것이 더욱 合理的인 考察이다. 그러면 經驗 乃至 環境은 무엇을 素材로 하여, 또 環境의 어떠한 條件이 어떠한 過程을 밟아서, 人間의 社會的인 動機 乃至 二次的인 傾性을 形成해 내는 것일까?

4) 慣習

앞서 言及한 웰스의 所見, 即 長老의 威壓이 一族의 行動을 統制하는 制約이었다는 見解도, 二次的 傾性(이것이 經驗的으로 習得되는 것임이 分明히 됨에 따라서 우리는 이 말 代身 '習性(traits)'이라는 槪念을 代置해야 할 것이다)을 造成하는 한 가지 社會的 條件을 提示한 것이었다. 最初엔 自己의 生命을 保全하기 爲하여서 長老의 意思에 順從하던 것이, 오래 繼續되는 동안에 順從이 習慣化하고 長老를 偶像視하는 固定觀念이 생긴다는 것은 可能한 일이기 때문이다. 그러나 長老의 威壓은 二次的 傾性을 造成

하는 한 가지 條件은 되었을지라도, 唯一한 條件은 아니리라는 것은 이미 論及한 바 있다. 이에 比하여, 듀이(J. Dewey)와 『倫理學(*Ethics*)』을 共著한 터프츠(J. H. Tufts)의 研究는, 人間의 二次的 傾性이 發生하는 事情을 좀 더 깊이 把握하고 있다.

原始社會에 있어서 二次的 傾性 乃至 社會的 動機가 가장 具體的으로 나타난 것은 慣習(customs) 또는 風習(folkways)이다. 터프츠는 慣習의 起源을 다음 세 가지 要因을 들어 說明하고 있다.[7]

(1) 原始的 欲求와 本能에 依하여 誘發된 行動(the activities induced by the great primitive needs and instincts)

어떤 行動은 成功하고 다른 어떤 行動은 失敗한다. … 사람들은 成功的인 行動의 方式을 讚辭와 더불어 後世에 傳하는 同時에 失敗的인 方式은 이를 廢棄한다.

(2) 吉凶의 運數(good luck and bad luck)

原始人의 生活에 있어서는, 禍福이 그들의 知識으로는 到底히 알지 못할 原因에 依하여 發生한다. 無知한 原始人은 그들의 禍福에 關하여 烏飛梨落格의 因果關係를 想定한다. 某月 一日에 東方으로 旅行한 사람이 病들었다면, 一日에 東方으로 出發함은 忌避해야 할 行動이다. 더구나 原始人의 信念에 依하면, 行爲가 招來하는 禍福의 運數는 그 行爲者 一個人에게만 떨어지는 것이 아니라, 一家族 또는 一部族 全體에 미친다. 그러므로 福을 부르고 禍를 물리치도록 行爲함은, 家族 또는 部族 全體의 連帶責任이다. 洞

---

7 J. Dewey and J. H. Tufts, *Ethics*, pp.53-54.

里의 守護神 — 洞口에 선 古木 — 의 가지를 벤 者는, 天罰을 當하기 前에 于先 洞里 사람들에게 處罰을 받아야 할 理由가 있다.

(3) 一定한 行爲에 對한 直角的 反應(immediate reaction to certain ways of action)

例컨대 勇敢한 行動이 그 有效性이나 禍福과의 關聯을 떠나서라도 그 自體 讚美의 對象이 되듯이, 어떤 行爲는 利害를 떠난 그 自體의 價値로써 보는 이에게 讚美 또는 非難의 感情을 일으킨다. 터프츠에 依하면, 이는 어떤 行爲에 對하여 어떤 個人이 偶然히 내린 價値判斷이 周圍에 傳播되고 反復될 때, 그것이 慣習에까지 이른 것이다. 여기서 터프츠가 道德的 行爲의 '客觀的 價値'라든지 道德的 價値에 對한 '叡知的 直觀'이라든지 하는 따위의 것을 意味한 것은 아니다. 다시 말하면 一定한 行爲는 萬人에게 普遍的으로 一定한 價値感을 일으킨다는 것이 아니라, 偶然히 내려진 價値判斷이 模倣되고 反復되어 慣習에까지 이르는 수가 있다 함에 不過하다.

섬너(W. G. Sumner)의 著書에 材料를 얻은 터프츠의 慣習 起源에 關한 論說이, 修正의 餘地가 없도록 完璧하고 못하고는, 지금 우리들에 있어서 關心의 焦點이 아니다.[8] 터프츠의 論說이 우리의 關心을 끄는 것은, 그것

---

8 特히 第三項目에 對하여는 批判의 餘地가 크다. 어떤 行爲에 對하여 讚揚 또는 非難하는 反應이 '偶然히' 생긴다는 것은 首肯하기 어려운 見解이다. 一定한 行爲에 對하여서는 一定한 價値判斷이 先天的 必然的으로 連結된다고 보거나, 그렇지 않으면 어떤 經驗的 條件이 一定한 行爲에 對한 價値判斷의 制約이 된다고 보아야 할 것이다. 萬若 同一한 行爲가 各人에게 주는 價値 印象이 區區하다는 事實이 어떤 行爲에 對한 價値判斷이 先天的으로 決定된다는 立論을 拒否한다면, 原始的 欲求의 滿足, 禍福, 其他 어떤 結果에도 關聯시킴이 없이, 卽 利害打算을 完全히 떠나서 그 行爲 自體에 對하여 直接 내려지는 듯이 보이는 價値判斷일지라도, 亦是 內面的으로는 經驗的인 基因을 가진 것으로 豫想해야 할 것이다.

이 한 가지 重要한 見解 即 慣習이 衣食住 같은 基本生活을 確保하고자 하는 基本的 欲求에 起源한다는 見解를 民俗學的 資料로써 支持하고 있기 때문이다. 터프츠 自身도 이 點을 다음과 같이 言明하고 있다. "生存에 必要한 活動이 이 過程의 出發點이다. — 基本的으로 必要한 것은, 個人이 生命을 維持해야 하는 限, 食料와 居處와 敵에 對한 防備다. 種族이 存續하기 爲하여서는, 또 生殖과 幼兒의 保護가 必要하다. … 이 必要를 滿足시키기 爲하여, 사람들은 集團生活 안에서 일하고 싸움하고 사냥하고 祭祀하고 保育한다. … 이러한 活動은 모두 生存競爭에 도움이 된다. 그러나 여기에 勞動者, 戰士, 歌手, 父母들은 또 그 以上의 것을 장만하고 있다. 即 그들은, 그 自體를 바로 道德이라고 부를 수는 없을지 모르나, 眞正한 道德을 爲하여 不可缺한 몇 가지 重要한 特質을 形成하고 있는 것이다. 따라서 우리는 人間의 意識的 意圖의 參與 없이 自然이 道德進化의 이 部分을 擔當하고 있다고 말할 수가 있다."[9]

生存을 爲한 必要가 慣習의 出發點이라는 터프츠의 見解는, 長老의 威壓이 家族 內 行爲規範의 要石이 되었다는 웰스의 見解와 根本에 있어서 一致한다. 그리고 이 一致는, 慣習에 있어서 典型的인 具現을 보는 社會的 欲求 乃至 二次的 傾性의 源泉에 關한 하나의 結論을 示唆한다. 그것은, 環境 또는 經驗이 그것으로써 社會的 欲求 乃至 二次的 傾性을 形成하는 素材는 적어도 그 大部分이 人間에 있어 生得的인바 生理的 欲求 乃至 一次的 傾性이라는 結論이다. 이와 같은 結論은 神學이나 形而上學이 볼 때에는 異端일지도 모르나, 오늘날 人間을 對象으로 삼는 諸科學에 있어서는 平凡한 常識에 不過하다.

---

9 J. Dewey and J. H. Tufts, *Ethics*, p.39.

人間의 '評價에 關한 二次的 傾性'의 起源을 살피게 된 우리의 當初의 動機는, 道德의 起源을 究明하기 爲한 것이었다. 다시 말하면 評價에 있어서의 二次的 傾性 또는 이 傾性의 가장 代表的인 具現으로서의 慣習이, 道德現象의 母體였으리라는 豫見下에서, 二次的 傾性의 起源을 묻게 된 것이었다. 이제 生理的 欲求가 적어도 大部分의 社會的 欲求의 土臺라는 結論에 到達하였음은, 道德의 起源을 묻는 우리의 問題가 그 解決에로 相當히 接近했음을 意味한다. 그러나 問題가 完全한 解明을 보기 前에 아직도 重要한 고비가 남아 있다. 그것은 慣習의 大部分이 生理的 欲求에 起因한다는 것은 밝혀졌다 하더라도, 慣習의 全部가 生理的 欲求에 起因한다는 것은 아직 論證되지 않았으며, 그뿐만 아니라 慣習이 道德의 母體라는 것 自體도 아직 分明히 되지 않았기 때문이다. 오늘날 倫理學을 哲學의 一分科로서 探求하는 學者도, 慣習의 大部分이 生存을 爲한 必要에 根源을 두었다는 見解에 反對하지 않을 것이다. 그러나 그들은, 道德의 起源도 生存을 爲한 必要에 있다는 見解에는 依然히 反對할는지도 모른다. 大部分의 慣習은 生存의 必要를 土臺로 삼을지라도, 그 一部는 生存을 爲한 必要 以外의 根源에 立脚하고 있으며, 慣習의 이 特殊部門이야말로 道德의 基盤이라고 보는 學者도 있을 것이다. 甚至於는 慣習과 道德을 本質的으로 判異한 것으로 보고, 眞正한 道德은 經驗的 社會現象에 不過한 慣習과는 何等의 內面的 聯關性이 없다고 믿는 學者도 있을지 모른다. 따라서 "道德現象의 起源은 무엇일까?"라는 本章 最初의 設問에 對하여 "道德現象은 生存의 要求에 起源을 둔다."고 對答할 수 있기 爲하여서는, 앞으로 다시 다음 두 개의 命題가 論證될 必要가 있다.

(1) 모든 慣習은 例外 없이 '生存의 必要'라는 根源에서 出發한다.

(2) 道德現象과 慣習과는 그 根本에 있어서 同一한 原理에 屬한다.

"모든 慣習은 生存欲에 根源을 둔다."라는 全稱判斷을 論證하기 爲하여서 모든 種類의 慣習을 남김 없이 檢討할 수는 없으며, 또 그럴 必要도 없다. 다만 生存에 必要한 生理的 欲求와는 가장 距離가 먼 듯한 慣習, 卽 個體의 生存이나 種族의 維持와는 全혀 關聯性이 없고 오로지 그 行爲 獨自의 價値에 依據하는 듯한 慣習을 例로 들어, 그것이 亦是 '生存의 必要'에서 派生 發展한 것임을 밝히는 길밖에 없으며, 또 그것으로 足할 것이다.

[例一] 割腹自殺

武家時代의 日本에 있어서, 上殿이나 一族에 對하여 面目 없는 行爲를 저지른 사람이 割腹함으로써 謝罪한 例가 많다. 그리고 一般은 이 自決行爲를 거룩하다고 稱頌하였다. 現代 우리 社會에 있어서도 過誤를 犯한 사람이 죽음으로써 贖罪함을 讚揚하는 氣風이 없지 않다.

自殺은 事情 如何를 莫論하고 生理的 欲求에 逆行하는 行爲임에 틀림이 없다. 정말 現實的인 贖罪나 補償이라면 오히려, 生存함으로써만 可能하다. 引責自殺을 是認하는 慣習은 一見 分明히 生存을 爲主하는 利害打算을 超越하고 있다. 그러나 省察하건대 引責自殺이 稱頌을 받는 元來의 理由는 그 動機에 內包된 責任感이다. 그리고 責任感은, 確實히 公共의 福利를 爲하여 가장 重要한 習性(traits)의 하나이다. 勿論 引責自殺을 是認하는 評價者들이 自殺動機로서의 責任感과, 責任感 尊重의 理由가 된 責任感의 公共生活을 爲한 實用性을 반드시 意識하지는 않는다. 오히려 本來의 動機를 忘却하고 過去에 反復된 行動을 機械的으로 踏襲하는 것은 慣習의 特徵에 屬한다. 그리고 本來는 責任感 强한 行爲가 社會生活 안에 일으킨 有效한 結果에 對하여 내려지던 높은 評價가, 다음에는 有用한 結果를 떠나서 責任感 自體로 돌아가게 되고, 더 나아가서는 責任感의 動機조차 떠나서, 恒常 責任感의 表現으로서 認定되어 온 '割腹'이라는 外面的 行動 自體에 對하여도 稱頌의 評價가 내려지게 되는 것은, 心理學의 基本原理의 하나인

條件反應(conditioned response)의 現象 以外의 것이 아니다.[10]

[例二] 守節

우리나라에 固有한 婦女道德에 依하면, 靑春寡婦도 再嫁하지 않는 것이 '守節'이라는 美德이다. 靑春寡婦가 獨身을 지키는 것은 本人의 生理的 欲求로 보거나 種族維持라는 全體의 立場에서 보거나 生物學的 基本欲求에는 逆行하는 짓이다. 그러므로 守節을 崇尙하는 舊來의 慣習은, 守節에 말미암는 어떤 結果 때문이 아니라, 守節하는 그 心情을 高貴하게 여기기 때문임이 分明하다. 그러나 '守節崇尙'이라는 慣習이 생기게 된 當初의 事情을 돌이켜 보건대, 人間의 原始的 欲求가 그에 關聯되어 있음을 推定하지 않을 수 없다. 그것은, 守節이라는 婦德이 寡婦된 婦人들의 自發的 要求에서 우러난 것이 아니라, 男便이나 媤父母의 要求가 젊은 女性 위에 反映된 것이라는 證據가, 守節이라는 舊習이 次次 脫皮되어 가는 過渡期에 있어서, 이 革新運動의 先鋒의 所任을 맡아 보는 것이 젊은 女性들 自身이요, 이 運動에 對하여 制止의 意思를 表示하는 것이 男便이나 媤父母들이라는 現象 안에 나타나고 있기 때문이다. 嫉妬心 섞인 男便의 生理的 欲求가, 妻

---

10 條件反應의 基本形式은 다음과 같이 表現된다. "어떤 反應 R_1을 일으키기에 (生理的 必然性을 가진 意味에서) 自然的으로 充分한 刺戟 S_1과, R_1과는 必然的 關係가 없는 다른 刺戟 S_2, S_3 … 等을 同時에 주기를 充分히 거듭한 다음에, 自然刺戟 S_1은 除外하고, 條件刺戟 S_2 또는 S_3 … 만을 주어도 該反應 R_1은 일어난다."
우리 例에 붙여 말하면, 稱頌(R_1)이라는 反應을 일으키기에 元來 充分한 自然刺戟(S_1)은 社會生活에 미치는 有用한 結果이다. 이 有用한 結果에는 언제나 責任感이라는 心情이 附隨條件의 刺戟(S_2)으로서 同伴하였다. 이러한 事情이 거듭되는 동안에, 有用한 結果라는 自然刺戟이 脫落되고 條件, 刺戟, 卽 '責任感'이라는 心情만을 接하여도 사람은 亦是 '稱頌'이라는 反應을 일으키게 된다. 더 나아가서는 '責任感'(S_2)까지도 忘却되고 責任感의 外的 表現인 '割腹'(S_3)만으로도 元來의 反應稱頌이 일어나게 된다.

의 貞節이 自己의 死後에까지라도 繼續되기를 願하는 것은 오히려 自然스러운 傾向이다. 그리고 子婦가 勞動力을 意味하던 未開社會에 있어서는, 子婦의 守節이 媤父母에 對하여 '利益'을 意味한 것도 事實이다. 男便이나 媤父母의 壓力이 妻나 子婦의 行爲規範으로 化할 수 있는 것은, 웰스가 指摘한바 長老의 威壓이 一族의 行動을 制約한 것과 같은 傾向이며, 男便이나 媤父母의 壓力이 消滅된 뒤에까지도, 妻나 子婦가 그 因襲에 사로잡히지 않을 수 없는 것은, 條件反應의 現象이다.

[例三] 容儀

夏節 炎熱에도 옷끈을 끄르거나 버선을 벗는 것은 兩班의 禮節이 아니다. 體溫調節이라는 生理的 欲求와 背馳되는 이 容儀觀念도, 上述한 바와 同一한 原理로 說明할 수가 있다. 一般的으로 禮儀라는 現象이 秩序 있는 社會生活의 必要와 便宜를 爲하여 發端했으리라는 것은, 只今까지의 우리 論述을 背定하는 限, 수월히 容認될 것이다. 具體的으로 어떠한 禮儀가 遵行되는가는 多分히 偶然的 要素(例컨대 迷信 指導者의 着想, 模倣 等)에 左右될 수 있는 問題이다. 더운 날에도 옷끈을 團束하는 慣習이 形成됨에 있어서도, 여러 가지 因子가 混合되어 있을 것이다. 다만 그 中에 한 가지 重要한 因子로서 推測되는 것은 性과의 關聯性이다. 衣服을 端正히 차리는 것이 性生活의 秩序를 爲하여 도움이 되었을 것은 分明하다. 그리고 性生活의 秩序에 對한 要求는 人間의 生理的 欲求에서 距離가 멀지 않다.[11]

---

11 男權이 優勢한 封建社會에 있어서 女性의 服裝問題가 더욱 까다로운 것은, 興味 있는 現象이다. 그리고 性道德의 理想이 開放的 方向으로 變遷해 감에 따라서 衣裳에 對한 嚴格한 制約이 緩和되었다는 事實도, 性道德과 依服에 關한 禮儀와의 깊은 關聯性을 明示한다.

其他 어떠한 慣習을 들어 考察의 對象으로 삼더라도, 우리는 根本에 있어서 同一한 說明을 適用할 수가 있을 것이다. 이리하여 "모든 慣習은 生存欲에 起源을 둔다."는 우리의 첫째 命題가 論證된 것으로 보아도 좋을 것이다. 이제 우리의 다음 課題는 "道德과 慣習은 根本에 있어서 同一한 原理에 屬한다."는 命題에 根據를 주는 일이다.

5) 慣習과 道德(良心의 經驗性)

터프츠는 人間의 行動 乃至 行爲를 세 가지 段階로 나누었다.

(1) 本能 및 基本的 欲求에서 일어난 行動(Conducts arising from instincts and fundamental needs)

(2) 社會的 標準에 依據한 行爲(Conducts regulated by standards of society)

(3) 社會的 合理的 標準에 依據한 行爲(Conducts regulated by a standard which is both social and rational)[12]

터프츠가 分類한 第一段階는, 生理的 欲求에 直接 對應하는바 所謂 '動物的'인 行動이다. 第二段階는 慣習에 盲從하는 段階이며, 第三段階는, 터프츠 自身도 '良心의 水準(the level of conscience)'에 達한 行爲라고 註釋한바, 倫理學에서 말하는 道德的 行爲(moral conducts)에 該當함이 分明하다. 우리는 이미 第二의 段階, 卽 慣習的 行爲가 第一의 段階, 卽 이른바 本能的 行動에 起源을 두고 있다는 것, 다시 말하면 第二의 段階가 第一의 段階에서 發展 또는 派生된 것임을 論證하였다. 이제 第三의 段階, 卽

---

12 J. Dewey and J. H. Tufts, *Ethics*, p.33.

道德的 行爲가 第一 或은 第二의 段階에 그 根源을 두고 있음을 밝히려는 것이 우리의 當面한 課題이다.

　道德의 絕對性을 主張하는 學者들은, 道德的 行爲가 先天的 原理에 依하여 統禦됨을 主張하고, 生理的 要求나 社會的 經驗이 道德發生의 根柢라는 것을 容認하지 않는다. (우리는 그 代表로서 칸트를 보았다.) 素朴한 思想家들에 있어서 道德의 絕對性 乃至 先天性의 論據가 된 것은, 道德觀念 또는 良心의 絕對普遍性이었다. 素朴한 觀察에 依하면, 個個人이 實踐하는 行爲는, 或은 善하기도 하고 或은 惡하기도 하여, 同一한 事情下일지라도 一定하지 않으나, 一旦 利害關係를 떠나서, 卽 感性的 欲求의 煩惱를 벗어나서, 行爲의 是非를 分揀하는 境遇에는, 正常的인 사람들이라면 모든 判斷이 同一한 結論에 到達한다. 옳은 行爲는 누가 보아도 옳고 그릇된 行爲는 누가 보더라도 그르다. 暫時 判斷을 그르쳐 非道의 行爲를 犯하는 것은 肉體에 拘束된 情慾의 所致요, 極惡無道한 人間일지라도 그 人格의 深奧한 바탕에 잠겨 있는 良心 自體는 聖賢의 그것과도 다를 바가 없다. 그러나 狹少한 範圍에 局限된 이 素朴한 觀察은, 더 廣範하고 透徹한 觀察에 依하여 轉覆되었다. 歷史學의 硏究가 時間이 오랜 옛 사람들의 良心의 記錄을 判讀하고, 民俗學의 硏究가 空間的으로 멀리 떨어진 異域의 道德觀念을 探索했을 때, 다 같은 人間일지라도 그 生活하는 時代나 地域이 다르면 그 信念에도 놀랄 만한 差異가 있다는 事實이 드러났기 때문이다.[13]

　良心 乃至 道德觀念의 先天性을 主張하는 學者들도 道德現象의 多樣性과 現實的 良心의 變遷을 否認하지 않는다. 그러나 그들은 道德의 普遍性이나 良心의 先天性만은 如前히 固執한다. "果然 現實에 나타난 良心은 時代나 地域을 따라 變遷이 있고 差異가 있다. 그러나 그 變遷과 差異는 現實 위에 나타난 面에 關한 事實이다. 人間의 本性 안에 潛在해 있는 良心 自體만은 恒常 不變하고 同一하다. 다만 그 潛在해 있는 良心이 恒常 完全하고

純粹하게 現勢化하는 것은 아니다. 時代와 地域의 經驗的 要素에 따라서, 그것이 어느 程度 完全하게 또 어느 程度 純粹하게 現勢化되는가가 決定된다. 모든 經驗的 制約을 克服하고, 우리의 良心을 理想的 良心에 가깝도록 實現하는 것이 우리 人間의 崇高한 義務이다." 論者는 이와 같이 辨明한다. 그러나 이러한 論調는, 直視된 事實에 依據하여 立論된 것이 아니라, 良心은 絕對的이라는 先入觀念으로부터 出發하여, 經驗되는 諸事實을 이 先入觀念에 알맞도록 說明하려는 詭辯이다. 따라서 飛躍과 歪曲을 免하지 못한다. 그들은 먼저 萬人에게 普遍的인 良心이 潛在해 있다는 證據를 提示했어야 할 것이다. 萬若 論者들에게 '理想的 良心'의 理念을 描寫시킨다면, 그들의 描寫는 全혀 無內容한 抽象圖가 되거나, 그렇지 않으면 論者들

---

13 道德觀念 乃至 良心의 變遷을 證左하는 事例는 드물지 않다.

(A) 封建社會에 있어서 君主에 對한 忠誠은 非單 强者의 壓力에 對한 被動的 服從만은 아니었다. 그것은 臣下 自身의 良心의 命令이었으며, 臣下의 自由意志가 選擇한 바였다. 그것은 現代 民主主義 社會에 있어서의 爲政者에 對한 尊敬과는 本質的으로 判異한 心情이다. 民主主義 社會에는 '忠誠'이라는 良心이 없다.

(B) 徹底한 基督敎人의 良心은, 心中에서 淫蕩을 想像만 하더라도, 姦淫의 苛責을 받는다. 한便 사모아島의 少女들은, 結婚 前에 數人의 愛人을 가져도 非難을 받지 않으며, 따라서 스스로 良心의 苛責을 받는 일도 없다(S. H. Britt, *Social Psychology of Modern Life*, p.48). 이것은 極端의 對照이다. 그러나 性道德에 關한 良心이 時代와 地域에 따라 크게 差異 있음은, 구태여 極端한 例를 들지 않더라도 우리 身邊 가까이 이를 觀取할 수 있는 平凡한 事實이다.

(C) 오스트레일리아(Australia)의 어느 族屬은, 自己 族屬 中에서 누가 죽는 것은 隣近의 種屬이 咀呪했기 때문이라고 믿는다. 따라서 그들은 隣近 種族의 一員을 殺害하는 것은 親近者의 死亡에 復讐하는 神聖한 義務라고 생각한다. 西部 오스트레일리아에서 裁判官 노릇을 하던 英國人의 農場에서 일하던 土人 한 사람은, 病死한 妻의 怨讐를 갚기 爲하여 떠나려고 하였으나, 裁判官의 制止를 받고 中止하였다. 그러나 義務를 履行하지 못한 土人은 良心의 苛責에 못 이겨 次次 衰弱해 가서 마침내 寢食을 못 이룰 地境에 達하였다. 어느 날 土人은 자취를 감추었다. 그는 約 一年 後에 돌아왔는데 잃었던 健康을 完全히 回復하고 있었다. 그는 '神聖한 義務'를 다했던 것이다(J. M. Guyan, *Esguisse dune Morale sans Obligation ni Sanction*, p.44). 이야기에 나오는 土人의 義務感은 殺人을 極惡의 犯罪라고 믿는 文明社會의 良心과 좋은 對照를 이루고 있다.

은 各各 自己의 個性과 環境을 反映하여, 百人百色의 異夢圖를 나타낼 것이다.

다른 先天論者들은 或은 論鋒을 돌려 다음과 같이 抗辯할 것이다. "變遷과 差異를 나타내는 것은 良心의 內容이다. 그러나 良心의 形式만은 東西古今을 通하여 그 同一性을 保全한다." 그러나 그들이 말하는바 絕對不變의 '形式'이 아무 內容도 없는 形式만의 形式이라면, 그것은 空虛한 形式이며, 또는 그것이 어떠한 內容이라도 받아들일 수 있는 無制限的 形式이라면, 그것은 無意味한 形式이다.

形而上學的 信條에서 出發한 立場과 正面 對立하는 論戰은 終結될 날이 없다. 우리는 先天的 良心論에 對한 直接批判을 멈추고, 道德觀念 乃至 良心이 經驗的으로 形成되는 過程을 科學的 手法으로 곧장 論證하기를 試圖함이 可할 것이다. 그리고 道德觀念이 經驗的으로 形成됨을 論證하려는 우리의 課題는, 두 개의 針路를 通하여 追究할 수가 있다. 針路의 하나는 道德觀念이 이미 經驗에서 形成되었음이 밝혀진 '慣習'에서 發展한 것임을 說明하는 길이요, 針路의 또 하나는 基本的 生活의 欲求에서 發足하는 新生兒의 行動이 自律的 良心에 依據하는 道德的 行爲에까지 發達하는 過程을 心理學的으로 究明하는 길이다.

[慣習과 道德] 慣習과 道德과의 關係에 對하여서는, 존 듀이의 明快한 論述이 있다. 그는 道德問題에 關한 主著인 『人間性과 行爲(*Human Nature and Conduct*)』에서 다음과 같이 말하고 있다.

"實際에 있어서 道德은 慣習 乃至 風習, 卽 集團的으로 形成된 習慣(habit)을 意味한다. 이것은 人類學者들에게는 平凡한 事實이다. 다만 倫理學者들은, 自己自身의 社會와 時代만은 例外라는, 或은 例外여야 한다는 幻想에 사로잡혀 있는 것이다. 그러나 어느 때나 어느 곳에서나, 人間行爲

에 對하여 標準을 提供하는 것은 慣習이다. … 이것은 過去 어느 時代에도 事實이었듯이 오늘날도 事實이다. 다만 오늘날은 慣習의 變動性과 混雜性으로 말미암아, 各 個人에게 提示된 慣習範型(custom patterns)의 範圍가 莫大한 넓이를 가지고 있다. 따라서 各 個人은, 慣習의 諸要素를 選擇하고 再組織함에 있어서, 個人的 才幹을 發揮할 수가 있다. 簡單히 말하면 各 個人은 그럴 意思만 있다면 慣習을 事情에 適應시키고, 따라서 慣習을 改造할 수가 있는 것이다."[14]

慣習은 盲目的이요 因襲的이며 無批判的임에 그 特色이 있다. 道德은 合理的이요 自律的이며 批判的임에 그 生命이 있다. 그러면 이같이 矛盾對立하는 두 개의 槪念 ― 慣習과 道德 ― 을 어찌 根源에 있어서 同一하다고 主張할 수가 있는가. 우리는 듀이의 引用을 좀 더 繼續해 보기로 하자.

"未開한 社會에 있어서의 慣習의 地位를 認知한 사람들은, 大體로 慣習이 文明社會 안에 存在하는 것은 오직 그 殘滓에 不過하다고 생각한다. 또는 섬너와 같이, 慣習의 安住地를 認定하는 것은 모든 合理性과 道德의 原理를 否認하는 것이나 一般이라고 생각한다. (그러나) 이 見解는, 정말 對立하는 것은 理性(reason)과 習慣(habit)이 아니라 因襲的이요 非理知的인 習慣과 理知的 習慣, 또는 藝術(art)이라는 事實을 看過하고 있다. 未開人의 慣習일지라도, 그것이 社會的 要求와 必要에 適合하다는 點에 있어서는, 合理的이라고 볼 수가 있다. 經驗이 쌓여 감에 따라 이 適合性에 對한 意識的 認識이 생길 것이며 따라서 '合理性(rationality)'이라는 慣習이 在來의 慣習 위에 새로이 添加되는 것이다."[15]

---

14 J. Dewey, *Human Nature and Conduct*, p.75.
15 Ibid., p.77.

慣習이란 元來 生의 必要에 依하여 생긴 것이었다. 慣習은 그것이 生의 必要를 滿足시켜 주는 限 '合理的(reasonable)'이다. 어떠한 範型의 行爲가 生의 必要에 適合하다는 事實이 累次 經驗되는 동안에, 그 適合하는 事實을 意識하게 되며, 여기서 '適合性'에 對한 要求가 생기고, 이것이 '合理性'이라는 새로운 慣習을 形成한다는 것이다. 듀이는, 大膽하게도, '合理性'이라는 槪念이 人間精神 안에 미리 주어져 있는 것이 아니라, 外部事物의 合理性을 經驗함으로써 생긴 慣習이라고 明言하고 있다. "目的에 對한 現實的 妥當(external reasonableness) 또는 適合(adaptation)이 妥當性의 觀念(reasonableness of mind)에 先行한다. 이것은 道德界에 있어서도, 自然界에 있어서와 마찬가지로, 認識에 앞서서 對象이 있어야 한다는 것, 따라서 合理性의 觀念(rationality of mind)은 先天的 所與(original endowment)가 아니라, 客觀的 適合性 乃至 客觀的 關係와의 相互關聯(intercourse)의 所産임을 主張함에 不過하다."[16]

理性(reason)은 合理性을 追求하는 習性이다. 그것은 '期待와 觀望의 慣習(custom of expectation and outlook)'이요, '다른 慣習의 合理性에 對한 强力한 要請(the active demand for reasonableness in other customs)'이다. 一旦 形成된 理性이라는 習性은 '다른 모든 慣習에 對하여 革命的 影響力을 가진바' 人間의 가장 强力한 習性이다. 모든 習慣이 自己主張(self-assertion)을 하듯이, 理性이라는 習慣도 自己를 主張한다. 批判과 反省과 評價는, 모두 理性의 自己主張 ― 習慣的인 自己主張 以外의 다른 것이 아니다.[17]

---

16 Ibid., p.77.
17 Ibid., p.78.

過去에 있어서는 자못 有力하던 묵은 慣習이, 오늘날 '理性'이라는 새로운 慣習으로 批判할 때에, 不合理한 點이 있을 것은 不可避한 現實이다. 迷信을 土臺로 한 慣習은 科學을 基本으로 한 慣習으로 代置되어야 한다. 封建社會를 背景으로 한 慣習이 물러가고, 民主社會를 地盤으로 한 慣習이 들어서야 한다. 道德的 精神이란, 新時代에 맞지 않는 묵은 慣習을 批判하고, 現實에 適合한 새로운 慣習을 樹立하고자 하는 理性의 自己主張이다. 그리고 오늘날의 淸新한 道德도, 時代가 흐른 後世에 가서는 또다시 묵은 慣習으로 轉落하고, 그 時代의 새 精神으로부터의 批判을 받을 運命에 있음은, 過去 모든 時代의 道德 乃至 慣習과 一般이다.

듀이의 見解를 中心으로 한 以上의 論述은, 道德觀念 乃至 良心의 經驗性을 論證하여, 慣習과 道德이 同一한 根源에 屬한다는 것을 밝히고자 하는 우리의 目的을 充分히 滿足시켜 주는 것 같지는 않다. 理性을 經驗的 機能으로 보는 見解에는 簡單히 解決하기 困難한 問題가 包含되고 있을 것이다. '理性'이니 '合理性'이니 하는 어려운 槪念을 導入함으로 말미암아, 우리는 數많은 論爭의 資料를 準備하였다. 以上 論述의 不備를 補充하는 意味에서, '理性'이나 '合理性' 같은 어려운 槪念의 導入을 必要로 하지 않는 第二의 針路, 卽 道德觀念 乃至 良心의 發展을 發達心理學의 見地에서 考察하는 針路를 더듬어 보기로 한다.

[良心의 發達] 行爲의 結果를 眼中에 둠이 없이, 오로지 그 行爲 自體를 爲하여 行하여지는 行爲가 있다. 이러한 行爲는 그 行爲가 招來할 實質的 利害를 無視할 뿐 아니라, 行爲가 받을 評價, 卽 象徵的 報酬조차도 期待하지 않는다. 이와 같은, 이를테면 純粹한 行爲가 存在한다는 事實은, 良心先天論者들이 그 論據로 삼는 事實의 하나이다. 卑近한 實例로서 正直한 行爲 하나를 들어 보기로 하자.

어느 教師가 받은 臨時手當 封套에는 二萬圜의 金額이 加外로 들어 있었다. 教師는 이것이 會計員의 單純한 錯誤요, 故意로 한 짓이 아님을 確信할 根據가 있었다. 그리고 設令 그 二萬圜을 가지가 私用하더라도, 自己만 秘密을 지키면, 世上에 그 事實이 發覺될 理가 없다는 것을 믿을 만한 條件도 있었다. 또 그 金額은 返還함으로써 庶務職員들로부터 받으리라고 豫想되는 讚辭가, 薄俸敎師에게 二萬圜의 價値가 있다고는 생각되지 않았다. 그러나 그 敎師는 그 加外의 金額을 如何튼 庶務에 돌렸다.

二萬圜을 返還한 이 敎師의 動機에는, 後日에 發覺이 나서 社會的 非難을 憂慮하는 心事는 조금도 섞여 있지 않다. 그것은 오직 正直을 爲하여서 正直하였을 뿐이다. 그러므로 아무런 外部的 壓力도, 結果에 對한 利害打算도 없이, 오직 自律的으로 行하여진 이 敎師의 行爲는, 充分히 '道德的'이라고 말할 수가 있다. 金額을 返還하라는 內心의 要求를, 버틀러(Butler)라면 '良心(conscience)'의 命令이라고 말했을 것이며, 金額을 返還하지 않는 동안 不安하고 返還함으로써 비로소 輕快해지는 心情을, 칸트라면 '純粹理性의 事實(Das Faktum der reinen Vernunft)'이라고 불렀을 것이다. 그러나 이 內心의 要求를 單純히 先天的인 것 또는 純粹한 것이라고 斷定하기 前에, 우리는 이 行爲의 性質을 새로운 角度에서 分析하기를 꾀해 볼 必要가 있을 것이다.

正直한 行爲에는 一般的으로 두 가지 社會的 結果가 隨伴된다. 첫째는 正直한 行爲가 大體로 社會共同生活에 對한 利益을 助長한다는 것이며, 둘째는 正直한 行爲者에 對하여는 大體로 是認 乃至 稱讚의 評價가 내려진다는 事實이다. 特殊한 事例에 있어서는 正直한 行爲가 社會共同生活에 損害를 끼치는 境遇도 생각할 수가 있다. 그러나 大體로 볼 때에, 正直이 社會生活의 安全과 秩序를 爲하여 바람직하다는 事實을 否認할 수는 없다. 그리고 正直이 社會共同生活에 對하여 利益을 意味한다는 事實은, 바로 社會

로 하여금 正直한 行爲者를 是認하고 稱讚하게 하는 根據가 된 것이다. 社會가 그 利益을 意識하지 않더라도 正直을 是認하고 稱讚하게 되는 事實 및 正直이 結果에 있어서 損害를 招來하는 境遇일지라도 사람들은 利害를 떠나서 그 正直 自體로 말미암아 이를 是認하고 讚揚하게 되는 過程에 對하여서는, 앞서 慣習의 形成 一般을 '條件反應'으로 說明한 그 說明이 그대로 適合한다.

正直한 行爲를, 그 行爲를 當하는 立場에서 볼 때, '有利한 行爲'라고 規定한다면 그 行爲者 自身의 立場에서 볼 때엔 '稱讚을 받는 行爲'라고 規定할 수가 있다. 그런데 正常的인 人間은 누구나 是認과 稱讚 받기를 願한다. 셰퍼(F. Shaffer)는 '社會的 是認의 動機(social approval motives)'를, '支配欲(mastery motives)'과 아울러 가장 '普遍的이요 確乎한' 人間의 欲求라고 論斷하였다.[18] 是認과 稱讚을 받는 것이 人間의 基本的 欲求라면, 그리고 正直한 行爲가 是認과 稱讚을 招來함이 確實하다면 人間은 分明히 正直하게 行爲할 動機를 가졌다. 是認이나 稱讚보다도 더 强한 動機가 對立하는 境遇가 있을 것이므로, 實際에 있어서는 不正直하게 行爲하는 수도 많을 것이다. 그러나 正直하고자 하는 動機는 恒常 多少間의 힘을 가지고 作用할 것이다. 이제 萬若 다음 두 개의 命題가 論證만 된다면, 正直하게 行爲하고자 하는 우리의 意欲이 基本的 生理的 欲求를 土臺로 하고 經驗的으로 發達하였다는 것을 說明하려 하는 우리의 目標가 完全히 到達될 것이다.

(1) 社會的 是認이라는 報酬를 全혀 度外視하고 行하여지는 正直한 行爲, 例컨대 그 行爲가 全혀 世上에 알려질 機會가 豫想되지 않는 境遇에 하는

---

18 F. Shaffer, *The Psychology of Adjustment*, p.103.

正直한 行爲도, 亦是 社會的 是認을 받기 爲하여 行하여지는 正直한 行爲와 同一한 根源에서 出發하고 있다.

(2) 社會的 是認 또는 稱讚을 받고자 하는 動機는, 人間의 生得的 傾向性이 아니라, 經驗을 通하여 習得된 社會的 動機에 屬한다.

우리는 以上 두 개의 命題를 亦是 條件反應의 原理에 立脚하여 說明하기를 試圖하기로 한다. 우리는 正直을 爲한 正直한 行爲의 分析으로부터 始作한다.

正直한 行爲에는 恒常 社會的 是認과 稱讚이 同伴하였다. 그리고 社會的 是認과 稱讚은 받는 이에게 滿足感을 일으킨다. 滿足感이라는 反應을 일으키기에 元來 充分한 刺戟, 卽 自然刺戟은 是認 乃至 稱讚이다. '正直한 行爲'는 是認 乃至 稱讚이라는 自然刺戟에 同伴하는 條件刺戟이다. 自然刺戟과 條件刺戟이 同伴하여 一定한 反應을 일으키기를 거듭한 다음, 自然刺戟이 脫落되고 條件刺戟만 홀로 주어질 때에도 그 反應이 亦是 일어나는 것은, 條件反應의 公式이다. 正直한 行爲와 關聯하여 是認 또는 稱讚이라는 報酬를 累次 經驗한 사람은, 마침내 '社會的 是認'이라는 自然刺戟 없이 '正直한 行爲'라는 條件刺戟만으로도 '滿足感'이라는 反應을 일으키게 된다. '社會的 是認'이라는 自然刺戟에 同伴하는 條件刺戟은 勿論 '正直한 行爲'뿐만은 아니다. 社會的 是認에 同伴되는 '自己自身의 是認'도 重要한 條件刺戟의 하나이다. 따라서 人間은 他人의 是認에 뿐만 아니라 自身의 是認에 對하여도 滿足을 느끼게 된다. 世上에 알려질 可能性이 全혀 없지만 自己自身의 良心에 忠實하기 爲하여 正當하게 하는 行爲란, 自己自身의 是認을 求하는 行爲 以外의 다른 것이 아니다. 問題를 消極的 側面에서 考察하여도 根本은 一般이다. 卽 不正直한 行爲가 暴露되는 날 받을 非難과 處罰의 威脅에 눌려서 正直하게 行爲해 버릇한 사람은, 非難 乃至 處罰이라는 自然刺戟이 脫落되어도, 如前히 正直하게 行爲하기를 繼續할 것이다. 原

理는 猛犬에 놀란 어린이가 강아지만 보아도 자지러지는 心理와 一般이다.

上述한 바를 一般化할 때에, 우리는, 모든 利己性을 벗어난 '착한' 行爲가 그 發生의 始初를 따지고 본다면, 社會的 是認을 받고자 하는 動機에 起源을 두었다는 結論을 얻는다. 이제 우리는 社會的 是認을 얻고자 하는 動機의 經驗性을 論하는 問題로 옮겨 간다.

新生兒는 自己自身의 힘만으로는 生存을 繼續할 可望이 없는 無力한 狀態로 出生한다. 그는 生存이 要求하는 모든 시중을 父母 其他의 成人에게 依賴하지 않으면 아니 된다. 幼兒는 자라는 동안의 體驗을 通하여 母親을 爲始한 家族 어른들의 重要性을 깨닫게 된다. 그러나 幼兒에 對한 어른들의 援助는 어느 때나 한결같이 施與되지는 않는다. 더 親切한 同情이 쏟아질 때도 있고, 援助를 冷靜히 拒絶 當하는 境遇도 있다. 幼兒의 年齡이 높아 감에 따라서 이 傾向은 漸漸 커간다. 幼兒가 귀여운 재롱을 피면, 어머니는 稱讚하는 言辭와 더불어 愛撫하는 動作을 주고, 讚揚하는 表情과 아울러 먹을 것이나 장난감을 提供한다. 이때 幼兒는 滿足과 기쁨을 느낀다. 이와 反對로 幼兒가 일을 저지르거나 미운 짓을 하면, 어머니는 叱責하는 言動과 더불어 或은 때리고 或은 給與를 拒絶한다. 이때 幼兒는 不滿과 苦痛을 느낀다. 幼兒로 하여금 滿足과 기쁨의 情緒反應을 일으키게 한 元初의 刺戟(自然刺戟)은, 稱讚하는 言辭나 表情이 아니라, 愛撫하는 動作이었고(皮膚에 對한 가벼운 摩擦은 生理的 快感을 일으킨다) 먹을 것이었고 장난감이었다. 不滿을 일으킨 것은 叱責하는 言辭나 表情이 아니라, 때리는 動作이요 給與의 拒絶이었다. 그러나 어떤 反應을 일으키기에 元來 必然性을 가진 어떤 刺戟, 卽 自然刺戟과 다른 附隨的인 刺戟, 卽 條件刺戟과를 同時에 받은 經驗이 거듭된 다음에는, 自然刺戟이 脫落되고 條件刺戟만 받아도 該反應을 일으키는 것은 條件反應의 現象이다. 이리하여 幼兒는 어느 時期에 達하면, 直接 生理的 滿足 또는 不滿을 일으키는 刺戟 없이, 오직

言辭와 表情만으로 된 稱讚이나 非難에 對하여도, 滿足 또는 不滿을 일으키는 것이다.

以上의 說明은 典型的 條件形成(conditioning)의 境遇를 例로 든 것이다.[19] 勿論 實生活에 있어서의 兒童心理의 發達은 훨씬 複雜微妙한 過程을 밟을 것이다. 그러나 그 過程이 아무리 複雜하고 微妙하다 하더라도, 그 根本原理는 上述한 條件反應의 原理를 멀리 떠나지 않을 것이다. 如何튼 우리는 社會的 是認을 爲한 動機의 '經驗性'을 否認할 수가 없다.

社會的 是認과 稱讚을 招來하는 것은 正直한 行爲뿐만은 아니다. 所謂 '道德的'이라고 認定되는 모든 行爲는 是認과 稱讚을 받는 것이 原則이다. 同一한 社會 內에서도, 一般이 '道德的'이라고 讚揚하는 行爲를 非難하는 人士가 있다. 그러나 그는 그 行爲를 眞正한 意味에서 道德的이라고 認定하지 않는 사람이다. '是認'한다는 것과 '道德的'이라고 認定한다는 것은 元來 같은 뜻의 말이다. 이제 우리는, 正直하게 行爲하고자 하는 意欲에 對하여 論한 바를, 무릇 道德律에 妥當하도록 行爲하고자 하는 意欲 一般에 넓혀서 다음과 같이 結論지을 수가 있다.

"道德律을 따라 行爲하고자 하는 모든 意欲은 社會的 是認을 願하고 社會的 非難을 꺼리는 情緒的 動機에 起源을 갖는다. 그리고 是認을 願하고 非難을 싫어하는 社會的 動機는 基本的 生理的 欲求에 起源을 둔다. 따라서 모든 道德的 傾向性은 發生的으로 볼 때에는 基本的 生理的 欲求에서부터 출발하였다."

---

19 人間性의 條件形成의 過程을 比較的 簡明하게 說明한 敍述로서는 셰퍼의 *The Psychology of Adjustment*의 第一部 第三章(pp.52-82)과 第四章(pp.100-108)을 들 수가 있다.

2. 道德의 本質

道德現象은 '生'에서부터 出發하였다. 道德現象은 生과 더불어 發展한다. 道德의 目標 亦是 生을 떠나서 그 밖에 있을 곳이 없다. 藝術, 宗敎, 科學 等과 더불어, 道德은 文化의 一環이요 歷史의 一斑이다. 文化가 生成하고 歷史가 變遷함에 따라서, 道德도 生成하고 또 變遷한다. 文化의 創造者요 歷史의 主人公인 人間이, 또한 道德의 創造者요 道德의 主人公이다. 文化 創造의 條件이요 歷史發展의 制約인바 自然은, 道德에 있어서도 또한 그 條件이요 그 制約이다. 人間의 欲求와 人間 相互間의 關係와, 人間과 그리고 自然과의 交涉이, 道德의 方向과 形態를 決定해 왔으며, 앞으로도 決定해 갈 것이다. 道德은 人生 그 自體의 一部分이다.

道德現象은 人間性의 反映이요, 社會相의 反映이다. 道德은 人間性의 生成과 步調를 같이하여 生成하고, 社會相의 變遷과 呼吸을 같이하여 變遷한다. 우리는 道德現象의 普遍性에 가까운 側面을 看過하지 않으며, 不變性에 가까운 要素를 否認하지 않는다. 그러나 이것은 道德 全般의 普遍性과 不變性을 主張할 根據는 되지 않는다. 道德現象의 거의 普遍的이요 거의 不變的인 側面은, 人間性 自體의 거의 普遍的인 側面의 反映이요, 社會生活 條件의 거의 不變的인 要素의 反映임에 不過하다. 人間은, 東西古今의 區別 없이, 衣食을 要求하고 異性을 그리워하고 子孫을 生殖하였다. 이와 같은 生의 基本欲求가 普遍的인 限, 自他의 財産을 尊重하며 異性을 思慕하며 子孫을 保護하는 道德도 또한 普遍的이다. 모든 人種은 옛날부터 오늘까지 集團的 共同生活 안에 生活해 왔으며, 모든 共同社會는 秩序와 協同의 惠澤을 입어 왔다. 人類가 集團的 共同生活이라는 基本生活 樣式을 維持하는 동안, 社會의 秩序와 協同을 強調하는 道德이 持續 要求될 것이다. 經濟事情이 物質의 浪費를 許諾하지 않는 限, '節約'이 善行으로서 尊

重될 것이며, 人生이 鬪爭을 要求하는 동안, '勇氣'가 美德으로서 鼓吹될 것이며, 國內外에 貧民과 孤兒가 자취를 감추지 않는 限, '慈善'이 道德法典에서 削除되지 않을 것이다. 道德은 人間性과 社會相의 變遷하는 側面을 反映하여 變遷하고, 恒存하는 側面을 反映하여 恒存한다.

道德은 生理的 欲求 또는 生存의 要求를 源泉 삼고 發生하였다. 그러나 道德의 起源이 生理的 欲求에 있다는 事實은, 道德의 價値가 生理的 欲求의 價値에 依存한다거나, 道德의 使命이 生理的 欲求를 滿足시킴에 있다는 것을 意味하지는 않는다. 繪畵의 價値가 畵具의 價値에 依存하지 아니하며, 胡蝶의 美가 그 幼虫의 美 안에 跼蹐하지 않듯이 무릇 發展된 事物의 價値는 그 起源의 價値 안에 局限되는 것이 아니다. 道德도, 그 起源은 비록 生理的 欲求에 있었으나, 一旦 形成된 然後에는, 그 起源의 外殼을 벗어나, 道德 獨自의 價値를 保有한다. 天文學은 그 起源을 占星術에 두었으나, 오늘날 天文學의 使命이 占星術의 使命을 踏襲하지 않듯이, 무릇 發達된 段階의 使命은 그 原始的 段階의 使命을 반드시 固執하는 것은 아니다. 道德은 비록 그 起源을 生理的 欲求에 두었으나, 오늘날 發達된 道德은 生理的 欲求의 使命을 超脫하고, 그 獨自의 使命 아래 獨自의 行路를 걷게 된다. 道德의 起源이 生理的 欲求에 있다는 主張은 道德이 原始社會로의 復歸를 理想으로 삼아야 한다는 것을 意味하지 않는다. 다만 道德의 經驗性을 肯定하는 主張은, 道德을 함부로 絕對化하고 化石化하려는 根據 없는 態度를 警戒할 뿐이다.

道德의 起源이 '生'[20]에 있다는 前提는, 道德의 使命이 人類의 生活을 原

---

20 여기서 '生'은 超自然的 形而上學的 槪念이 아니다. 新陳代謝하고 生殖하고 死亡하는바 生物學的인 '生'을 意味할 뿐이다.

始的 未開狀態로 後退시킴에 있다는 結果를 正當化하지 않는다. 原始人의 生活이 가장 健全하고 高貴한 生活이라고 생각되지도 아니하며, 動物界의 生態가 오늘날 우리 人間에 對하여서도 가장 自然스러운 生態라고 보이지도 않기 때문이다. 그러나 道德의 起源이 '生'에 있다는 認識과, 道德이 生을 超越하여 또는 生에 앞서서 獨自의 領域을 가지고 있다는 信念은, 道德의 使命에 關하여서 各各 別途의 見解를 示唆할 것이다. 道德이 生을 超越하여 超經驗的이라는 信念으로 본다면, 道德은 '生' 밖에서 生을 引導하는 慧星이다. 道德은 生의 價値를 判定하는 標尺이며, 道德實現이 人生 最高의 目的이라는 피히테(J. G. Fichte)의 見解가 妥當하다. 그러나 道德이 生에 起源하고 經驗과 더불어 變遷한다는 우리의 立場으로 본다면, 道德은 '生'의 內部에서 生을 調整하는 自律의 原理이다. 道德이 生의 價値를 決定하는 것이 아니라, 生이 道德의 價値를 評定한다. 피히테의 見解보다는 차라리, 人生이 道德에 奉仕할 것이 아니라 道德이 人生에 奉仕해야 한다는 니체(F. Nietzsche)의 思想이 더 合理性에 가깝다. 그러나 嚴密하게 말하자면, 道德과 人生은 對立시켜 생각할 槪念이 아니라, 道德이 人生 안에 包攝되는 槪念이다. 藝術, 宗敎, 科學 等과 同等한 層位에서, 道德도 人生의 一部分이다. 道德的 行爲도 넓은 意味로는 一種의 藝術이다.[21]

---

21 道德과 藝術은 原始的 欲求의 昇華(sublimation)라는 點에 있어서 本質的인 共通性을 갖는다. 兩者는 다 같이 精神的 價値의 實現을 目標로 삼는다. 다만 道德은 그 價値의 實現을 實生活 안에서 企圖하는 데 反하여, 藝術은 그것을 한갓 '表現의 世界'에서 꾀하는 差異가 있다.

四章
倫理學의 方向

四章 倫理學의 方向

　現實的인 道德現象을 떠나서, 倫理學의 地盤이 될 만한 어떤 다른 世界에 關하여 우리는 아는 바가 全혀 없다. 그리고 우리는 全혀 알 수 없는 것을 土臺로 한 學問을 '學'으로서 받아들이기를 拒否했던 것이다. 이제 萬若, 우리가 容納하는 倫理學이 可能하려면, 그것은 우리가 어느 程度 알 수 있는 現實, 卽 道德의 現象을 발판으로 삼을 수밖에 길이 없다. 그러면 道德現象을 根據로 삼는 學問의 成立이 果然 可能할 것인가? 可能하다면 그것은 어떠한 方向과 構想을 가질 것인가?

　萬一 '道德現象'이라는 現象이 絕對不變하는 目的이나 法則 아래 展開되는 것이라면, 卽 道德現象 背後에 時間과 空間에 無制約的으로 妥當하는 行爲의 目的이나 法則이 있다면, 그 目的 乃至 法則의 究明은 倫理學의 課題가 될 것이요, '人生의 窮極目的' 또는 '行爲의 絕對法則'이라는 確固不動한 對象을 가진 倫理學은, 버젓한 學으로서 問題 없이 成立할 것이다. 實은 從來의 傳統的인 諸倫理說이 構想한 것은 바로 이와 같은 倫理學이었다. 그러나 우리는 앞서 '道德現象의 本質'을 考察할 때에, 道德現象이 時代와 地域을 따라서 歷史的으로 變遷하는 經驗的 事實이라는 結論에 達하

였다. 그리고 이것은 從來의 傳統的인 倫理說에 對한 不信을 意味하는 것이었다. 그러나 여기서 우리가 倫理學이라는 것은 都是 學으로서 成立할 수 없다고 斷定하기 前에, 새로운 原理 위에서 새로운 方向과 構想을 가진 倫理學의 可能性 與否를 愼重히 檢討하는 것이 正當한 順序일 것이다.

무릇 어떤 現象이 있는 곳에는 그 現象을 '現象'으로서 記述, 分類하고, 可能하면 그 通則을 發見하는 科學이 成立할 수가 있다. 따라서 萬若에 '道德現象'이라는 現象이 人間生活에 있어서 없어질 수 없는 必然性을 가진 現象이라면, 우리에게는 적어도 道德現象에 關한 社會科學과 心理學이 可能할 것이다. 그것은 마치 人間生活에 經濟, 政治 等의 現象이 必然的인 限, 그 現象을 對象으로 삼고 經濟學, 政治學 等의 社會科學이 可能한 것과 같은 論理에 屬한다. 따라서 '道德에 關한 學'의 可能性을 밝히기 爲하여, 우리는 먼저 '道德現象의 必然性'을 論考하기로 한다.

'道德現象의 必然性'이 肯定的으로 論證된다면, 그것으로써 道德에 關한 存在(Sein)를 밝히는 一種의 社會科學과 心理學의 可能性은 保障될 것이다. 그러나 우리는 道德現象을 單純한 現象으로서 밝히는 科學의 成立만으로 滿足하지는 않을 것이다. 倫理學의 動機는 元來 不動하는 實踐의 原理를 把握하자는 데 있었다. 우리는 道德을 그저 있는 그대로의 現象으로서 밝힘에 그치지 않고, 한 걸음 나아가서 마땅히 있어야 할 實踐의 理想을 밝히는 '當爲의 學'에 到達함으로써 窮極의 目標로 삼는다. 그러므로 道德에 關한 '存在의 學'이 可能하다는 것이 밝혀진 다음에는, 우리는 行爲에 關한 當爲의 學이 可能한가 可能하지 않은가를 묻는 段階로 넘어갈 것이다.

1. 道德의 必然性

經驗을 超越하여 絶對的 義務를 賦課하는 行爲의 客觀的 法則이 없다 함

은, 人間에게 한便으로는 無限한 自由를 意味하는 것이나, 또 한便으로는 無限한 重擔을 意味하는 것이다. 人間이, 이미 所與된 法則에 拘碍할 必要 없이, 自己自身의 行爲를 自意로 決斷할 權利가 있다는 點에서, 그것은 無限한 自由를 意味한다. 그러나 길 없는 處女地를 새로이 길을 열며 걸어야 한다는 點에 있어서, 또는 너무 여러 갈래로 길이 뚫린 交又點에 서서 오직 한 갈래의 길을 選擇해야 한다는 點에 있어서, 그리고 自己가 열고 或은 自己가 選擇한 길에 對하여서, 卽 그 길을 걸음으로써 일어나는 모든 結果에 對하여서, 自己 스스로가 責任을 져야 한다는 點에 있어서, 그것은 無限한 重擔을 意味한다. 法則이 이미 주어져 있을 때에는, 于先 立法의 수고를 덜 수가 있었다. 또 所與된 法則대로 行爲만 한다면 責任은 그것으로 끝나는 것이요, 法則대로 行爲하여 設令 現實的 不幸을 招來하더라도, 그 結果에 對하여서 아무런 責任이 없다. 萬事를 運命에 내맡기고 諦念할 수 있으며, 甚至於는 '惡夢에 善解夢' 格으로, 그 現實的 不幸이 深奧한 窮極에 있어서는 도리어 幸福을 意味하는 것이라고 스스로 慰安할 수도 있다. 그러나 法則이 所與되어 있지 않은 以上 立法의 難題를 自己가 맡아야 하며, 그 立法에 對하여는 스스로가 全責任을 져야 한다.

그러나 所與된 法則이 없으면 瞬間 瞬間의 氣分을 따라 恣意로 行爲할 뿐이지, 또 새삼스럽게 立法이 必要하다 함은 무슨 까닭인가? 그리고 絶對的 義務가 賦課되지 않은 以上, 行爲의 結果에 對한 '責任'이란 무엇을 意味하는 것일까?

첫째로 人間이 언제나 氣分에 따라 欲望대로 行爲할 能力을 가졌다면, 人間에게는 行爲의 法則이 必要하지 않았을 것이다. 그러나 人間이 各 瞬間에 있어서 欲望대로 行爲한다는 것은 事實上 不可能하다. 欲望대로 行爲함을 不可能하게 하는 첫째 因子는, 欲求에서 欲求滿足에로 이르는 行路를 가로막는 障碍다. 行爲를 妨害하는 障碍에는 여러 가지가 있다. 運動會를

不可能하게 하는 雨天과 같이, 外部 環境에서 오는 障碍(environmental obstacle)도 있고, 敏捷한 行動을 不可能하게 하는 身體의 不具와 같이 一身上의 缺陷에서 오는 障碍(thwarting from personal defects)도 있다. 그러나 倫理學의 見地에서 볼 때 가장 重要한 意義를 가진 것은 動機의 衝突(confrict with antagonistic motives)에서 오는 障壁이다.[1] 우리의 動機는 一時에 반드시 한 가지만 나타나지는 않는다. 例컨대 日曜日이면 映畵도 보고 싶고 讀書도 해야 하며 散步도 하고 싶다. 그러나 이 여러 가지 欲求를 한목에 滿足시킬 道理는 없다. 一定한 時間을 爲하여서는 오직 한 가지 動機만을 選擇해서 行하지 않으면 아니 된다.[2] 萬若 이 動機의 選擇을 單純히 그때그때의 氣分에만 依하여서 決定하려면, 우리의 健全한 生活은 不可能할 것이다. 動搖하는 氣分은 우리의 神經을 分裂狀態에 빠뜨릴 것이며, 우리는 高度로 緊張된 生存競爭에서 淘汰를 當할 것이다. 우리는 躊躇없이 動機를 決定할 수 있는 選擇의 原理, 卽 '價値의 尺度'를 가질 것이, 生活 그 自體를 爲하여 必要하며, 또 實際에 있어서 우리는, 意識的이든 無意識的이든 間에, 各者의 價値의 尺度에 비추어 動機를 選擇하고 있다.

欲求대로 行爲함을 不可能하게 하는 둘째의 因子는, 社會 內 存在로서의 個人 相互間 또는 集團 相互間의 欲求의 對立이다. 同一한 利權을 中間에 두고 甲과 乙이 다투며, 文學을 志望하는 아들에게 醫學工夫를 要請하는 아버지가 있다. 欲求의 對立은 集團과 個人과의 사이에도 있고, 集團과 集

---

1 障碍를 이같이 세 種類로 나눈 것은 셰퍼의 *The Psychology of Adjustment*(p.117)에 依한 것이다.
2 勿論 여기서 選擇된 한 가지 動機일지라도 恒常 滿足될 수 있는 것은 아니다. 讀書하기로 決定하였으나 來客이 있어 뜻을 이루지 못하는 수도 있으며(外的 環境의 障碍), 散步가 하고싶어 門 밖까지 나서 봤으나 아직 健康回復이 完全치 않음을 깨닫고 中止하는 境遇도 있다(一身上의 缺陷에서 오는 障碍).

團 사이에도 있다. 우리는 이와 같은 對立이 平和的으로 解決되기를 願하며 (平和的 解決은 大體로 兩側의 利益을 意味하기 때문에) 對立이 平和的으로 解決되기 爲하여서는, 이 對立을 折衷 乃至 揚棄하는 어떤 原理 또는 法則이 있어야 한다. 社會的 對立을 平和的으로 解決함이, 다름 아닌 秩序요 治安이며 國際間의 友好關係이다. 그리고 바로 이 社會的 折衷의 原理로서, 慣習이 있고 道德이 있고 또 法律이 생긴 것이다.

人間에게 先天的으로 所與된 義務的 法則은 없다. 그러나 人間은 自我 內部의 動機의 對立과 自我 對 他我의 欲求의 對立을 合理的으로, 卽 生存이라는 基本欲求에 合目的으로 解決하기 爲하여서, 人間 自身이 어떤 法則을 創造할 必要에 直面하게 되며, 또 現實에 있어서, 이 必要에 따라 사람들은 여러 가지 法則을 만들어 가지고 있다. 行爲의 法則을 가지고 있음은 人間의 現實이요 人間存在의 基本方式이다.

다음에 '行爲의 結果에 對한 責任'이라 함은, 人間이 目的意識, 따라서 價値觀念을 떠날 수가 없다는 必然的 心理的 事實을 가리키는 것으로서, 人間이 人間 自身에 對하여 지는 責任을 말한다. 意識的 行爲란, 主觀的으로는 動機로부터 出發하여 動機滿足에서 終結되는 對應의 過程이다. 그리고 動機의 特色은, 行爲의 出發點인 그 動機 안에 이미 行爲의 終結點인 '目的'이 意識되어 있다는 點이다.[3] 人間이 目的觀念을 가졌다는 事實은, 人間으로 하여금 事物을 그 目的觀念의 尺度로 評價하게 한다. '評價的 態度'는, 欲望과 目的觀念을 가진 人間이 事物을 對하는 基本的 態度이다. 自他의 行爲를 評價的으로 對하는 人間의 基本的 態度가, 意志를 自由라고

---

3 目標가 意識되지 않은 欲求를 心理學者들은 動因(drive)이라고 불러 動機(motive)와 區別하고 있다.

認定하는 一般的 信念과 結合할 때에, ‘責任(responsibility)’이라는 觀念이 생긴다. 높이 評價되는 行爲를 한 사람은 讚揚을 받고, 낮게 評價되는 行爲를 한 사람은 叱責을 當하는 것은, 그 讚揚과 叱責의 客觀的 妥當性 如何를 莫論하고, 人間生存의 基本形式의 하나이다. 人間은, 生存을 繼續하는 동안, 行爲의 結果에 對한 考慮, 卽 目的觀念을 벗어날 수가 없을 것이며, 따라서 評價, 是認, 非難 等의 現象이 社會生活에서 抹殺되지도 않을 것이다. 行爲에 對한 評價的 態度는, 그 是非를 論議할 ‘權利’의 問題가 아니라, 人間生活의 基本形式으로서 주어진 事實이다. (評價的 態度의 是非를 論議하는 것 自體도 이미 하나의 評價的 態度임은 勿論이다.)

人間이 行爲를 妨害하는 內外의 障碍를 克服하기 爲하여 스스로 法則을 세운다는 事實과 自他의 行爲를 評價하고 問責하는 事實과는 內面的으로 密接히 關聯되어 있다. 더 嚴密하게 말하자면, 이 두 가지 基本事實은 同一한 根本事實의 兩面이다. 行爲에 關한 立法이란, 곧 行爲選擇의 原理를 決定함을 意味하는 것이니, 目的觀念과 評價作用이 그 안에 內包되고 있다. 反對로 評價라는 것은 어떤 標準을 豫想하는 것이니, 그 안에 벌써 法則이 包含되고 있다. 評價作用은 곧 立法作用이다. 人間이 自他의 行爲에 關하여 立法하고 評價하는 이 基本現象은, 바로 넓은 意味의 道德現象이다. 道德現象은, 누가 그 有用 無用을 論할 餘地도 없이, 人間生活 안에 必然的으로 주어진 基本現象이다. 道德現象은 人間의 歷史와 함께 生成하였으며, 앞으로도 人間性에 本質的인 變化가 오지 않는 限 오래 存續할 것이다.

2. 倫理學의 可能性

우리는 道德이라는 現象이 人間生活에 있어서 必然的이라는 것을 認定하였다. 이것으로써 우리는 道德現象에 關한 ‘存在의 學’이 可能할 根據를 잡았다. 이제 우리가 當面한 問題는, 行爲에 關한 '當爲의 學'이 可能한가 可能하지 않은가에 있다. 다만 道德現象을 하나의 現象으로서 그 있는 事實대로를 記述하고 說明함에 그치지 않고, 나아가서 앞으로 있어야 할[4] 道德現象을 究明하는 學, 卽 規範學으로서의 倫理學이 可能할 것인가.

우리는 南洋群島 오스트레일리아 其他에 居住하는 原始部族의 道德現象에 對하여서 純客觀的 態度를 取할 수가 있다. 사모아島의 靑年男女들이 아무리 紊亂한 性生活을 하더라도, 또는 도부안스族이 反逆과 詐欺를 當然한 것으로 認定하더라도, 우리는 冷靜히 그것을 傍觀할 수가 있다. 그러나 우리 自身이 그 中의 한 成員이 되고 있는 우리 自身의 社會의 道德現象에 對하여서는, 그와 같이 冷靜한 態度로 이를 傍觀할 수가 없다. 外部社會와 完全히 絕緣하고 孤身隱居나 한다면 모르거니와, 社會 안에 사는 以上, 그 社會의 道德現象에 對하여 全혀 沒價値的 態度를 取할 수는 없는 것이다. 우리는, 우리 社會에 詐欺와 掠奪이 橫行하기를 願하지 않는다. 우리는 우리나라 靑年의 氣風이 씩씩하기를 期待하며, 우리나라의 商人이 正直하기를 要望한다. 우리는 우리 社會의 道德現象이 公正한 原理 위에 서기를 願하며, 우리 社會의 倫理가 國家社會의 富强과 福祉를 助長하는 種類의 것이기를 要求한다. '生'에 對한 關心이 道德現象에 對한 意見을 갖게 하며 輿論에 參加하게 한다.

個個의 道德現象에 對한 意見 乃至 輿論을 蒐集하여도, 그것이 바로 學問이 되지는 않는다. — 마치 新聞의 總和가 歷史學을 이루지 않듯이. 그러나 人間에 있어 根本的인 '合理性'에 對한 要求는, 道德現象이 全體로서 同

---

4 여기서 '있어야 할' 道德現象이라 함은 時空에 無制約的으로 妥當하는 '絕對的 道德'이라는 뜻은 아니다. 그것은 오직 우리 人間의 立場에서 人間의 意慾이 決定하는 理想的 道德現象을 意味할 뿐이다.

一한 原理 아래 發展하기를 願한다. 個別의 道德現象이 相互間에 矛盾 없이 整合하기를 要望한다. 道德 單獨으로서 뿐만 아니라, 道德, 法律, 政治, 經濟, 其他의 社會制度가 總體로서 同一한 原理 아래 整合되기를 理想으로 삼는다. 한마디로 말하자면 우리는 體系(system)를 要求한다. 實踐問題에 關한 우리 思想이 하나의 體系를 이룰 때, 그리고 그 體系에 對하여서 (設令 그 體系에 包含되는 評價의 原理가 必然的으로 主觀性의 要素를 띤다 하더라도) 一種의 妥當性이 認定된다면 그 體系는 '學(Wissenschaft)'의 이름에 該當할 것이다.

道德은 人間生活에 있어 必然的인 現象이었다. 이 必然的으로 주어지는 道德現象에 對하여 우리가 評價的 態度를 取하며 道德에 關한 理想的 體系를 希求하는 것도 亦是 必然的이다. 우리가 行爲에 關한 價値論的 思想體系를 要求하고 또 그것을 實現하는 것은, '生存'과 '合理性'에 關한 人間의 基本的 欲求에 立脚하는바 必然的 事實이다. 問題는, 이와 같이 欲求 — 그것은 必然的으로 主觀性을 包含한다 — 를 地盤으로 삼고 實現되는 價値論的 思想體系에 어떠한 意味의 妥當性을 認定할 수가 있느냐에 있을 것이다. 그리고 이 妥當性의 認定 與否가, 그 體系의 '學'으로서의 成立 與否를 決定하는 關鍵이 될 것이다.

어떠한 實踐規範도, 그것이 萬人의 義務라는 것을 客觀的으로 論證할 수는 없을 것이다. 그러나 어떤 實踐法則이 人間의 眞正한 欲求를 反映하는 것이며, 欲求充足에 合目的的이라면, 그것이 人間의 眞正한 欲求와 一致하고 또 그 欲求에 合目的的이라는 意味에서, 그것은 一種의 妥當性을 갖는다고 認定할 수가 있다. 道德은 元來 社會的 現象이다. 따라서 道德에 關한 思想體系는, 그것이 少數人의 欲求보다도 넓은 範圍의 眞正한 意慾을 反映한 것일수록, 그 妥當性이 크다. 또 道德의 目標는 本來 그 實踐에 있다. 따라서 實踐性이 確實한 思想體系일수록 그 妥當性도 크다고 認定된다. 人間

의 有限性이 人類 全體의 意慾을 如實히 反映했을 뿐 아니라 또 完全히 實現시킬 수 있는 思想體系(即 絕對的으로 妥當한 實踐的 思想體系)를 拒否할지도 모른다. 그러나 우리는 어느 程度 넓은 範圍의 意慾을 反映하고 同時에, 어느 程度의 實踐性을 가진 實踐的 思想體系를 이룩할 수는 있을 것이다. 그리고 모든 學問이, 가장 精密한 種類의 自然科學까지도, 完成途中에 있는 思想體系라는 것이 事實이라면, 우리는 이 制限된 範圍의 妥當性을 갖는 實踐的 思想體系에 對하여, '倫理學'의 이름을 容認할 수가 있을 것이다. 倫理學은 可能할 뿐만 아니라 合理性에 對한 人間의 要求가 그것을 必然的으로 要望하고 있다.

오늘날 純理論科學이라는 認定을 받는 諸科學도, 그 發生의 動機를 캐어 본다면, 그 背後에는 恒常 現實生活에 對한 應用을 企圖하는 關心이 있다. 經濟學은 오로지 經濟現象의 있는 그대로의 모습을 밝히자는 것이 아니고, 生理學의 動機는 生理現象을 事實 그대로 敍述하는 데서 그치지 않는다. 理論經濟學의 背後에는 經濟政策論이 있고, 基礎學으로서의 生理學은 臨床醫學을 豫想하고 있다. 純理論科學이란 實은 分業의 結果임에 不過하다.

萬若에 經濟政策論이, 臨床醫學이, 그리고 造林學이, 또는 一般的으로 應用科學이 버젓한 '學'으로서 認定된다면, 行爲가 依據할 根本原則을 論究하는 當爲의 學으로서의 倫理學이, '學'으로서의 權威를 疑心 받을 아무런 根據도 없는 것이다. "脚氣病에는 비타민 B_1를 攝取해야 한다."는 命題가 堂堂한 科學的 命題라고 認定하는 사람들이, 무엇 때문에 "約束은 지켜야 한다."는 命題의 科學性을 疑心하는 것인지 理解하기 困難하다. "脚氣病에는 비타민 B_1를 攝取해야 한다."는 命題의 妥當性은 "비타민 B_1를 攝取하면 脚氣病이 낫는다."는 科學的 事實이 立證한다고 주장하는가? "約束은 지켜야 한다."는 命題의 妥當性은 "約束을 지키는 社會는 秩序가 保全된다."는 科學的 事實이 立證한다. 그러면 "脚氣病을 고쳐야 한다."는 것은 客觀的으로 自明한 眞理이나, "社會의 秩序가 保全되어야 한다."는 것은 主觀的 意見에 不過하다고 主張할 것인가? 그러나 "社會의 秩序가 保全되어야 한다."는 것도, "脚氣病을 고쳐야 한다."는 것이 客觀的인 것만큼 客觀的이며, "脚氣病을 고쳐야 한다."는 것도, "社會의 秩序는 保全되어야 한다."는 것이 主觀的인 것만큼 主觀的인 意見이다.

倫理學과 醫學 사이에 差異가 있다면, 그것은 醫學이 自明한 眞理로서 默過하는 大前提를 倫理學은 一旦 懷疑의 態度로 그 根據를 물어보는 點에 있을 것이다. 醫學은, "脚氣病은 고쳐야 한다."는 것은 當然한 理致로서 前提하고 나온 것이다. 그러나 倫理學은, "社會의 秩序가 保全되어야 한다."는 것은 어떤 根據를 가진 命題인가 하고 끝없이 거슬러 올라가서 묻는 態度를 取한다. 이 差異로 말미암아, 醫學은 單純한 科學의 位置에 머물러 있고, 倫理學은 科學의 範域을 넘어서서 哲學의 領域에로 뚫고 들어가는 것이다. 그러나 倫理學이 哲學性을 띠었다는 事實은, 決코 倫理學의 學으로서의 資格을 減少하지 않는다.

여기서 意志決定論者의 反駁이 있을지도 모른다. "人間의 道德律을 立法하고 是非善惡을 評價하는 것은 人間과 環境과의 客觀的 諸條件에 依해서 必然的으로 決定되는 것이요, 人間이 自由로 裁量할 수 있는 것이 아니다. 따라서 우리가 道德現象의 當爲(Sollen)를 論議하는 것은 無意味한 노릇이다. 道德現象은, 우리가 그것을 願하고 안 하고에 拘碍치 않고, 自己의 必然的인 路線을 따라 生成할 뿐이다."라고. 이에 우리는 意志決定論者와 더불어 意志가 自由냐 또는 必然이냐에 關하여서 길게 論爭할 必要는 없다. 그것은 '自由(Freiheit, freedom)'와 '必然(Notwendigkeit, necessity)'과는 서로 矛盾되는 槪念이 아니기 때문이다.

自由라는 槪念에는 두 가지 本質的인 徵表가 있다. 하나는 行爲의 原因이 自我 內部에 있음이요, 또 하나는 그 行爲를 自發的으로 했다는 意識이다. 行爲가 原因 없이, 卽 完全히 偶然하게 發生했다는 것은 自由의 必須條件이 아니다. 다만 行爲가 自我 內部에 基因하고 그것을 스스로 했다는 意識이 同伴할 때에, 우리는 그 行爲를 '自由'라고 부른다. 어떤 行爲가 外部의 刺戟으로부터 影響을 받음이 전혀 없이 純粹히 自我만의 原因으로 이루어질 수는 거의 없을 것이다. 그러므로 行爲의 原因이 오로지 自我 內部에만 있다는 意味로 完全한 自由란 事實上 있을 수 없을 것이다. 그러나 行爲가 적어도 그 一部의 原因은 恒常 自我 內部에 가지고 있음은 分明한 事實이다. 그리고 個人의 自我意識이 어느 程度 發達하면, 行爲의 原因은 그 一部만이 自我 內部에 있더라도, 그 行爲를 自發的이라고 意識하는 것도 누구나 經驗하는 事實이다. 우리의 모든 意識的 行爲는 적어도 多少間의 自由를 갖는다.

　設令 決定論者가 말하듯이 모든 行爲가 因果律的 必然에 依하여 決定된다 하더라도, 그것이 倫理學 成立의 可能性이나 倫理學의 意義를 妨害하지는 않는다. 모든 道德現象이 刺戟과 反應에 關한 必然의 法則을 따라 決定된다고 하더라도(其實은 嚴密히 必然的으로 決定된다기보다는 어느 程度의 確率的인 法則을 따라 決定된다고 보는 見解도 있다), 倫理學은 不可能하지도 않으며 無意味하지도 않다. 道德에 關한 價値論的 思想體系가 要求되고 있다는 現實이, 倫理學의 可能性의 根據이며, 그 思想體系에 對한 要求가 必然的으로 決定된 것이면 必然的일수록, 倫理學의 成立도 必然的이다. 또 道德現象이 內外의 諸條件을 따라 必然的으로 決定되는 것이라면, 어떠한 倫理思想이 存在한다는 事實 自體도 그 社會의 道德現象 決定에 參與하는 한 가지 條件이다. 어떤 倫理思想이 表明되는가는 必然的으로 道德現象 發展에 影響을 줄 것이며, 따라서 倫理學의 存在는 決코 無意味할 수가 없다.

　우리의 論述은, 道德이 人間社會에 있어서 必然的인 現象이요, 따라서

倫理學도 必然的으로 要求되는 學問의 하나라는 것을 認定하였다. 그러면 現代 우리의 立場에서 볼 때, 倫理學의 問題는 具體的으로 어떠한 것이며, 또 倫理學은 어떠한 構想을 가질 것인가?

3. 倫理學의 問題

倫理學이란 元來 哲學의 實踐的 部門 全體로 意味하였다. 從來 倫理學의 對象을 '道德'이라고 規定한 것은, 道德을 人生의 最高原理로 보는 見地에 서였다. 人間의 萬般活動의 窮極目的이 眞正한 道德을 實現함에 있다면, 道德을 對象으로 삼는 倫理學 乃至 道德哲學은 곧 人生의 實踐問題 全般을 硏究하는 學問이 될 것이다. 그러나 우리는 日常用語에서 말하는 道德이 人生의 全部를 意味하는 것이 아니라, 藝術, 宗敎, 科學 等과 同列에 서는 人生의 一部라는 것을 指摘하였다(第三章). 따라서 人間行爲의 窮極的 原理의 究明을 目標로 삼는 倫理學이, 오늘날 그 對象을 狹義의 '道德'에만 局限할 수는 없을 것이다. 倫理學이 對答하고자 하는 窮極의 問題는 "우리는 어떻게 行爲할 것인가?"에 있었다(第一章). 그러나 모든 分野에 걸쳐 行爲의 技術的 細則을 作定하는 것은 倫理學의 任務가 아니다. 技術的 細則에 關하여서는 各 分野에 따라 專門的 學術이 있다. 畵筆을 어떻게 움직일 것인가는 美術學이 硏究할 問題이며, 機械의 運轉에 關한 問題는 機工學이 맡아 볼 分野에 屬한다. 그런데 技術의 問題란, 事物을 單純히 手段으로서 對하는 方法에 關한 問題이다. 그리고 行爲란 事物에 對하는 有意的 反應을 意味한다. 이제 單純한 手段으로서의 事物에 對하는 行爲의 問題가 倫理學으로부터 除外된다면, 남는 것은 그 自體 內에 目的이 認定되는 事物에 對하는 態度決定의 問題뿐이다. 卽 倫理學의 問題는, 單純히 手段으로서만이 아니라 그 自體를 하나의 目的으로 認定할 수 있는 事物에 對하여 어떠한 態度로 行爲할 것인가에 있다.

　人間의 立場에서 볼 때, 그 自體 內에 目的이 認定되는 것은 于先 自己自身이다. 다음에 自己自身과 同一한 또는 近似한 組織과 作用을 가졌다고 認定하지 않을 수 없는 他者, 卽 自己 以外의 모든 人間에 對하여서도 우리는 目的性을 否認할 수가 없다. 그 다음에 一般動物 또는 生物 全體에 對하여 目的性을 認定할 것인가 아닌가는 論爭이 될 수 있는 問題이다. 認定할 것인가 말 것인가 하는 理論의 問題를 떠나서 現實을 觀察한다면, 人間과의 親近性에 따라서(家畜, 飼鳥는 가장 親近한 動物이다) 또는 人類와의 生物學的 近似性에 따라서(哺乳類 特히 靈長屬은 大體로 人間에 가깝다) 多少間의 目的性을 認定하는 것이 心理的 事實인 듯하다. 그러나 一般動物에 對하여 認定되는 目的性이란 人間에 對한 그것에 比하여 極히 微弱할 뿐만 아니라, 人間의 아직까지의 生活樣式은 無生物뿐만 아니라, 牛馬 같은 高等動物까지도 單純한 手段으로 利用하기를 强要하고 있다. 따라서 原理的으로는 論議의 對象이 될 수 있는 이 問題를, 우리는 便宜上 一旦 括弧 안에 넣어 두기로 한다. 以上의 推論으로 우리는 倫理學의 問題를 다음과 같이 規定할 수가 있다. "우리는 自己自身 및 他人에게 어떠한 態度로 對할 것인가?"

　自己에 對한 態度決定의 問題와 他人에 對한 態度決定의 問題는 內面的으로 相互滲透한다. 問題의 出發點은 "내 自身이 어떻게 살 것인가? 내 自身이 어떻게 行爲할 것인가?"에 있었다. 내 自身의 삶이, 내 自身의 行爲가, 내 個人 안에만 局限될 수 없다는 事實이 判明될 때, 卽 내가 社會的 存在라는 것을 反省할 때, 他人의 存在 및 他人과 自己와의 關聯性이 問題가 된다. 自己가 他人에게 對하는 態度는, 直接 反射하여 他人이 自己에게 對하는 態度를 左右한다. 따라서 내가 남에게 對하는 態度는, 넓은 意味로 보면, 내가 나 自身에게 對하는 態度의 一部이기도 하다. 나의 存在는 내 個

人만으로 孤立된 存在가 아니다. 내 自身의 成敗는 내 家庭의 盛衰를 左右하고, 내 國家의 興亡에도 多少間 影響을 끼친다. 따라서 나의 내 自身에 對한 態度 如何는, 卽 나 自身을 어떠한 人物로 만드는가는, 크게 보면 내가 他人에게 對하는 態度의 一部이기도 하다. 그뿐 아니라, 나의 나 自身에 對한 態度와 나와 남과의 關係는 또 남과 남과의 關係에도 影響을 주며, 反對로 남과 남과의 關係도 亦是 나의 나에 對한 態度, 또는 남과 나와의 關係를 決定하는 因子의 하나이다. 우리는 남과 남과의 關係를, 全혀 他人들만이 關係하는바, 나에게 無關心한 關係라고 볼 수가 없다. '社會性'을 基本으로 삼는 人間生活에 있어서, 나의 나 自身에 對한 態度, 나와 남과의 關係, 그리고 남과 남과의 關係는 따로따로 떼어 볼 수 없이 서로 엉킨 關係이다. 倫理學은 人間關係의 모든 面을 研究對象 안에 包含한다.

倫理學의 問題가 人間關係에 있다고 보는 見解 自體는 別로 새로운 생각이 아니다. 倫理學을 人間關係의 學으로 보는 것은, 오히려 傳統에 屬하는 見解라 하겠다. 그러나 從來의 倫理學은 大體로 人間關係의 나와 남과의 側面을 中心으로 考察하고, 나와 나 그리고 남과 남과의 側面은 比較的 疎忽히 한 느낌이 있다. 人間關係를 그 一側面에서만 考察하는 態度는 自然 倫理學을 抽象的 思辨의 學으로 기울어지게 하고, 倫理學이 實踐의 學이면서 實踐性이 缺如된 學으로 轉化하게 된 契機의 하나라고 생각된다. 우리는, 人間關係를 究明의 對象으로 삼되, 人間關係의 모든 側面과 모든 角度에서 이를 고루 考察하지 않으면 아니 될 것이다.

'나와 나'의 關係의 側面이란 自愛의 原理에 關한 側面이다. 從來 自愛를 主張한 思想은 大體로 他愛를 鼓吹한 思想에 壓倒된 感이 있다. 孝經은, "身體髮膚는 受之父母하니 不敢毀傷은 孝之始也니라."고 하여, 自愛의 原理를 他人에 對한 義務로서 正當化하였다. 벤담의 功利主義와 칸트의 形式主義는, 正面으로 對立하는 面도 있으나, 自愛와 他愛를 同一한 水準에 놓

으려 한 點에 있어서는 共通性을 가졌으며, 또 이 點에 있어서 두 倫理說은 共通된 卓見을 보여주었던 것이다.

自愛에 關한 實踐的 問題는 自愛 自體의 是非를 云謂하는 따위의 抽象的인 것이 아니라 더 具體的이요 日常的인 것이다. 나는 어떤 學校를 志望할 것인가, 나는 무슨 職業을 選擇할 것인가, 나는 어떤 趣味를 살리고 어떤 藝術을 즐길 것인가 等等의 가장 切實한 關心은, 또 가장 實踐的인 問題이기도 하다. 實踐의 學으로서의 倫理學은, 이와 같이 具體的인 實踐問題에 對하여서도 힘이 되지 않으면 안 될 것이다.

우리가 道德을 갖게 되고 따라서 倫理學이 要求된 것은, 人間에 欲求의 對立이 있다는 事實에 出發點이 있었다. 그리고 欲求의 對立은 非單 對外的으로, 卽 他人과의 關係에 있어서만 있는 것이 아니라, 내 自身 內部에도 여러 가지 動機의 對立이 있었다. 倫理學은 이 對內的 對立을 어떻게 調和시킬 것인가 하는 問題를 應當 重要한 問題의 하나로서 容認해야 할 것이다. 이 問題를 論究함으로써, 倫理學은 日常生活의 問題에 뿐만 아니라 自己 人生觀의 樹立이라는 根本問題에 對하여서도 合理的 地盤을 提供할 것이다.

우리는 倫理學의 任務가 그 普遍性의 要求에만 치우쳐 時代性과 地域性을 無視하고, 實踐性이 稀薄한 抽象論에 始終할 것이 아님을 指摘한 바 있다. 各其 特殊性을 가진 時代와 地域社會의 具體的 把握 위에 이루어진 實踐理論만이 眞實로 實踐的이다. 이 特殊性의 方向을 끝까지 追究할 때, 우리는 個人의 個性에까지 到達한다. 社會的 存在인 同時에 個別的 存在인 人間에게 實踐의 길을 밝히려는 倫理學은, 個人이 그 中의 一成員인 共同體 全般의 現實을 土臺로 삼는 同時에, 各 個人의 特殊性 現實, 卽 個性에도 依據하지 않으면 아니 된다. 勿論 共同의 文化財로서 世上에 公表되는 倫理學은 社會 全體에 關한 一般論에 그칠 것이다. 그러나 單純히 理論的

關心에서가 아니라 自身의 切實한 實踐의 要求에서 出發된 倫理의 學說에는, 世上에 公開되는 一般論 以外에 自己만이 간직하는 特殊部門이 成立할 餘地가 있다.

모든 實踐的 科學에는 그것에 從事하는 專門的 實踐家가 있다. 醫學은 醫師의 專門分野요, 工科의 諸科學은 工業技師의 專門分野이다. 그러나 '行爲師' 또는 '道德家'라는 專門家는 없다. 卽 倫理學의 理論을 實踐하는 專門家는 따로 없다. 모든 行爲者는 道德의 實踐家이다. 따라서 적어도 一定한 體系的 理論 위에서 條理 있는 行爲를 가지려 하는 사람은 누구나 自己의 倫理觀을 가져야 한다. 勿論 모든 사람이 徹底한 意味의 倫理學者가 될 수는 없다. 그러나 自身이 直接 關係하는 實踐問題에 關하여서는, 一定한 原理 위에서 統一된 見解를 가질 수 있는 것이며, 또 實際에 있어서 어떤 意識的 立場을 가지고 人生을 산다는 사람들은, 不徹底하나마, 어느 程度 統一된 倫理觀 乃至 人生觀을 가진 사람들이다. 一般人에게 倫理觀 乃至 人生觀을 세움에 基礎가 되는 一般的 知識을 提供하는 것은 專門的 倫理學徒의 使命이다. 그러나 "내가 어떻게 살 것인가?"라는 問題에 最後의 決斷을 내릴 수 있는 것은 오직 나 自身뿐이요, 어떠한 倫理學者도 이를 代行할 수는 없다. 이것은 이미 주어진 '義務의 道德'을 否認한 우리의 必然的 歸結이다.

個人은 自己의 行爲를 自意로 決定할 權利가 있다. 그러나 生을 肯定하는 限, 어떠한 個人도 이 權利를 濫用하여 自己의 生命을 스스로 否定하는 結果를 招來하고자 願하지 않을 것이다. 各者는 누구나 自己로서는 가장 賢明하다고 믿는 길을 擇한다. 主觀的으로 가장 妥當하다고 믿고 行한 行爲가 實은 不當하였다고 事後에 뉘우쳐지는 것은, 行爲를 決斷하는 瞬間에 있어서, 그 決斷의 地盤을 이룬 現實把握이 正確하지 못하였기 때문이다. 그러므로 누구나 態度를 決定하는 最後의 決定權을 可能한 限 正確한 現實

把握 위에서 行使하고자 願하지 않는 사람은 없다. 人間과 社會의 一般的 特質에 關한 現實을 正確히 把握하여, 一般人에게 態度決定의 地盤을 提供하는 것은, 專門的 學者들의 使命이다. 各 個人은 專門家가 提示하는 一般的 原理를 土臺로 삼고, 自己 스스로가 把握한 自己 個性의 現實을 媒介로 하여 自己의 倫理觀 乃至 人生觀을 세울 것이다. 이와 같이 볼 때, 人間關係에 있어서 나와 나 自身의 關係에 對한 問題, 卽 나 自身에 對한 態度決定의 問題는 倫理學의 一般論에는 屬하지 않을지라도, 行爲를 實地에 決斷하는 各 行爲者의 直接的 準則의 決定에 關한 것으로서, 看過할 수 없는 問題라고 생각된다.

'나와 남'의 關係는 從來 倫理思想에 있어서 가장 힘이 기울어진 方面이다. 그러나 從來의 倫理思想은 나와 남과의 關係를 主로 一方的 見地에서 考察한 느낌이 있다. 卽 '義務'의 見地에서 自他의 關係를 오로지 論하였다. 그 結果는 柔弱한 者로 하여금 自己의 義務에만 神經이 過敏하여 服從의 道德을 崇尙하게 하였으며, 反面에 狡猾한 者들에게는, 表面上 義務를 大義名分으로 내세움으로써 內實은 自己의 權利를 主張하는 欺瞞의 道德을 助長하였다. (例컨대 子息보다도 父母가 孝道를 强調하였고, 아내보다도 男便이 婦道를 鼓吹하였다.)

'滅私'를 理想으로 삼는 利他主義(altruism)은 本來 지나친 利己主義(egoism)에 對한 反動이다. 그러므로 利他主義에도 反動主義에 一般的인 偏僻性이 있다. 사람이 自己의 利己性에 嫌惡를 느끼고 이 醜惡하다고 認定되는 利己性의 克服을 自我形成의 目標로 삼는 것은 自然스럽게 생길 수 있는 일이며, 또 이와 같은 愛他의 態度를 '거룩하다'고 讚揚하는 것도 自然스러운 社會現象이다. 그러나 自我의 人格形成의 意慾에서 일어난 克己의 理想이 誇張되어, 利他 그 自體가 至上目標로 化할 때는 盲目的이 아니면 僞善이 結果的으로 생긴다. 더욱이 '利他'가 自己 스스로의 內面的 要求

로서 우러나기 前에 外部로부터 이를 强要 當한다면, 그것은 不自然할 뿐만 아니라 不道德的이다.

사람이란 自我를 中心으로 살기 마련이다. 다만 '自我'라는 것이 一定한 範圍, 即 固定的인 外延을 가진 槪念이 아니라, 그것은 伸縮이 自由로운 하나의 '意識'이다. 五尺短身 안에 용솟음치는 나의 情欲이 나의 '自我'가 될 수도 있으며, 내 나라 내 社會 全體가 나의 '自我'가 될 수도 있다. '自我를 克服한다' 함은, 自我의 좁은 外廓을 무너뜨리고 더 넓은 範圍를 自我 속에 同化시킴을 意味하는 것이다. 거룩한 人格이 實現되는 것은, 自我를 抛棄함으로써가 아니라, 同化에 依하여 自我를 擴大함으로써 可能하다. 이른바 '사랑'이라 함은 바로 이 同化作用에 不過하다. 사랑의 對象은 사랑을 받는 瞬間에 벌써 自我의 一部로서 包攝되는 것이다. 他愛란, 實은 넓은 自愛에 不過한 것이다. '사랑'의 넓이와 깊이를 따라서 '自我'의 넓이와 깊이가 決定되고, '自我'의 넓이와 깊이를 따라서 '人格'의 넓이와 깊이가 決定된다.

그러나 사랑은 스스로 우러나는 感情이요, 마음대로 左右되는 意志가 아니다. 사랑하고자 하는 意志는 나의 사랑의 制約이 될 수는 있다. 그러나 그 意志가 바로 사랑의 感情으로 化하는 것은 아니다. 스스로 우러나는 사랑이 있어 自我가 넓어지고 人格이 커진다면 좋다. 그러나 無理한 意志가 사랑을 强要하고 人格의 完成을 躁急히 굴 때, 不自然과 僞善이 結果하는 것이다. 나와 남과의 關係를 두고 아름다운 理想을 세우는 것은 좋다. 그러나 이 理想이 한갓 空想이 되지 않기 爲하여서는, 나와 남의 關係를 現實的으로 制約하고 있는 有限한 人間性의 諸特質을 看過해서는 안 될 것이다.

社會構造의 有機的 聯關性을 考慮할 때, 우리는 '남과 남'의 關係가 單純히 第三者들만의 關係가 아님을 깨닫는다. '남과 남'의 關係를 純全한 남의 일처럼 생각하고, 남의 關係에 介入하지 아니함을 人權의 原則으로 믿었던 個人主義 思想은, 過去의 倫理說이 人間關係의 個人的 側面만을 抽象해 보는 偏頗된 傾向을 助長하였다. 그러나 現實的인 倫理學은 人間의 關係를 社會 全體로서의 集團的 聯關性의 側面에서도 考察해야 할 것이다. 이와 같은 見解는 必然的으로 倫理學이 政治, 經濟, 法律 其他의 全體的 社會問題에 對하여서도 無關心할 수가 없다는 結論으로 이끈다. 倫理學은 理論에 있어서도 一般 社會科學과 連結되어야 할 것이며, 그 實踐에 있어서도 一般 社會制度와 協同해야 할 것이다.

4. 倫理學의 構想

倫理學의 窮極問題는 "人間의 關係는 어떻게 있어야 할 것인가?" 하는 當爲의 問題이다. 그러나 當爲의 法則은 先天的으로 所與되어 있는 것이 아니라, 人間이 그것을 作定해야 한다. 어떠한 法則을 세우는가는 制限된 意味에 있어 人間의 自由이다. 그러나 이 自由는 無根據하다는 意味의 自由는 아니다. 人間의 未來를 決定하는 根據가 되는 것은 人間의 現在이다. 다시 말하면 人間의 存在(Sein)가 人間의 當爲(Sollen)를 規定하는 根據가 된다. 다만 人間의 現在가 人間의 未來를 規定함에 있어, 人間의 意識(consciousness, Bewusstsein)이 重要한 役割을 한다는 點에 있어서, 現在가 未來로 넘어가는 瞬間에 人間의 自由가 認定된다.

人間의 自由意志가 스스로 當爲를 決定함에 있어서 根據로 삼는 것은, 人間의 存在에 關한 認識이다. 勿論 存在에 關한 認識에서 當爲에 關한 認識이 形式論理學的으로 推論되지는 않는다. 그러나 自由意志가 '生'의 基本要求의 路線을 따라 스스로의 態度를 決定함에 있어 判斷의 資料로 삼는 것은 存在에 關한 認識이다. 따라서 現在 어떻게 '있는가'에 對한 認識이 正確하고 廣範할수록, 將次 어떻게 '있어야 할 것인가'에 關한 判斷이, 그 判斷을 내린 人間의 本意에 가까워질 것이다. 그러므로 人間의 當爲問題를 밝히고자 하는 倫理學이 그 地盤으로 삼을 것은, 人間의 存在에 關한 認識이다. 人間이 어떻게 '있어야 할 것인가'를 묻기 前에 人間이 現實에 어떻게 '있는가'가 밝혀져야 한다. '人間의 存在에 關한 學'은 倫理學의 基礎部門이다.

人間의 現實이 어떻게 있는가를 밝히고자 하는 '人間의 存在에 關한 學' ─ 簡單히 '人間存在의 學'이라고 불러 둔다 ─ 의 問題는, 便宜上 두 개의 觀點에서 이를 考察할 수가 있다. 첫째는 意識의 單位를 이루고 있는 '個人'을 中心으로 보는 觀點이요, 또 하나는 人間存在의 基本形態인 '社會生活'을 巨視的으로 보는 觀點이다. 前者는 個人으로서의 人間이 어떻게 行爲하고 있는가, 卽 個人 안에서 일어나는 欲望과 그 對應이 어떠한 調和와 秩序를 가지고 이루어지는가를 밝히는 立場이다. '人間存在의 學'의 이 部門을 우리는 '人性論'이라고 부를 수가 있다. 後者는 人間의 具體的 全體로서의 社會가 어떠한 對立과 秩序의 關係를 가지고 運營되고 있는가를 把握하고자 하는 立場이다. '人間存在의 學'의 이 部門을 우리는 '社會學的 人間論'이라고 부를 수가 있다. 個人을 對象의 單位로 삼는 '人性論'은 生理學的 心理學的 土臺 위에 서야 할 것이다. 特히, 行動의 過程을 欲求에서 出發하여 그 滿足에서 終結되는 對應過程(adjustment process)으로서 硏究하는 對應心理學(psychology of adjustment)과, 人間을 受胎로부터 死亡에 이르는 發達過程으로서 探求하는 發達心理學(developemental psychology)은, '人性論'에 貴重한 基礎를 提供할 것이다. 人間을 全體的 具體相에서 보는 '社會學的 人間論'이 社會學的 地盤 위에 서야 할 것은 勿論이다. 特히 社會의 秩序的 關係의 基盤을 이루는 道德現象의 樣相을 究明하는 道德社會學(moral sociology)은, '社會學的 人間論'의 重要한 根幹이 될 것이다. 그러나 道德現象 그것만이 抽象的으로 考察될 것이 아니라, 道德意識의 具體的 表現이요, 同時에 道德意識의 制約根據인바 政治,

法律, 經濟 等의 諸現象과의 關係下에서 把握되어야 할 것은 勿論이다. 그리고 人性論과 社會學的 人間論이 嚴密히 區分되는 두 分野를 갖는 것이 아니라, 相互交錯하고 長短相補하여 人間存在의 實相을 밝히는 두 部門임도 두말할 것이 없다. 人性論과 社會學的 人間論과의 綜合의 土臺 위에서, 具體的인 人間存在의 本質을 밝히는 것은 哲學的 方法의 導入을 要請할 것이며, 이에 새로운 哲學的 人間學의 基本課題가 있을 것이다.

人間關係의 存在는 그 안에 벌써 當爲를 內包하고 있다. 人間存在는 實踐的 存在이다. 人間關係가 어떠어떠하게 있다는 事實 自體 안에 바로 如斯 如斯하게 있어야 한다는 意味가 包含되어 있다. "敎室 內에서 담배를 피우지 않고 있다."는 事實 背後에는 "敎室 內에서 담배를 피우면 안 된다."는 規範의 힘이 作用하고 있는 것이다. 現在 授業 中에 담배 피우는 사람이 없다는 事實은, 우리가 全혀 無關心할 수 있는 事實, 卽 相關없는 것으로서 無視할 수 있는 事實이 아니라, 우리에게 '敎室 內 禁煙'을 强制하는 '힘'을 內包하고 肉迫하는 事實이다. "敎室 內에서는 禁煙해야 한다."는 先天的 法則이 있는 것은 아니다. 우리가 "卷煙을 피워 가며 講義를 들어도 좋다."고 생각하기는 어렵지 않다. 그러나 實際로 그것을 斷行하기는 困難한 것이다. 보이지 않는 힘이 그것을 막는다. 이 힘은 良心에서 나오는 것은 아니다. 이 힘의 根源은 社會的 現實이다. — 人間存在이다.

우리는 存在 안에 當爲가 內包된 顯著한 例로서 言語와 文法과의 關係를 볼 수가 있다.[5] 文法이라는 規範이 먼저 있고, 그것을 따라서 言語가 생긴 것은 아니다. 言語라는 現實 가운데 秩序가 깃들었고, 그 깃들어 있는 秩序를 發見해 놓은 것이 文法이다. 文法 그 自體는 하나의 있는 事實이다. 文法대로 말해야 한다는 義務는 없다. 觀念上으로는 文法을 無視할 수도 있다. 그러나 實際에 있어서 文法을 無視하기는 困難하다. 文法에 意味를 붙이는 人間的 現實이 그것을 가로막는 것이다. 言語 相互間에 存在하는 關

係, 卽 文法이 우리의 表現活動을 制約하듯이, 人間 相互間에 存在하는 關係, 卽 慣習 乃至 道德이 우리 行爲에 規範을 提示한다. 여기에 存在가 當爲를 規定하는 一面이 있다.

現實에 存在하는 人間關係는 그것이 現實에 存在하는 것이기 때문에, 마땅히 있어야 할 人間關係, 卽 當爲의 因子를 內包한다. 現社會에 어떠한 慣習 乃至 道德이 支配하고 있는가를 밝히는 것은, 將次 또 어떠한 慣習 乃至 道德이 遵守되어야 할 것인가를 暗示하는 意味를 갖는다. 그러나 現存하는 慣習 또는 道德은 그대로 完全하거나 絶對的인 것은 아니다. 우리가 現在를 遵守해야 할 義務는 없다. 다만 現在가 가진 實力이 우리를 制約할 뿐이다. 慣習 乃至 道德 其他의 規範이 貴重한 것은, 그것이 人生을 豊富하게 하고 潤澤하게 하는 限에 있어서다. 萬若 現存하는 秩序 中에 生命의 發展을 阻害하는 因子가 있다면 그 因子는 破棄되어야 한다. 더 有能한 秩序가 더 無能한 秩序를 물리치고 恒常 代置되지 않으면 아니 된다. 現實은 언제나 우리가 밟고 디뎌야 할 발판이다. 그러나 現實은 우리가 畢竟은 그 위로 밟고 넘어가야 할 그 무엇이다. 現實의 克服을, 더 높은 것을 希求하는 人間의 精神이 要望한다.

人間的 自覺이 높아짐에 따라서, 過去人이 지어 놓은 秩序보다도 더 合理的인 秩序를 創造할 可能性이 늘어간다. 또 한편 人口의 增加, 産業機構

---

5 이 比喩에 힌트를 준 것은 듀이의 다음과 같은 敍述이다.
"人間은 言語를 意圖하지 않았다. 人間은 말을 始作했을 때 社會的 目的을 意識에 두지 않았으며, 또 言語에 앞서서 이 意思疎通의 方途에 規律을 세우기 爲한 文法 乃至 發音規則을 미리 가졌던 것도 아니다. 文法이나 發音規則은 이 (言語라는 一譯註) 事實이 있은 뒤에, 또 이 事實로 말미암아, 생긴 것이다. 言語는 알 수 없는 중얼거림, 本能的인 손짓 발짓 또는 周圍의 壓力으로부터 發生한 것이다. 그러나 一旦 形成된 言語는 言語요 言語로서 行勢한다."(J. Dewey, *Human Nature and Conduct*, p.79)

의 革新, 生活樣式의 變遷 等 歷史的 變動은, 旣存하는 秩序에 龜裂을 招來한다. 이리하여 새 時代는 새 秩序를 要求한다. 새 時代가 要求하는 새 秩序를 發見하는 것은 바로 倫理學이 窮極의 目標로 삼는 바이다. 이에 '人間存在의 學'의 뒤를 이어서 '人間當爲의 學', 卽 人間關係의 當爲를 究明하는 學이 오지 않으면 아니 된다. 그리고 後者가 前者의 土臺 위에 서야 할 것은 勿論이다.

우리는 人間存在의 學을 人性論과 社會學的 人間論의 두 部門으로 나누어서 생각하였다. 이 存在의 學을 土臺로 삼는 當爲의 學도 또한 두 部門으로 나누어질 것이다. 人性論을 基礎로 하는 當爲의 學의 問題는 "나는 어떻게 行爲해야 할 것인가?" 더 具體的으로 말하면, "個人 內部에 惹起되는 動機의 矛盾對立을 어떻게 調和시킬 것인가, 卽 나는 어떠한 人格이 되어야 할 것인가?"에 있다. 이것은 우리가 崇尙할 德目에 關한 問題, 다시 말하면 理想的 人格의 類型에 關한 問題이다. 우리는 人間當爲의 學의 이 部門을 '理想的 人格論'이라고 부를 수가 있다. 한편 社會學的 人間論을 基礎로 하는 當爲의 學의 問題는 "人間과 人間은 어떠한 關係를 가져야 할 것인가?" 더 具體的으로는 "社會 內에 惹起되는 人間的 欲求의 對立을 어떻게 合理的으로 調和시킬 것인가, 卽 우리는 어떠한 社會를 가져야 할 것인가?"에 있다. 이것은 社會的 秩序의 問題, 卽 우리가 建設할 理想的 社會에 關한 問題이다. 우리는 人間當爲의 學의 이 部門을 '理想的 社會論'이라고 부를 수가 있다.

勿論 以上의 區分은 嚴密한 限界線을 가진 것은 아니다. 學問의 區別이란 恒常 便宜上의 것임에 不過하다. 個人 內部의 動機對立을 調和시키는 心理的 秩序와, 社會 內에 있어서의 人間的 欲求의 對立을 解消하는 社會的 秩序와는, 相互間에 內面的으로 密接히 關聯되고 있다. 따라서 人性論과 社會的 人間論 및 理想的 人格論과 理想的 社會論도 縱橫으로 錯綜한

關聯性을 갖는다.

理想的 人格論 및 理想的 社會論의 '理想'은, 人類가 到達해야 할 窮極目標라든지 絕對善 따위의 形而上學的 槪念을 意味하지 않는다. 그것은 우리가 人類歷史의 將來를 透徹히 豫見하지 못하는 限, 時間과 空間의 制約을 가진 우리 時代 우리 地域社會가 指向할 目標에 不過하다. 그것은 遙遠한 彼岸에 가로놓인 理想이 아니라, 우리가 當場에 그 實現을 爲한 努力에 着手해야 하며, 또 實現시킬 수 있는 目前의 目標이다. 人間當爲의 學은 時空에 無制限한 普遍妥當性을 要求할 수 없으며, 또 그것을 要求할 必要도 없는 것이다. 우리는 우리가 살고 있는 우리 社會의 問題를 解決하면 足하며 그 以上의 무엇을 바라는 것은 有限者 人間의 힘을 넘는 것이다. 다른 時代와 다른 地域의 社會問題는 그 時代 그 地域의 사람들이 自己네의 知慧와 意思에 따라서 決定할 問題이다.[6]

'人間當爲의 學'은 '人間存在의 學'을 土臺로 삼는다. 그러나 前者는 後者로부터 直接 推理되지는 않는다. 存在判斷과 當爲判斷과는 本來 異質的인 것이며, 그 中間에는 함부로 넘나들 수 없는 間隙이 가로막고 있다. 어떠한 第三의 存在判斷도, 存在判斷에서 當爲判斷을 推理하는 媒介가 될 수는 없다. 이 媒介가 될 수 있는 것은 오직 또 하나의 當爲判斷뿐이다. 人間存在의 學에서 人間當爲의 學을 推論하는 媒介가 되는 또 하나의 當爲判斷은, 倫理學徒의 人生觀이요 世界觀이다. 人生觀 乃至 世界觀이 當爲를 論하는 모든 倫理說의 大前提가 되고 있다. 人間存在에 關한 把握은 恒常 그

---

6 이 事情은 倫理學의 權威를 떨어뜨리는 것이 아니라, 도리어 倫理學徒의 使命에 恒常 새로운 生命을 넣어 준다. 萬若 어떤 倫理說이 萬世를 通하여 絕對妥當한 實踐規範을 밝힐 수 있다면, 後世의 倫理學徒에게 賦課된 任務는 오직 先哲이 發見한 眞理를 祖述하고 註釋하는 데 그칠 것이다. 그러나 道德을 時空의 制約下에 妥當한 것으로 볼 때, 모든 時代 모든 地域社會의 倫理學徒에게는 恒常 새롭고 獨特한 使命이 賦課되는 것이다.

小前提의 任務를 맡아 볼 뿐이다.[7]

　人間當爲의 學의 主張이 論者의 人生觀 乃至 世界觀을 大前提로 삼는다는 事實은, 當爲를 論斷하는 倫理說의 主張이 그 論者와 大同한 人生觀 또는 世界觀을 가진 사람들에게만 妥當한다는 것을 意味한다. 一定한 言語가 文化的 傳統이 全혀 다른 異邦에 가면 通用될 수 없듯이, 一定한 倫理說은 人生觀 乃至 世界觀이 全혀 다른 個人이나 社會에 對하여서는 妥當性이 없다. 어떠한 人生觀 乃至 世界觀을 갖는가의 마지막 決斷은 各 個人의 自由 意思에 달려 있다. 아무도 남에게 人生觀이나 世界觀을 强要할 權利는 없기 때문이다. 同一한 時代 同一한 地域社會 內에서도, 서로 다른 人生觀이나 世界觀이 對立할 수가 있다. 따라서 同一한 社會 內에서 서로 다른 倫理說이 彼此 同等한 權利를 가지고 主張될 수도 있다. 또 現實에 있어서도 同一한 社會 內에 相反되는 人生觀 또는 倫理說이 對立 抗爭하고 있는 것이 歷史的 事實이다.[8] 그러나 우리가 自己의 人生觀을 自己의 自由意思로 決定할 수 있다고 말할 때, 그 '自由'는 制限된 意味의 自由이다. 各 個人은

7　例컨대 "國產品 愛用은 國民經濟의 健全한 發展의 必須條件이다."라는 存在判斷에서, "國民은 國產品을 愛用해야 한다."는 當爲判斷이 推理되는 背後에는, "國民經濟는 健全하게 發展해야 한다"는 當爲判斷이 大前提의 役割을 하고 있다. 또 "經濟의 自立이 없이는 國民의 完全한 獨立은 없다."는 存在判斷에서, "國家는 經濟的으로 自立해야 한다."는 當爲判斷이 推論되는 것은, "國家는 自主獨立해야 한다."는 人生觀이 大前提로서 待期하고 있기 때문이다.

8　同一한 社會 內에서 抗爭하는 人生觀 乃至 倫理說의 對立이 解決되는 方式에는 여러 가지가 있다. 兩說이 對立하다가 一方이 他方의 優越性을 認定하고 스스로 讓步하는 境遇도 있을 것이며, 兩者가 各各 一部式을 讓步함으로써 折衷되거나 第三의 立場으로 揚棄되는 수도 있을 것이다. 또는 周圍의 支持의 强弱을 따라 勝敗가 決定되는 境遇도 있을 것이며, 一方이 武力이나 權力으로 他方에 緘口를 强要하는 事例도 있을 것이다. 如何튼 그 社會에서 가장 適性을 가졌다는 意味로 가장 實力이 있는 主張이, 그 社會 一般에 通用되는 人生觀이나 倫理觀으로서 生命을 持續할 것이다.

觀念上으로는 自由意思에 따라 제멋대로 人生觀을 樹立할 權限이 있다. 그러나 이 權限을 實際로 行使하는 마당에 있어서는 現實의 制約을 받는 것이다. 우리는 이 微妙한 關係를 既存하는 言語와 新造語와의 關係에 比喩할 수가 있다. 觀念上으로 생각한다면, 우리는 어떤 固定된 言語를 使用해야 한다는 義務가 없으며, 또는 一定한 言語에 있어서 그 現在의 文法을 遵守해야 한다는 法則도 없다. 우리는 제멋대로 新語를 造作할 權限이 있으며, 文法을 無視하고 제멋대로 文章을 엮을 '自由'도 있다. 그러나 이 權限이나 自由란 한갓 觀念上의 것이요, 現實에 있어서 無作定하고 行使되는 絶對的 自由는 아니다. 實際에 있어서, 客觀的 條件을 無視하고 제멋대로 新語를 造作한 사람들이 있다. 그러나 社會가 그것을 認定하지 않는 까닭으로 저절로 消滅되곤 하였다. 事情은 人生觀이나 倫理說에 있어서도 一般이다. 우리가 自由로 人生觀을 選擇하고 倫理說을 樹立한다 하되, 亦是 現實의 客觀的 事情을 基盤으로 삼고, 生의 論理를 따라서 이 自由를 行使하는 것이다. 客觀的 事情과 生의 論理를 無視하고 나온 人生觀이나 倫理說은 自然 消滅되고 말 뿐이다. 人生觀이나 倫理說은, 그것이 어느 個人의 個性을 如實히 反映한 側面으로 보면, 個人의 人生觀이요 個人의 倫理說이다. 그러나 그것이 社會 一般의 客觀的 事情을 必然的으로 反映하고 있다는 側面에서 본다면, 社會 全體의 文化財에 屬하는바 共同의 人生觀이요 共同의 倫理說이다. 人間이 各其 孤立된 個人으로서 生活하는 것이 아니라, 社會라는 共同의 地盤과 組織 위에 살고 있다는 現實이, 우리에게 共通된 人生觀 또는 倫理說의 可能性을 示唆한다.

倫理學徒가 現存하는 秩序를 발판으로 삼고 새로운 秩序를 構想하는 活動은, 文學者가 既存하는 言語와 文法에 依據하면서도 그것을 넘어서 새로운 表現과 새로운 語法을 發見하는 創作的 活動에 比할 수가 있다. 時代의 變遷에 따르고 새로운 事態에 適合한 새로운 表現만이 오랜 生命을 지니듯이, 새 時代의 社會形便이 要求하는 人生觀 乃至 倫理說만이 그 時代의 그 社會를 이끄는 炬火가 될 수 있을 것이다. 時代와 社會의 要求에 適合하다 함은, 반드시 그 時代 그 社會에서 好評을 받고 勢力을 떨친다는 것을 意味하지 않는다. 偉大한 思想이 大衆의 無知에 依하여 默殺될 수도 있으며, 暴力에 依하여 迫害를 받을 수도 있다. 그러나 眞實로 偉大한 思想이라면, 一時的으로는 默殺을 當하고 或은 迫害를 받을지라도, 새 時代의 새로운 要求가 좀 더 分明히 表明되는 날, 亦是 偉大한 思想으로서 認定을 받고 社會를 이끄는 偉大한 力量을 發揮할 것이다.

以上에 略述한바 우리 倫理學의 構想을 表示하면 다음과 같이 된다.

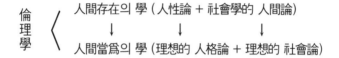

5. 方法 小考

以上의 論述은 倫理學의 方法에 關한 大綱을 暗示한다. 卽 '人間存在의 學'에 關하여서는 歸納을 主로 하는 科學的 方法이, '人間當爲의 學'에 關하여서는 演繹을 主로 하는 哲學的 方法이 各各 適用될 것이다.

人性論에 있어서는 一般心理學의 方法이 그 基礎가 될 것이다. 卽 實驗的 方法(the experimental method), 測定法(the method of measurement), 統計法(statistical method) 等이 고루 使用된다. 人性論이 特히 人間行爲의 情意的 側面을 根幹으로 하여 人間精神의 全體的 把握을 꾀해야 할 것인 만큼, 情意의 微妙한 움직임을 記述하는 內觀法(the method of introspection), 人間의 行爲 乃至 性格과 環境과의 關係를 數字的으로 處理하는 相關關係法(co-relation method), 그리고 個人의 性格 乃至 人格形成의 過程을 發生學的으로 追究하는 事例 硏究法(the method of case study) 等은, 一般心理學에 있어서보다도 이 人性論 硏究에 있어서 特히 重要한 役割을 할 것이다. 近來 人間精神의 深奧한 內面을 探求함에 있어 놀라운 功績을 남긴 精神分折學(psychoanalysis)의 諸槪念은, 重要한 假說 또는 暗示로서 尊重될 것이다. 그러나 그 方法은 더 客觀的인 方法에 依하여 代置되어야 할 것으로 생각된다.

社會學的 人間論에 있어서는, 一般社會學의 方法이 그 基礎가 될 것이다. 社會發展의 一般的 原則을 밝히는 以外에 時代와 地域의 制約을 가진 特殊社會의 現存하는 人間關係를 記述的으로 把握하는 努力이 必要할 것이다. 家族制度, 禮儀的 慣習, 道德思潮의 一般的 特質, 宗敎的 信念, 法律, 政治, 經濟 等 諸制度, 諸機構에 나타난 各種 人間關係 等이 廣範한 資料蒐集下에 分類, 記述되고, 또 可能하면 因果的으로 說明되어야 할 것이다. 社會學뿐만 아니라 民俗學, 經濟學 等 社會科學 一般이 社會學的 人間論을 爲하여 補助의 任務를 맡아 보아야 한다.

'人間當爲의 學'은 그 本質에 있어 創作的 活動이다. 時代에 對한 銳利한 洞察力, 涵養된 情操(sentiment), 其他 온 人格과 思想의 總力이 動員되어 人生觀이 樹立될 것이다. 그러나 이 人生觀 樹立의 地盤이 되는 것은 亦是 '人間存在의 學'이 提供하는 現實에 對한 認識이다. 個別的 事態에 處하는 行爲의 準則은 人生觀이 주는 大前提와 '人間存在의 學'이 提示하는 小前提 아래 演繹的으로 推理될 것이다.

方法의 詳細한 部分은 各 部門에 있어서 個別的으로 깊이 硏究될 問題이다. 詳細한 論究를 各 部分에 맡기기로 하고, 여기서 한 가지 附言할 것은, 倫理學의 課業이 一個人의 그것이 아니라는 點이다. 行爲의 問題는 一部

專門家에게만 局限된 問題가 아니라, 모든 部類의 사람들이 直接 關係하는 廣範한 問題이다. 따라서 行爲를 硏究하는 學問도 少數의 學者만으로는 다루기 過重한 廣範한 問題를 包含하고 있다. 專門的 倫理學徒뿐만이 아니라, 心理學, 社會學을 비롯한 諸般 人間의 科學이 協同하여 이 크고 切實한 問題의 究明을 圖謀해야 할 것이다.

人格 또는 社會에 關한 좋은 理想이 섰다 하더라도, 그것만으로 現實이 움직이는 것은 아니다. 理論이 現實化하기 爲하여서는 特別한 技術과 制度가 必要하다. 勇敢함이 高貴한 德目으로서 認定되고, 우리가 勇敢하기를 希望한다 하더라도, 그것만으로는 現實에 勇敢한 性格이 涵養되지 않는다. 性格은 一時的인 深刻한 體驗으로 말미암아, 이를테면 靈感에 依해서 形成되는 수가 있다 하더라도, 그것은 特例에 屬하는 것이며, 原則으로는 오랜 習慣에 依하여서 形成되는 것으로 보아야 한다. 그리고 習慣을 기르는 것은 넓은 意味의 敎育過程이다. 훌륭한 習慣의 形成을 意味하는 敎育의 課業은, 被敎育者의 理解力에 呼訴하는 說得의 問題이기보다는 오히려 肉體的 組織에 工作하는 技術의 問題이다. 또 어떠한 社會的 關係가 實現되기를 公衆이 熱望한다 하더라도, 그 實現을 爲한 政治力의 發動이 있고, 또는 法律이 制定되어 그것을 實現하기 爲한 具體的 制度가 서기 前에는, 그 希望은 한갓 空想에 가까운 것이다. 倫理學의 理想을 實現化하는 것은, 敎育, 政治, 法律을 擔當하는 社會制度 全般과 社會人 一般의 協力이 있은 다음에 비로소 可能할 것이다. 一國에 美風을 기르고 道義를 세운다는 것은 決코 一部 學者들만의 일이 아니다. 從來의 倫理學이 實踐의 學이면서도 其實은 實踐力이 薄弱했던 原因의 하나는, 倫理學이 現實社會를 實際로 움직이고 있는 諸力量, 諸制度와 緊密히 連結되지 못했던 點에 있다고 생각된다.

五章
人間性과 行爲의 世界

五章 人間性과 行爲의 世界

　前章에서 論한 倫理學의 構想에 依한다면, 人間存在의 個人的 側面을 考察하는 '人性論'과 人間存在의 社會的 側面을 考察하는 '社會學的 人間論'이 各各 試圖되고, 다음에 可能하면 人間을 個人的, 社會的 存在로서 綜合的으로 把握하는 方向으로의 努力이 이루어질 것이다. 以上의 努力이 어느 程度의 成果를 보면, 그때 우리는 個人과 社會의 不可分의 關係를 考察하면서, 理想的 人格과 理想的 社會에 關한 試論을 꾀하는 段階로 넘어가게 된다. 以上에서 便宜上 네 가지로 나누어 본 課題는, 各各 그 對象探求에 適合한 方法에 따라 各各 別個의 部門으로서 論究해야 할 커다란 課題들이다. 따라서 이들 課題에 對한 論考는, 倫理學의 過去를 簡略히 回顧하고, 現代에 있어서 앞으로 倫理學이 取할 方向과 構想의 輪廓을 그려 보고자 한 基礎的 試論에 지나지 않는 이 小著 안에 包含시키기에는 適合하지 않다. 따라서 우리에게 남은 問題는, 앞으로 새로운 硏究로 引繼되어야 할 것이다. 그러나 主로 初步者를 倫理學으로 案內함을 그 任務로 삼는 이 小著가, 主로 倫理學의 學的 性格을 究明하는 일에만 치우치고, 行爲의 單位的 主體인 個人과 行爲의 世界인 社會에 關하여 全혀 論及하지 않는 것도 不

適當하다고 생각되므로, 人間存在의 基本構造를 便宜上 個人的 側面과 社會的 側面으로 나누어 그 輪廓만을 살펴보기로 한다.

1. 行動

1) 行動의 意義

'自然'을 넓은 意味로 解釋한다면, 사람은 自然의 一部임에 不過하다. 客觀的으로 본다면, '세계'는 곧 하나의 自然이다. 그러나 사람에게는 '自我 (self, ego)'라는 意識이 있는 까닭으로, 自我와 自我 以外의 存在者, 卽 他者를 分離해서 보는 傾向이 있다. 主體(subject)와 客體(object)가 나누어지는 瞬間이다. 自我意識을 中心으로 본다면, 世界는 自我와 他者와의 對立이다. 이때 自我가, 自我와 同類라고 認定되는 다른 모든 사람들을, 自己까지 包含하여 '人類'라는 概念으로 包括한다면, 世界는 人類와 自然과의 對立으로서 經驗된다.

世界 全體로서의 自然의 各 部分은 相互間에 作用한다. 그리고 이 相互作用은, 自然界에 있어서 끊임없는 '變化'의 正體이다. 이 相互作用은 原子와 原子 사이에도 있고, 分子와 分子 사이에도 있고, 人體 內에서도 일어나고, 사람과 狹義의 自然 사이에도 있으며, 사람과 사람 사이에도 일어난다.

어떤 生命體를 中心으로 볼 때, 世界는 生命體와 그 環境으로 나누어진다. 앞서 말한 相互作用은 勿論 모든 生命體와 그 環境과의 사이에도 일어난다. 生命體는 그 環境으로부터 影響을 받는 同時에, 環境에 對하여 影響을 끼친다. 그런데 生命體가 環境의 作用을 받아들이고 또는 環境에 作用을 加하는 方式은, 物體의 溫度와 그 體積과의 關係에 있어서와 같이, 單純히 機械的이 아니라, 그것은 生物로서의 一定한 目的에 適合하려는 傾向을 가지고 이루어진다. 우리가 '行動(behavior)'이라고 부르는 것은, 바로 높은 發達段階에 達한 生命體로서의 人間이나 一般動物이, 自己의 生物學的, 心理學的 目的에 適合하고자 하는 傾向을 가지고, 環境과 相互作用하는 이 現象을 意味하는 것이다. 人間이 行動할 때, 그 行動의 生物學的, 心理學的 目的을 意識하는 同時에 有意的으로 行動을 調整하는 境遇가 있다. 倫理學이 그 規範을 밝히고자 하는바 '行爲(conduct)'라는 것은 바로 이 '有意的으로 調整된 行動'을 가리킨다. 따라서 우리는 行動을 行爲의 原初形態라고 볼 수가 있다.

"우리는 어떻게 行爲할 것인가?"라는 倫理學의 基本問題를 追究하기 爲하여, 우리는 먼저 "우리는 어떻게 行爲하고 있는가?"를 살펴야 하며, 現實에 하고 있는 行爲의 本質을 알기 爲하여서는, 行爲의 原初形態요, 널리는 行爲까지도 그 속에 包含하는 '行動'에 對한 心理學的 理解가 앞서야 할 것이다. 우리는 生得的 行動으로부터 始作한다.

2) 生得的 行動

從來 人間의 여러 가지 行動이 '本能(instinct)'이라는 말로 說明되었다. 例컨대 싸움은 鬪爭本能의 탓이요, 勉學은 愛知本能이 結果라는 것이다. 協同, 所有, 蒐集, 父性愛 等 여러 가지 行動이 모두 本能에 起因한다고 생각되었다.

여기서 '本能'이라는 말이 어떤 社會 안에 傳統을 가진 一般的 習性을 意味한다면 모르거니와, 이것을 모든 人類에게 有史 以前부터 現今까지 遍在하는 先天的 原理, 다시 말하면 絶對不可變한 人類의 本性으로 보는 從前의 見解를 쫓는다면, 이 本能說에는 여러 가지 難點이 있다.

(1) 아메리칸 인디언(American Indian)의 一種인 주니族(the Zuni)에 있어서와 같이 競爭意識이나 攻擊性이 全혀 缺如된 部族의 存在, 또는 마조히즘(masochism) 氣質의 存在[1] 等은 '攻擊性(agressiveness)'의 先天的 普遍性을 否認한다. 近來의 民俗學이나 心理學에서는 從來 先天的, 永續的인 것으로 믿어 오던 攻擊性, 支配欲, 協同性 等을 後天的, 社會的 習性으로 보고 있다. 姙娠의 經驗이 없는 女性의 母性的 行動도 從來는 母性本能의 先天性을 立證하는 것으로서 認定되었으나, 뉴기니아의 마누스族(the Manus)에 있어서, 女兒보다도 男兒가 人形에 對한 關心이 컸다는 事實의 發見은 이 信念을 뒤집었다. 卽 마누스族에 있어서는, 女子가 戶外에서 勞動을 하고 男子가 어린애를 보살피는 社會的 慣習이 幼兒들의 母性愛的 態度를 規定한 것이다.[2]

(2) 學者들의 擧示한바 本能의 種類는 그 內實과 數爻에 있어 千差萬別하다. 버나드(L. L. Bernard)의 調査에 依하면, 本能說을 主張하는 數百卷의 心理學 書籍 中에 나오는 本能의 種類는 都合 一萬四千四十六種이나 되는데, 그 中 어떤 學者들은 不過 四五種類의 本能을 認定하는가 하면, 다른 어떤 學者는 數百種의 本能을 計上하고 있다. 같은 '人間의 本能'에 對해서 學者들의 見解가 이토록 差異가 많다는 것은, "本能이 嚴密히 科學的인 概念이 못 된다는 證左이다."[3]

---

1 크레츠머(E. Kretschmer)에 依하면 모든 사람에게는 多少間의 사디즘 氣質과 마조히즘 氣質이 混合되어 있다.
2 南博, 『社會心理學』, p.72, M. 미드의 硏究에서.
3 F. Shaffer, *The Psychology of Adjustment*, p.24.

(3) 行動을 本能의 發露로 보는 說明은 매우 簡便한 것이기는 하나, 其實인즉 아무 說明도 안한 것에 가깝다. "사람은 왜 稱讚을 받으면 기뻐합니까?" 하고 묻는 사람이, "그것은 人間의 本能입니다."라는 對答을 받아 봐야 質問者의 知識에는 別로 增加가 없을 것이다.

'本能'이라는 觀念의 이와 같은 難點을 避하기 爲하여, 近來의 心理學은, 本能 代身에 '生得的 行動(native behavior)'이라는 槪念을 가져온다. 生得的 行動이란, 사람이 胎兒期 또는 新生 當初부터 할 수 있는 行動을 意味한다.[4] 따라서 生得的 行動은 가장 原初的인 것이요, 앞으로 複雜하고 洗鍊된 行動이 그것으로부터 發達해 나올 母體가 되는 것이다.

生得的 行動의 種類는 成人의 行動의 그것에 比하면 極히 少數이나, 그 細細한 이름을 網羅하는 것은 우리에게는 必要하지 않은 煩雜이다. 여기서는 生得的 行動을 大別하여 세 가지 部類로 나누어 본다.

(1) 生理的 反射(physiological reflex)

感官이 받은 刺戟이 神經中極(意識)에까지 到達하지 않고, 直接 筋肉이나 腺으로 傳達되어, 反應을 일으키는 것을 '反射(reflex)'라고 부른다. 新生兒가 하는 反射運動은 主로 生理的인 것으로서 하품, 재채기, 기침, 唾液 分泌 等 數十 가지가 있다. 反射에는, 生後의 經驗을 따라 變化하는 것이 있어 後日의 複雜한 行動의 基礎가 되기도 한다. 奏樂, 運動競技 等에서 볼 수 있는 專門的 技術은 主로 習得된 反射의 連續이다.

---

4 出生 當時에 바로 하는 行動일지라도, 이를 반드시 '生得的'이라고 斷定할 수 없다는 見解가 있다. 胎生學者들은, 胎兒의 發達도 그것이 받는 刺戟에 따라서 影響을 받는다고 指摘한다.

(2) 全體反應(mass reaction)

行動은 客觀的으로는 刺戟에 對한 反應이며, 主觀的으로 본다면(元來는) 生物로서의 어떤 目的을 達成하기 爲하여 일어나는, (人間을 包含한) 動物의 運動이다. 따라서 感官이 받는 刺戟은 그 生命體에 對하여는 一種의 '問題'를 意味하는 것이요, 刺戟에 對한 反應은 本來는 이 問題解決을 爲한 運動이다. 生命體가 當面한 問題를 解決하는 方策이 그 生命體에게 알려져 있다면, 問題解決策으로서의 生命體의 反應은, 가장 經濟的이요 效果的인 路線을 擇할 것이다. 例컨대 이마 위에 앉은 모기를 處置하기 爲하여서는, 한 팔의 筋骨을 若干 動員시키는 程度로 그칠 것이다. 그러나 經驗이 貧弱한 新生兒에게는 問題解決의 方案이 알려져 있지 않다. 그러므로 손가락 하나만 움직이면 解決될 問題를 當해서도, 全身의 筋骨을 움직인다. 新生兒는 손등 위에 앉은 모기를 쫓기 爲하여서 全身을 버둥거리는 것이다. 이와 같이 部分的 反應이 要求되는 刺戟에 對하여 온몸을 不規則하게 움직이는 反應을 全體反應(mass reaction)이라고 한다. 全體反應은 人間이 胎兒 때부터 할 수 있는 基本的 行動으로서, 經驗이 늘어 감에 따라 次次 分化하여, 將次 洗鍊된 行動을 習得하는 土臺가 되는 것이다.

(3) 感動(emotion)

成人社會에서 볼 수 있는 感動 乃至 情緒는 기쁨, 슬픔, 노여움, 사랑, 미움, 부끄러움, 두려움, 嫉妬 等 매우 여러 가지가 있으나, 그 모두가 生得的인 것은 아니다. 行動主義 心理學(behaviorism)의 元祖 왓슨(Watson)이 生得的 感動의 種類를 急激한 變動, 特히 큰 音響에 對한 두려움(fear), 身體拘束에 對한 노여움(anger), 皮膚에 주는 가벼운 摩擦에 對한 性的 快感(lust)의 세 가지로만 局限한 것은 極端한 例라 하겠으나, 大體로 生得的이라고 認定되는 感動의 種類는 그리 많지 아니하며, 매우 單純한 것 몇 가지

뿐이다. 이러한 單純한 感動에 經驗的 因子가 結合되어, 나중에는 虛無感, 法悅, 人類愛 等의 複雜微妙한 情操(sentiment)까지 생기게 되는 것이다.

3) 成熟과 學習

新生兒도 할 수 있는 生得的 行動은 매우 單純 拙劣하고 그 範圍도 자못 좁다. 그러나 成人의 行動은 매우 複雜하고 洗鍊되었을 뿐만 아니라, 行動의 種類와 範圍에 있어서도 놀라운 發展을 보여준다. 新生兒로부터 成人에 이르는 동안에 이와 같이 行動이 發達하는 現象을, 心理學者들은 成熟(maturation)과 學習(learning)의 두 側面으로 나누어 본다.

'成熟'이라 함은, 新生兒 때 또는 그 以前부터 生得的으로 潛在해 있던 素質이, 나이가 참에 따라서 自發的으로 外部에 나타나는 現象을 말한다. 齒牙의 發生, 걸음마 始作, 思春期 少年의 變聲 等은 成熟의 代表的 現象이다. 行動成熟의 基礎가 되는 것은 筋骨의 成長을 비롯한 肉體的 成熟이다. 全體로서의 性格發達에 特히 重要한 役割을 하는 것은 內分泌腺(endocrine glands)의 成熟이다.

成熟의 時期와 程度는 個人에 따라 差異가 있다. 또 같은 사람에 있어서도, 成熟이 빠른 部分과 늦은 部分이 있다. 成熟의 時期와 程度에 決定的 影響을 미치는 것은 遺傳(heredity)이다. 그러나 經驗의 影響, 卽 學習과의 關聯 없이 成熟만이 홀로 이루어지는 境遇는 드물다. 心身의 發達에 있어 成熟과 學習은 密接히 相互滲透한다.

成熟의 過程은, 經驗的 條件의 影響을 받는 바 없지 않으나, 大體로는 內在하는 素質의 自然的 發現이었다. '學習'이라 함은, 이와 反對로, 過去의 經驗이 後日의 行動에 對하여 繼續的인 變化를 일으키는 效果를 말한다.

學習은 여러 가지 經路를 통해 이루어진다. 周圍 사람들에 對한 模倣

(imitation)이 習慣으로 化하는 境遇도 있고, 거듭된 試行과 錯誤(trial and error)로 目標에 達하는 行動의 捷徑이 發見되고, 發見된 捷徑이 後日에 繼續 活用되는 境遇도 있으며, 洞察(insight)에 依한 問題解決이 以後 行動의 指針이 되는 境遇도 있다. 그러나 學習에 있어서 가장 基本的인 因子가 되는 것은 條件反應의 現象이다. 特히 條件反應에 있어서의 '區別(differentiation)' 乃至 '禁止(inhibition)'의 作用은 學習過程에 있어서 重大한 所任을 본다.

學習은, 새로운 經驗이 從來의 行動에 變革을 招來하는 現象이라는 面으로 본다면, 人間行動에 있어서 改新의 過程이라고 볼 수가 있다. 그러나 學習은, 一旦 얻어진 經驗이 오래오래 살아서 繼續的인 行動傾向을 決定한다는 面으로 본다면, 保守의 原理요, 習慣(habits) 乃至 習性(traits) 形成의 過程이라고 볼 수가 있다. 學習은, 習慣을 形成하는 固定力인 同時에, 過去의 習慣을 깨고 새로운 길을 開拓하는 革新力이기도 하다. 우리는 이 關係를 流水와 水路와의 關係에 比할 수가 있다. 흐르는 물은 이미 過去가 決定한 地形, 地物의 影響을 받는다. 그러나 過去의 水路를 嚴格히 遵守하지는 않는다. 洪水 其他에 따르는 새로운 水勢는, 水路 自體에 일어난 새로운 條件들과 어울려서, 새로운 水路를 開拓해 나간다. 그리고 새로운 水路는 다음에 따르는 流水에 對하여 繼續的 制約이 되고자 한다. 우리의 行動도 從來의 習慣이 決定해 놓은 行動路線을 따른다. 그러나 우리가 받은 새로운 刺戟은 過去의 習慣을 깨뜨리고 새로운 行動路線을 開拓하게 한다. 그리고 새로이 開拓된 行動路線은 뒤에 따르는 行動들에게 繼續的 制約이 되고자 한다. 이와 같은 進行은 個人의 行動을 에워싸고서만 생기는 것이 아니다 社會 全體의 歷史的 흐름에 있어서도, 文化와 政治를 에워싸고 이와 같은 保守와 改革의 兩勢力이 對立하며 調和되는 辨證法이 進行되고 있다. 倫理學의 根本問題는, 行爲의 世界에 있어서, 바로 이 묵은 要求와 새 要求와를, 어떻게 調和시키고 어떻게 揚棄시키느냐에 있다고도 볼 수가 있다.

2. 欲求

1) 動因과 動機

前節에서 우리는 行動의 發達을 發生學的으로 略察하였다. 發生學的으로 본다면, 成人의 行動은, 生理的 反射, 全體反應 感動 等 生得的 行動이 成熟과 學習의 두 契機를 通하여 分化發達한 것이다. 그러나 觀點을 바꾸어 行動을 斷面的으로 본다면, 모든 瞬間의 모든 行動에는 그 行動을 일으킬 만한 動力이 背後에 있어야 할 것이다. 이제 우리는 行動을 일으키는 原動力으로서의 '欲求(needs)'에 對하여서 考察하기로 한다.

앞서도 말한 바와 같이 行動이란 어떤 刺戟에 對한 反應이다. 그런데 刺戟은 行動하는 生命體의 外部에서 뿐만 아니라 內部로부터도 온다. 例컨대 장발장으로 하여금 한 조각의 빵을 훔치는 行動을 일으키게 한 刺戟은, 그가 손 닿는 곳에 빵이 있었다는 外的 刺戟보다도, 굶주려 못 견디게 된 生理的 狀態에서 온 內的 刺戟이 더 컸던 것이다. 行動을 일으키는 刺戟 中에서 生命體의 內部로부터 오는 것을, 心理學은 '動因(drive)'이라고 부른다. 動因은 行動을 誘發하는 內部로부터의 動力이다. 그리고 이 動力의 出處는, 生命體 內部에 生理的 均衡이 깨졌을 때, 그 均衡을 回復하고자 하는 一般的 傾性에 있다. 動因에 主觀的인 意識이 結合되었을 때, 이것을 '欲求'라고 부른다. 動因은 生理的 均衡이 回復될 때까지, 또는 欲求가 滿足될 때까지 作用하며, 生理的 均衡이 回復되면 終熄한다.

그러나 內部刺戟으로서의 動因이 單獨으로 行動을 일으키는 境遇는 드물다. 內部의 刺戟은 恒常 外部의 刺戟, 卽 環境과 서로 呼應하여 行動을 일으킨다. 內部의 刺戟인 動因 自體가 外部의 刺戟인 環境에 依하여 誘發되는 것이며, 一旦 誘發된 動因은 環境 안에서 그 解消의 手段을 求한다. 쉽게 말하자면 環境은 우리의 欲求를 決定하는 主要한 因子인 同時에, 우리의 欲求를 滿足시키는 主要한 手段이기도 하다.

우리가 動因解消의 手段을 環境 內의 一定한 事物에 發見할 때, 그 事物은 該動因이 誘發하는 行動의 目標가 된다. 이리하여 動因과 目標가 內外 呼應하여 行動의 態型(behavior pattern)을 決定한다. 一定한 目標와 連結된 動因을 '動機(motive)'라고 부른다. 動機는 一定한 行動方向을 가진 動因이다.

그러나 有意的 行動, 卽 行爲를 問題 삼는 倫理學에 있어서, 動因과 動機를 따로 分離하여 생각할 必要는 없을 것이다. 이제 우리는 '動因'과 '動機'를 통틀어서 '欲求'라는 槪念으로 代置하고, 人間이 가진 欲求의 系列을 살펴보기로 한다.

2) 生理的 欲求와 社會的 欲求

우리는, 사람이 가진 여러 가지 欲求를 生理的 欲求(physiological needs)와 社會的 欲求(social needs)의 두 系列로 나누어 볼 수가 있다.

'生理的 欲求'라 함은, 生理的 基礎를 가진 것으로서 動物一般에게도 있는 것이다. 따라서 이것은 人類에 普遍的인 것이요, 이른바 '先天的'인 欲求에 該當한다. 生理的 欲求는 그것이 充足되지 않는 境遇에는, 個人의 生命 또는 種族維持에 支障을 招來하는 性質의 것이다. 食欲, 渴症, 性欲, 苦痛回避, 體溫調節, 呼吸欲, 休息欲, 睡眠欲, 排泄欲 等은 生理的 欲求의 代表的인 것들이다.

生理的 欲求는 이를테면 生存欲에 該當하는 것이다. 이를 表現하는 樣式

이나 充足시키는 手段에는 個人差와 文化的 差異가 있으나, 그 欲求 自體는 人類에 先天的이요, 普遍的이다. 따라서 이 欲求를 어떻게 合理的으로 充足시킬 것인가 하는 手段方法의 問題는 생기나, 이들 欲求 自體가 善인가 惡인가 하는 倫理問題는 생길 수가 없다. 이 系列의 欲求는, 原則的으로 物質로써 또는 肉體的으로 滿足되는 것이며 性欲을 除外하고는 代償的 滿足(compensation)이 不可能하다.[5]

'社會的 欲求'라 함은 社會生活을 通하여서, 다시 말하면 環境 乃至 經驗의 影響 밑에서, 이를테면 後天的으로 習得된 欲望이다. 따라서 生理的, 解剖的 基礎가 없으며, 特定한 社會集團 內에서는 共通의 일 수 있으나, 全人類에게 普遍的인 것은 아니다. 社會的 欲求는 그 大部分이 社會生活을 營爲하는 데 있어서 充足시킬 必要가 있는 것이며, 間接的으로는 生命保全에도 必要한 것이 있으나, 直接은 生命保全이나 種族維持와 關係가 없다. 支配欲, 協同性, 名譽欲, 服從欲, 所有欲, 蒐集欲, 父性愛 等은 社會的 欲求의 代表的인 것들이다.

生理的 欲求가 體內의 生理的 均衡의 喪失을 基礎로 하고 생기는 것이라면, 社會的 欲求는,'生理的 均衡의 喪失'이라는 基礎 없이, 社會的 關係에 連結되는 心理的 均衡의 喪失에서 생기는 欲求라고 볼 수가 있다. 다시 말하면 社會的 欲求는 大體로 情緒緊張에서 오는 欲望에 一致한다. 生理的 欲求는 物質的으로 充足시키는 수밖에 道理가 없었으나, 生理的 基礎 없이 單純히 情緒緊張에 起因하는 社會的 欲求는 이를 直接的으로 充足시키는

---

5 셰퍼는 人間의 欲求를 '生存欲에서 오는 動機(subsistence motives)'와 '情緒緊張에서 오는 動機(motives from emotional tensions)'의 두 가지로 나누고, 性欲을 後者에 屬하는 것으로 보고 있다. 本著書에서 欲求를 生理的인 것과 社會的인 것으로 區分한 것은, 오히려 常識的인 見解에 가까운 것이다.

以外에, 代價的 滿足의 길이 있다. 例컨대 憤怒를 解決하는 本來의 方法은, 그 憤怒를 일으킨 相對便을 打倒하는 일이다. 그러나 오늘날 文明人은 絶交, 中傷, 第三者 攻擊, 自己批判, 慈悲 等 여러 가지 代理方法으로 이를 解決한다. 이와 같이 한 가지 情緒緊張을 풀 수 있는 여러 가지 方途 中에는, 適當한 것도 있으나 不適當한 것도 많다. 여기서, 社會的 欲求를 어떠한 手段으로 滿足시킬 것인가 하는 行動調整의 問題는, 우리가 어떻게 行爲할 것인가 하는 倫理學의 基本問題와 相接한다. 그리고 社會的 欲求는 生理的 必然性을 가진 것이 아닌 만큼 支配欲, 名譽欲, 協同性 等 그 自體가 批判과 評價의 對象이 된다.[6]

以上에서 우리는 欲求를 便宜上 生理的인 것과 社會的인 것으로 區分해 보았다. 그러나 實際生活에 있어서 純粹히 生理的인 欲求와 純粹히 社會的인 欲求를 따로따로 經驗하는 事例는 드물다. 具體的 動機에는 生理的 欲求와 社會的 欲求가 서로 錯綜複合되는 것이 普通이다. 우리들의 衣裳은 體溫調節만을 爲한 것이 아니고, 우리의 食生活은 單純히 榮養補充만으로 足하지 않다. 生理的 欲求와 社會的 欲求의 이와 같은 錯綜은 이 두 가지 欲求의 內面的 關聯性을 示唆하는 것이다.

우리는 이미 第三章에서 道德現象의 本質을 考察했을 때, 行爲評價의 一次的 傾性이 生理的 欲求에 應하는 것이며, 行爲評價의 二次的 傾性이 社會的 欲求에 應하는 것임을 말하고, 이 二次的 傾性이 저 一次的 傾性에서 派生된 것임을 論하였다. 이것은 바로 人間의 社會的 欲求가 그 根柢를 生

---

6 生理的 欲求와 社會的 欲求와의 區分規準에 關하여서는 南博의 『社會心理學』, 第一部 第一章 參照. 그리고 代價的 滿足에 關하여서는 F. Shaffer, *The Psychology of Adjustment*, 第四章 參照.

理的인 것에 두고 있다는 것을 意味한다. 大體로 우리의 社會的 欲求는, 一見 生理的 欲求와는 無關係한 듯하고, 甚至於는 生理的 欲求와 矛盾되는 듯이 보이나, 그 根柢에 있어서 生理的 欲求에 連結되고 있다. 祖國을 爲하여 一身을 犧牲하는 愛國者의 情熱, 또는 俗世의 苦樂을 達觀하고 無의 世界를 觀照하는 佛敎徒의 情操 等은, 一見 우리의 生理的 欲求, 例컨대 飢渴, 性欲 等과는 全혀 關聯이 없는 것같이 생각되나 그 發生의 起源을 살피면, 아무리 高尙하고 複雜한 行爲일지라도, 그 根柢에는 亦是 原初的인 生理의 欲求가 가로놓여 있음을 알 수가 있다. 이같이 生理的 欲求에서 社會的 欲求가 派生發達하는 契機에, 條件反應과 模倣이 있고 習慣과 流行이 있다(第三章, 1, 3) 參照).

3) 對應

欲求는 行動의 原動力 卽 出發點이다. 行動은 大槪 一定한 目標를 가지고 있으며, 그 目標가 達成되면 그 行動을 일으킨 欲求는 充足되고, 그로 말미암은 行動도 一旦 終熄한다. 目標는 行動의 終點이다. 萬若에 行動의 出發點인 欲求에서 그 終點인 目標에 이르는 路程이 恒常 平坦하여 無條件 通過할 수 있는 것이라면, '對應(adjustment)'이라는 現象은 일어나지 않을 것이다. 그리고 對應이라는 現象이 아니었다면, '道德'이라는 現象도 없었을 것이며, 따라서 倫理學의 問題도 생기지 않았을 것이다. 元來 全知全能한 神에게는 道德이나 倫理學이 必要하지 않다. 그러나 實際에 있어서, 欲求로부터 그것을 充足시킬 目標에까지 이르는 途程에는, 大體로 어떤 障碍가 가로막고 있는 것이 通例이다. 여기서 어떻게 해서 그 障碍를 克服할 것인가 하는 '問題'가 생긴다.

動機의 充足을 꾀하고 일어난 行動이, 그 行動의 길을 가로막는 障碍, 卽

問題에 當面했을 때, 그 行動은 갖은 方向으로 障碍의 克服, 卽 問題의 解決을 試圖한다. 甲이라는 方法으로 解決되지 않으면 乙이라는 方法으로 交替하고, 乙의 方法이 失敗하면 다시 丙, 丁의 方法으로 옮겨 간다. 이리하여 어떠한 方式으로라도 當初의 動機가 充足되는 것을 보고야 마는 것이다. 이와 같이 動機에서 出發한 行動이 當面한 障碍를 가지가지의 反應으로 克服하고 드디어 動機解消라는 목표에 到達하는 過程을, '對應過程(process of adjustment)'이라고 부른다.

行動路程을 가로막는 障碍가 單純히 物理的인 것이라면, 그때 우리가 當面하는 問題는 技術的인 問題요, 倫理道德에 關한 것은 아니다. 倫理學의 問題가 생기는 것은, 行動을 가로막는 障碍가 動機 乃至 欲求의 矛盾對立을 包含하는 境遇에 있어서다. 學藝의 길을 精進하고자 하는 나의 意慾을 安逸과 遊興을 貪내는 또 하나의 欲望이 妨害할 때, 道德의 問題가 생긴다. 담 너머로 늘어진 果實을 따 먹고 싶은 나의 欲望을 그 果實에 對한 所有權을 主張하는 他人 乃至 社會의 意思가 隱然히 가로막을 때, 倫理의 問題는 생긴다. 倫理學의 問題는, 結局 自我 內部에 또는 自我와 他人과의 사이에 複數의 欲求가 對立했을 때, 그 對立을 合理的으로 克服할 原則을 發見하는 問題였다(第四章, 3).

意慾과 意慾의 矛盾對立을 當面하여, 이에 對應하는 方式에는 여러 가지 類型이 있다. 自己自身 안에 意慾의 對立을 經驗할 때는, ① 더 感情的이요 肉體的인, 따라서 現在的인 欲求에로 기울어지는 態度, ② 더 知性的이요 精神的인, 따라서 未來的인 欲求에로 기울어지는 態度, ③ 上述한 두 가지 態度 사이를 右往左往하여 逡巡不斷한 態度, ④ 두 가지 欲求를 調和 있게 折衷하는 態度, ⑤ 其他 여러 가지 中間型 等이 있다. 自我와 他我의 意慾이 對立하는 境遇에는 ① 相對便을 攻擊하여 끝내 自己의 意慾을 固執하는 態度, ② 相對便에게 服從하거나 또는 相對便을 回避함으로써 競爭對立의

狀態를 緩和하고자 하는 態度, ③ 協同 乃至 妥協으로 折衷線을 發見하려는 態度, ④ 自我의 意慾을 昇華(sublimate)시키거나 他我를 自我 안에 包攝시킴으로써, 自他의 對立을 揚棄하려는 態度, ⑤ 其他 여러 가지 中間型 等이 있다.[7]

以上은, 사람이 道德的인 問題를 當面하여 取하는 態度를 抽象的으로 分類해 본 것에 不過하다. 具體的 情勢에 있어서 사람들이 取하는 態度는 類型의 範疇를 넘어서 形形色色이다. 個人行動의 一般的 傾向을 決定하는 것은 그 個人의 '사람됨(personality)'(앞으로 性格이라는 말로 通用한다)과 社會環境의 生活樣式(文化)과의 相互關聯이다. 우리는 먼저 性格의 形成에 關하여 一瞥하고, 다음에 人間存在의 社會的 側面을 論及하여 보자.

3. 性格

性格이 形成되는 過程을 全面에 걸쳐 仔細히 살피는 것은 이 자리에서 다루기엔 지나치게 厖大한 일이다. 우리는 다만, 遺傳的 諸因子를 括弧 안에 넣고 볼 때, 人間의 性格形成이 習慣을 中心으로 이루어진다는 事實을 指摘하는 것만으로 그친다.

가난한 살림엔 밥알 하나 흘린 것도 주워 먹는다. 아침에도 그렇게 하고 저녁에도 그렇게 하고, … 이것이 여러 날 거듭하면 흘린 밥을 주워 먹는 習慣(habit)이 形成된다. 같은 形便에서, 조밥을 먹을 때면 턱 밑에 왼손을

---

7 여기서는 便宜上, 意慾이 對內的으로 對立하는 境遇와 對外的으로 對立하는 境遇를 나누었다. 그러나 實際에 있어서 對內, 對外 두 가지 對立은 相互關聯한다. 例컨대 對外的 對立에 當面한 사람은, 그 對立에 있어서의 自己의 立場을 背定-否定하는 對內的 對立을 아울러 體驗한다.

받친다. 이것이 버릇이 되면, 끈기 있는 쌀밥을 먹을 때도 왼손을 받친다. 또 하나의 習慣이 생긴 것이다. 鉛筆이 달아서 짧아지면 붓뚜껑을 이어서 쓰는 習慣이 생기고, 벨벳 치마를 입고 座席에 앉을 때면 뒷자락을 올리는 버릇이 생긴다. '習慣'이라는 말을 좁은 意味로 解釋할 때, 그것은 以上에 例를 든 바와 같은 斷片的 動作에 關한 反復傾向이다. 斷片的 動作에 關한 여러 가지 習慣이 相互間에 內面的 關聯性에 依하여 一定한 系列을 지어 綜合될 때, '習性(trait)'이 생긴다. 例컨대 밥알을 아끼고, 鉛筆을 아끼고, 치마를 아끼는 等의 習慣들이 '吝嗇', '규모', '알뜰함' 等으로 불리는 習性을 形成하는 것이다.

같은 經路를 밟아, 다른 여러 가지 習性이 생긴다. 일찍부터 小便을 가리는 버릇, 아침마다 洗面하는 버릇, 장난감이나 옷가지를 다독거려 整頓하는 버릇 等에서, '깔끔하다'고 불리는 習性이 생기고, 낯선 사람을 보면 얼굴을 가리는 버릇, 강아지를 보면 달아나는 버릇, 理髮所에 가면 울고 야단치는 버릇 等에서 '緊張性', '恐怖性' 等의 習性이 생긴다. 한 사람 안에 形成되는 여러 가지 習性은 相互間에 內面的인 聯關性을 갖는다. 그리고 個人에 따라서 가장 支配的인 習性이 있다. 가장 支配的인 習性을 中心으로 하고, 다른 習性들이 相互關聯하면서 一種의 關係로서 綜合된다. 이와 같이 한 個人이 가진 모든 習性이 綜合統一된 것이, 바로 우리가 말하는 '性格(personality)'의 意味內容이다. 그리고 이 퍼스낼리티의 自覺이 바로 自我의 意識이다.

그러나 이 順序를 反對로 생각할 수는 없을까? 卽 '人格'이라는 統一實在가 先天的으로 所與되어 있고, 그 人格에 包含된 여러 가지 性質이 分化發達하여, 習性에 該當하는 여러 가지 特質로서 나타나고, 이 特質에 따라서 여러 가지 習慣이 形成되는 것이 아닐까? 例컨대 손발을 자주 씻는 버릇에서 淨潔의 習性이 생기는 것이 아니라, 淨潔한 性質이 天品으로서 먼저 있기 때문에 손발을 깨끗하게 씻는 것이 아닐까?

勿論 生命體는 出生 以前부터 하나의 統一體이다. 萬一 '人格'이 生物學的 統一性의 原理를 意味하는 것이라면, 우리는 分明히 習慣形成에 앞서 人格을 갖는다. 그리고 新生兒는 이미 여러 가지 素質的 制約을 타고난다. 우리는 모든 新生兒를 自己가 願하는대로의 體格과 性格을 가진 사람으로 育成할 수는 없는 것이다. 神經質이 되기 쉬운 素質이 있으며, 느긋한 性格이 되기 쉬운 素質도 있다. 또 一旦 形成된 習性은, 그 다음의 習慣을 形成시킴에 있어서 重要한 因子가 된다. 두세 살 때에 손과 낯을 깨끗이 씻어 버릇하여 깔끔한 習性이 생긴 어린이는, 八九歲 되어서 齒牙를 깨끗이 닦는 習性을 들이기 容易할 것이며 學校에 들어가면 册을 깨끗하게 保存하는 버릇이 생기기 쉽고, 甚至於는 精神的 方面에 있어서도 潔白한 人物이 되기 쉽다.

'人格'의 先天性에 對한 主張이 以上의 程度를 意味하는 것이라면 좋다. 그러나 이 程度를 넘어서 精神的 意味의 統一된 人格性이 出生과 더불어 具備되어 있다든지, 사람의 性格은 先天的 素質만으로 決定되는 것이라든지, 깨끗한 性質을 가진 사람은 모든 境遇에 깨끗하게 行動한다고 主張한다면 그것은 容認되지 않는다. 첫째로 아직 羞恥感이나 名譽心을 모르는 어린이에게는 成人에게 보는 바와 같은 自我意識이 없다. 그리고 幼兒에게는 大體로 食欲. 睡眠欲 等 部分的인 欲求는 있으나, '人間'으로서의 理想이나 抱負는 없다. 이와 같은 事實은 幼兒에게 人格的 統一性이 缺如되어 있음을 意味한다. 둘째로 사람의 性格은 어느 程度 可變的이다. 그리고 新生兒의 生活에서 '厭世觀'이라든지 '責任感'의 싹을 指摘하기는 어렵다. 이것은 性格이 先天的 素質만으로 決定되는 것이 아님을 意味한다. 셋째로, 學校에서 잘 웃고 잘 떠드는 사람이 집에서도 반드시 잘 웃고 잘 떠드는 것은 아니다. 一般的으로 物件을 아끼지 않는 사람이, 册만은 아끼는 習慣을 갖기도 한다. 이것은 習慣이 어떤 全體的 素質에서부터 一律的으로 決定되는 것이 아니라, 各其 具體的인 狀位에 따라서 形成되는 것임을 意味한다.

人格이 先天的으로 決定되는 것이 아니라 함은, 그것이 經驗의 影響을 받는다는 뜻이요, 따라서 可變的이라는 것을 意味한다. 그러나 性格이 經驗에 따라 可變的이라는 것은, 우리가 自己의 願하는 대로의 性格이 될 수 있다는 것을 意味하지는 않는다. 우리가 努力에 依해서 性格 乃至 人格을 어느 程度까지 願하는 方向으로 形成할 수는 있으나, 이 可能性은 極히 制限된 範圍 內에서만 現實化할 수가 있다.

性格形成을 制約하는 첫째 契機는 遺傳(heredity)이요, 둘째 契機는 넓은 意味의 文化(culture)이다. 遺傳이 性格形成의 先天的 制約이라면, 文化는 그 後天的 制約이라 하겠다. 오늘날 人類에게 傳해지는 遺傳은 有史以前부터의 오랜 歷史를 가졌다. 人類의 生活이 元來 社會的이었다는 點으로 보면, 그것은 悠久한 社會生活의 記錄의 一面이다. 人間의 文化도 亦是 人間의 歷史와 같이 오랜 過去를 가졌다. 遺傳이 人間의 社會生活의 物質的 記錄이라면, 文化는 그 精神的 記錄이라고 볼 수 있다. 遺傳과 文化는 다 같이 歷史的이요, 따라서 社會的이라는 點에 共通性을 가졌다. 人間性格의 形成이 遺傳과 文化의 制約을 받는다 함은, 곧 性格의 形成이 '人間存在의 基本形態'로서의 社會性의 制約下에 있다는 뜻이다.

4. 人間存在의 社會性(行爲의 世界)

1) 槪說

"나는 생각한다. 그러므로 나는 있다(Cogito ergo sum)." 데카르트(R. Descartes)의 이 有名한 말은, 그가 모든 存在를 疑心한 끝에 가장 먼저 그

存在性을 認定한 것이 '나'라는 뜻으로 알려지고 있다. 그러나 데카르트가 "나는 모든 것을 疑心한다."고 斷言하던 그 瞬間에, 이미 그는 他人의 存在를 認定하고 나온 것이다. "모든 것을 疑心한다."고 主張하는 것은 그 主張을 들어 줄 相對를 豫想하고 있기 때문이다. 무릇 自己의 主張을 들어 줄 사람 또는 읽어 줄 사람을 豫想하지 않는다면, 우리는 어떠한 意見도 말하거나 쓰지 않을 것이다.

어떤 意見을 表示하려면 우리는 言語를 使用한다. 言語라는 것은 말하는 이와 듣는 이의 兩者가 있음으로써 비로소 成立하는 것이요, 혼자만이라면 言語라는 것 自體가 생길 수 없다. cogito, ergo, sum이라는 세 單字는 데카르트가 새로 지어 낸 말들이 아니라, 그 以前에 이미 있었던 것을 데카르트가 엮은 것에 지나지 않는다. 言語가 萬若에 어느 個人이 지어 내는 것이라면, 그 個人만이 그것을 理解할 수 있을 것이요, 言語가 意思를 疎通하는 媒介가 될 수는 없을 것이다. '言語'라는 것이 있다는 事實 自體가 벌써 人間存在의 社會性을 가리킨다.[8]

여기 冊床머리에 홀로 앉아서 講義案을 作成하는 敎授가 있다. 그의 行動은 完全히 個人的인 行動인 것 같다. 아무도 이 敎授의 行動을 妨害하는 사람은 없기 때문이다. 그러나 조금만 살피면, 講義案은 敎授 單獨의 힘으로 作成하는 것이 아님을 알 수가 있다. 講義案을 쓰는 敎授는 그 講義를 들을 學生들을 念頭에 둔다. 學生들이 興味를 느낄 수 있는 思想을 다루고 싶으며, 學生들이 理解할 수 없는 어려운 表現은 避하고 싶다. 다시 말하면 學生들의 存在가 보이지 않는 곳에서 敎授의 붓대를 制約하고 있는 것이

8 　以上과 같은 見解는 이미 日本學者들이 發表한 지 오래다. 特히 和辻哲郞의 『倫理學(上)』, 高山岩男의 『哲學的 人間學』에는 비슷한 見解가 詳細히 論述되어 있다. 本節은, 以下에 있어서도 이 兩書籍을 參考한 바 적지 아니함을 明記하여 둔다.

다. 이를테면 敎授와 學生들이 힘을 合하여 講義案을 作成하고 있는 셈이다. 講義案 作成에 參與하는 것은 敎授와 學生뿐만도 아니다. 講義內容이 敎室 밖에까지 나갈지도 모른다고 생각할 때, 敎授는 더 넓은 社會의 意見을 念頭에 두지 않을 수 없다. 先輩나 同僚에게서 惡評을 받을 內容을 적어서는 안 된다. 當局의 誤解가 있을 말은 더욱 삼가야 한다. 講義內容의 根幹으로 말하더라도, 敎授가 혼자서 생각해 낸 獨自의 思想은 아니다. 그가 읽고 들은 先哲들의 思想과, 그 社會의 傳統的인 觀念이, 直接 間接으로 影響을 미치고 있다. 敍述에 使用하는 言語부터가 歷史的, 社會的 産物이다. 人間의 모든 行爲에는, 孤立한 사람의 單獨行爲에까지도, 오랜 歷史와 넓은 社會가 隱密히 參與하고 있다.

　敎室에서 敎壇에 선 사람은 '敎師'로서 서 있고, 聽講席에 앉은 사람은 '學生'으로서 앉아 있다. 單純히 抽象的인 '個人'이 서 있고 또는 個人들이 앉아 있는 것이 아니다. 서고 앉은 사람 사이에는 '師弟間'이라는 特殊한 關係가 成立하고 있다. 이 特殊한 關係가, 敎壇에 서 있는 사람과 敎室에 앉아 있는 사람과의 行動을 制約한다. '敎師'라는 立場이 이야기하는 사람에게 一定한 規範을 强要하며, '學生'이라는 身分이 듣는 이들에게 一定한 態度를 要求한다. 行動을 制約하는 이와 같은 關係는 敎室 안에만 있는 것이 아니다. 家庭에 돌아오면 父母와 子息의 關係가 있고, 兄弟姉妹의 關係가 있다. 市場에 가면 파는 이와 사는 이의 關係가 있고, 學生들끼리는 上下級生의 關係가 있다. 모든 사람들은 여러 角度로 여러 가지 關係에 매여 있다. 아무런 關係의 制約도 받지 않는다는 意味로서의 '自由人'이라는 것은 存在하지 않는다.[9]

9　和辻哲郎, 『倫理學(上)』, p.76.

雇傭主와 雇傭人과의 關係 또는 政黨關係와 같이, 個人들이 모여서 人爲的으로 맺고 또 풀 수 있는 人間關係도 있다. 社會란 個人들이 自由契約에 依하여 結成한 것이요, 社會에 앞서 個人이 根本的이라는 思想은, 人間關係의 이러한 側面에 着眼한 것이다. 그러나 人間의 모든 關係가 個人들의 自由契約으로 成立되는 것은 아니다. 父母와 子息의 關係, 男性과 女性의 關係, 祖國과 國民의 關係 等 人生에 있어서 가장 重要한 關係들은, 도리어 個人의 意思에 앞서서 이를테면 '運命的'으로 決定된다. 우리는 出生과 同時에 어떤 父母의 子息으로서, 男子 或은 女子로서, 그리고 一定한 國家나 民族의 一員으로서 存在한다. 簡單히 말하면, 出生과 더불어 社會의 一成員이다. 그리고 後天的 人間關係에 있어서도, 設令 그것이 自由意思로 左右할 수 있다 할지라도, 그 自由에는 制限이 있는 것이다. 우리가 어떤 商人과 賣買契約을 맺는가, 또는 어느 下宿에 主人을 定하는가는 어느 程度 個人의 自由意思로 決定할 수 있다. 그러나 賣買 또는 主客이라는 社會關係 自體를 떠나서 生活할 수는 없는 點에 있어서, 個人의 自由는 必然的 制約을 받는다. 萬若 어떤 特殊條件下에 있는 사람이, 모든 物質生活을 自給自足하고, 또 모든 訪問客을 謝絕하여 隱居하기를 願한다면, 그는 賣買나 主客의 關係를 떠나서 살 수도 있지 않을까. 어느 程度 可能할 것이다. 그러나 隱居를 願한다는 것 自體가 特殊한 社會關係를 經驗한 사람이 아니고는 가질 수 없는 所願이다. 다시 말하면 隱居의 所願 自體는 社會的 關係를 通하여 생긴 것이니, 社會性은 隱者의 깊은 內面에까지 滲透되고 있다.

人間의 社會關係는, 個人들이 單純히 便宜를 爲하여서 지어낸 偶然한 關係가 아니다. 사람은 出生하자 곧 社會的 關係 안에 놓인다. 社會性은 人間存在에 있어서 必然的이요 根源的이다. 그리고 個人과 個人을 社會的으로 連結시키는 基本的인 紐帶가 되는 것은, 于先 血緣과 性別이다.

2) 血緣과 性

民主主義의 出發點은 萬人이 自由平等(free and equel)하다는 信念이다. 그러나 이것은, 人間이 生存함에 있어 自由와 平等한 權利를 가져야 한다는 當爲의 主張이요, 人間이 現實에 있어서 完全히 自由롭고 또 平等하다는 事實의 主張은 아니다. 社會的 存在로서의 人間의 自由와 平等을 制限하는 因子는 無數하다. 그 中에서도 가장 根本的이요 또 運命的인 것은, 人間을 社會的으로 連結시키는 가장 基本的인 紐帶인 血緣關係와 男女의 性別이라고 볼 수 있다.

사람은 出生과 더불어, 或은 그 以前부터, 어떤 父母의 子女로서 存在한다. 即 사람은 처음부터 어떤 사람들과 血緣關係를 가지고 出生한다. 血緣關係는, 아무도 그것을 떠나서 사람이 될 수 없는 必然的 自然의 關係이며, 個人의 生涯와 運命을 左右하는 根本的인 關係이다. 血緣關係는, 父母와 子息을 連結할 뿐만 아니라, 個人을 家族 乃至 氏族과 連結시키고, 나아가서는 民族과도 連結시킨다. 血緣關係는, 現存하는 人間들을 橫的으로 連結시킬 뿐만 아니라, 過去의 人間과 現在의 人間, 그리고 未來의 人間을 縱的으로 連結시킨다. 血緣關係는, 遺傳을 通하여 個人의 容貌와 體軀와 그리고 才質 等을 大部分 決定하며, 性格을 大體로 固定시키는 幼兒期의 環境을 決定한다. 이와 같이 決定된 容貌, 健康, 才質 그리고 性格 等은 그 사람의 生涯와 運命을 支配하는 基礎가 되는 것이다.

男女의 區別도 또한 人間에 있어서 必然的이요 自然的인 存在樣式이다. 人間은 必然的으로 男性 또는 女性으로서 存在하는데, 個人이 男性인가 女性인가는, 어느 便이 되든지 마찬가지인 副次的인 關係가 아니라, 個人의 生涯와 運命의 方向을 決定함에 커다란 힘이 되는 本質的인 關係이다. 男女는, 하나의 '人格'이라는 點에 있어서는, 同等한 權威를 認定받아야 한다. 그러나 男女同等의 理念이, 男女間의 先天的인 素質의 差異를 忘却하는 것이어서는 안 된다. 男女의 性別은, 社會生活에 있어서 分業을 決定하는 重要한 契機이며, 人間의 結合과 分離를 促進하는 前個體的 要因이다.

[戀愛] 兩性의 結合은 生物界 一般에서도 볼 수 있는 한갓 自然現象이다. 그러나 人間에 있어서의 兩性의 結合은 單純한 自然現象에 머물지 않고, 自然 以上의 것을 指向함에 있어, 社會的 存在로서의 人間의 特殊性을 보여주고 있다. 人間의 性結合이 單純한 自然 以上의 것을 指向한다는 것은, 單純히 自然스러운 性의 結合을 妨害하는 많은 社會的 干涉이 있다는 事實과, 또 結合하는 當事者들도 單純히 自然的인 結合만으로는 滿足하지 못한다는 事實 위에 如實히 나타난다.

人間의 結合이 單純한 自然 以上의 것을 希求한다 함은, 거기에 肉體的인 結合뿐만 아니라, 人格的인 結合까지도 要求되고 있다는 뜻이다. 男女는 單純히 性衝動에 依하여 움직이는 雌雄과는 다르다. 男女가 動物的인 性衝動에 依하여 接近하기 前에, 높은 人格을 憧憬하는 人間的인 要求에 依하여, 미리 心理的인 接近이 先行하는 것이 普通이다. 普通 '戀愛'라고 불리는 關係는, 바로 이 人格的인 結合의 要求와 性衝動的 結合의 要求가 합쳐져 있는 人間關係를 말하는 것이다.

戀愛는 人格에 對한 사랑과 肉體에 對한 사랑과의 結合이다. 人格에 對한 사랑이란 個性에 對한 사랑이다. 個性에 對한 사랑인 까닭에, 戀愛의 相對는 第三者로서 代置할 수 없는 獨特한 價値의 所有者가 된다. '友情'도 亦是 人格個性에 對한 사랑이다. 그러나 友情에 있어서는 肉體가 關聯되어 있지 않기 때문에, 第三者가 그 中間에 參加하더라도, 友情은 그 價値를 損傷함이 없이 存續할 수가 있다. 그러나 戀愛에 있어서는 肉體에 對한 사랑이 兼하고 있다. 그리고 肉體의 特質의 하나는 그 有限性이다. 有限한 肉體

는 그 價値를 덜지 않고 分有할 수가 없다. 여기서 友情에서는 보지 못하던 獨占의 要求가 戀愛에 있어서는 絕對條件이 된다. 사랑하는 心情으로 볼 때 愛人의 肉體와 心靈은 不可分의 同一體이다. 그러므로 愛人의 人格的 個性에 對한 사랑은 바로 肉體的 個性에 對한 사랑이기도 하다. 따라서 愛人의 肉體를 分有함은, 그 肉體의 價値만을 減少하는 것이 아니라, 그의 人格價値 全體의 破壞를 意味하는 것이다. 第三者의 介入을 嚴重히 排除하는 獨占의 要求는, 個性의 사랑으로서의 人格愛와 有限한 肉體에 對한 사랑을 兼한 '戀愛'에 있어서의 必然的인 것이다.

戀愛가 가진 第三者 排斥 또는 獨占의 要求는 自然히 戀愛로 하여금 '私的 性格', 卽 一種의 '利己性'을 갖게 한다. 戀愛는 第三者를 — 널리는 社會一般을, 眼中에 두지 않고, 自己네 두 사람의 關係에만 온갖 熱誠을 쏟아 버리는 閉鎖的 關係이다. 여기에 戀愛가 갖는 反社會性이 있다. 戀愛가 人性의 뿌리 깊은 自然現象이요, 人類歷史 以來의 普遍的인 現象임에도 不拘하고, 傳統的 思想이 이를 '墮落'이니 '煩惱'니 불러 罪惡視하는 傾向이 있는 것은, 바로 戀愛가 갖는 이 反社會性에 緣由하고 있다. 基督敎, 佛敎, 儒敎, 其他 모든 宗敎思想과 倫理思想이, 한편으로 가장 自然스러운 '性의 사랑'을 共通的으로 嫌惡했다는 事實은 決코 偶然히는 생길 수 없는 일이다.[10]

和辻 敎授도 指摘한 바와 같이, 그 私的 性格으로 말미암아, 社會人으로서의 建設的인 活動을 阻害하는 '男女愛'는, 應當 排斥을 當할 理由가 있다. 그러나 男女愛를 全的으로 否定할 수는 없다. 그것은 自然의 길이요, 人倫의 길이다. 男女愛는 否定 當해야 할 一面을 가지면서도 亦是 肯定하지 않을 수 없는 必然的 關係이다. 이에 한便으로 男女愛에 있어서 否定 當할 面, 卽 反社會的인 利己性을 克服하면서, 또 한便으로는 男女愛가 가진 人倫的인 使命을 살릴 수 있는 方案으로서 人間이 發見한 것이, 곧 '結婚

이라는 制度이다.

[結婚] 結婚은 私的 關係이던 男女의 結合을 社會가 公認함으로써 成立한다. 私的 關係로서의 男女愛는 元來 二重의 不安에 싸여 있다. 그 하나는 獨占欲에 必然的으로 連結되는 것으로서, 第三者의 競爭에 對한 恐怖에서 오는 疑惑과 嫉妬의 不安이요, 또 하나는 社會의 否定的 態度에 對應하는 '秘密'의 不安이다. 二重의 不安은 當事者의 愛着을 더욱 病理學的으로 强調하는 反面에, 社會共同事業에 對한 參與를 漸漸 게을리하게 한다. 여기에서 社會는, 特定한 男子와 女子와의 結合을 固定的 關係로서 公認하는 同時에, 第三者의 侵入으로부터 이를 保護한다. 男女 두 사람은 獨占欲의 滿足을 社會的으로 保障받는 代身에, 自己네의 性生活을 두 사람 사이에만 局限할 것을 社會에 公約한다.[11] 이와 같은 公約은, 다른 사람들의 立場에서 볼 때는, 亦是 自己네의 性的 獨占欲에 對한 保障이기도 하다. 이를테면 性的 不可侵의 連帶的 默約과도 같다. 如何튼 男女愛는 結婚을 通하여 私的 關係에서 公的 關係로 轉換한다.

結婚을 通하여 公的 關係로서 새 出發한 男女의 사랑은 이제 安定된 狀

---

10 東京大學의 和辻 敎授는 戀愛가 갖는 私的 性格을 다음과 같이 論述하고 있다. "男女가 사랑에 있어 存在를 같이할 때, 그들은 心身의 全體로서 서로 參與한다. 그들은 存在의 구석구석까지 相對에게 公開하고, 相對의 參與를 拒否하는 어떠한 點도 없다. 그러나 이 相互參與는 第三者의 參與를 嚴密히 拒否한다. 相對에게 나의 全體를 주었다는 것은, 同時에 第三者에게 그것을 拒否함을 意味한다. 두 사람 사이에 完全히 '私'가 消滅되기 爲하여서는 그 共同存在가 第三者에 對하여 完全히 私的이 아니면 아니 된다. 여기에 性的 共同存在의 顯著한 私的 性格이 있다. … 그렇다면 男女間의 사랑의 合一은 正常的으로 이루어진 境遇에도 顯著한 '私'를 나타내고 있으며, 다시 그 '私'가 지켜지지 않는 境遇에는, 사람으로 하여금 甚한 主觀的 苦悶에 빠지게 한다. 이 側面을 注目한다면, 男女愛에 있어서의 存在共同은 넓은 人間愛를 妨害하고, 人間의 客觀的 創造活動을 阻害하는 것으로서 排斥 當할 수밖에 없을 것이다."(『倫理學(中)』, pp.39-40)

態에 놓인다. 第三者의 侵入을 두려워하는 不安感이 解消되고, 情熱 代身에 理知가 두 사람을 묶는 새로운 紐帶로서 作用한다. 理知的이요 不安感없는 關係이기 때문에, 結婚한 男女는, 情熱에 사로잡힌 戀愛關係의 男女와는 달리, 社會 全體의 建設事業에 參與할 心身의 餘裕가 생긴다. 自然發生的인 男女愛는, 結婚으로서 制度化함으로써 그 閉鎖性을 克服하고 安定되는 同時에, 두 사람에게, 하나의 새로운 單位로서, 社會共同事業에 積極參與할 길을 연다. 結婚은 男女의 私的 要求와 社會의 公的 要求와를 棄揚하는 人倫의 制度이다.

[家族] 第三者 排除를 固執하는 私的 結合으로서의 男女愛는, 結婚을 通하여 夫婦가 됨으로써, 公的 關係로 轉換하였다. 이제 夫婦는 子女를 生産하여, 처음에 頑强히 排除하던 第三者를 스스로 導入함으로써 그 社會性을

---

11 結婚에는 二重의 約束이 包含되고 있다. 하나는 當事者 되는 男女 相互間의 約束이요, 또 하나는 結婚하는 두 사람 對社會 全體의 約束이다. 그 約束의 內容은 文化와 慣習에 따라 若干의 差異가 있을 것이나, 大體로 獨占的인 相互參與와 第三者의 排除를 그 中心內容으로 삼는다. 두 사람은 性的 結合이 두사람 사이에만 局限될 것을 約束하는 代價로서 이 私的 結合의 公認을 받으며, 두 사람 사이에 第三者가 侵入하는 境遇에는 社會는 이 第三者 排擊에 協助한다는 默約이 成立된다.
무릇 道德性의 根本은 '約束의 履行'에 있다. 夫婦의 道德도 夫婦間에 맺어진 約束을 지킴에 根本이 있다. 設令 그릇된 約束일지라도, 그것을 지키는 것은 約束을 지킨다는 그 點으로 볼 때엔 善이다. 그러나 約束이 너무나 그릇된 境遇에는, 그 約束 自體에 包含된 惡이 約束을 지킴으로써 實現되는 善보다도 더 큰 境遇가 있다. 夫婦間의 破約을 意味하는 離婚이 是認되는 것은, 그 約束 自體에 包含된 過誤가 破約으로 생기는 過誤보다도 더 크다고 認定되는 境遇에 있어서다. 그리고 約束은 兩便 當事者가 合意하면, 이를 解約할 수가 있다. 이것이 結婚에 適用된 것이 協議離婚이다. 그러나 結婚은 當事者들만의 約束으로 成立한 것이 아니라, 當事者間 및 當事者 對社會라는 二重約束으로 成立한 것이다. 따라서 協議離婚이라 할지라도, 그것을 社會가 옳다고 認定하지 않는 限, 社會에 對한 約束을 一方的으로 破棄했다는 非難을 免치 못한다. 結婚에 關聯된 惡을 行하지 않기 爲한 最善의 길은 輕率한 約束을 맺지 않는 일일 것이다.

더욱 强化한다.

夫婦를 連結하는 自然的 契機는 性別이었으나, 父母와 子女를 連結시키는 自然的 契機는 血緣이다. 元來 自然에서 出發한 性的 關係가 自然 以上의 것으로 發展했듯이, 元來는 自然으로서 맺어진 血緣關係도 單純한 自然關係에 머물지 않고, 自然 以上의 關係, 卽 '社會'로 發展한다. 性으로 結合된 夫婦關係에 血緣으로 連結된 父母 子女 關係가 參加하여서 생긴 社會가, 곧 '家族(family)'이다. 家族은, 個人과 個人을 連結하는 가장 原初的인 두 개의 紐帶, 卽 性과 血緣으로 엉킨, 社會를 構成하는 가장 基本的인 單位이다.

家族은 單純한 自然的 結合團體에 그치는 것이 아니기 때문에, 거기에는 여러 가지 人倫에 特有한 關係가 생긴다. 經濟的 共同과 扶養의 關係가 생기고, 夫婦와 父子, 兄弟間을 規律하는 各種 慣習과 道德이 생긴다. 親族法, 相續法 等이 規定하는 法律關係도 생긴다. 性이나 血緣의 關係가 單純한 自然關係로서 그칠 수 없고, 반드시 道德, 法律, 經濟 等의 人倫關係가 이에 關聯하게 되는 것은 社會的 存在로서의 人間生活의 特徵이다.

家族에 있어서의 自然의 契機, 卽 生物學的 關係는, 이를 因果律的 普遍의 關係라고 볼 수 있을 것이다. 그러나 家族에 있어서의 人倫의 契機, 卽 社會的 關係는, 經驗的 歷史의 産物이며 時代와 地域에 따라 그 形態가 一定하지 않다. 다시 말하면 家族에 關聯된 慣習, 道德, 經濟, 法律 等의 關係는 地域에 따라 差異가 있고, 時代에 따라 變遷이 있다. 새로운 文化가 交流되고, 政治, 經濟 等의 變動과 아울러, 時代의 새로운 慣習, 道德, 法律 等이 要求될 때에는, 家族을 둘러싼 慣習, 道德, 法律 等에도 이를 어떻게 改新할 것인가 하는 倫理問題가 생긴다.

子女가 成長하여 結婚함에 이르러 그들은 새로운 世代의 中心이 된다. '分家'의 現象을 通하여 하나의 家族이 數個의 家族으로 늘어 가면, 家族은

親族(kin) 또는 氏族(clan)으로 擴大된다. 古代社會에 있어서, 氏族은 같은 地域에서 集團生活을 營爲하여 經濟生活을 共有하며, 氏族의 長을 政事의 首位로 모시고, 氏族의 神을 宗敎的 信仰의 對象으로 삼는 等 緊密한 組織 社會를 形成하였다.

氏族을 形成하는 成員은 반드시 같은 血族뿐만은 아니었다. 血統이 다르더라도 偶然한 機會에 같은 地域에 살림하게 된 사람들은, 같은 氏族團體 속에 編入될 수가 있었다. 卽 地域的 連結性은 氏族을 形成시키는 또 하나의 契機였던 것이다. 地理的 隣近性, 卽 '地緣'은 血緣, 性別과 아울러 人間을 結束하는 또 하나의 紐帶였다. 氏族社會가 部落社會, 市民社會 等으로 變遷해 감에 따라서 社會的 紐帶로서의 地緣의 意義는 漸漸 增大해 갔다.

3) 地緣

[勞動] 우리가 그 위에 살고 있는 '땅'은 單純한 自然物은 아니다. 우리가 알고 있는 땅은 田畓, 山野, 住宅地, 道路 等 一定한 資格을 가진 땅이요, 單純히 抽象的인 '흙', 卽 化學的 物質의 合成에 不過한 것은 아니다. 우리가 理解하는 땅은 人間에 對하여 一定한 價値 乃至 用途를 가진 땅이다. 땅이 人間에 對하여 一定한 價値를 가질 수 있는 것은, 그것을 利用할 수 있는 人間의 '技術' 때문이다.

田畓으로 하여금 糧穀을 供給하게 하고 山野로 하여금 禽獸나 薪炭을 供給하게 하는 것은, 單純한 自然으로서의 土質이나 樹木이 아니라, 그 自然에 作用하는 人間의 技術이다. 그리고 技術은, 한 個人 또는 한 家族이 單獨으로 案出하는 것이 아니라, 그 背後에는 오랜 歷史와 넓은 社會의 協同이 있다. 그러므로 技術의 媒介를 通하여 形成된바, 人間의 生活地盤으로서의 '땅'은, 여러 사람이 共同으로 參與하는 場面이다. 田畓의 耕作은 그

地方에 共通된 道具와 技術의 使用, 그리고 이웃사람들의 共同作業을 通하여 이루어진다.

같은 땅 위에 산다는 것은 같은 技術을 使用한다는 것을 包含하며, 같은 技術을 使用한다 함은, 같은 勞動에 共同參與한다는 뜻을 갖는다. 土地의 共同과, 技術의 共同, 그리고 勞動의 共同은 같은 人間生活의 세 가지 側面이다. 勿論 人類가 아직 定着生活을 하지 않던 遊牧時代나 狩獵時代, 或은 그 以前을 생각한다면, 土地의 共同에 앞서서 技術의 共同이 있었고, 技術의 共同에 앞서서 勞動의 共同이 있었다. 共同勞動의 經驗이 技術의 發達을 招來했으며, 技術의 發達이 人類의 先祖로 하여금 固定된 地域에 定住함을 可能하게 한 것이다. 그리고 人類가 定住生活을 開始한 것은 人間의 社會性을 發展시키는 飛躍的 契機였다. 從前에는 性과 血緣만이 個人 相互間을 連結하는 紐帶였으나, 이제 定住를 契機로 '地緣'이 사람과 사람을 連結하는 새로운 媒介로서 登場한 것이다. 性과 血緣만을 紐帶로 삼고 形成된 社會는, 좁은 範圍의 人員만이 參與할 수 있는 小規模의 社會였다. 그러나 地緣이 사람과 사람을 連結하는 媒介가 되면서, 人間의 社會는 훨씬 廣範한 共同體를 形成할 可能性을 얻는다. 實로 地緣은, 人間의 社會로 하여금 家族이나 氏族이 가진 閉鎖的 境界를 넘어서서, 村落l이나 都市로 發展하고, 마침내 國家와 같은 巨大한 共同體를 組成하게 한 擴大의 契機였다.[12]

[經濟] 같은 地域에서 共通된 技術로 共同으로 勞動하는 人間의 集團은, 經濟的 組織을 가진 共同體이기도 하다. 各 集團의 傳統과 自然的 條件 等에 따라서, 그 集團에 特有한 生産方式이 發達한다. 生産의 目標가 定해짐

---

12 勞動, 技術, 道具 等에 關하여서는 高山岩男, 『哲學的 人間學』, 第二章 參照.

에 따라서 生産의 技術的 手段이 硏究되고, 이어서 勞動의 分擔이 마련된다. 다음에 亦是 그 集團의 傳統과 特殊性을 反映하는 一定한 方法으로 生産品 或은 그 價値가 分配된다. 將來에 對한 念慮에서 物品의 貯蓄이 勵行된다. 財物의 所有가 欲望充足의 手段으로서의 價値를 넘어서서 權力이나 名譽를 意味함에 이르러, 所有를 爲한 所有가 努力의 對象이 된다. 所有를 爲한 所有의 努力과 生産技術의 發達은 特定 生産品의 過剩을 招來하며, 特定 生産品의 過剩은 交通의 發達과 아울러 物品의 交易을 可能하게 한다. 未開의 段階에 있어서는, 生産, 分配, 所有, 交易 等 經濟活動의 秩序를 調整하는 것은 主로 慣習이다. 社會組織의 複雜化와 生存競爭의 激化에 따라서, 慣習만으로도 經濟生活의 秩序가 保障되기 困難한 段階에 이르면, 慣習은 强化되어 '法'으로 發展한다. 그리고 經濟生活을 둘러싼 慣習과 法의 背後에, 經濟生活을 둘러싼 道德觀念이 形成된다. 勿論 慣習과 法, 그리고 道德觀念의 이와 같은 形成은, 人間生活의 經濟面에서 뿐만 아니라 모든 部面에서 볼 수 있는 一般的 現象이다. 經濟的 活動은, 그 元來의 動機로 본다면, 人間의 生理的 欲求에 對應하는 것이다. 萬若 人間의 生理的 欲求가 人間의 欲求에 있어서 基本的인 것이라면, 그 基本的인 欲求에 對應하는 經濟活動도 亦是 人間의 活動 中 基本的인 것이라고 보아야 할 것이다. 이 點을 忘却한 從來의 倫理說이 現實性을 잃은 空論이 된 것은 自然스러운 일이었다. 現代의 倫理學은 經濟生活에 對하여 無關心할 수가 없다.

그러나 經濟生活의 重視가 精神生活의 輕視를 意味해서는 안 된다. 經濟生活이 人生에 있어 基本的이라 함은, 經濟生活이 人生의 全部임을 意味하지 않는다. 經濟生活의 重要性을 强調하는 一部의 思想家는 物質的 條件이 人間의 精神的 狀態를 一方的으로 決定하는 것처럼 생각하고자 한다. 그러나 物質的 條件과 精神的 狀態는 相互關係下에 있다. 經濟活動 自體가 單純히 物質만을 爲한 活動은 아니다. 經濟活動 가운데 이미 物質을 넘어서는 精神의 契機, 卽 '文化(culture)'의 契機가 있다.

[文化] 같은 地域에서 共通된 技術로 共同으로 勞動하는 人間의 集團은, 또한 文化的 共同體이기도 하다. 人間의 勞動은 그 原初의 出發點으로 본다면, 生理的 欲求의 充足을 爲한 手段이었다. 그러나 人間은 끝까지 生理的 欲求의 充足만을 爲하여 勞動하는 것은 아니다. 條件反應의 現象은 人間으로 하여금 象徵的 報酬(symbolic reward)를 爲하여도 努力하게 한다. 生理的 欲求의 充足을 爲하여 勞動하던 人間은, 一轉하여 生理的 欲求의 充足과는 關係없는 物品의 生産을 爲하여 勞動하게 되고, 나아가서는 狩臘의 스포츠化에 있어서 볼 수 있듯이, 勞動 그 自體를 爲하여 勞動하게까지 된다.

비록 原始部族의 農耕일지라도, 單純히 生存이 要求하는 農産物의 生産을 爲하여 必要한 最小限의 勞力만을 바치는 것은 아니다. 民俗學者들의 報告에 依하면, 그들은 自己네의 耕作地를 美化하는 데도 相當히 힘을 기울인다. 밭둑을 깨끗하게 整理하고 農産物을 보기 좋게 쌓는 데도 關心이 깊다. 오늘날은 한갓 營利를 爲하여 花草를 栽培하는 '園藝農業'이라는 것이 있다. 그러나 뜰앞이나 밭머리에 花草 및 나무를 가꾸는 元來의 心情에는 營利的 打算은 없었다. 또 園藝農業이 營利的으로 經營될 수 있는 것 自體가, 生存과 直接 關係없는 花草를 사랑하는 다른 사람들이 있기 때문이다. 우리의 住宅에는 비바람을 가리기에는 何等의 必要가 없는 여러 가지 裝飾이 있다. 우리의 衣裳은 單只 體溫만을 調節함으로 足할 수가 없다. 이와 같이 人間의 勞動이 生理的 欲求 滿足과는 直接 關係없는 對象에까지 波及되는 事實은, 人間生活은 '文化'라는 現象이 생기는 첫째 契機이다.

勞動은 非但 人間에만 特有한 現象은 아니다. 그러나 人間의 勞動은, 動物一般의 그것과는 한 가지 根本的인 差異를 가짐으로써, 人間으로 하여금 모든 動物 中에 特異한 存在로서 發展하게 하는 重要한 契機를 주었다. 人間勞動의 特質이란 人間의 勞動이 道具를 使用한다는 事實이다. 人間을 '道具를 만드는 動物' 또는 '工作人(homo faber)'으로 規定한 것은, 實로 人間本質의 一面을 把握한 洞察이었다. 人間이 道具를 만들 수 있는 것은 人間이 特別한 손을 가진 德澤이다. 人間이 特히 솜씨 있는 손을 가진 것은 人間이 知性 높은 動物이라는 事實의 裏面이며, 人間의 知性이 높은 것은 人間이 卓越한 손을 가졌다는 事實의 他面이다. 人間의 頭腦와 손은 相互 關聯下에 發達하여, 人間을 생각하면서 만들고 만들면서 생각하는 動物로 發展시켰다.[13] 人間이 知性과 技術을 가졌다는 事實은, 言語의 使用과 아울러, 人間生活에 '文化'라는 現象이 일어나게 된 契機 中에서 根本的인 것이었다.

原始部族에 있어서 宗敎的 活動은 生活의 重要한 部分을 차지한다. 播種 時에는 發芽를 祈禱하는 呪術的 儀式이 있고, 秋收期에는 多收獲을 感謝하는 祭祀가 施行된다. 가뭄에 祈雨祭, 建築에 上樑祭, 其他 時機 時機에 따라서 定期와 臨時의 宗敎的 儀式이 그칠 사이 없다. 宗敎儀式에는 彩色丹粧이 準備되고, 歌舞와 音曲이 隨伴한다. 人間의 歷史와 함께 長久한 傳統을 가진 人間의 宗敎觀念은, 人間生活에 文化라는 現象을 發展시킴에 있어 또 하나의 中心的 役割을 하였다.

文化財는 그것이 人工으로 만들어졌다는 點에서 純粹한 自然物과 區別된다. 自然物과 區別되는 文化財는 人間性의 가장 直接的인 表現이다. 다

---

13 일찍이 아낙사고라스(Anaxagoras, 500-428 B.C. 頃)는 人間은 손을 가짐으로써 動物 中 가장 知性 높은 存在가 되었다고 主張했다 하며, 아리스토텔레스는 反對로 人間은 가장 知性이 높은 까닭에, 卽 '생각하는 사람(homo sapiens)'인 까닭에 손을 가졌다고 主張하였다. 人間理性에 關한 經驗論과 先天論의 對立은 오늘도 哲學의 어려운 問題 中의 하나다.

시 말하면 文化는 가장 包括的인 意味에서 '人間的(human)'이다. 우리는 文化를 通하여 人間性의 具體相을 가장 如實하게 看取한다. 다음에 文化財는, 그 價値가 生理的 欲求를 充足시킬 수 있는 效能에 依存하지 아니함으로써, 單純한 物質과 區別된다. 文化財의 價値가 生理的 欲求의 充足을 떠나서 있다 함은, 그 價値가 社會的 欲求를 充足시키는 效能에 달려 있음을 意味한다. 或 價値의 純粹한 客觀性을 믿는 사람은, 文化財의 價値는 어떠한 欲求와도 關係없이, 그 自體가 擔持한다고 主張할는지도 모른다. 그러나 價値는 恒常 어떤 欲求 乃至 意志를 前提하고서 成立하는 것이다. 元來 人間的인 '文化'의 價値는 人間의 意慾을 떠나서 생각할 수가 없다. 文化財의 價値가 人間의 社會的 欲求를 充足시키는 效能에 달려 있다 함은, 文化가 '社會的' 産物임을 意味한다.

文化는 元來 社會的이다. 文化財의 價値는 그것이 他人에게 理解되는 데서 생긴다. 다시 말하면 그 '意味'가 他人에게 傳達되지 않는 文化財는 있을 수가 없다. 文化財를 만드는 사람은 반드시 그것을 鑑賞하고 理解해 줄 他人의 存在를 豫想하는 것이다. 讀者를 豫想하지 않고 글을 쓴다든지, 보아 줄 사람을 생각하지 않고 그림을 그릴 수는, 正常的으로는 없는 일이다. 秘密히 혼자 쓰는 日記에도 그것을 읽어 주는 空想의 人物이 있고, 혼자서 부르는 自慰의 노래에도 그것을 들어 주는 假想의 人物이 있다. 社會性은 文化財를 鑑賞하거나 理解하는 사람의 立場에도 나타난다. 아무리 좋은 映畵도 혼자 보아서는 興味가 없다. 혼자서 읽는 讀書도 讀後의 感想이나 知識을 他人과 交換할 可能性을 豫想함으로써 더욱 興이 있다. 같은 心理는 讀書 傾向에 流行性이 있다든지, 全혀 理解 못하는 音樂會를 能히 즐길 수 있다는 事實 等에 더욱 뚜렷이 나타난다.

文化는 '表現(expression)'을 通하여 文化가 된다. 文化에 있어서 表現되는 것은 人間性이요, 表現된 人間性의 가장 基本的인 特質은 그 社會性

에 있다. '人間的'이라는 것과 '社會的'이라는 것은 거의 相通하는 말이며, 文化가 人間的이요 同時에 社會的이라는 事實 위에 人間存在의 社會性이 如實히 나타나고 있다.

文化가 表現과 傳達에서 成立한다 함은, 文化가 사람과 사람을 連結하는 또 하나의 紐帶라는 것을 意味한다. 血緣, 性別, 地緣, 그리고 經濟關係가 사람과 사람을 連結시킴에 있어서는, 언제나 生理的인 欲求가 直接 關聯性을 가졌다. 그러나 文化가 社會的 紐帶로서 作用함에 있어서는 生理的인 要素는 直接 表面에 나오지 않는다. 따라서 우리는 '文化'의 紐帶를 '精神生活의 紐帶'라고 부를 수가 있다. 萬若 人間을 一般動物과 區別하는 特質이 人間의 '精神生活'에 있다면, 人間은 '文化'라는 紐帶를 가짐으로써 '人間'이 되었다고도 볼 수가 있다.

性은 가장 自然스럽고 緊密한 紐帶이기는 하나, 原則的으로 '두 사람'을 連結하는 閉鎖的 紐帶이다. 血緣은 團結의 範圍를 家族과 親族에까지 擴大하는 紐帶이기도 하나, 亦是 閉鎖性을 免치 못하였다. 地緣과 經濟關係는 莫大한 範圍를 連結할 수 있는 開放的 紐帶이나, 主로 利益社會 (Gesellschaft)를 形成하는 媒介이므로 內面的 必然性이 稀薄하다. 이에 比하여 文化는 가장 넓은 世界를 包攝하면서도 物質的 利害關係를 넘어서서 人間을 連結하는 데 그 特色이 있다. 性과 血緣이 좁은 共同社會 (Gemeinschaft)를 形成하는 紐帶라면, 文化는 넓은 共同社會를 形成하는 紐帶라 하겠다. 人間은 文化를 通하여 그 狹窄性을 克服한다.

經濟와 文化를 紐帶로 삼는 人間의 集團은, 그 理念으로 말하면, 全人類를 하나의 團體 안에 包攝할 때까지 擴張될 수 있을 것이다. 그러나 歷史的 現實에 있어서는 人間集團의 無限한 擴大를 制止하는 因子들이 있다. 例컨대 人間集團의 地域性, 民族性, 政治勢力의 傳統 等이다. 이러한 因子들의 制約을 받아 가며 자라난 人間의 集團이 歷史的 現段階에 있어서 到達한

最高의 經濟的, 文化的 地緣團體는 '國家(state)'이다.

[國家] 같은 地域에서 共通된 技術로 共同으로 勞動하는 人間의 集團, 即 地緣團體는 物質的 側面으로 본다면 經濟的 協同體였고, 精神的 側面으로 본다면 文化的 共同體였다. 物質의 生産, 分配, 所有, 交易 等에 關與하는 人間의 經濟的 關係는 一面으로 보면 相互協助的인 關係이기도 하나, 他面으로 보면 利害對立的인 關係이기도 하다. 經濟生活에 利害對立의 一面이 있음은 物質의 有限性에 基因하는 必然的 現象이다. 이와 같은 利害의 對立을 調停하는 基準으로서 慣習이 있었고, 法律이 있었고, 또는 道德觀念이 있었다. 이때 慣習, 法律 또는 道德觀念으로 하여금 現實的인 規範으로서 行勢하게 하려면, 이 規範的 意思를 代辯할 만한 實力을 가진 指導勢力 乃至 統制勢力이 必要하다. 그리고 이와 같은 指導나 統制의 任務를 맡아보는 中樞勢力은, 모든 團體에 있어서, 自然發生的으로 생기거나 또는 人爲를 加하여서 作定된다. 家族에 있어서 指導權을 잡는 것은 家長이요, 氏族에 있어서는 氏長者이다. 地緣團體에 있었서도 各其 團體의 規模에 따라서 特色 있는 中心勢力이 생긴다.

指導勢力 乃至 統制勢力은, 地緣團體의 精神的 側面인 文化活動에 있어서도 作用한다. 文化는 元來 '社會的'이었다. 元來 社會的인 까닭에 文化는, 設令 어떤 個人을 通하여 表現되는 境遇에도, 그 表現된 內容은 全體로서의 社會性을 잃지 않는다. 이에 文化에 있어서 가장 優勢하게 表現되는 것은, 大體로 그 社會에 있어서 가장 優勢한 思潮를 反映하는 것이라고 볼 수 있다. 그러므로 어떤 社會에 있어서 實權을 잡은 中樞勢力이 그 社會에서 가장 優勢한 思潮를 掌握하고 있는 동안, 그 中樞勢力은 經濟生活에 있어서 指導的 任務를 擔當할 뿐만 아니라, 그 文化活動에 있어서도 指導的 立場에 서는 擁護者가 된다. 그러나 時代의 變遷이 從來의 支配的 勢力의

意思와 背馳되는 思潮를 惹起하는 境遇에는, 支配的 勢力은 새로운 思潮를 反映하는 새로운 文化에 對하여 彈壓의 立場을 取하는 것이다. 이와 같은 事情은, 古來로 政治와 宗敎의 關係에 있어서 가장 如實히 나타나고 있다. 原始的 部族社會에 있어서 政事를 맡아 본 사람이 宗敎的 行事까지 兼擔한 것은 前者의 典型이요, 歷史上의 大部分의 政權이 所謂 '異敎'에 對하여 苛酷한 彈壓者였다는 事實은 後者의 典型이다.

經濟와 文化 兩面에 對한 統制力이 가장 強한 團體로서 '國家'가 있다. 國家는 地緣團體 中에 가장 巨大하고 複雜한 組織을 가진 團體이다. 國家는 一定한 地域을 領土로 삼고, 그 領土 위의 住民을 原則的으로 全部 그 成員으로서 包攝한다. 國家가 다른 地緣團體에 比하여 特異한 點은, 그 領土 內의 國民生活을 統制하는 權力, 卽 統治權이, 그 領土上에 存立하는 어떠한 團體보다도 優越한 絕對性을 가질 뿐만 아니라, 그 領土 밖에 있는 어떠한 團體로부터도 支配 當하지 않는 獨立性을 가졌다는 點에 있다.

國家의 統治權이 保有하는 이와 같은 絕對性은, 國家 그 自體를 絕對視하는 數많은 國家論을 빚어내는 心理的 根據가 되었다. 論者들은, 或은 國家를 '人倫(Sittlichkeit)'의 最高 發展段階라고 부르고(Hegel), 或은 "私我를 完全히 超克하여 徹頭徹尾 公的인 共同體"(和辻)[14]라고 論斷하였다. 이와 같은 論說의 存在는, 國家統治權의 威力이 그 國民의 思想 위에 莫大한 影響을 미친다는 것을 立證하는 좋은 事例라고 볼 것이다.

全體主義的 國家絕對論에 對稱的인 것으로서, 國家를 個人의 安寧과 福祉를 爲한 手段이라고 보는 思想이 있다. 그러나 國家는 元來 個人을 爲한 手段으로서 만들어진 것은 아니다. 아무도 幸福의 手段으로서 國家를 創設한 사람은 없다. 國家는 人間에 있어 必然的인 存在樣式이다. 國家는 하나의 現實이요, 個人에 對하여서는 運命的인 所與이다. 人間은 個人의 意思를 超越하여 血緣과 性으로 連結되었고, 地緣으로 連結되었다. 人間의 生

活이 必然的으로 社會生活인 까닭에, 거기에는 必然的으로 經濟라는 現象이 생겼고, 또 文化라는 現象이 생겼다. 그리고 經濟現象과 文化現象을 가진 團體生活에 있어서, 自然히 支配와 被支配의 關係가 생겼고 '政治'라는 現象이 必然的으로 發生한 것이다. 政治는 人間의 社會性과 物質의 有限性이 빚어낸 必然的 歸結이다. '國家'란, 바로 '政治的 獨立性을 가진 地緣團體'를 意味하는 것이다. 따라서 國家도 社會的 動物로서의 人間의 必然的인 存在樣式이다.

性別과 血緣關係는 人間에 있어 必然的인 制約이다. 그러나 性과 血緣으로 連結된 人間社會를 어떻게 組織하는가, 例컨대 어떠한 家族制度를 갖는가는 人間이 歷史的으로 作定하는 것이다. 政治, 따라서 國家라는 現象도 人間에게 必然的인 制約이다. 그러나 우리가 어떠한 政治 또는 어떠한 國家를 갖는가는, 人間이 歷史的으로 決定한다. 여기에 人間的 自由의 出發點이 있다.

---

14 和辻哲郎은 그의 『倫理學』 中卷에 있어서 人間社會의 發展段階를 家族, 親族, 地緣共同體, 文化共同體, 國家로 區分하고, 各 段階는 上記한 順序에 따라 大體로 包攝關係에 있는 것같이 보고 있다. 그는 地緣團體를 一種의 共同體(Gemeinscheft)로 보고, '鄕土'를 그 典型的인 것으로 본다. 그는 文化共同體의 最高發展體로서 民族을 보고, 國家는 諸民族을 統合하는 最高의 共同體라고 認定하였다.

그러나 文化共同體와 地緣團體로 國家 안에 包攝되는 槪念으로 보기는 困難하다. 도리어 國家가 地緣團體의 一種이라고 보아야 한다. 그리고 그는, 文化共同體는 '閉鎖的'인 團體이나 國家는 그보다 훨씬 '開放的'인 絕對的 團體라고 主張하였다. 그러나 이것도 亦是 首肯하기 困難하다. 文化에는 恒常 國境을 넘어서서 普遍의 世界로 달아나려는 一面이 있다. 文化에도 勿論 地域性이 있다. 그러나 國家에 比한다면 더 開放的인 것이다. 그리고 그는 國家를 '私我'를 떠난 共同體라고 보고 地緣團體는 國家 內部에 包含되는 것으로 보았기 때문에, 地緣團體도 亦是 私利를 超越한 '共同體'로 보지 않을 수 없었다. 그러나 地緣團體를 함부로 '共同體'로 規定하기도 困難하다. 地緣團體에는 共同社會的인 面과 利益社會的인 面이 아울러 있기 때문이다. 그의 以上과 같은 國家觀에서 우리는, 所謂 大東亞戰爭을 惹起하고 '八紘一宇'를 꿈꾸던 當時 日本의 皇國主義의 反映을 看過할 수가 없다.

NATURALISM AND EMOTIVISM

— SOME ASPECTS OF MORAL JUDGMENTS —

ABSTRACT

The main purpose of this dissertation is to approach one of the basic problems in ethics, *whether, and to what extent, moral judgments can be justified or rejected on empirical grounds*. But since any approach to this problem naturally presupposes the clarification of the meaning of moral expressions, I have been obliged to give considerable space to a study of evaluative language.

In view of the difficulty of my subject I have found it necessary to begin with a careful tracing of some great writers' achievements in the same subject. Among contemporary ethical philosophers I have chosen three American writers, Dewey, Perry and Stevenson. As a matter of fact, the greater part of the present thesis consists of a study of these three men's ethical views. In this sense my present work is only preliminary.

After analyzing each theory I attempted an evaluation or criticism of it. On the basis of my evaluation of the three chosen theories I have tried, in the last chapter, tentatively to orient my own view-point. But the phrase "*my own* view-point" is misleading; for what I call "mine" has been remarkably conditioned by the three writers as well as by some others.

As far as the problem of the meaning of moral expressions is concerned, the view which I have defended in my concluding chapter is close to Stevenson's position. Yet it disagrees with his in some significant aspects. In those respects where I parted from Stevenson, "my" view seems to have been influenced by such philosophers as R. M. Hare and J. L. Austin. But I have never intended simply to combine or compromise several more or less different thoughts. I have endeavored, first of all, to follow the line that my criticisms in the earlier chapters suggest.

As for the methodological problem of the justification of moral utterances, perhaps I have been more influenced by Dewey than by any other writers. In connection with this problem, I think, my last sections involve also some independent ideas, though not original.

My last chapter has been led by the conviction that it is advisable for a student to have his own tentative position provided he is willing to correct or give it up whenever reasons require. Thus "*Concluding Remarks*" is not a very good name for the chapter, which concludes this dissertation but nothing else.

Contents

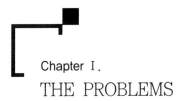

Chapter I.
THE PROBLEMS

1.

The fact that every kind of science must be based upon certain assumptions, and that consequently even those proposition which are recognized to be "scientific" cannot, unless they are tautological, be completely proved, constitutes one of the most unfortunate limitations of human knowledge. Unless we trust either the senses or the intellect or some other faculty of the human mind we can assert nothing. Moral philosophy, or ethical science, then, is not the only field of human investigation the reasonings of which can be verified only when we assume to be true those principles which play (explicitly or implicitly) the part of major premises in our thinking. But it does not seem to be quite without reason that traditional ethical theories have been charged with being "unscientific" or "dogmatic." In other words, it might well be argued that the assumptions on which traditional ethical theories have been based are *more* unhappy than those which have become the "first" principles of other branches of science or philosophy.

When an assumption or a hypothesis, though it cannot be strictly proved in principle, is taken to have some kind of intuitional or empirical ground, then we might accept it as "tenable." The assertion that assumptions on which traditional ethics is founded are more unhappy must mean that they cannot be credited with even such unsatisfactory tenability as is recognized in connection with the basic principles of non-value sciences. Since traditional moral philosophers found their final objective in answering those normative problems which are essential to human situations, they looked for the justifying ground of their theories mostly in the intuitional evidence of their fundamental principles. (For, a normative conclusion must have a normative principle as its major premise, and those normtive principles on which traditional philosophers based their maxims, while refusing any empirical proof, seemed to them intuitionally true.) Traditional ethical theories were fortunate enough to enjoy a long period of devotion to the "self-evident" truth of their basic principles. Some philosophers believed that the truth of moral principles was as obvious as that of mathematical principles. Some of those rationalists who held that sense perceptions were exceedingly misleading might have maintained, for instance, that the ultimate end of human beings (e.g., to realize men's potential functions) was more evident than the fact that an elephant is larger than an ant. When, however, the self-evidence or the intuitional obviousness of moral principles once became doubtful, the predicament which endangered the status of ethical philosophy seemed much more serious than those which other branches of philosophy or of science had to encounter in connection with Skepticism.

Students who were engaged in the investigations of non-value problems, when they became desperately skeptical about their "a priori" principles which had been held "self-evident," could finds alternative ways of verifying their assertions by relying upon certain empirical methods. Students who concerned themselves in other fields of the science of values than ethics (e.g., political economy) could manage to maintain their professions by promptly shifting the focus of attention from a normative to a descriptive point of view. It seems, for example, that Plato did not consider esthetics to be primarily a descriptive science. For him such normative problems as "What kind of poetry is to be admitted in the ideal state?" or "What should an artist regard as the criteria of good works of art?" remained important to the last. Again, classical philosophers such as Aristotle, Hobbes and Spinoza, when they were engaged in the problems of politics, seem to have had in mind "What is the *good* polity?" as the final question of political philosophy. However, modern philosophers of art might find it unwise to be too much occupied in the attempt of finding criteria of beauty. It would seem safer for them to concentrate rather on the study of the process of the creative activity or on the psychological analysis of the work of art. Few modern writers seem to consider political science primarily a normative science. Many would hold that historical descriptions, some kinds of classification, finding some sorts of causal relations, and so on, are enough to make a political theory "scientific."

Many students of moral philosophy, however, find difficulty both in establishing alternative ways of verifying their assertions by relying on certain empirical methods and in maintaining their profession by simply shifting their viewpoints. The claim that an ethical utterance such as "X is good" or "Y is our duty" does not convey any factual information and, accordingly, is neither true nor false is by no means an entirely negligible objection against the foundation of ethical philosophy. It may well be argued that most moral utterances contain some cognitive factors and that their truth or falsity can be examined in terms of these cognitive factors. Indeed it seems broadly admitted that the logical positivists were wrong when they held that the moral utterance implied no descriptive factors at all, but it seems also undeniable that those descriptive factors which are included in an ethical utterance do not constitute the *whole meaning* of that utterance. It seems difficult even to show that the descriptive factors in an ethical statement constitute the main elements which compose the meaning of that statement. It is quite problematic, therefore, whether we are entitled to claim that we have established an ethical statement when we proved all the descriptive factors in the statement to be true. In any case it seems clear that we cannot test a value–judgment in the light of "observation" as easily as we do in the case of a fact–judgment.

And this difficulty which is peculiar to the establishment of a value-judgment seems to have its root in the peculiar nature of the assumption on which the value-judgment is based.[1]

Students of moral philosophy also find it difficult to give up entirely all attempts to lay a foundation for the solution of normative problems of human conduct. It is, of course, not impossible to confine ourselves to the mere description of moral phenomena, and some writers actually have tried to establish the "science of morals" by shutting off all kinds of normative problem. But the attempt to exclude normative problems from the field of ethics seems to involve at least two difficult points. In the first place, this attempt might be in danger of resulting in the suicide, so to speak, of ethics. What peculiar realm remains to be investigated by ethics distinct from psychology, sociology and anthropology or from their combinations, if ethics confines itself to the mere description of moral phenomena? Secondly, this attempt, if successful, would not satisfy that dearest desire of mind which originally drove man toward the study of ethics.

A man might indeed begin to interest himself in ethical study merely from cognitive curiosity concerning phenomena of morals; or it might be also conceivable that even a trivial motive, such as getting a job in a college, can help a man to choose the field of moral philosophy. But it seems hardly probable that mere cognitive curiosity, interest in one's

---

1 What is the peculiar nature of the ethical assumtion will be considered later. (Ch. V)

maintenance, and such are the main motives which caused the origin of ethical philosophy in the history of ideas and has made this prosaic and painstaking study continue for almost twenty–five centuries. It is a deep–rooted activity of human mind to long for some ideal, and the motive which drives a man to moral philosophy seems to be closely connected with the ideal–longing passion.

It would be admitted then that ethics has its origin in normative questions and has its final objective in normative answers. We may possibly establish a system of ethical study without bothering ourselves with that annoying problems of "What ought to be?" But it would be a poor performance for an artist who started with an intention of painting a tiger to end by picturing a cat even if it were a successful picture of a cat. It is true that meta–ethics has come to claim its own independent value. Paradoxically enough, some ethical theories have come to fame by plausibly negating, in effect, the possibility of ethics. Again, the *technical* advance of philosophy has been sometimes promoted by philosophers' losing sight of their original objectives. But it is suspected that a technically advanced ethical theory might involve some deformity in its advancement if it had nothing important to say concerning the serious problems of practical life.

2.

A foundation of normative ethics would be laid, if a method were given by which ethical statements could be justified or rejected. Those who can *see*, following the intuitional tradition in ethics, the "self-evidence" of some moral principles have already gained what they needed; for those who can, following the metaphysical tradition, commit themselves to some dogmatic principles the foundation is already laid; those who can simply give up normative problems are not concerned here. Troubled are those who can, being empirically minded, neither see any self-evident principle nor commit themselves to any metaphysical principles, but who, as human being, find it none the less difficult to clearly cut off their lingering attachment to the finding of a theoretical foundation for a "better" life. The present dissertation is concerned with just the problems those troubled people are obliged to encounter.

It is quite natural for empirically-minded students to try to find principles of ethics on some empirical ground; and the empirical tradition of ethics is as old, at least, as the Sophists. The classical empiricism in ethics, however, seems to have involved some fundamental defects. Firstly, the psychological knowledge on which classical empiricists grounded their ethical systems was so naive and mistaken that their theories have proved to be untenable in the light of modern psychology. The fallacies of psychological hedonism and of psychological egoism are good examples of this sort. The belief that the prescriptions of conscience are uniform everywhere and at all times might be added for another example. Secondly, the classical empiricism seems to have more or less confused the descriptive and normative problems in ethics. (Though some of the classical empiricists implicitly assumed the distinction between meta-ethics and normative ethic, it was far from being complete enough.) And this confusion often helped philosophers to jump from non-value premises to value conclusions. John Stuart Mill's reasoning that general happiness is *desirable* because each person *desires* his own happiness might be considered as an example of this kind of confusion.[1]

It seems to have been just this logical confusion between "what is" and "what ought to be," together with the immature conclusion that human nature is uniform, which enabled some classical empiricists to believe that they had established a firm foundation for the universally binding normative ethics on the base of empirical facts. In short, they believed that they could directly derive the universal prescription of conduct from the universal description of human nature.

When critical minds among ethical empiricists notice the above mentioned serious defects in its classical version, they are obliged to search for some new scheme, unless they agree with the position that the ethical statement is neither true nor false in any sense. Is it the inevitable conclusion empiricists or naturalists must reach that there can be no standard of value, if it is admitted that different people feel, desire and think different things? Is it the necessary conclusion that human nature is quite irrelevant to the decision of what we ought to do, or rather is it to be claimed that there is nothing in the world which we ought to do, if we admit that there is an insurmountable gap between the realm of *is* and that of *ought*?

There is something in us which strongly rejects each of the above suggested conclusions. It is noteworthy that, even among those who believe there is no value apart from sentient being's feeling, thinking, or interest, a strong conviction is still attached to the following ideas: i) There must be some standard of values which is not altogether a reflection of individual taste or caprice. ii) There are things which we ought, or ought not, to do; even though we may well reject all sorts of heteronomous obligations such as are derived from theological or political authorities of from some metaphysical beliefs, we cannot entirely deny the reality of the *autonomously* charged obligations, whether they are based on human nature or on some necessary modes of human life.

That the aforesaid conviction-like ideas have no tenable ground, of course, is not inconceivable. But it would not be entirely meaningless to try once again to find whether there are any grounds to support these ideas, even though there might be some chance for the attempt to be ended simply with some psychological explanation. Thus, we ask: (Provided we avoid all psychological errors classical empiricists used to fall in, and provided we do not smuggle in any normative factors in the discussion of purely descriptive facts;) i) Can we verify or justify any standard of moral values on an empirical basis? Can we show some empirical ground why we ought to act in this or that way? Or rather we may unify or fuse these two questions into one by putting them in another way; namely, would it be possible to find some empirical way of justifying (or rejecting) ethical utterances without committing any psychological or logical errors? And these are the central problems with which the present thesis is concerned.

It seems advisable for a student of ethics to study, before attempting to wrestle with these difficult problems by himself, what modern empiricists say or suggest about those problems. I shall choose three big figures among contemporary American ethical writers: John Dewey, Ralph B. Perry, and Charles L. Stevenson. These three philosophers seem to have something in common in their basic standpoints while disagreeing in some important ways. It is hoped that a careful study of their works will prove to be a good starting–point for our fundamental problems.

Since the present dissertation is not primarily concerned with historical exposition, the following chapters will not touch upon every aspect of the three ethical theories under consideration. Attention will be concentrated on some major points which have direct connections with our problems.

The difficulty of verification which is peculiar to value statements seems to be rooted in the peculiarity of the value–predicate. There is no difference between the forms of the value judgment and those of the non–value judgment; besides one and the same concept can be a subject of both kinds of the judgment. Accordingly the characteristic of the value statement is to be found in its predicate. It follows, therefore, that special attention should be paid to the meanings and natures of ethical predicates. "The fundamental problem of theory of value," says Perry, "is to define the *concept* of value."[2]

Since all of our three philosophers take the teleological point of view, more attention will be given to the concept of Good. The status of "good," especially whether it has an objective status in the universe, independent of interest, desire, feeling or valuation, will be carefully considered. The problem of "intrinsic" versus "extrinsic" good will also be touched. Other moral concepts such as Right, Ought, and Duty will also be studied, though with less emphasis. Perhaps some attention should be paid to the relations between ethical terms, especially to the relations between "good" and other concepts.

If we could clarify what meanings each of our philosophers finds or gives to those main ethical concepts, the nature of the ethical utterance, namely, whether it conveys some information about facts, simply expresses the utterer's feelings or wishes, or has some still different meaning, would be brought to light. But some of our philosophers might hold that ethical concepts are not to be defined as such; they might rather maintain that the natures of ethical terms are better understood through the analysis of the act of valuation itself. Or again, some of our philosophers might hold that the meaning or nature of an ethical predicate can be properly understood only when the meaning of the statement in which that predicate is involved is clarified, and that the analysis of the ethical *statement*, not that of the term, is primary. If this happens to be the case we must, of course, follow their own lines.

If the meanings of ethical concepts and ethical statements could thus be brought to light the cognitive status of the ethical statement would become clear, and then we would be ready to proceed toward our main problem, that is, "Would it be possible to find some empirical way of justifying (or rejecting) ethical statements?"

Perhaps, some comparison between our three philosophers might be made in the course of discussion. But with the comparison as such the present thesis is not primarily concerned.

Now we shall begin with Perry and through Dewey come to Stevenson.[2]

---

2 This order is not exactly in accord with the chronological one. It is chosen because some advancement, from the present thesis' point of view, seems to be recognizable in that order.

Chapter Ⅱ.
PERRY: VALUE AND INTEREST

1.

For Perry the problems of "value" and the problems of "moral value" are to be distinguished, and the solution of the latter must be grounded on that of the former. Value in the *moral* sense, he holds, begins with the bearing of "lower" values, upon "higher" values. Moral judgments are concerned with "organizations of values, whether in the personal or in the social life."[1] Morality then, it might be argued, consists in pursuing some sort of "higher" or "greater" values. If so, the meaning of moral concepts, the clarification of which Perry would think to be the primary concern for an ethical investigation since he holds that "the fundamental problem in theory of value … is the problem of definition,"[2] must be defined in terms of "higher" and "lower," or "greater" and "smaller," values. Accordingly, before the definitions of moral concepts are attempted the definition of "value" *in its generic sense* must be achieved. If we could define the genus and could discover the differentia of the species the definition would be logically complete. Thus Perry's study begins with the definition of value in general. "What is value generically?"

Before setting about the task of defining value, Perry deems it necessary to dispose of the challenge by those who assert the indefinability of value. The main points in his answer to this challenge are: i) The assertion that value is adjectival rather than subjective and that a predicate cannot be defined in terms of that of which it is predicated, is sound. But this does not prove that an adjectival term, or a predicate, must be indefinable, because a concept is indefinable only when it is unanalyzable, and because it is not always the case that a predicate is unanalyzable. (Whether a given predicate is simple or complex is a question of fact.)[3] ii) Though Moore, Russell, Santayana and Brentano claim that the value character is unanalyzable, none of them has proved its unanalyzability; what they have proved is, at best, that most alleged definitions of good (or value) were unacceptable, which is not the proof of the indefinability of that term.[4] iii) Moore's assertion that if good could be defined it must be equated with a set of other concepts than good, and that this is impossible because, given any set of concepts not containing good, it is always pertinent to inquire whether it is good, is, though it deserves "more serious consideration," not decisive; for this assertion owes its plausibility to its overlooking the fact that one and the same thing can be both good in some sense and not good in some other sense.[5]

Perry's arguments here summarized are only negative; for what they prove is, at best that Moore and other writers could not prove the indefinability of good. In other words, his arguments do not, in themselves, prove the definability of good. This would be proved if he could present us an acceptable definition. Let us proceed to see how he himself define "value" in its generic sense.

2.

In one of his later works, the *Realms of Value*, Perry remarks two quite significant things at the outest of his attempt to define "value." In the first place, he makes it clear, by reffering to the distinction between the questions, "What does 'value' mean?" and "What things have value?", that what he is seeking for is to define "value" *in terms of its connotation*, but not in terms of its denotation.[6] This remark seems to be noteworthy because, while it apparently suggests that Perry takes care to avoid the so-called Naturalistic Fallacy, it might become one of the criteria by which the success or the failure of his attempt to define value can be estimated. In the second place, Perry points out that there is no "established and universal meaning" of value, and that the problem of its definition is not to *discover* a present meaning — since "there are only too many meanings" — but to *give* a meaning to the term, "either by selecting from its existing meanings, or by creating a new meaning."[7] This point is not explicitly mentioned in his earlier works. It is not necessary to affirm whether Perry was influenced here by Stevenson's criticism in terms of "persuasive difinition" or not. What is more important for us is: how does he, admitting the absence of the universal meaning, justify his own definition as an "unemotional" and "scientific" one, which he had proposed to establish in the *General Theory of Value*[8] and never gave up attempting to do? In any case Perry's position, which not only declares that theory of value is "in search of a preferred meaning," but also claims that the task of defining "value" is not an arbitrary matter,[9] must be subtle.

Among problems concerning the definition of value perhaps the most crucial is the problem whether value has its objective status in the world independent of some sentient being's feelings, desiring, thinking or any other motor–affective experience, or whether on the other hand it owes its status to some being's attitudes or experience — the problem which is straightforwardly expressed in that commonplace puzzle, "Is a thing valuable because it is valued, or is a thing valued because it is valuable?"

If we employ the term "interest" to represent the all aspects of the motor–affective life — "desire, feeling, will and all their family of states, acts and attitudes," theories concerning the definition of value may be classified in terms of the relation of value to interest as follows:

a) Theories which hold that value is *irrelevant to interest*.

b) Theories which hold that value is *the qualified object of interest*.

c) Theories which hold that value is *the object of qualified interest*.

d) Theories which hold that value is *any object of any interest*.[10]

(A) Among the first type of theories are included, for example, those which view value as "immediately perceived" empirical quality, as a "logical indefinable," as "help" or "fitness," as "self-realization and unity."[11] Theories of this type are, according to Perry, all unacceptable, because they either fail to apply to "value" at all or smuggle some sorts of interest into their definitions.

The doctrine which maintains that values are immediately perceived empirical qualities is an example of those which are entirely inapplicable to value. If value is a perceptual quality it must be actually given in our perception; but, Perry argues, we do not see any such

> a distinct quale which appears in that region which value terms roughly indicate, and which is different from the object's shape and size, from the interrelation of its parts, from its relaton to other objects, or to a subject; and from all the other factors which belong to the same context, but are designated by words other than "good."[12]

Nor is Moore's comparison of "good" and "yellow" quite sound; for the former does not possess the self-evidence of the latter.[13] Almost all normal people agree over the meaning of the term "yellow," and as to the distribution of that quality; but why there is so much difference of opinion in connection with "good?"

The fundamental misconception of the theory under consideration, Perry continues to criticize, consists in its failure to recognize the peculiar nature of the so-called "tertiary" qualities. The advocates of the theory, having affirmed the extra-mental existence of what are called "secondary qualities," proceed a step further to admit the same objectivity to the "tertiary" qualities. A little consideration, however, will suffice to show that the "tertiary" qualities are strongly affected by some reactions of subjects. This is manifested by the fact that when we closely examine the "tertiary" qualities they clearly appear "to be either modes of attitude or impulse, and thus motor; or sensory qualia which are localized in the body," while we fail when we, by an act of attention, "endeavor to localize the red of cherry in the subject."[14]

An example of the first type theories which bring in interest in their definition without admitting the fact, can be found in the "self-realization" view. One version of this theory maintains that goodness consists in the complete exemplification of those attributes or capacities which are peculiar to the kind to which the thing in question belongs. The good for man, for example, is to realize the peculiar faculty of man, namely, "reason." But this view involves "a disguised circularity." Reason is by no means the only faculty peculiar to the human being; man is, for instance, often said to be the only animal which can laugh. However, no self-realizationist claims that the best man is he who laughs "longest and loudest." Here it is evident that the goodness of reason has been already taken for granted before "good" is defined in terms of "self-realization." In other words, for the self-realizationist goodness lies not in the bare realization of *any* faculty peculiar to the kind, but is borrowed from the nature of some *selected* faculties. And through the hole of "selection" interest is stealthily introduced, for it is the *interested* being who selects![15)](15)

Another example of the class in question is the view which defines goodness as the relation of *fitness*—the view which is familiar even in common sense in the popular expression of "good for." But goodness does not, Perry criticizes, consists in the bare relation of "fitness" itself. If A is fit for B, A is good when and only when B is recognized as good. But B's goodness, in turn, is not finally defined in terms of fitness. It is a fact of experience that fitness for one thing is judged good, while fitness for another thing bad. Here, again, selection comes in, which presupposes participation of interest.[16)](16) One might object that there are cases in which fitness is judged to be good for itself. But Perry would answer that it is the case because man sometimes *is interested in* or desires fitness itself.

(B) The basic assumption of the second type of theories, namely, that which maintains that value is the qualified object of interest, is that certain objects are *qualified* to evoke interest, while other ones are not. As there is the "true north" as the right direction which every compass should point to, even though some actual compasses may point to some other directions, there are *right* objects to which interest should be directed. This means that cases are conceivable in which interest is *mis*-directed. It is obvious that in this view the final defining principle of value is not interest; goodness lies in the nature of objects. Some relation, to be sure, is recognized between value-objects and interest. But this relation is not essential for the goodness of the objects.

What then are the "right" objects of interest? And on what ground are those "right" objects entitled to the monopolization of interest? Perry refers to four conceptions in terms of which the "right" of certain objects to demand interest has been defended. They are: i) the conception of "purposiveness," ii) the conception of the "desirable as power to move desire," iii) the conception of the "desirable as capable of being desired," iv) the conception of the "ought−to−be."[17]

Perry, however, finds that none of those conceptions proves the normative nature of certain objects; for all of them are based on some metaphysical principles which are by no means well−established.

The notion of "purposiveness" appears in various forms of teleological interpretations of the universe, of which Platonic metaphysics is a notable instance. According to these views, everything in the world exists for some pre−established purpose, and therefore a subject's interest ought to be directed to objects in accordance with its given purpose. But Perry sees no warrantable grounds for any of those teleological interpretations of the universe. He suspects that the teleological views are promoted by what he calls the "pathetic fallacy," namely, by the "tendency on the part of a purposive being to impute to another purpose that which coincides with his own, but which has not, as a matter of fact, resulted from it."[18]

The conception of the "desirable as power to move desire" appears in the notions of Aristotelian God, the Thomistic Unmoved Mover, and so forth. Such phrases of customary speech as "repelling ugliness" and "irresistible temptation" can be regarded as the expression of the same notion in the common sense level. In this notion also Perry recognizes the same "pathetic fallacy." The force of desire lies not in the desired object but in the disposition of the desiring subject. "That in temptation which a man finds it difficult to resist," tells Perry, "is not the strength of the object, but the strength of his own appetite. The object releases this strength but does not supply it."[19]

According to the class of views which interpret the "desirable" as *capable* of being desired, "there is a specific *capacity* to be desired, which is complementary to the faculty of desire, and by virtue of the possession of which, things are held to be good."[20] There are several versions of this type of view. Some hold that "self" is the only thing which can be desired; some others maintain that only "satisfaction" can be desired; and still others name still other things — "existence," "the intelligible" etc. — as the only object capable of being desired. And Perry finds for each of these views some reasons which make it unacceptable.[21] But we need not follow his somewhat verbal discussions here. In fact, it was not necessary for Perry to have troubled himself to reject the present class of views, as far as the problem at issue, the *meaning* of value, is concerned. For, from the formal point of view, there is no incompatibility between the view that "only some qualified object can be desired" and the view that "value is any object of any interest" — out fourth type of theories.[1] Let us then proceed to the notion of the "ought-to-be."

According to this last version of the "qualified object of interest" theory, the valuable is that which *ought to be*. Value stands between being and nonbeing; value has a claim upon existence. But this "oughtness" does not come from any subjective ideal. It is not because some one aspires after an ideal that the ideal ougut to be. On the contrary, we should aspire after an ideal because it is, in its own nature, something which ought to be. But how do we know that something ought to be? "It is known," they answer, "by direct acknowledgments."[2]

But the difficulty involved in this view is "quite palpable," Perry criticizes, because it must meet the same objections which have confronted all sorts of intuitive and formalistic doctrines of value. The "direct acknowledgments," first of all, do not always agree with each other. Thus it becomes necessary to provide some criterion by which the validity of the acknowledgments is to be judged. But if we try to find this criterion on the side of the objective being, we must commit ourselves to some unwarranted metaphysical principle; while if we attempt it on the side of the acknowledging subject, we must admit some absolute or standard act of mind which is not discovered in experience.[22)]

(C) Our third type of view holds that only the object of some qualified interest is the valuable. The basic assumption of this class of views is

---

1 The same argument could have been applied to the aforesaid dispution concerning the conception of the "desirable as power to move desire."
2 Perry refers to W. M. Urban as a writer who holds this kind of view. *General Theory of Value*, pp.77-79.

that there are qualificatory differences between various interests. In other words, they maintain that "the modes of the motor—affective life, the desires and affections of living creatures, are not to be accepted as they stand, but condemned as partial, blind, apparent or unauthorized as compared with some standard will which is complete, enlightened, real or imperative."[23] Consequently that which is good, or valuable, is that which is the object of a "real" or "higher" will. As for the question, "What kind of will is credited with that honorable qualification of superiority," there are pretty many different answers; they include the conceptions of the "final will," the "harmonious will," the "absolute will," the "self—conscious will," and so on.[24]

Perry finds this third type of theories also unacceptable; for they either depend upon some doubtful metaphysical principles or else apply only to some special classes of values instead of to value in general. Perry's criticism against this type of views, which appears in his *General Theory of Value*, Ch. IV, and in his article "Definition of Value" (*Journal of Philosophy*, XIV, pp.156—159), may be boiled down into two major point:

i) The existence of such wills as the advocators call by the names of "the final will," "the harmonious will," "the absolute will," "the common will" etc., is quite doubtful. The will which we are familiar with in experience is the individual will.[3] If, for instance, the

---

3 Whether an "individual will" is an entity or simply a mode of behavior, is another question. But Perry does not touch this problem in this connection.

"universal will" or the "common will" does not mean the collection of individual wills, these phrases can be nothing but poetic or religious expressions, "for there is, strictly speaking, no such will."[25] To this tendency of personification or anthropomorphism too, Perry's notion of the "pathetic fallacy" might be applied, though he did not refer to it. Anyhow, doubtless we see, in those conceptions of "the final will," "the absolute will," "the universal will" and so forth, the reverse side of teleological interpretation of the universe which Perry rejected above in connection with the notion of "purposiveness."

ii) Perry does not see why a desire (or will) A could properly have a claim to precedence in comparison with another desire (or will) B *except on quantitative grounds*. It is commonly held, for example, that the satisfaction of an organized whole self is better than that of isolated or momentary impulses. But the only reason which can be set forth for the justification of such estimation is that the satisfaction of an organized self is "a more conserving and fruitful fulfilment of an aggregate of interests than is possible when these interests are unorganized."[26] To take another example, some proposes to define good in terms of "collective" interest, or of "general" happiness. Here again no reason is found why the happiness of the whole society can be regarded as more properly significant with respect to the value than that of an individual, save that the former is *greater* in the quantitative sense. Variety in the forms of interest can perhaps be the ground on which the varieties or grades of values are defined, but it cannot be the ground for the definition of value itself. Hence Perry's conclusion:

A universal will that would be entitled to preeminence in determining values would be a will that took up into itself or facilitated all interests. But the nits preeminence would be based on the assumption of the value of all interest–fulfilment, and would signify simply the comparative value of more and the superlative value of most. In short, there is no specific kind of interest — personal, social, or metaphysical — that can be said to determine value exclusively; or even preeminently, save in so far as it sums or enhances the fulfilment of more limited interests.[27]

3.

Since the possibility of defining value was assumed, and since three out of the four possible alternatives have been successively eliminated as illegitimate, it follows that the residual last alternative must be adopted as the legitimate form of the definition of value. Thus Perry is led to define value as "the peculiar relation between any interest and its object; or that special character of an object which consists in the fact that interest is taken in it."[28]

Value then is any object of any interest. "X is valuable = interest is taken in X."[29] Any kind of object may become the possessor of value, whatever ontological status it may have — whether real or imaginary — as far as it may be interested in by some subject.

As value is thus defined in terms of interest, its more precise meaning must depend upon the definition of "interest." According to

Perry's definition given in the *Realms of Value*, interest is "a train of events determined by expectation of its outcome."[30] It is the "all-pervasive characteristic of the motor–affective life" — the "state, act, attitude or disposition of favor or disfavor."[31] It is noticeable that Perry endeavors to interpret "interest" in behavioristic terms, avoiding the unverifiable introspective interpretation. This reveals his strong hope of establishing a science of value on an objective ground. This objective interpretation of interest suggests an emphasis on the motor aspect of the motor–affective life. Here we see the point where Perry's "interest theory" of value parts with the so-called "affective theory" of value, in spite of their common belief that the ground of value is to be found in psychological facts of motor–affective experience.

The word "interest" is not a new one, and in our ordinary language it is used both in broader and narrower senses. Perry advises his readers, therefore, to be careful not to confuse what he means by "interest" with certain too broad or too narrow senses of the word. A too broad sense to be excluded is given when interest is used as a synonym of "attention." Sheer attentiveness is not the sufficient condition for the arising of value. A too narrow sense to be excluded is given when the word is used in reference to selfishness, as is the case when it is used to mean "self-interest." The same use is involved in the word "disinterestedness" which signifies interest directed to others. Another excessively narrow use of word "interest" is seen when it refers to the "collective, and more or less permanent, interest of a social group," as when a feminist speaks of "the interest of women" or when a socialist claims "the interest of labor."[32]

The word "interest," in perry's usage, reflects the polarity of living mind — the common characteristic of *being for or against*, which is posessed by a certain class of acts or states. "Interest" is a class name for such names as "liking" — "disliking," "loving" — "hating," "hoping" — "fearing," "desiring" — "avoiding."[33]

If the possibility of properly defining value had been established, and if the elimination of the three out of the four alternatives of its possible form had been decisive, Perry's definition of value could be accepted as proved. But what Perry did show was that the indefinability of value had not been established either by Moore or by some others. (See above Ch. II, Sec. 1) Again, Perry did not shut out with logical conclusiveness the three alternative forms of the definition of value. What he did was to criticize *some* examples of theories which he deemed to belong to each of these three categories. Even his criticisms of these chosen examples could not be conclusive, for these examples of theories usually contained some metaphysical assumptions which can neither be established nor be rejected completely, as far as the present human knowledge is concerned. (See above Ch. II, Sec. 2) Here then Perry stands in the need of showing some positive grounds in the defence of his own definition as the legitimate one. Moreover, Perry admitted that there are "too many meanings" of value and that "theory of value is in search of preferred meaning."[34] (See also above Ch. II, Sec. 2) How then can he advocate his definition as *the one to be preferred*?

Perry indicates three criteria by which the legitimacy of a definition is to be judged, namely, "linguistic, formal, and empirical."[35] Words used in a definition must be appropriately judged by their history of usage and their suggestiveness. The definition must satisfy certain formal and epistemological requirements; for example, it must not be circular or self-contradictory. A good definition must fit a certain body of selected empirical facts.

For the first criterion, Perry argues that his chosen words "value" and "interest" largely accord with the popular usage and that they are comprehensive convenient and "the least misleading."[36]

For the third criterion, Perry claims that his proposed definition will turn out to be "descriptive" or "real" definition.[37] In other words. he claims that his definition will prove to be adequate to describe systematically the realms of value — realm of morals, of polity, of religion, of economy, of art, and so on. To follow his application of this test would mean an exposition of almost the whole volume of his *Realms of Value*, which is beyond what the present thesis attempts. Let us be satisfied for the present by refering to a passage in the *General Theory of Value.*[4] In this book Perry, after reaching his definition through a process of "systematic elimination," comments that there is a "certain presumption" in favor of his definition not only because it belongs to the last alternative remaining after the

---

4 A little more will be supplemented in this connection when we study his conception of "moral goodness."

elimination of unsuitable ones, but also because there is a certain *positive* plausibility in its support. This plausibility is given by

> the fact that in order to create values where they did not exist before it seems to be sufficient to introduce an interest. The silence of the desert is without value, until some wanderer finds it lonely and terrifying; ⋯ There is no entity that can be named that does not, in the very naming of it, take on a certain value through the fact that it is selected by the cognitive purpose of some interested mind. As interests grow and expand, ⋯ the store of cosmic values is enriched and diversified.[38]

For the second criterion, Perry endeavors to show that his definition is logically sound, by answering some objections. In the first place, Perry feels it necessary to reject the objection from the so-called emotivists. The main theses Perry claims in this connection seem to be: i) Most statements possess both a descriptive and an emotive meaning. "Statements which employ such terms as good and bad may, and usually do, convey objectively meaningful concepts." When we state, for example, that Lincoln was a "good" man, we are usually refering to some objective facts such as Lincoln's hatred of war, his emancipation of the slaves, or his compassion for soldiers.[39] ii) The fact is not that a value term has no descriptive meaning, but that it has so many meanings in common usage. Such terms as "good" and "bad" are used in different meanings in different situations, so that there are no invariable objective meaning attached to them. But this fact no more prevents a philosopher from giving an invariable meaning to a value term than the fact that the word "matter" has no common objective meaning in current usage prevents a physicist to give an objective meaning to it.[40]

The second objection which Perry cares to answer is the charge of circularity. This objection consists in asserting that it is an remarkable fact of moral experience that only objects of good interests are recognized to be good and, accordingly, to define good in terms of interest is, if the definition is to accord with our experience, to define "good" in terms of good. To this Perry answers by saying that this charge arises from the objector's failing to notice that the proposed definition can be also applied to an interest itself. An object A is invested with positive value when a positive interest B is taken in it; but interest B may be invested with negative value by another interest C which is negative. When the negative value of B overrules the positive value of A, A is often carelessly judged to be "bad."[41]

In opposition to this answer a third objection comes out. It protests by asking whether it is not contradictory to affirm that one and the same thing is both good and bad. But this charge is, Perry answers, simply based on a misconception of "contradiction." To assert that "one man's meat was not that man's meat" would be contradictory; however, "meat to one man" and "poison to another" are not con-tradictories, but are "two different and consistent propositions."[42] In the same way, there is no contradiction in asserting that the same object is good from one point of view, and bad from another point of view.

Lastly, Perry takes up the charge of relativism. Perry admits that his theory of value *is* relativistic in the sense of *relationalism*, namely, in that it asserts that value of an object is determined by the relation between the object and some interest. But he sees no reason why this sort of relativism is disgusting. The only objectionable kind of relativism is the so-called "vicious relativism," that is, sceptical relativism. But nothing sceptical, Perry claims, is involved in his theory. His theory would be sceptical if it meant that value is relational to the interest of the judge. But he defined value as any object of *any* interest. Consequently, the judge is bound by the definition to judge a thing good if an interest is taken in it *whoever's interest it may be*. "The evidence of its goodness or badness is the observable fact of interest, which is just as objective, and just as open to agreement, as any other fact of life or history."[43] [5]

4.

It would be appropriate to refer to Perry's conception of "comparative value" before proceeding to his interpretation of *moral* concepts. For

---

[5] The problem whether here outlined series of defences are adequate to justify Perry's definition of value, will be touched when the general criticism of his position is attempted.

evidently morality has much to do with such concepts as "better" or "best." Though Perry does not dare to define "moral goodness" as the "maximum of generic good possible in a given situation," he explicitly states that the moral value "begins with the bearing of a *lower* interest upon a *higher* interest."[44] Perry interprets "morality" in a rather strict sense taking the realm of morals for one section of the whole realm of value, on the same level with the realms of polity, economy, art and so forth. Hence, from his point of view, the problem of comparative value possesses a much wider scope than the problem of morals. But the close relation between these two problems is quite obvious.

The gist of the problem of comparative value is to determine the meaning of "better," "best," "worse" and "worst." (Hereafter let us speak only of "better" leaving others to be understood.) "What is that condition of an object in virtue of which it may be said to be better?" "Better" is "more good" or "more valuable." From the fact that "value" was defined as "any object of any interest" it follows that "better" can be defined only in terms of a quantitative comparison of interests concerned. If interest is the only source of value, and if no qualification is required for an interest to be a source of value, evidently nothing but the quantitative difference of interests can cause any difference of values. Thus the problem of comparative value turns out to be the problem of the measurement of interests.

In the *General Theory of Value* when Perry's critical analysis of traditional views has eliminated their alleged criteria for the measurement of value, he finds four notions left as possible standards of comparative value, they are: Correctness, Intensity, Preference, and Inclusiveness.[43][6]

The standard of *Correctness* is a measure of the truth of the judgment by which an interest is mediated, and is quite different from other three standards in that the former is not a quantitative measure of interest. Strictly speaking the standard of correctness is not a measure of value at all, though since it has a bearing on the stability of the interest, it clearly controls the duration of the value. But to make this point clear we must turn for a while to his view concerning the interdependence of interest and cognition.

If value is to be defined as any object of any interest, a further explanation of the nature of value would require to answer the question, "What actually determines the object of interest?" Perry finds two basic factors as the determinants of the object of interest at the human level. They are "a governing propensity" and "expectation." A *governing propensity* is "a determining tendency or general *set* which is at any given time in control of the organism as a whole."[46] We might interpret this factor to be largely coincident with what psychologists call "drive." It is a general tendency of behavior universal to the animal life. On the other hand, *expectation* is the act of foreseeing "what is to come next." This factor presupposes intelligence

---

6 In the *Realms of Value*(Ch. 4, p.53) Perry suggests seven criteria, namely: preference, intensity, strength, duration, number, enlightenment, and inclusiveness. But, it seems, no drastic change has been made in this connection.

or the notion of causation; thus this can be considered to be that peculiar function which largely characterizes the behavior *at the human level*. We might then formulate the relation between governing propensity, expectation and interest as follows: Governing propensity is the biological tendency which inheres in every unbalanced state of organism and which perpetually seeks the rebalance; expectation is the anticipation of the means to the attaining of the rebalance; and "an act is interested insofar as its occurrence is due to the agreement between its accompanying expectation and the unfulfilled phases of a governing propensity."[47]

Expectation is evidently a form of cognition.[48] This means that, at the human level, no interest occurs without judgment. Cognition is inherent in interest; or to put it more precisely, every interest is "mediated" by some judgment. This mediating judgment Perry calls the "interest−judgment."[49] Thus it is manifest that interest and value are necessarily modified by cognition. But the relation between value and cognition is, so to speak, indirect. The mediating judgment itself is by no means a part of the interest or of the corresponding value. In short, it is solely interest, and not cognition, that gives rise to value.

Now we are ready to come back to our study of the standard of "correctness." This standard refers to the truth or falsity of the interest−judgment or the mediating judgement. The correctness or the incorrectness of an interest−judgment, however, does not influence the magnitude of the interest concerned, and consequently does not modify the degree of the corresponding value; for the interest−

judgment is not a part of the interest, and is by no means a determinant of the value. Thus the standard of correctness is simply the method of criticizing whether a given value is founded on a true or false belief; but it has nothing to do with the quantitative measurement of the value itself.[50]

To understand the principle of correctness properly, Perry warns, we must distinguish "sharply and tenaciously" between the judgment of value and the interest-judgment. The judgment of value is that which asserts that a certain thing is an object of interest.[51] Value is more closely connected with the interest-judgment than with the judgment of value. The falsity of the judgment of value makes no difference to the value. But the falsity of the interest-judgment may prove to be the source of an alteration in the value; for when the interested subject comes to notice the falsity, his interest mediated by that false judgment might be altered.[52] Because of this intimate relation between the value and the interest-judgment, it is customary to speak of the value itself as true or false, though, strictly speaking, only judgments can be true or false.[53]

The other three standards, namely, Intensity, Preference and Inclusiveness, are principles to measure *quantities* of interest, and consequently, of value. "Intensity" refers to the variation in the degree of excitement of a given interest. Physiologically defining it is "a ratio of the elements which are acting under the control of the interest, to the totality of the elements of the organism."[54] "Preference" refers to the cases in which a single interest sets, from among its eligible objects in all of which it is interested, "one above or below another."[55] This standard can be applied only for the comparison within the range of a single interest. The principle of "Inclusiveness" can be expressed in the statement that "if a certain interest is included as part of a totality of interests, then, however the magnitudes are measured, there is an excess ⋯ in the totality as compared with any part."[56] This principle is implied in the claims of the superiority of the total "personal will," and that of the total "social interest." Now, in terms of these three standards, the meaning of "better" can be stated as follows:

An object, wine, is better than an object, water: i) if the interest in the wine is more intense than the interest in the water; ii) if the wine is preferred to the water; and iii) if the interest in the wine is more inclusive than the interest in the water.[57]

The next question which suggests itself after plural standards for the estimation of comparative value has been proposed, is naturally concerned with the problem of the commensurability of these measures. A little consideration, however, would show us that the above mentioned three standards cannot be unified into a single, or general, standard. They are independently variable, and measure respectively different aspects of value. This respect may become plain if we stop to reflect the meaninglessness of the saying that "what an object loses by a decline in intensity can be offset by a rise in the order of preference," or that "the including interest is seven times as great as the included." In Perry's own words: "They cannot be multiplied or divided into one another, for lack of the equal units which would be necessary to render them commensurable."[58]

Though these three standards of the interest measurement are incommensurable, Perry holds, there is a proper order of their application for the cases when interests conflict one another. According to the order, "preference" takes precedence to "intensity," while "inclusiveness" takes precedence to "preference." For the justification of this order Perry presents the following reasons: i) Intensification interferes with the exercise of preference, cutting off better possibilities, and the exercise of preference precludes a harmonious integration, while the converses are not the case.[59] ii) The standard of intensity can be applied only to a particular interest in a particular object, while the standard of preference can be applied to several eligible objects of a given interest; but the standard of inclusiveness is "relative neither to interests nor to objects, but may be applied absolutely."[60]

The principle of inclusiveness, which is the basis of the "harmonious integration of all interests," is by far the most important of the three standards. The principles of morals which seek the highest good as their ideal, must hinge upon this supreme principle of comparative value. Let us now proceed to his conception of "moral good." But to define the meaning of moral terms we must first clarify the nature of morality itself.

5.

A purely mechanical world as interpreted by the inorganic sciences is, according to Perry, devoid of value. With the introduction of life, which necessarily involves some "bias" or "interest," nature becomes "a new system with a new center,"[61] and value makes its appearance. But the bare introduction of "interest" does not invest nature with the "moral" character. An interest itself, or its corresponding value, is neither moral nor immoral. "The moral drama," says Perry, "opens only when interest meets interest; when the path of one unit of life is crossed by that of another."[62]

"Conflict of interests" is a necessary condition for the formation of morality; but it is not the sufficient condition. Morality presupposes the possibility of the reconciliation of interests. Thus morality occurs "only when there is such dividing and compounding of interests as to permit of some interplay of part interests and whole interests, of exclusiveness and considerateness."[63]

If conflict of interests is the starting point of morality, harmony of interests is its ideal goal. Asceticists are mistaken, Perry argues, when they take the denial of inclinations as such for duty. "Morality is an organizing of interests in order that they may flourish. The denials derive their only *moral* justification from the affirmations for which they make room."[64] Preceptualists are confused in their claim that precepts of conduct, such as the scriptual commandments, are the ultimates of morality "shining in their own light." Indeed precepts are valuable, but only as "the instruments by which the good life is achieved."[65]

Conflict of interests occur both within one and the same person and among interpersonal relations. To remove these conflicts, and to integrate antagonistic interests into a harmonious whole on both individual and social level, is the business of morality. But the integration itself is not the final objective of morals. The ultimate of morality remains to the last in the constituent interests themselves, for they are the only source of value. "In moral organization," says Perry, "the whole serves the parts, or the whole only for the sake of the parts."[66] Perry recognizes the superiority of an "interest of the totality" to its parts. But this superiority is grounded on the fact that the whole is greater than any of its parts; in other words, it is based on the principle of inclusiveness.

Now morality requires the integration of interests. But how can this integration be achieved? According to Perry, the integration is effected by a rational procedure which he calls "the method of reflective agreement." This procedure appears both in the personal will and in the social will. Perry's own description of the process of "reflective agreement" in the formation of the personal will reads as follows:

> In the creation of the personal will there occurs a thinking over, in which the several interests of the same person are reviewed, and invited to present their claims. Reflection overcomes the effects of forgetfulness and disassociation. It corrects the perspectives of time

and immediacy, ···. It brings to light the causal relations between one interest and another. From reflection there emerge decisions which fulfill, in some measure, the purpose of harmony: ···.[67]

The procedure by which the social will is effected, is somewhat similar to the case of the personal will. In the former case communication and discussion play the part which reflection performes in the latter case. But there is a "profound difference" between these two levels of will. That is, while the personal will is the will of a person, the social will is not strictly the will of a society. It is "several personal wills which are peculiary modified and interrelated" that composes the so-called "social will."[68]

It is "benevolence" which enables several personal wills to advance into a social moral will. Benevolence consists in "one person's positive interest in another person's interest."[69] When you and I are both benevolently disposed to each other's interests we stand on a common ground for the formation of a social will. Then we will come to have a socialized common purpose which will be dominant over your or my original interests. Thus the social moral will might be described as an "agreement of personal will" achieved chiefly by virtue of benevolence and reflection, though these are not the all factors conducive to such an agreement.[70]

Reflective agreement of personal wills can be achieved in every type of society — from the most intimate group like family to the most remote association like mankind. But Perry, of course, does not claim that the application of "the principle of reflective agreement" is made in all situations, nor that this method is always successful when it is applied. There are many antagonistic situations which are even devoid of the desire to agree. And in most cases where this method is actually applied, the agreements resulted are incomplete; there are levels of agreement. What Perry claims is that to apply this method more or less successfully is within the reach of human beings. "Morality," he says, "is a *pursuit*, not an infallible recipe."[71]

Now, the meaning of "moral goodness" naturally follows, so Perry conceives, from the meaning of the two concepts which we have so far studied, the concepts of "generic value" and of "morality." Moral goodness is a special kind of value characterized by the moral quality. Thus we may express the relation of these three notions in a form of equation: Moral goodness = Value(Good) + Moral quality. Now, as we have seen, value is a character which an object comes to possess when some interest is taken in it; and the moral quality lies in the harmonious integration of interests. Hence Perry's definition of moral good: "Morally good is the character imparted to objects by interests harmoniously organized."[72] This definition is inevitable for Perry, because for him the quality of goodness or value lies not in the nature of any objects, but is imparted by interest, and consequently there can be nothing except interest itself which can invest a value with the quality peculiar to morality.

We are tempted to say that the object of *moral interest* is morally good, while the object of cognitive interest is cognitively good, and the object of esthetic interest is esthetically good. This would be true indeed if we define "moral interest" as the harmoniously organized interest. But Perry does not define it in that way. And he seems to be wise in this point. For if we define moral goodness as "the object of moral interest," it might sound that moral goodness hinges on some special quality (which is characterized as "moral") of a special kind of interest (which is called moral interest), and this definition would seem to be in accord with one of the views Perry rejected already when he discussed the definition of generic value — the view which defines good as "the object of qualified interest."

For Perry, "moral interest" means rather the *harmony seeking* interest. Hence Perry's another way of defining moral goodness reads: "A total life in which all interests endorse one another is morally good when it is the object of the moral will."[73] It should be remembered that the moral goodness, as well as the generic value, lies neither in the nature of the object nor in the quality of the interest, but in the special relation between the interest and its object.

Since a harmonious integration of interests indicates a situation in which each component interest is invited to claim itself without thwarting other interests — a situation where all constituent interests are organized into a whole without losing their identity, it is obvious that the basic principle of moral goodness is identical with the supreme principle of comparative values, namely, with the principle of inclusiveness. And the general tendency of the moral experience which considers the personal good morally better than the good of any of its constituent interests, and which considers the social good better than the personal good, can be regarded as to be coincident with the present position; for the broader the scope of an integration is, the greater degree of harmony it must contain. "There must be a harmony of harmonies."[74]

The recognition of the doctrine of harmonious integration as the basic principle of morality, directly leads us to the conception of the "highest good." The highest good as an ideal must not allow any single individual's[7] unhappiness. "The highest good is not sheer satisfaction of maximum intensity." Bentham's greatest happiness principle is mistaken in that it provides no logical ground to refuse the majority's egoistic enjoyment at the expense of the minority's suffering. In the ideal state of the highest happiness all individuals must attain what they desire from their deepest hearts. The highest good is "the object which satisfies all individuals, when individuals are both personally integrated and harmoniously associated," it is the "joint and inclusive satisfaction of all individuals."[75]

7　Whether this "individual" is to be limited to the *human* individual, or must include even *animal* life, is a "troublesome question." In the *General Theory of Value* Perry does not apparently refer to the moral status of animals, but in the *Realms of Value* he explicitly mentions that he sees no reason why the objects of benevolence is to be limted to responsible moral agents. (p.114)

6.

Other moral terms such as "right," "wrong," "ought" and "duty" are defined by Perry in terms of "moral goodness."

As for the meaning of "right" and "wrong" Perry follows on the whole the traditional teleological interpretation. "'Right' means," we are told, "conduciveness to moral good, and 'wrong' means conduciveness to moral evil: the one to harmony, and the other to conflict."[76] The phrase "conduciveness to moral good" here implies not only the causal relation between an act and its effects, but also the subsumptional relation between part and whole. In other words, an act is to be called "right" either when it (by *causing* somebody's happiness) "makes for," or when it (by being *embraced* within the agent's happiness) "goes into the making of," harmonious happiness.[77]

Besides the root meaning of "right" mentioned above, there are several derived meanings of the term. When A conduces to a greater good than B, A has "superior" rightness than B. When good results are foreseen as following from an act, the act has "intentional" rightness.[8] When an agent erroneously believes his act to be conducive to moral goodness, the act has "apparent" rightness. Apparent rightness is contrasted with "true" rightness. As the precipitation of past

---

8 But it is not intentionality but the *consequences* intended from which "the right thing," or "the wrong thing," derives its ultimate meaning. (*Realms*, p.107)

experience concerning results of actions, most societies have some generalized and stereotyped rules of conduct, and acts are frequently judged according to these rules. When an act conforms to such conventional rules it possesses "formal" rightness. When an act or a set of acts, though it does not directly conduce to the moral good, creates certain preliminary conditions helpful for the realization of the moral good, that act or set of acts possesses "interim" rightness. Interim rightness is contrasted with "ultimate" rightness.[78]

Though Perry thus defines "right" and "wrong" as extrinsic value, he does not overlook the fact that what is right or wrong may come to be loved or hated for its own sake and obtain "intrinsic" value. Perry refers to the "widely pervasive" phenomenon of the mutation of interest in which means become ends in themselves, or dependent interests become independent. This mutation of interest from the dependent to the independent is ethically significant, because "the new independent interest thus generated may then supersede the original interest by which it was generated."[79]

The terms "ought," "duty," and "moral obligation" have a basic idea in common, while they imply more or less different shades of meaning.[9] Moral obligation is "what is called for by the end of the

---

9　According to Perry "the term 'duty' is applied primarily to the moral agent, and only secondarily to acts⋯. It is a stronger term than 'ought' since it is associated with an implied promise by which the agent has bound himself." (*Realms*, p.109) But as for the specific meaning of "obligation" Perry, to my knowledge, says little.

moral good."[80] Whenever one seeks an end in a given situation, there is a "right" act which is required by the fact that the end is sought. And the rightness of the act, or the requirement made by the pursued end, put the man seeking the end under an obligation. Thus "an obligation may ⋯ be said to exist wherever there is an interest operating in an environment."[81] And if the end sought possesses the moral character the accompaning obligation is what is called "moral obligation." Obligation, or oughtness, might be defined, from Perry's point of view, as a character invested to a certain class of actions by virtue of some determinate relation which connects those actions to interests on the one hand, and to their environment on the other.[82] Hence, from Perry's point of view, to say that an act ought to be performed, primarily indicates some objective fact of relation, not merely the "feeling of obligation."

It is evident, from what has been mentioned above, that Perry's interpretation of "ought" or "obligation" is grounded on his "assumption that good means what ought to be." The concept of "ought" is not the ultimate of morals in Perry's theory. "Ought is by nature an implication," says Perry, "there is an ultimate premise which is not similarly implied. That from which all moral oughts are derived is not itself a moral ought."[83] And doubtless Perry finds that ultimate premise in the principle of harmonious integration of interests.

The dependent relation in which "ought" stands against "good" forces ought, obligation, and duty to give up the claim of being "categorical" or "unconditional." But the fact that "ought" is conditional, we are told, is not prejudicial to the validity of an obligation. "My moral obligation to act in a certain manner is not more unreal for being conditioned by my desires and circumstances, than is the gravitation of the earth for being conditioned by the mass of the sun."[84] If, however, the oughtness of moral oughts is not proved by the moral oughts themselves or by an ultimate ought, is not the most basic problem of ethics left unanswered? *Why* ought the moral good to be? *Why* ought we to be harmoniously happy? To this objection Perry answers simply by contending that such a question of "why?" is "meaningless."[85]

Nor Perry's conception of moral obligation leads to an egoism. Indeed duty hinges on the good; and the good hinges on interests; but since the good is any object of any interest, I have no reason to justify my egoism. Situations are often encountered where duty requires even the negation of myself, for the call of a larger good overrules the call of a smaller good.

7.

We have so far surveyed Perry's view concerning the meaning of some basic value terms—generic value, moral good, right, ought and duty. Now, it is understood that when the definition of a value term is given, the meaning of a statement or an utterance which contains the term, is also given at the same time. Thus, for Perry, "X is valuable" means, or should mean, that interest is taken in X; "Y is morally good" means that a harmoniously integrated interest is taken in Y; "Z is right" means that Z is conducive to moral good, or that Z is conducive to the fulfillment of a harmoniously integrated interest; "A is a moral obligation" means that A is called for by the end of the moral good. It is remarkable that in Perry's view all sorts of value-statement or value-utterance can be translated into descriptive judgments which are verifiable on some empirical ground. That troublesome difference between value and non-value judgments, which has seriously threatened the establishment of a science of value, seems to be only apparent. We can test, according to Perry, the truth or falsity of a moral statement exactly in the same way as we do in the verification of a non-value judgment. Thus, to see whether an object is valuable or not we have only to examine through observation whether an interest is actually taken in that object. If we are to test whether an end is morally good or not, we have simply to study whether the end is, as a matter of fact, an object of a harmoniously organized interest.

If Perry's definitions had been proved to be *the* legitimate definitions of value terms, we could conclude here that the foundation of value theory, and specially of ethics, is firmly established. But the question whether Perry's definitions are legitimate or not, is left open. Perry's defence for his definition of "generic value" was already mentioned, leaving the business of examining its soundness for our later criticism. Let us postpone our criticism once again. What is here to be noticed is that even if Perry's definition of generic value is taken to be established it is not enough for the foundation of ethics. For the justification of his definition of generic value does not include the justification of his definitions of moral predicates. The legitimacy of the former is necessary for that of the later, but not sufficient.

Perry holds that the most basic problem in ethics is the problem of defining "moral good." That which "constitute the primary subject matter of moral theory" is the question, "In what does moral goodness consist?"[86] And he has suggested a definition of this basic concept in terms of the principle of harmonious happiness. But Perry himself does not think that his definition indicates the established and universal meaning of the concept. As in the case of "value" there is no established meaning of "moral good." Different persons mean different things by the same phrase "moral good." Among many conceivable meanings Perry suggested one as *the* meaning to be preferred. Thus it is his responsibility to justify the preference he made.

The significance of the justification under consideration is manifest. To define "moral good" is to determine the moral standard, for the phrase "morally good" is normative in nature. Therefore the justification of a definition of "moral good" implies the justification of the moral standard implied in it. And the justification of a moral standard implies the establishment of the foundation which would enable the proof of moral knowledge to be possible. Or, to be more exact, to justify the definition of "moral good" is, in itself, to establish the "first or basic judgment" of morals — the most fundamental knowledge of morality.[10]

Thus for Perry the justification of the definition of "moral good," the justification of the moral standard, and the establishment of moral knowledge ultimately are one and the same problem. In the *Realms of Value*, where Perry's fully mature moral view appears, he takes up this triple problem as the problem of "moral knowledge," and endeavors to show that "knowledge of morality differs from other kinds of knowledge not qua knowledge," but only in its subject matter,[87] by establishing his principle of "harmonious happiness" as *the* moral standard.

If a proposed principle is to be truly accepted as *the* moral standard, Perry suggests, it must satisfy the following conditions: i) "It must so agree with human nature and the circumstances of human life that men can adopt it by education, persuasion and choice; and, having adopted it, can govern their conduct in accordance with its requirements." ii) It must possess "further and unique qualifications" so that it can claim not to be merely one among many possible standards, but to be *the* moral standard with *theoretical* precedence.[88] Perry hesitates to affirm that his proposed standard of harmonious happiness can be completely verified to the satisfaction of everybody, but he believes that his principle can be defended with arguments

---

10 Perry asserts that there are two kinds of moral knowledge, basic and derivative. The basic moral knowledge is the first judgment which provides the standard of morals; the derivative moral knowledge is the judgment which applies the established standard. And Perry maintains that the fundamental question of moral knowledge concerns the proof of the standard. (*Realms*, pp.122–123)

which "at least have the merit of being appropriate to the thesis which is to be proved."[89)]

Perry's arguments in support of his standard are of three kinds: the argument from the evidence of agreement, the argument from the evidence of opinion, and the argument from empirical proof. Let us survey them one by one.

i) "The standard of harmonious happiness," contends Perry, "is *capable of* being agreed on — both theoretically and practically."[90)] It is theoretically capable of being agreed on, because it meets the fundamental requirement of cognition, that is, universality and objectivity. The principle of harmonious happiness is free from that egocentricism which has been a chronic obstacle to the *objective* consideration of moral problems. It is completely impartial and can be applied universally — "to all interests and persons." The standard of harmonious happiness is also practically capable of being agreed on, because it can, by inviting everybody to reflect on his own interests, and by providing some stake for every person, obtain a broad support. Being thus "doubly universal" the principle of harmonious happiness is "a norm on which all man can unite and agree — both theoretically and practically."

ii) The principle of harmonious happiness is largely in line with most of generally respected moral opinions. It "reaffirms" the time-honored doctrine of the cardinal virtues — courage, temperament, wisdom, and justice. It also "endorses" the three virtues Christianity has extolled — faith, hope, and love. Take any other maxims which are widely accepted and are alive in our tradition because of their reasonableness, you will find it, in most cases, difficult to indicate any contradiction between the proposed principle and them.[91] [11]

Of course the agreement with the generally accepeted opinion, Perry seems to admit, is not an adequate proof for a norm to be the moral standard. But an opinion does not survive long without reason. Opinion is corrected in the course of history, and the more correct or reasonable an opinion is, the more chance for it to be "traditional." If so, Perry asserts, "it may properly be argued for any theory that it agrees with widespread opinion."[92]

iii) Perry's proposed standard, we are told, is "empirically" supported in that it can describe with adequacy and correctness the data given in our moral experience. According to Perry, the ultimate data of moral science are conflicts of interests, and the organizations of interests. And he believes that his theory is most appropriate to deal with these "ultimate" data.[93]

———

[11] Here Perry seems to believe that his theory of harmonious happiness is in agreement with such traditional moral thoughts as the ancient Greek or the Christian conception of "virtue." But we may properly ask him, "*In what sense* does your view agree with the traditional moral thoughts?" Perry's answer to this question would be that the realization of harmonious happiness requires such virtues as the traditional thoughts have admired. (Cf. *Realms of Value*, p.134) This answer, however, is not adequate to affirm the real agreement between his and the traditional views; for the traditional views have admired those virtues *as ends in themselves* while Perry deems them *as means* for the ideal of harmonious happiness. Perry might attempt to solve the difficulties involved here by means of his conception of "mutation of interest." But I doubt whether that conception can work here satisfactorily.

When Perry asserts that his principle of harmonious happiness is in accord with the moral experience, he does not mean that men are actually harmoniously happy. What he invites our attention to is the fact that "there is a prolonged and widespread attempt to be harmoniously happy; that men are capable of such an attempt; that they can and do take steps in the direction of harmonious happiness; ⋯." And on the ground of this fact of human endeavor, he claims that his doctrine describes "a peculiarly widespread, fundamental, and persistent human pursuit for which 'moral' is the most appropriate name."[94]

8.

Since we have studied Perry's basic ideas concerning the definition of moral predicates the meaning of moral statements (or utterances), and the verification of moral knowledge, it might be proper for our next step to return to our initial problems and examine what light his theory throws on them — a step which would naturally imply some criticism. Our fundamental problem was, it is remembered, whether we can find some empirical method of justifying, or rejecting, ethical utterances. And this problem involved such questions as, "Can we establish any standard of moral values on an empirical basis?" and "Can we show some empirical ground why we ought to act in this or that way?" (See above Ch. I, Sec. 2)

We see that Perry's view is, in several aspects, in line with what we are seeking for. In the first place, his theory is thoroughly empirical; he has rejected all kinds of unwarranted metaphysical assumptions; he has discarded the claim of the intuitionistic "self-evidence" which can be grasped only by some limited people with self-assurance. Perry makes what is given in our experience his starting point, and his definitions of value terms seem to be largely in accord with the actual usage of them. Above all, his assertion that value involves a certain subjective factor, namely, that the existence of some sentient being's attitude, or what he calls "interest," is the necessary condition for the occurrance of value, seems to be sound.

Whenever we are concerned with the controversy between realistic and non-realistic views of value, we are reminded of the name "Moore." Moore's exhaustive rejection of the intimate relation between value and desire might be considered as a good contrast with Perry's "relational" theory of value. Moore's main argument against the view that "good" is what is desired, or what is desired for its own sake, consists in claiming that there are cases in which a man believes that a thing or a state of things is desired, and even desired for its own sake, and yet does not believe that it is intrinsically good. Moreover, Moore adds, a man may even believe a thing to be positively bad in spite of the fact that it is desired for its own sake. To my knowledge, however, Moore has offered no satisfactory instances of such cases, though he insists that it is "undeniable."[95]

To show that intrinsic goodness is independent of any mental attitude, Moore suggests in his *Principia Ethica* to imagine a completely beautiful world and to compare it with another imaginary world which is the ugliest we can possibly conceive. (pp.83–85) Moore's point here is that he "cannot help thinking" that, supposing these two worlds quite apart from any possible contemplation by human beings, it is better that the beautiful world should exist, than the one which is ugly. This illustration, however, does not seem quite convincing; for Moore assumes here that such value as beauty or ugliness can exist without any sentient beings to feel or contemplate it — the very point at issue. Since Moore's own example is not suitable let us consider some other instances which Moore might be willing to admit, with a view to the consideration of the pros and cons between Perry and Moore. Perhaps "friendship" can be considered one of the examples we are looking for. Now we can neither prove nor disprove the statement or utterance that friendship would be intrinsically good even if no one were interested in it. The only thing that can be argued for the vindication of our proposition seems to be to say, "I *see* that friendship is intrinsically good, whether any one desires it or not." But the simple fact that there are many persons who do not have that kind of intuition, may suggest that some difficulty is involved in this argument. Moore would attempt to tide over the difficulty by charging those people without the intuition with "moral blindness." Unfortunately, however, he does not provide us with an unmistakable method to decide whether a man with a certain moral intuition is suffering from an illusion, or another man without it is to be diagnosed as "morally blind." And one suggestive fact in this connection is that many moral opinions which had passed for intuitive truths in former days have lost their unquestionable authority nowadays when the advancement of social sciences is remarkable.[12] At any rate it might be admitted that Moore's intuitionism cannot adequately explain the well-known fact that different people's moral judgments, even if they appeal to their "intuition," widely vary in their contents, and that his argument is far from being satisfactory to show the existence of an intrinsic good quite independent of all kinds of human attitudes. There are, on the other hand, some psychological facts which seem to suggest that intrinsic goodness and certain mental attitude are necessarily related. For example:

i) Those who strongly desire friendship usually recognize it to be intrinsically good, while those who are little interested in it are less ready to admit that it is so. Moore, of course, would insist that this kind of fact does not prove anything against his position, arguing that it simply shows that a man may not be interested in a certain object until he is aware of its value. It seems by no means easy to give a

---

12 It was not very long ago that Korean people believed it self-evident that a woman should not marry twice. If a girl was rumored to have been in love with a boy she had little chance to marry unless her home removed to some distant place, because even the boy's parents would never accept such an "indecent" girl. (Even a piece of love-letter, and nothing more, was enough to prove a girl to be indecent.) They seem to have had no teleological consideration concerning sex morals. For them, the *intrinsic* value of women's chastity was simply unquestionable. To give another example, most Samurais of the feudal Japanese did not stopped to doubt why they were obliged to give up their lives for their masters. It must have been too obvious to be questioned.

decisive argument to solve the old puzzle, "Does a man desire a given thing because he recognizes it valuable, or does he consider it valuable because he or others desire it?" — a puzzle analogous to the chicken-egg problem. But a little consideration of some clear-cut cases might suggest that, as far as an intrinsic value is concerned, desire is primary. Ask yourself, for instance, whether boys ordinarily experience their first love after and because they recognize the valuableness of love, or they evaluate the value of love according to their love-experience; and consider also the suggestive fact that a man's appreciation of the value of love can be more remarkably changed in accordance with the psychological development of his personality, the basic conditions to determine his interest in love or in girls, than a man's interest in love is modified in accordance with his appreciation of the value of love.

The plausibility of the proposition, "I desire X because X is valuable (or good)," may probably be connected with the ambiguity of the proposition. a) When the proposition means, "I desire X because X is good for Y," and Y is something I desire for itself, it is doubtless true that the valuableness of X is the reason of my desiring it. In this case, however, X's value is instrumental, and the position that nothing can be intrinsically good without being desired still remains unexpelled. b) When the proposition, "I desire X because it is good," means, "I desire X because X *possesses* some good quality" (as is the case when I say that I like Mr. Smith because he is delightful), it is also true that the valuableness of X is the reason of my liking it. But in this case the proposition does not tell why I like the good quality which is the real object of my liking. When I say, "I like Mr. Smith because he is delightful," my liking of delightfulness is antecedent, and my statement does not tell why I like delightfulness. c) The proposition under consideration can, of course, also mean, "I desire X because it is intrinsically good." In this case, however, it seems quite difficult to think of any instance in which the proposition sounds plausible, but its opposing proposition, "X is good because it is desired," is less plausible.

ii) Different things belonging to the same class are often valued differently in consequence of different human attitudes towards them; for example, most of us are ready to admit that a *man's* health is intrinsically good, but we are inclined to hesitate to assert that a *malaria-mosquito's* health is so, too. Many people hold that "knowledge" is intrinsically good, but it is doubtful whether they include in the list of their *valued* knowledge someone's knowing the date of birth of a wild kitten which has no special connection with any man at all.

It seems fundamentally difficult to offer a conclusive argument for or against the realistic interpretation of the nature of value. For, among other things, even the problem whether such a term as "value" has only one legitimate meaning, in spite of its various usage, is still left open. But it is hardly deniable that there is some real and important connection between what we usually call "value" or "good" and the motor-affective aspect of living beings. Perhaps it might be argued that this inseparable relation between good and desire proves not that good is "something that is made what it is by our desires," but rather that good is "something into accord with which we should bring our desires."[96] This is another example of that kind of arguments which can be hardly proved either positively or negatively. But obviously the responsibility of verifying the assertion seems to sit more heavily upon the shoulders of the part who argues it positively than that of disproving the proposed assertion lies upon the part who feels doubt against it. Furthermore, it should be noticed that the very assertion that "good is something we *should* desire" is remarkably charged with emotion, desire, or interest!

In the second place, Perry's theory possesses some notable advantages over other psychological value theories, besides sharing with them the soundness of their non-dogmatic approach toward value experience. His careful application of recently developed psychological knowledge enables Perry to be free from those errors to which I referred in the introductory chapter. Indeed it would be precipitate to consider the biological-psychological foundation on which Perry's value theory is based to be complete, when biology and psychology themselves are still at the level of "young sciences," but no one would deny the remarkable advantage Perry possesses over classic ethical empiricists.

Even compared with some other contemporary psychological views of value such as the "affective theories," Perry seems to stand on a more or less advantageous position. First, Perry's interest theory is free from the egocentrism by which the affective theory is apt to be bothered, and which prevents the "feeling theory" from an adequate explanation of the altruistic aspect of moral experience. Second, though Perry's theory is "relativistic" in a sense, it offers a standard, or a set of standards, by means of which the normative problems of morals, which are mostly troubled by conflicts of interests as well as by disagreements of opinions, might be, theoretically at least, resolved; while such affective theory as, for example, Prall's throws little light on the solution of conflicts the moral life inevitably involves. For Prall, who defines value exclusively in terms of feeling or liking, reflection or cognition has, strictly speaking, no part to play in the constitution of value. Thus, to make distinction between higher and lower values on the ground of reflection is precluded already in his conception of value, and consequently to give any standard for the comparison of the degrees of values proves to be impossible. For Perry, who defines value solely in terms of interest, also no cognitive factors *directly* participate in the formation of value. But by introducing the concept of "interest judgment" and the "standard of correctness" Perry provides a way for reflection or cognition to take part in the constitution of value. And the standard of inclusiveness and the principle of harmonious happiness present a method which, if adopted, may throw light, in a way which cannot be expected of Prall's theory, on the solution of social problems.

Possibly many other merits of Perry's view could be pointed out. But let us close our approval of Perry by adding only one more remark, that is, his theory's advantage over Utilitarianism. It is understood that the "greatest happiness" principle of Utilitarianism involves a logical difficulty in connection with the problem of doing justice to handicapped individuals or groups. But since Perry's principle of "harmonious happiness" allows every interest to reflect its own claim, it enables even lesser interests to have, theoretically at least, a chance to take a share in that supposed "harmonious happiness."

Though Perry's theory contains some remarkable contributions, we find that it is not able to give a satisfactory solution to our fundamental problems. According to Perry, the statement, "X is valuable," is proved, when it is shown that some interest is actually taken in X; the utterance, "Y is better than Z," is established when it is shown that the interest taken in Y is quantitatively greater than the interest taken in Z. If this is the truth the following must be also true, namely: When all disputants admit that some interest is taken in X, there can be no real disagreement about the valuablensss (or goodness) of X; when all debaters come to agree that the interest taken in Y is greater than the interest taken in Z, then there can be no real denial of Y's being better than Z. That this is not the case, however, might become clear if we imagine some extreme situations.

Suppose a small number of people are living in a small solitary island known only by its inhabitants. They are living together on fishing and farming. But all the inhabitants, except one, hate to work, being lazy and aggressive. These lazy rascals have succeeded in conditioning, through the method of praise and punishment, one of their companions, who is the only diligent, meek, and somewhat stupid man among them, to be *interested* in hard work. The lazy fellows enjoy their leisure time playing checker and cards, but the diligent fellow, not knowing how to play them, is little interested in the games. Besides, this diligent man, thanks to his inherent good health and his subnormal intelligence, has no complaint about his being exploited and is happy in a sense. Now our question is this: What kind of moral judgments would people pass on the situation just described? Would they judge that the rascals' inactivity at the expense of the meek fellow's overwork is good? Or would they insist that all the islanders should work in co-operation with the diligent one? Apparently opinions would *not* agree with one accord; some would approve the islanders' peculiar mode of life, and others would disapprove it. Perry himself might find nothing wrong in their way of living; but some others, even if they are not socialists, might blame the islanders. Does this disagreement of opinions come from the disagreement of the disputants' beliefs on the psychological facts concerning the islanders' interests? Probably, even if all of the disputants well understand the situation and completely agree about the psychological facts involved, the disagreement of their moral evaluation would not be terminated. If Perry and his followers argue that, since everybody in the island is satisfied, nothing more is necessarily required there, their opponents might insist that the rascals should not make a profit of the meek fellow's ignorance. They might contend that the islanders should try to make the meek fellow be interested in the games they play, and give him chances to participate in their enjoyment. Those who hold that morality requests "justice" for justice's sake, would assert that all the islanders ought to work in co-operation even if we do not take into consideration the many generally desired effects which might possibly be caused by their co-operation, such as having more fish.[13]

If some other illustrations with a little more conceivable situation is requested, we may well consider that quarter of moral problems in which the disagreement of opinions has been perhaps most remarkable, namely, the problems of sex morals. Concerning sex morals, an extreme position holds that adultery is a sin even if it is only imaginary, while another extreme maintains that husbands

---

13 Since someone might maintain that the above mentioned illustration is too far removed from actual human situations to be suitable, it would not be superfluous to introduce here a story which might show that our supposed situation, though such an extreme and clear-cut case might rarely occur, is not altogether inconceivable.

In the days of Lee Dynasty, Korean people were divided into two large classes, the privileged and the ordinary. The privileged were called Yangban, and the ordinary were called Sangno. Both Yangban and Sangno were sub-divided into several sub-classes forming a line of ranks from the bottom to the top. Only some higher classes of Sangno could have the honor to enter the higher Yangbans' room in some special occasions such as when cleaning was required. (Some were allowed to approach as far as the hall; some others were permitted to come only to the garden.) When a new year came every man-Sangno (women were excluded) was granted the special favor to come into the Yangban's home to which he belonged and to bow from the garden towards the Yangban's room in the expression of "Happy new year." Now, at the end of the Lee Dynasty, I heard, there was an enlightened Yangban. When one of his favored Sangno came into his garden for the new-year-salute, the enlightened man suggested him to come into the room. However, the Sangno answered with great surprise, "No, it is impossible, Sir." I refer to this story because this "impossible" type of Sangnos usually believed that to serve for their "neverwork" type of Yangbans was their sacred duty, and accordingly never thought of complaining against their "duty," whatever overwork it might have required.

might properly make their sexual life more enjoyable by sometimes exchanging their wives in the same way as friends make their dinners more enjoyable by means of inviting each others, provided that kind of practice does not result in making "wrong" children. (I remember B. Russell suggested something similar to this latter position in his *Marriage and Morals*.) Evidently such remarkable disagreement on sex morality does not come from mere disagreement on the psychological or sociological *facts* concerning sex. Even if a complete agreement on facts of sex were reached, some disagreement of sex morals might remain, for the time being at least.

For the sake of clearness we have considered some extreme examples. But the disagreement of moral judgments or opinions is not exclusively related to certain extraordinary situations. Perhaps we may safely argue that in any moral situation a valuational disagreement may occur, however completely people might agree about the psychological facts of interests involved in the given situation. That agreement of beliefs on facts does not always bring about agreement of beliefs on values indicates the inadequacy of Perry's definitions of value terms, for, if as Perry holds what the value utterance means is nothing but mere psychological facts, a complete psychological agreement must be accompanied by a complete moral agreement.

Moore's notion of "Naturalistic Fallacy" implies at least one admirable contribution. It would be indeed unfair if the name of "fallacy" were given exclusively to ethical definitions simply because they are *incomplete*. Strictly speaking, it seems, most definitions, unless they are merely nominal, are more or less incomplete. (For example, to say "X is a man" is not exactly the same thing as to say "X is a rational animal;" for the phrase "rational animal" does not represent the *whole connotation* of a "man.") And it is also true that, when a definition which clarifies the whole connotation of the concept to be defined (let us call it "definition by connotation") is unavailable, even a definition which indicates the whole denotation of it (let us name it "definition by denotation") is better than nothing. But the real shortcoming of those ethical writers who have been charged by Moore with the "Naturalistic Fallacy," does not consist in the fact they gave *incomplete* definitions, but in the fact that they *mistook* their definitions by denotation for definitions by connotation. And it was Moore who pointed out this mistake most clearly.

Perry himself, perhaps on the basis of his knowledge of Moore, was quite careful not to make the same mistake and to reach a definition which truly indicates the connotation when he declared that "What does 'value' mean?" is not the same as the question, "What things have value?" (See Ch. II, Sec. 2) His achievement, however, could not keep up with his ambition. If Perry's definition of value means that any object of any interest is, *as a matter of fact*, a value-holder, it is evidently a definition by denotation; if, on the other hand, his definition means that any object of any interest *should be* regarded as valuable, obviously it is, to borrow Stevenson's terminology, "persuasive." Indeed Perry would assert that his definition of value means none of these things; he might claim that what his theory holds is that "X is valuable" *means* "Interest is taken in X." But this assertion of Perry's seems untenable.

As Moore would hold, to say that "X is valuable" is not the same as to say that "interest is taken in X," because the former means *more* than the latter. The utterance "X is valuable" includes, to use P. B. Rice's terms, both "descriptive" and "prescriptive" elements, but the statement "Interest is taken in X," when it is uttered as a detached proposition, includes descriptive elements only. The former expresses the speaker's attitude toward X, as well as conveying other facts, while the latter does nothing but conveying certain psychological facts. Thus we might conclude that Perry's definitions of value terms, which utterly neglect the prescriptive elements in the terms, are remarkably inadequate. And it is inevitable that the inadequacy of his definitions undermines his whole theory, for Perry holds that the crucial problem of theory of value is the problem of definition.

Among the derivative shortcomings originated in Perry's neglect of the prescriptive elements in valuational utterances, perhaps the most serious is the confusion between the purely *analytic* aspect and the *normative* aspect of ethics — the defect which was criticized by Stevenson as "a confusion which at once distorts analysis and hampers well-defended evaluations."[97]

As long as a writer confines himself to the study of the actual use of moral terms, his study remains purely analytic; but, it seems, as soon as he dares to give the "proper" or "true" definition of an ethical concept in terms of nonethical concepts, his attempt introduces, implicitly at least, a normative element into his theory. To give a definition of an ethical concept as "the true" one is neither a pure analysis of language nor a mere description of facts. It is a normative, or a prescriptive, conclusion based on linguistic analysis and factual informations. Perry was, on the one hand, quite eager to establish his ethics as an objective science; and he believed firmly, on the other hand, that the foundation of ethics is the definition of "moral good." Unfortunately, however, Perry overlooked the fact that *the* definition of "moral good" is not the foundation of "meta-ethics," but rather of "normative ethics." It is not difficult to imagine that an attempt to establish the objective science of morals upon a normative foundation is necessarily led to a confusion between two specifically different aspects of ethics.

Since Perry wanted a purely objective science of value he consciously took pain to rule out all subjective elements. But his own persuasive attitude, which is necessarily subjective in a sense whatever true judgments might have "mediated" it, betrays itself in connection with many crucial points.

As one of the occasions where Perry's persuasive attitude is most clearly revealed we might indicate the place in which Perry discusses the "standards of comparative value." Explaining that the proper order for the application of the three standards of quantitative measurement is i) inclusiveness, ii) preference, and iii) intensity, Perry tells us as follows:

A system of interests which shall be the greatest in all three senses can be achieved only by first achieving a harmonious integration of all interests. Component interests being so compounded as to realize the greatest inclusiveness, the resultant interests may then exercise preference, each choosing its best; and having so chosen, each interest may then be brought to its maximum of intensity.[98]

Judging from this passage, Perry doubtless takes it for granted that interest or value is *something we should endeavor to maximize*. But however carefully we may analyse his conception of "interest" or of "value" we can never find any ground which necessitates the conclusion that interest or value should be maximized. If we interpret Perry's definition of value literally we cannot even tell which is better, "more value" or "less value;" not to mention the reason why each interest should be "brought to its maximum" after a "harmonious integration of all interests" is achieved. To justify what Perry believes to be the proper order of the application of the three standards, we must, besides his definition of value, admit a certain assumption — an assumption which Stevenson would characterize as "persuasive."

Perry's "persuasive" tendency appears also in his conception of "moral goodness." To define "moral goodness" in terms of "harmonious happiness," Perry had to take morality as "that organization of life by which conflict is escaped and by which co-operation. is achieved." However, among the phenomena which we may recognize to be "moral" there are many other aspects than what Perry's view of morality referes to; for example, love of justice for justice's sake, pangs of a guilty conscience, and the sense of duty cannot be perfectly described as simply conflict-avoiding or co-operation-seeking phenomena. When we choose some aspects of morals to name as "the ultimate data of moral science" or as "the essence of morals," our *attitude* is introduced as one of the determinant factors in our moral theory.

Again, though Perry presented several evidences (the evidence of agreement, the evidence of opinion, and the fitness for the description of experience) to establish his standard of "harmonious integration of interests,"[99] they do not really prove that his proposed standard is *the* moral standard. Even if we admitted his arguments on this point to be sound,[14] Perry's arguments for the defense of his moral standard are not solely based on objective facts, but also on his moral *ideal*.

Perry's "persuasive" attitude can be seen also in connection with his conception of "ought." For Perry, the ultimate ground of moral obligation was moral *goodness*, which consists in the harmonious happiness. And to the question, "Why ought the moral good to be; why ought we to be harmoniously happy?" he simply answered that such a question of "why" was "meaningless." (See above, Sec. 6 of this Ch.) But it is difficult to see why this question is so "meaningless," as far as we stick to Perry's completely "objective" point of view. The question

---

14   See above the last footnote put in Sec. 7 of the present chapter.

would be meaningless if human beings *necessarily* desired the "harmonious happiness," and if there were no tendency which conflicts with the principle of harmonious happiness. But to endeavor for the harmonious happiness does not seem to be the naturally given universal state of human beings; it is rather an ideal state. Hence only with some persuasive conviction we can assert that men ought to be harmoniously happy. How can this persuasive conviction be justified, is naturally another question. In any case, however, it might be admitted that Perry's initial position of "objective science" cannot adequatly deal with the problem of "ought."

Chapter Ⅲ.

DEWEY: VALUE AND PROBLEMATIC SITUATION

.1.

Morton White indicates that the general position of John Dewey's ethics is located somewhere between the view of G. E. Moore and that of R. B. Perry.[1] This comment of White's seems to be particularly true in connection with the controversial problem of the definability (or indefinability) of "good" or "value." Dewey, though he is regarded as one of the eminent defenders of the so-called naturalism in ethics, never offers any clear-cut definition of "good," or of "value." At some place he even seems to be asserting the indefinability of "value" with almost the same tone as was employed by Moore when he denied the definability of "good."[1] But whoever surveys Dewey's general position concerning the nature of value easily finds that his view is far removed from Moore's and rather agrees with Perry's in some basic assumptions.

Dewey, to be sure, seems to admit that the innermost essence of "value" is indefinable. But he never agrees with the doctrine that values have a real status independent of all human activities such as desiring, liking, judging and so forth. "Valuity, the quality," says Dewey, "may be undefinable and simple, like any ultimate empirical quality, but the thing which possesses the undefinable is two things-in-relation, one the object, the other the *human attitude.*"[2)] Values are not immediately given *a priori*, they are something which arise in experience."[2] Values arise under certain conditions and as the outcome of a process of human attitude. If, therefore, we could clarify under what conditions and after what kind of process of human attitude things or acts or events come to have value, we might well claim to know something about the nature of value. When a logical definition cannot be given directly a genetic definition often proves to be helpful. Thus, Dewey, from the early days of his activity, was concerned with the *logic of valuation* which he believed to be the most crucial factor for the occurrence of values, when a number of writers were busying

---

1 In his *Experience and Nature* Dewey says, "Values are values, things immediately having certain intrinsic qualities. Of them as values there is accordingly nothing to be said; they are what they are." (Dover edition, p.396)
And, also in an article written in 1923 he explicitly asserts that "as a quality it [value] is ultimate, simple and undefinable." (*Journal of Philosophy*, XX. p.622)
2 Dewey's rejection of the absolutism in ethics appears in many places. See, for example, the Ch. VII of the *Reconstruction in Philosophy* (esp. p.165 ff) and the Ch. X of the *Quest for Certainty* (esp. pp.250−252 of the George Allen & Unwin ed., 1930).

themselves with the endless controversy about the *nature of value*. In 1915 he explicitly declared:

> I am not concerned with the *nature* of value as that has recently been the object of controversy. For my purpose, it makes no difference whether value is comprised within consciousness, independent of consciousness, or a relation between an object and some form of consciousness. I am going to deal with valuation, not with value.[3]

How then do values arise in experience? Under what conditions or situations do they come into being? What does valuation do for the rise of value? And what is the logic of valuation? Let us follow Dewey's own thoughts concerning these questions.

As long as every thing is going well and smoothly with us, so Dewey holds, there is no occurrence of value, whatever strong feeling of enjoyment or satisfaction may accompany that troubleless experience. But such an absolutely smooth and calm situation, even if it is experienced, cannot last long. Because of the change and flux both in ourselves and in our environment all experience is exceedingly unstable. Hence some trouble is introduced into the situation together with the change of circumstances. Moreover, most acts or events have a series of diverse effects. Some of them are sweet, but others are bitter. We might be, at first, transported with the sweet effects, but it would require but a brief time to notice the bitter ones. Thus, in many cases, even without essential change in the objective circumstance the "troublesome and uncertain quality" latent in the situation might be brought to light.

When a man is conscious of the troublesome quality of his situation, "the natural tendency of man" is to do something at once, because there is impatience with unsettledness. An immediate action, however, does not always bring the wanted solution. The outcome might be even worse than the present situation. Hence the agent must choose a *right* action to acquire the desired result. In other words, he must know, before starting an overt action, what is the right kind of response. Here the situation becomes a "problem" for him.

Confronted with a "problematic situation" a man's action thus "centers upon finding out something about obstacles and resources and upon projecting inchoate later modes of definite response"[4] instead of rushing to "do something about it." The agent must, after studying the conditions of the situation, predict what kind of results would be brought about by this or that response, and then appraise and compare these probable results to decide which course of action is to be chosen. This act of appraisal and comparison is nothing but the act of "valuing" in the primary sense of the term "value,"[3] for it is

---

3 Dewey admits that the verb "to value" is used, in common speech, in two different meanings, "to prize" and "to appraise." (*Theory of Valuation*, p.5, and *Journal of Philosophy*, XII, p.520) But, as we shall see, Dewey's theory of valuation has more to do with the latter usage.

Dewey's belief that "'value' is a noun established by the verb or action of evaluating."[5] Here we have reached the concept of "value." Value is something which comes into being as the result of valuation; and valuation takes place when and only when the situation is problematic in nature. In short, value is something which arises in a problematic situation as a result of valuation, which is necessarily connected with human nature.

This conclusion seems to suggest that Dewey's theory of valuation occupies the central position in his theory of morals. Since Perry held that the fundamental problem of theory of value is to *define* the concept of value and developed his theory in accord with this assumption, we, when we were concerned with him, concentrated our attention on his definitions of value terms. As for Dewey, however, we seem to be obliged to employ ourselves chiefly in a careful analysis of his theory of valuation. Perry analyzed the meaning and nature of the value utterance through the definition of "value" and proceeded to the question whether there can be knowledge of value. Dewey, on the other hand, believing that valuation is fundamental, directly tackles the logic of the value utterance. Hence we may, even without bothering ourselves very much with the puzzling problem of the definition, study his answer to our main question in the present thesis, "Can a value utterance be justified or refuted on an empirical ground?" But we should recall that we have left an important point which seems to require being dealt with before we set about that central task of studying his conception of valuation; that is, Dewey's rejection of the view which identifies value with immediate enjoyment or with a kind of aesthetic quality immediately enjoyed, or the view which holds that feeling or liking or interest can *solely* constitute value.

Since we have studied Perry's "interest theory" of value it would be appropriate to refer briefly to the so-called "affective theory" as a preparation for the study of Dewey's criticism against the "motor-affective" theories. David Wight Prall, one of the distinguished defenders of the affective theory, holds that values are based on the instinctive life of impulse, and that "the feeling of the animal that has any feeling is all that is needed to give a situation where there is value."[6] If value is constituted by mere feeling or liking, reflection or thought-process is not a necessary constituent of it, Prall even deliberately argues against the suggestion that reflection is essential for the occurrence of value. Prall admits that reflection or judgment is "in some cases" at least one of the many causal conditions which help the occurrence of a value situation. But it is no more a causal condition than "eyes and ears and violins and perhaps pianos and piano-movers" are sometimes conditions for a certain kind of value experience. If reflection is a condition of value it is so only in an indirect way.[7] In other words, reflection may become a part of the background which helps the causation of the value-experience; but even without it value can be well constituted. Reflection is not necessary, if it is sometimes helpful, for the occurrence of value.

Dewey's argument against Prall's position is, in effect, as follows:

i) Prall's thesis that liking *constitutes* values would be acceptable if it simply meant either (a) that liking is *one of the conditions* of an object's acquiring the quality of value, or (b) that liking is an ingredient, a constituent part of the total situation possessing the quality. But the thesis cannot be accepted so long as it means that liking is all that is needed for a situation to obtain the quality of valueness. "Liking is necessary but not sufficient condition of the occurrence of a thing with value quality."[8]

ii) Reflection or thought as well as liking is *always* the condition of the occurrence of value-things. A motor-affective act which has no element of reflection is a "purely animal act." Only when the motor-affective act contains discriminating *meaning* due to reflection, it can constiute that kind of an act which determines the existence of *a* value, namely, "appreciation."[9] It should be admitted that the only way by which "the pallid remoteness of the rationalistic theory, and the only too glaring presence of the institutional theory of transcendental values" can be avoided, is to connect the theory of values with concrete experience of desire and satisfaction. But the true way of escaping from the defects of transcendental absolutism is not to be found in "setting up as values enjoyments that happen anyhow, but in defining value by enjoyments which are the consequences of intelligent action."[10]

But what is the ground for Dewey to insist that mere liking or immediate enjoyment is not sufficient, and that some activity of intelligence must participate, for a situation to obtain the quality of "valuity?" The main points of Dewey's argument answering this question would be:

i) To identify merely liked, or immediately enjoyed, objects with values is not in accord with the proper usage of language. This view overlooks the important difference between descriptive terms and evaluative ones. To say "X is enjoyed" is not the same thing as to say "X is enjoyable;" there is essential difference of meaning between "desired" and "desirable," between "satisfying" and "satisfactory." To say that something is desired is to make a statement about a bare fact, "something already in existence." But to claim that something is desirable is "to assert that it satisfies or fulfils certain conditions." To say that something is desired is "to report something as an isolated finality," while to say that something is desirable is "to define it in its connection and interactions."[4] An evaluative proposition is primarily concerned with a future; it contains a prediction, as well as "it denotes an attitude *to be* taken."[11)]

To put it in another way, to call something satisfactory is equivalent to saying that the thing is satisfying as a matter of fact, and that this satisfaction is to be cared for, or preserved. And the decision whether a satisfaction is to be cared for or not, is evidently hinged upon the consideration, or reflection, about the various relations in which the satisfaction stands. In short, we judge things loved and cherished to be

---

4 For Dewey this search for "connection and interactions" is nothing but *thinking*. (*The Quest for Certainty*, London, 1930, p.254)

valuable only when we have in mind some "reason for their being loved and cherished."[12] Even Prall himself seems to admit, Dewey argues, that not all satisfying things are real values; for he "insists upon the importance of the cultivation of taste" on the ground that "values are satisfactory or unsatisfactory according as a subject's faculties are acute or not ⋯."[13]

ii) As a matter of a psychological fact, human appreciation or enjoyed contemplation in a concrete situation usually includes some reflective factor. It is a matter of "every matured sane experience" that "after the first dumb, formless experience of a thing as good, subsequent perception of the good contains at least a germ of critical reflection."[14] Writers who assert the irrelevance of thought to the occurrence of a value seem unduly to assume an insulated wall between the immediate and the reflective in human experience; for if desire[5] and thought are inseparably interwoven what is the point in excluding so eagerly the reflective element from the constitution of value? But the true "contrast, or conflict, is not to be found between desire and reason, but between a less thoughtful desire and a more thoughtful one. "There can be no separation morally of desire and thought because the union of thought

---

5 In the *Theory of Valuation*, Dewey emphasizes that "desire" is to be distinguished from mere impulse. We are told that "the whole difference between impulse and desire is made by the presence in desire of an end-in-view, of objects as foreseen consequences," (p.30) and that "some degree of intellectual respect for existing conditions and consequences does operate as a control factor in formation of desires⋯." (p.56)

and desire is just what makes an act voluntary."[15]

iii) The view which deems a bare enjoyment to be a value in itself, makes it impossible to find any guiding principle in practical life. The conflict between desires, or between enjoyments, is a matter of everyday's experience. But if all desired things, or all enjoyments, are indiscriminatingly values, how can we have any standard by which we can settle the conflicts between them? In Dewey's own expression:

> If enjoyment are value, the judgment of value cannot regulate the form which liking takes; it cannot regulate its own conditions. Desire and purpose, and hence action, are left without guidance, although the question of regulation of their formation is the supreme problem of practical life.[16]

Dewey declares it to be a "serious matter" that the "most widely held empirical theory," by identifying values with all sorts of enjoyments, is in effect justifying "the greater part of the activities of the greater number of human beings" who are beside themselves "to seize upon and hold on to such enjoyments as the actual scene permits."[17]

It is apparent that at this third point of his argument Dewey is revealing his attitude or ideal as a practical thinker. We recall White's words: "Dewey was primarily a moral philosopher, an educator, and a political thinker."

We have so far studied Dewey's view concerning the relation of liking and thought to value chiefly through his criticism of Prall's position.

But it must be admitted that the criticism is applicable, in principle, to most of the so-called motor-affective theories including Perry's, so far as they hold that values are constituted solely by liking and enjoyment, or by interest. We have seen in the last chapter that Perry maintained that value may be "mediated" by judgments, but that the judgments which mediate interests are themselves no ingredient of the interests, which alone determine values.

2.

The fundamental problem of Dewey's ethical philosophy is whether a *science of morals* is possible, and its main objective is to give an affirmative answer to this controversial question on an empirical as well as logical ground. We have just seen that value are, for Dewey, something which arises in a problematic situation as a result of valuations. If Dewey could then establish i) that valuation is a kind of judgment, and ii) that the valuation-judgment possesses the same logical characteristics of those judgments which are already acknowledged to be the subject-matter of "scientific" treatment, his attempt in his ethical investigation might be said successful.

At the outset of the attempt to show that valuation is a kind of judgment, it seems necessary to define or limit the meaning of "valuation." "Unfortunately for discussions," the term "value" as a verb means "two radically different things: to prize and appraise; to esteem and to estimate."[18] When Dewey asserts that valuation is one kind of judgment his "valuation" is used, of course, in the second sense of the term, namely, in the sense of "appraisal" or "estimation." It is not required for Dewey to show that valuing in the sense of "prizing" or "esteeming" is also a sort of judgment, for he has never admitted that mere liking or prizing is the sufficient condition for the happening of a value.

That valuation is a kind of judgment might be best established through the rejection of the logical positivist position, or emotivism, which affirms that value-expressions are purely ejaculatory and cannot be constituents of proper propositions that affirm or deny something; and this view would be neatly rejected by pointing out that even gestures or exclamations, to which the view likens value-utterances, "say something and are of the nature of propositions" when they are made on purpose.[19]

When, for example, a little child purposely cries, this phenomenon is "social" in the sense that it is made "as a sign" to communicate something to other persons and interpreted by them as having some meaning, evoking their responses accordingly. Made as a sign, or taken as a sign, a cry is a "linguistic symbol" analogous to a proposition; for it communicates some information, or expresses some prediction, whose truth or falsity can be empirically tested. The child's cry might inform, for example, that he is confronted with a strange dog, and it might predict that he will be hurted unless somebody helps him quickly.

The analogy between value-utterances and gestures or exclamations is obvious. In gestures and exclamations there are indeed no explicit value-expressions; but we can read some implicit valuing words in them. The cry for aid, to use the same example again, might be interpreted as an assertion "that the situation with reference to which the cry is made is 'bad'."[20] If value-utterances and exclamations are essentially analogous, and if exclamations are of the nature of propositions, there would remain no ground for emotivists to claim that evaluative utterances are by no means judgments but mere expressions of feelings which cannot be either true or false. Evaluative utterances, or valuations, *are* a kind of judgment.[6] Let us, then, proceed to Dewey's next point, namely, to his discussion asserting that valuation-judgments are an authentic subject-matter of scientific treatment.

There are many writers who, admitting that valuative utterances are one kind of judgments, assert that valuative and scientific judgments are basically different in kind. They hold that moral judgments are of such peculiar character that the methods which have proved to be successful in the treatment of "scientific" propositions are not available for them. They recognize, or assume, an insurmountable logical gulf

---

6 Dewey seems to have thought that it is not necessary to illustrate, in this connection, an interpretation of a value-utterance into empirically verifiable propositions. But if someone asks him the interpretation of such an utterance as "You acted wrongly in stealing that money," he would answer that it contains such judgments as "You stole the money," "The situation became still more troublesome because of your stealing," etc.

between moral philosophy and natural science. This "split between the material, the mechanical, the scientific and the moral and the ideal," was so prevalent in his time that Dewey called it "the greatest dualism which now weighs humanity down," and considered it the "root difficulty" of the day.[21] And, as we know, he regarded it as one of his chief aims to do away with this "intellectual scandal ⋯ involved in the current and (traditional) dualism."[22]

The ground upon which the writers claim the seperation between scientific and moral judgments is, according to Dewey, that scientific judgments are universal, hence only hypothetical, and incapable of relating to acts, while moral judgments are categorical, and thus individualized, and hence refer to acts.[23] It is just these two commonplace antinomies (the separation between the universal and the individual; the separation between the intellectual and the practical) that Dewey has constantly objected to from the early days of his activity. Thus, in one of his writings intending to bridge between the scientific and the moral, "Logical Conditions of a Scientific Treatment of Morality" (1903), Dewey trys to establish that scientific and moral judgments are similar in source and kind, by showing: i) that "scientific judgments" are, at bottom, dealing with individual cases, for they begin with concrete experiences and end in "the testing and checking of the so-called laws and universals by reference to their application in further concrete experience," the generic propositions occupying a purely "intermediate position;"[24] ii) that even "scientific judgments" are conditioned by moral motivations, for every scientific judgment, as well as every moral judgment, must be regarded as an *act*, "the act showing itself both in the selection and determination of the subject and the predicate, and in the determination of their values with reference or respect to each other;"[25] iii) that ethical judgments, though individualized, not only require for their control generic propositions "which state a connection of relevant conditions in general (or objective) form," but are controllable in their formation through such universals.[26]

Even if scientific and ethical judgments have some fundamental characteristics in common, they cannot, of course, be of the exactly same nature in all aspects. What kind of differentia, then, does the ethical judgment have to distinguish itself from the scientific one? If the ethical judgment has some unique cbaracteristics, the way of the "scientific treatment" available for it might not be exactly the same with that available for ordinary descriptive judgments. Then, in what way, or in what sense, ethical problems can be treated by scientific methods? We shall study Dewey's matured views concerning these problems through his later works.

3.

For Dewey valuation is connected with desire and interest; desires and interests are "observable in themselves and in connection with their observed effects."[27] Thus, it is unquestioned that propositions *about* valuations are possible. This possibility, however, is not the sufficient condition of a scientific treatment of moral problems; for "moral problems" are not primarily concerned with *facts* of valuations but with the *validity* of them, while propositions *about* valuations tell only matter of facts. The possibility of a moral science, unless we mean by "moral science" pyschology or sociology of morals, can be guaranteed only when the possibility of some *valid* way of the *evaluation of valuations* is shown.

Most scientists believe that the validity of a descriptive proposition can be empirically tested through observation or experiment. For example, the validity of the proposition, "The diamond is harder than the gold," can be established inductively by repeating the experiment of rubbing a piece of gold with a piece of diamond. But when we come to an ethical utterance the matter seems to be not so simple. When we say, for instance, "Telling the truth is good," or "Stealing is bad," what are there to be observed or experimented with in the way of verifying the truth or falsity of the utterance? Those who give a negative answer to this question are not limited to "scientists" distinguished from "philosophers."

When we think of an ethical utterance in its abstract form, Dewey would argue in his answer to the just-mentioned objection, it would be indeed difficult to point out any observable criteria for the verification of the utterance, but if we bring the ethical utterance in a concrete situation and consider what is practically meant by it, we might find that the way to its verification is not so completely blockaded. When a man says *in a concrete situation*, "You should tell the truth," he is predicting some observable facts besides indicating some existing conditions in the situation which are also observable. But what kind of prediction and indication does an ethical utterance make in a concrete situation, and how can its prediction and indication be empirically tested? As a preparation for his answer to this question Dewey presents his analysis of the nature of "practical judgments," for he believes that judgments of value constitute a species of judgments of practice.

By "practical judgment" Dewey does not mean "an alleged type of judgment having a different organ and source from other judgments." He simply means a kind of judgment which has "a specific type of subject-matter," namely, the judgment of a situation which is "demanding action."[28] "He had better consult a physician;" "This is a good time to build a house;" and so forth, are specimens of practical judgments given by Dewey himself. They are "practical" because they are judgments of what *to do*, or what is *to be done*.

Among the characteristics of the practical judgment[7] the following three seem to be most noteworthy from our point of view: First, the situation which constitute the subject-matter of a practical judgment is incomplete or problematic. This incompleteness is not merely psychological. The objective situation itself is lacking in something and

---

7 In "The Logic of Judgments of Practice" Dewey characterized practical judgments under five items.

unsettled. "Only after this something else has been supplied will the given coincide with the full subject—matter." Since the subject—matter is unfinished and waiting for something to be done, it is connected with the future.[29]

Second, in a practical judgment the judgment itself, together with the judge's subsequent action, is a factor in completing the situation. In other words, the situation in question is more or less determined by the judgment.[30] Thus, it is clear that *some* propositions concerning an unfinished situation are *not* "practical;" for example, "It is about to rain," or "The girl is still crying."

Third, a practical judgment implies both a statement of the existing conditions of the situation judged and a prediction about the means for completing or resolving the situation.[31] For instance, "He had better consult a physician," implies that something in his physical conditions is out of order, and that the order will be recovered if he consults a physician.

From what has just been said by way of the analysis of the nature of practical judgments, particularly from the last remark, the criteria for the decision of the truth or falsity of a practical judgment is obvious. If the judgment's implicit statement about the existing conditions of the situation turns out to be false, the falsity of the whole judgment is decisive without waiting for any further consideration.[8] If, on the other hand, the judgment's statement about the existing conditions is unquestioned, the truth or falsity of the judgment is "constituted by the issue,"[32] namely, it is determined according to whether the predicted outcome is resulted by means of the suggested action. And the empirical verifiability of the statement and the prediction implied in the practical judgment might be taken for granted.

The recent development of so-called applied science is too remarkable to allow any doubt concerning the possibility of scientific treatments of practical judgments. A while's stop to consider what kind of practices physicians, engineers, architects and so forth are engaged in, and how their practices "rest upon scientifically warranted physical generalizations," would be enough to convince us of the point at issue. "Appraisals of courses of action as better and worth, more and less serviceable," says Dewey, "are as experimentally justified as are nonvaluative propositions about impersonal subject matter."[33] Is everything, however, that is true regarding practical judgments *also* true with ethical judgments? On what ground does Dewey affirm that ethical judgments are a species of practical judgments? Furthermore, even if it is established that ethical judgments are one kind of practical judgments, this is not a sufficient ground to assert that all which is true of applied science is also true of morals. For there might be *two kinds of* practical judgments, and the differentiae of them might make what is true about the one false about the other. In fact, what Dewey really did in his discussion which we have so far followed was to give

---

8 In "The Logic of Judgments of Practice" Dewey does not make any explicit mention of the case when the implicit statement about the existing conditions is questioned, but this point might be considered to be understood.

an analysis of the nature of *a certain kind of* practical judgments, which might be called "means–end propositions," for he considered there only such propositions as can be regarded as the alleged subject–matter of applied science, leaving all sorts of ethical judgments for his later consideration. Therefore, what Dewey has to do next for the completion of his argument is: i) either to show that means–end judgments and ethical judgments are of exactly the same nature concerning all logical characteristics of them, or ii) to show that the difference which exists between means–end judgments and ethical judgments is irrelevant to the verifiability or non–verifiability of them. Let us follow his further discussion.

It is understood that ethical judgments are judgments about what to do. When an ethical judgment is uttered in a concrete situation, Dewey holds, it is demanding an act. An act is required because the situation is lacking in something. In other words, whenever a situation finds itself to be incomplete or problematic, it requires the completion or the resolution; the main instrument which can effectively bring forth the resolution in a problematic situation is human activities; and an ethical judgment, for Dewey, is nothing but the judgment about the fit instrument, or proper means, required for the resolution of a problematic situation.

Interpreted in this way, the similarity between ethical judgments and "practical judgments" is obvious. In both cases the situations which constitute their subject–matters are incomplete and problematic. In both cases the judgments themselves are the factors in completing the situations. And in both cases the judgments explicitly suggest the proper way for the completion of the unfinished situations, implicitly indicating the existing conditions of the situations. Hence Dewey affirms that the ethical judgment is a species of practical judgments, since it is "never complete in itself, but always in behalf of determinig what is to be done," as well as it implies that "value is not anything as yet given, but is something to-be-given by future action, itself conditioned upon ⋯ the judgment."[34)]

A practical judgment such as, "He had better consult Dr. A than Dr. B," has an end to be accomplished, and what it is suggesting is the effective means to reach the "end-in-view." A reflective relating can always be found in this kind of practical judgment, and it is just what distinguish them from ordinary descriptive propositions. The verifiability of this kind of practical judgments is doubtless due to the fact that they can be tested by observation of results actually attained in comparison with those intended. Besides, the relation of means and end is controlled by the same principle which governs the relation of cause and effect. Thus, as far as "practical judgments" concern themselves in discovering serviceable *means* to given ends, it is safely asserted that "they are rules for the use, in and by human activity, of scientific generalization as means for accomplishing certain desired and intended ends."[35)]

Here, however, a crucial question presents itself; namely, "Do ethical judgments also primarily concern themselves in discovering useful means for given ends?" This question is crucial because if it is answered affirmatively, and can be adequately defended, Dewey's attempt to establish the possibility of the "science of morals" would remarkably approach its goal, while if it is answered negatively Dewey would have to introduce some other assumptions if he does not want to make a fresh start.

It is commonly held that the primary concern of ethics is "intrinsic" good (or right). When "X is good," is uttered as an ethical valuation, the "good" does not mean "good for" but what is good *in and of itself*. In other words, the proper object of an ethical judgment is, so we are told, a matter of ends, not of means. When the ends to be attained are known, the problem of discovering the fit means could doubtless be scientifically dealt with. But in the case of a genuinely ethical situation, so the popular view maintains, the end to be accomplished is not known; it is just the end that is questioned. If this widely held position is correct, what has been established by Dewey concerning "practical judgments" would evidently not be adequate to settle at a stroke that fundamental problem of ethics — "Is a science of value possible?" How, then, does Dewey tide over the difficulty suggested by this "standing objection?" Now, it seems, we have come to the point where we may aptly proceed to his conception of the relations between the categories of "means" and "end."

4.

To survey Dewey's conception concerning the nature of ends would be a good start for studying his view of the relation between means and ends. Dewey rejects, in the first place, the traditional notion of "fixed ends." Even after the intellectual revolution of the seventeenth century expelled from natural science the Aristotelian teleological view of the world, the doctrine of fixed ends−in−themselves has survived, at the expense of logical consistency, in the realm of philosophy as "the cornerstone of orthodox moral theory."[36] I do not want to engage in a ponderous argument against the notion of fixed ends. Let us, instead, simply ask the defenders of the notion two questions: i) What are *the final ends (or end) a priori* of human actions? ii) What ground do you have to verify that *they* are the final ends? So long as these questions are not convincingly answered the notion remains merely a metaphysical or religious assumption.

Ends, Dewey holds, are not "things lying beyond activity at which the letter is directed." They are imaginary pictures which the mind makes in the course of human activities. "In fact, ends are ends−in−view or aims."[37] Confronted with a problematic situation, a man reacts against the present state of things and wishes to have something different. He pictures in his imagination a scene which, if presented, would be satisfactory. But in itself this picture is a mere fancy. A mere fancy, a phantasy, or a day−dream does not constitute a true aim or end. An imaginary picture colored by wish, however, becomes an aim or end when, and only when, it is sincerely considered in terms of *means*. "It becomes aim or end," says Dewey, "only when it is worked out in terms of concrete conditions available for its realization."[38]

Dewey's arguments concerning the inseparability of means and ends, which is already suggested by his description of the nature of ends, and which constitutes the keystone of his answer to the objection made by the popular view which definitely distinguishes intrinsic and instrumental goods, can be summarized as follows:

i) Desires and interests, the matrix of the constitution of end-values, are not independent of the appraisal of the means to satisfy them, but are intimately modified by the consideration of the conditions which are causally related to the attainment of the desired goals. "The object finally valued as an end to be reached," says Dewey, "is determined in its concrete make up by appraisal of existing conditions as means."[39]

ii) The popular assumption that the separation between instrumental and intrinsic goods is undeniable is not, in fact, self-evident.

iii) The distinction between means and ends is "temporal and relational." Since experience is continuous, an end at a certain stage necessarily turns out to be one of the conditions which control the means for another end to be accomplished at the next stage.[40] This fact is reflected even in common sense which discriminates between "shortsighted" and "farsighted" desires. "Farsightedness" means nothing but the prudence which views a given end-in-view, or an aim, as a "conditioning means of further consequences."

iv) The absurdity of the sharp separation between means and ends becomes obvious when we think of its *practical* implication. What if, for example, a would-be artist professes his devotion to painting pictures on the one hand, but reveals his profound "contempt for canvas, brush and paints" on the other hand? "The ineffectiveness in action of 'ideals'," says Dewey, "is due precisely to the supposition that means and ends are not on exactly the same level with respect to the attention and care they demand."[41]

v) The popular view maintains that the values of means are necessarily instrumental and cannot be immediate or intrinsic because means are by definition relational, mediated and mediating. But the fallacy of this reasoning is manifest; for "the relational character of the *things* that are employed as means does not prevent the things from having their own immediate qualities."[42] Whenever an object is *prized* and *cared for*, even if the reason for the prizing the object lies in its usefulness for something else, the object necessarily possesses an *immediate* quality of value; for, according to the popular view, *prizing* applies only to *ends*, while *appraising* applies to things that are *means*.[43]

To push a little further, the view which identifies the *inherent* or the *intrinsic* with the *nonrelational* is incompatible with the view which connects the end–value of a thing with desire and interest. According to the latter view, all values are relational. Therefore, if to be intrinsic is equivalent to being nonrelational there can be no intrinsic value at all. Evidently all this absurdity originates in the undue separation of means and ends. To repeat once again, the distinction between means and end is relative. "If one has an ardent desire to obtain certain things as means," says Dewey, "for the time being, producing or obtaining those means *is* the end-in-view."[44]

Let us assume, for convenience sake, that Dewey's arguments about the inseparability of means and ends are, as such, sound, and see whether Dewey's attempt to establish the possibility of ethical science has reached its solid foundation by this, so to speak, last touch of the means-end arguments.

The fundamental points of Dewey's position under consideration might be put, if we borrow the form of syllogism, in this way:

i) All empirically verifiable propositions can be scientifically treated. All practical propositions are empirically verifiable. Therefore, all practical propositions are proper subject-matter of science.

ii) Practical propositions are judgments about the appropriate means to attaining ends-in-view. (Definition) Though all ethical utterances are judgments about the values of ends-in-view, not only are ends-in-view themselves inseparable from the means to accomplish them, but ends actually reached are, in turn, means to future ends; and consequently to judge the value of an end-in-view the judge must take into consideration both the means by which the end-in-view is to be accomplished and the future ends for which the attainment of the end-in-view must turn out to be either favorable or unfavorable. Therefore all ethical utterances are practical judgments.

iii) From i) and ii) it is clear that a scientific treatment of all ethical utterances *is* possible.

The first syllogism would not be open to objection provided that we admit the verifiability of "scientific" judgments. And the last conclusion would be established if it is shown that the second syllogism is also acceptable. But the second proposition of the second syllogism is rather complicated, and it seems difficult to affirm or negate on the spot its suitability as the minor premise required to make the reasoning sound. Therefore, a little further analysis of the second proposition in question is necessary.

The perfect minor premise for our second syllogism would be this: "All ethical utterances are judgments about the appropriate means to the accomplishment of some end or ends." Thus, the essential point of our analysis of the second proposition must be to find whether the proposition is equivalent to the above suggested model of the perfect minor premise.

The equivalency at issue would be affirmed when, and only when, it is proved that *all* ends-in-view are, in their ultimate nature, instrumental. That all ends-in-view are instrumental, namely, that all ends-in-view are after all means for something beyond themselves, might seem, at first sight, to be a self-contradictory assertion. For the "something" beyond all ends-in-view itself must be one kind of end-in-view. But when we survey Dewey's whole position carefully we find that he does affirm the instrumentality of all ends-in-view.

The *inseparability* of means and ends, however closely they may be related, does not necessarily make an end instrumental. For that an end-in-view is inseparably related with the consideration of means, does not exactly mean that the end-in-view itself is a means. As a matter of empirical fact, ends and means might be always inseparable;

but as logical concepts "means" and "end" are always distinguishable. Thus, the instrumental characteristic of all ends-in-view does not follow from the psychological fact of inseparable relation between ends and means. Whence then does it come?

The instrumental nature of ends-in-view seems to be found in Dewey's own conception of "ends-in-view." Ends-in-view, it should be remembered, are imaginary pictures which the mind makes in problematic situations. When there is some "trouble" in an existing situation, that is, when there is something lacking, or wanting in a given situation, the mind, wishing to resolve the trouble, or to supplement the lacking factors, pictures to itself a scene which would be realized when the problem is resolved. This imaginary picture of the future state naturally becomes the temporary aim, or end-in-view, of the activity caused by the "something the matter"[45] in the situation. Thus considered, the instrumental nature of the end-in-view begins to reveal itself; for the end-in-view is evidently one of those things *by virtue of which* the problem involved in the situation is resolved. The commonplace saying that the human being is the most powerful animal in the world primarily indicates the fact that he can resolve his problems most skillfully and effectively. And this skill and effectiveness are, of course, due to his intelligence. Now what intellect does in the course of problem-solving is, among other things, to judge what may follow from such and such an action. In other words, the power of intellect is most remarkably revealed when it predicts and plans. Predictions and plans are powerful instruments through which human beings resolve their problems skillfully and effectively. And an end-in-view is noting but a predicted future preferred as the best possibility. It is a part of a plan. Like a lighthouse in the ocean it helps the voyage of human life. Or we might better liken ends-in-view to milestones. As no milestone is the final end of travel, no end-in-view is the ultimate end of an action, nor even one of the *true* ends of human activities. *Ends-in-view are "directive means!"* The following quotations might suggest that the above-mentioned interpretation is not far removed from Dewey's own idea: (Italics are mine.)

> Ends are foreseen consequences which arise in the course of activity and which are *employed to give activity added meaning* and *to direct its further* course. They are in no sense ends *of* action. In being ends of *deliberation* they are redirecting pivots *in* action.[46]

> Even the most important among all the consequences of an act is not necessarily its aim. Results which are objectively most important may not even be thought of at all; ⋯. The end-thought-of ⋯ gives the decisive clew to the act to be performed under the existing circumstances. *It is particular foreseen object that will stimulate the act which relieves existing troubles*, straightens out existing entanglements.[47]

In the continuous temporal process of organizing activities into a co-ordinated and co-ordinating unity, a constituent activity is both an end and a means: an end, insofar as it is temporally and relatively a close; a means, insofar as it provides a condition to be taken into account in further activity.[48]

Ends-in-view, as distinct from ends as accomplished results, themselves function as *directive means*; or, in ordinary language, as plans.[49]

When our analysis of Dewey's position has reached this point we notice that there is one basic assumption which is supporting Dewey's whole theory of morals. The assumption tells: "Problems ought to be solved;" or "It is good to resolve troubles." Dewey himself has not explicitly set up this assumption, but if our interpretation of his view is acceptable, the existence of this assumption as a hidden base of Dewey's ethics might be consequently admitted. We saw that, for Dewey, all aims or ends-in-view were instruments for something, and now we see that the "something" can be indentified with "solving problems."

Some might be tempted to make an objection at this point by asking, "Is then problem-solving an intrinsic good? Do we prize problem-solving for its own sake, or do we desire to solve a problem as a means to something else such as, for instance, 'happiness' or 'troubleless life'?" But we can hardly think of anything which can be properly called "happiness" or "life" apart from the very process of man's problem-solving. If such terms as "happiness" or "human life" are to indicate something concrete they must be indentifid with the stream of activities which is nothing but the incessant process of problem–solving. The seemingly different two propostions, "We seek to resolve problems for the resolutions' sake," and "We seek to resolve problems for the sake of happiness (or troubleless life)," do not indicate quite different things.

Whether we call what is ultimately sought after "happiness" or "troubleless life" or "solution of problems," the matter is rather verbal. But there are at least two real, as well as fundamental, questions which must be asked in connection with Dewey's basic assumption we have just discussed. They are: i) Why ought problems to be solved? ii) Is there a *right* way of solving problems, as distinguished from a wrong way; and, if there is, what is it?

5.

The basic difference between Dewey's ethical doctrine and traditional ethics consists, in fact, not so much in his denial of the distinction between intrinsic good and extrinsic good as in his affirmation of the instrumental nature involved in what popular views usually hold to be "intrinsic values." The traditional teleological thinkers believed that the first problem of ethics was to find the ultimate end of human actions, and attempted to solve this problem through dialectical analysis of the nature of "value" (or "good"), or on the ground of metaphysical beliefs or psychological facts. But Dewey, finding the traditional approach futile, began with the empirical question, "How value occurs actually in experience?" Holding that values are caused by valuation he concentrated his attention on the analysis of the nature of *valuation* rather than that of "value." One of the important things Dewey found in his study of valuation was that our activity of valuation concerns itself primarily not with "absolute" ends (or *the* final end) which are desired for their own sake, but with ends–in–view, which, being "ends" only temporarily and relatively, are of an instrumental nature in their essence. Thus, Dewey came to recognize the importance of means–value, which had been generally neglected, and pushed his study accordingly. Meanwhile, the old problem which traditional teleologists deemed most fundamental, "What is the final end of human activity?" or "What is intrinsically good?" was, so to say, left behind the screen by Dewey. However, though Dewey did not tackle this problem from the front, the problem was implicitly answered. The answer was implied in his assumption that a problem ought to be solved. Then we may properly ask, with traditional thinkers, "Why problems ought to be solved? And what is the *right* way to resolve them?"

Dewey himself, to my knowledge, has not explicitly occupied himself with the problem of why we ought to solve our problems. Dewey might have thought it is even foolish to spend time asking such a question. Indeed the question at issue has been asked very often under wrong assumptions. It has mostly been asked either by those who believed in some absolute values or goods which exist *a priori* (i.e., independent of experience) and put human beings under obligation from the outside, or by those who thought that there is no obligation at all. Since Dewey considers the notion that "value-conceptions have to be imported from a source outside experience is one of the most curious beliefs the mind of man has ever entertained,"[50] he would consider it only foolish to seek for any transcendental reason why we should resolve our problems. If, on the other hand, the question is asked by a man of skeptical mood, Dewey would answer him by pointing out the *necessity* or *inevitableness* by which experience or nature is conditioned.

In "The Logic of Judgments of Practice" there is a passage which is suggesting that though there is no value, apart from objects' relations to some subject, in objects as such, a man has a reason to desire (or to do) something. We read:

> Why, it will be asked, does a man buy a suit of clothes unless that it is a value, or at least a proximate means to a further value? The answer is short and simple: Because he has to; because the situation in which he lives demands it. ⋯ While a man lives, he never is called upon to judge whether he shall act, but simply *how* he shall act. A decision not to act is a decision to act in a certain way, it is never a judgment not to act, unqualifiedly. It is a judgment to do something else ⋯ conditioned upon the necessity that irrespective of judging a man will have to act somehow anyway. ⋯[51]

This quotation is not from a context which is dealing with the problem of the ultimate ground of moral obligation. But it would not be quite far-fetched to connect this passage with our problem under consideration, and to affirm that, for Dewey, the final source of moral obligation is to be found in some biological necessity of human nature.

Morality is a cultural phenomenon which "grows naturally out of the very conditions of human life."[52] We cannot adequately consider moral problems apart from the basis out of which the phenomena of morals inevitably grow. Problems of morals are problems of living men. Since he is alive and his environment undergoes change, a living man is confronted with situations which require to be altered to recover the balance which is continuously disturbed by the fluctuation of the world. The required alterationa should be, in principle, brought about by actions. A man is prohibited from acting simply in accordance with sheer impulse, since by nature he is endowed with intelligence. Since an action is required as a means to change the given situation in a certain way, and since only some limited kinds of action can be suitable for the purpose to be accomplished, an intellectual being necessarily thinks over which action is to be chosen. But the choice is not between to act and not to act, but between several ways of acting. In other words, "the question" is not "to be or not to be" but "how to be." Thus, though we may ask, as a subject of an abstract discipline by formal discussions, whether we should resolve our problems or not, this question is not quite *practical*. To hold that the question, "Do I have to solve my problems," is so important that we must answer it, and to think that I may answer this question negatively, is evidently self-contradictory. If I need not solve my problems it would be superfluous even to ask why I ought to solve my problems; for, then, I would be raising a problem the solution of which is not necessary.

Moral problems are problems of living men. Living men are at bottom valuing creatures. They must value because they are alive; they ought to value because they are obliged by their own nature to value. The only thing which can be, for Dewey, the ultimate ground of the moral imperative is the nature of human beings. If we ask Dewey how he justifies his categorical imperative, "So act as to increase the meaning of present experience,"[53] he would simply answer: "We must act so because our own nature requires it."

For Dewey ethical judgments are, as a sort of practical judgments, hypothetical. They can be translated into the form of "If … then …." But, Dewey seems to believe, we living men cannot, as a matter of fact, refuse the conditional antecedent, "If …." If the antecedent is inevitably accepted, the whole hypothetical proposition which constitutes an ethical judgment must have one kind of absoluteness. It is this form of absoluteness, as distinct from a complete relativity, that I want to defend in the final chapter.

Our second question in connection with Dewey's basic assumption was, "What is the *right* way to resolve problems?" It is a commonplace that even one and the same problem can be solved in several ways. We can get a wanted book either by borrowing or by buying, or even by stealing. Even over-compensation and hysteria are recognized as ways of adjustment. Is there a specially right way to reach a desired end? Dewey's answer to this question might be found in his notion of the "continuum of ends–means." If a problematic situation were isolated and independent of all other situations, all kinds of means effective to solve the problem would be acceptable. But our situations are continuous like a stream and our problems are interrelated like an organism. A way of solving the present problem inevitably constitutes one of the conditions upon which the next situation depends. Thus, it is natural "that desires, ends–in–view, and consequences achieved be valued in turn as means of further consequences."[54] Burning down a house to obtain a roast pig cannot be regarded as the right method because it causes still more serious troubles. G. R. Geiger suggests to express the answer to our question, "with both bluntness and tautology," as follows: "The only 'good' solution to a problem is one which indeed solves it without still further enlarging the problem."[55] Whether Dewey likes this expression or not, his recommended "method of intelligent action" would not lead us a conclusion far from Geiger's. Of course, when we think of the endless chain of cause and effect as well as the complicated tangle of social relations, and when we bear in mind the limited power of human intelligence, it is obvious that very few ways of solution can be absolutely complete. Here too, what is allowed to human beings is only to seek for the approximation towards the ideal.

6.

Even with this much study of Dewey the possibility of the science of morals does not seem to have been established. It is undeniable that the phenomenon of valuation exists as an empirically observable fact, and that knowledge *about* valuations is accordingly possible. But it is admitted that a bundle of the knowledge about valuations does not of itself constitute the "science of morals" which Dewey has in mind. And it also has become clear, provided that Dewey's arguments so far surveyed are sound, that a valuation–judgment can be empirically tested (partly at least) by means of observing whether the consequences actually attained give the solution needed. Even this, however, does not provide the sufficient condition for the possibility of a scientific theory of morals; for *ex post facto* verifiability alone is not enough to make a proposition "scientific." The truth or falsity of such propositions as, "The first baby who is to be born in London next year will be a girl," or "Orioles will beat Yankees with the score of 11 to 9 in the first game to be played ten years from today," can be tested when the day concerned comes, but they cannot be called "scientific" unless their formation were methodologically controlled by other established judgments. A proposition can be properly called "scientific" only when it is available as a *valid rule for prediction*. This point is especially true with Dewey who believes that science is primarily method. "Scientific", says Dewey, "means the possibility of establishing an order of judgments such that each one when made is of use in determining other judgments, thereby securing control of their formation."[56] To put it in ordinary language, to be scientific is first of all to be able to foresee what would follow from a given course of action. In short, if the science of morals is to be possible, some *generic* propositions useful in moral situations must be attainable.

According to Dewey, even in physical science generic propositions occupy a purely intermediate position. "They are bridges by which we pass over from one particular experience to another."[57] Two particular experiences can be bridged because the controlling factors upon which the two experiences are hinged are basically common. For instance, we can formulate general rules of making ice-cream because the conditions under which A makes A's ice-cream are not so essentially different from the conditions under which B makes B's ice-cream that the same general rules cannot be applied to both cases. Since no two situations are exactly the same, there are of course differences between the two sets of conditions. But the difference is not fundamental as far as ice-cream making is concerned. The same thing might be asserted, in principle, about technology, architecture, medicine, and other fields of science. But can we extend the same logic to the formation of generic moral rules?

That it is difficult to answer this question in the affirmative without hesitation is suggested by Dewey's own emphasis about "the uniqueness of good." Since for Dewey values occur as, so to say, functions of situations, and situations are different from each other, the notion of fixed good or eternal value is naturally rejected. We are told:

> In quality, the good is never twice alike. It never copies itself. ··· It
> is unique in its every presentation.[58]

If the good is "new every morning, fresh every evening," it is
consequently difficult to set up general rules of actions to bring it
about. Dewey himself contends that "moral is not a catalogue of acts
nor a set of rules to be applied like drugstore prescriptions or cook-
book recipes."[59]

Even when the problems are simply of a technical nature the
situations are not exactly the same. One man may have to make plenty
of ice-cream for commercial purposes while another man may have to
make only a small amount of it for his family. The materials available
for each of them may be more or less different. One might have to use
powdered eggs, powdered milk, beet sugar etc., while the other will
have to use fresh eggs, fresh milk, cane sugar etc. They might have to
make ice-cream in different temperatures, under different
atmospheric pressure and so forth. But these differences are all
quantitative and they can be numerically defined. For example,
different bottles of milk might be composed of different proportion of
protein, fat, carbohydrate, water etc., but they can be difined in terms
of commensurable chemical elements. Since the differences involved in
the conditions of different ice-cream making situations are solely
quantitative they can be technically controlled. Of course the products

might be different in some measure from each other, but they are anyhow things which can be called "ice-cream."

As far as the "material" world is concerned, whether we consider practical problems or theoretical problems, the possibility of forming general rules or principles might be, to the extent that the assumption of the Uniformity of Nature is tenable, admitted from the pragmatic point of view at least. But as soon as we transfer our attention to the fields of "mental" and "social" affairs, we find that the matter is not so simple. The most excellent psychologist or psychiatrist cannot present a generic prescription to cure hysteria or schizophrenia or mania-depressive psychosis as confidently as a watch-repair-man at the back alley tells how to deal with various troubles of watches and clocks. As for social or political problems, the difficulty is even more striking, Think of the simple fact that to root out juvenile delinquency is much more difficult than to send a rocket to the moon. We have almost forgotten to think it strange that, even though most people on the earth have rightly found their common aim in the ideal of "world peace," no one can show the successful way to reach that earnestly desired end.

There cannot be, for Dewey at least, a definite demarcation between "moral" problems and "social" or "psychiatric" problems. All problems or troubles which stand in the way of human happiness must be managed through human actions, and can be considered "moral" in a very wide sense of the term. Anyway it is clear that Dewey's moral aim of actions, to remove troubles from situations concerned, includes the resolution of psychiatric and social problems. It is accordingly also clear that all the difficulties which men must meet on their way to a scientific solution of psychiatric or social problems must be met also when we attempt to solve moral problems through scientific method.

That moral problems are even more complicated than psychiatric and social problems, and that a science of morals had its peculiar difficulties will be suggested in the next section when we try a criticism of Dewey's position. It might, however, be appropriate to refer here to the cultural relativity of morals which has been often emphasized by those who denied the possibility of general principles in morals. Dewey himself is one of those who contend for the inseparable relation between custom and morality,[60] and the remarkable diversity of customs is a commonplace of folklore. Although custom as such cannot be identified with morals, it is indisputable that the same kind of conduct, for instance, to marry a widowed sister-in-law, may be morally acceptable in one society and unacceptable in another, as long as we, following Dewey, define "good" in terms of results of actions in problematic situations, and deem "right" and "duty" things which "arise from the relations which human beings intimately sustain to one another."[61] That one and the same sort of action can be, depending upon situations, both good and bad, or right and wrong, might be regarded as a fact suggesting the difficulty, if not impossibility, of scientific treatment of moral problems; for science is supposed to enable the formation of generic propositions.

Dewey's own view concerning the point at issue, namely, whether individual moral experiences can be regulated through the mediation of generic propositions, seems to be, in effect, that the formation of generic moral propositions is difficult but not impossible. This optimistic position of Dewey seems to be based mainly upon the following assumptions as well as upon those which were implied in the already studied discussions (such as that values occur in the context of human needs and desires).

The first assumption is that human beings can be defined, both psychologically and sociologically, in terms of universal elements or common conditions. According to Dewey there are at least two forces which make morals stable. One is "the psychological uniformity of human nature with respect to basic needs;" and the other comes from the sociological fact that "there are certain conditions which must be met in order that any form of human association may be maintained, whether it be simple or complex⋯."[62] By virtue of these two common factors the basic *framework* of morality is commonly shared by all sort of societies, and some moral laws are almost universally accepted.

The important implication of this assumption is that psychology and sociology, or anthropology in wider sense, can be an "explanatory science," if the use of a vague terminology is allowed. Of course Dewey would not assert that we can, at the present stage of psychological and sociological knowledge, completely analyze human nature and human society into common elements exactly defined, and that individual difference among men or societies can be described solely in terms of quantitative measurements of the commensurable elements, as is the case with physics or chemistry. What Dewey maintains would be that even the so-called social sciences *can approach* the ideal the pattern of which has been clearly shown by the advance of "natural science."

The second assumption which, in close connection with the first, sustains Dewey's optimistic position seems to be that the more we know about facts (especially facts of valuation and human nature in general) the more likely we are to make right or valid valuations in ethical situations. To be a little more detailed:

i) Though the factual knowledge about valuation does not of itself provide ethical propositions, it is not only a necessary but a fundamental *condition* of formulating valid ethical judgments. "The ability to form valid propositions about the relation of present desires and purposes to future consequences," says Dewey, "depends in turn upon ability to analyze these present desires and purposes into their constituent elements."[63] The knowledge about the past valuation-events clarifies the import of present valuations and places them in proper perspective. Since human activities are continuous, existing desires and interests and valuations can be properly revalued only when they are seen in the context of past conditions. When, for example, an existing moral law is known to be grounded upon some prejudice or superstition, this factual knowledge would prove to be an important condition of the proper reappraisal of the law.

ii) Existing valuations as such, of course, cannot be unconditionally accepted as valid rules of conduct. But there can be no abstract and transcendental theory of valuation which is entitled to be respected as the standard for the evaluation of existing valuations. "Improved valuation," says Dewey, "must grow out of existing valuations, subjected to critical methods of investigation that bring them into systematic relations with one another."[64] It is obvious that this recommendation of the method bringing existing valuations into connection with one another, is nothing but to suggest that the methods which have proved to be successful in the fields of physics and chemistry are to be carried over to the field of human or social study. The systematic advance of physical science "dates from the time when conceptions that formed the content of theory were derived from the phenomena themselves and were then employed as hypotheses for relating together the otherwise separate matters−of−fact."[65] In the field of humanistic studies the *certain* means for bringing factual elements into close relation with one another is at present lacking. But Dewey sees no reason why the same process of method cannot, in principle, be applied to this outstripped domain of investigations. He believes that "the propositions which have resulted and which now form the substantial content of physics, of chemistry, ⋯ provide the very means by which the change which is required can be introduced into beliefs and ideas purporting to deal with human and social phenomena."[66]

7.

We need not, it seems, spend much space to commend the

contributions of Dewey's ethical theory; partly because some of the merits we have already assigned to Perry are also shared by Dewey who, together with Perry, has brought the problems of morality from the height of metaphysical clouds down to the stern realities of the earth by deeming value essentially a matter of human experience; and partly because the hitherto presented exposition of Dewey's doctrine, if it is acceptable, might have implicitly suggested some excellences contained in the theory. It would suffice to itemize a few respects:

i) By indicating that the ultimate ground of morals is the necessary conditions under which human beings are obliged to live their lives, Dewey admirably clarified the very nature of morals themselves. This point is essential for ethics because the right understanding of the nature of morals are prerequisite to the proper setting up or choice of problems to be studied as "fundamental" by a theory of morals. ii) The intellectual aspect of valuation was aptly pointed out by Dewey, and the analogy he found between scientific and moral judgments is full of suggestions, if not completely sound. iii) Dewey's emphasis on the "uniqueness of good," his consideration of values in close connection with individual situations, seems to be in accord with our experience which abounds in varieties and diversification of human value, though the greater the emphasis on this point the greater might be the difficulties in finding the universal in morals. Anyhow, the creative aspect of moral activities has been clearly revealed by Dewey's penetrating observation. iv) Dewey properly demanded that we reconsider the commonplace conceptions concerning "end" and "means," "intrinsic value" and "instrumental value," though his thoroughgoing obliteration of the distinction between intrinsic and extrinsic values might be questioned.

It seems true that the distance to the ideal of "scientific ethics" has been shortened by Dewey's painstaking analysis of the nature of valuation. But we should also admit that Dewey's attempt to establish the possibility of scientific treatment of morality is far from being complete. This conclusive remark is sustained by the following considerations:

A) The first difficulty involved in Dewey's theory is connected with his conception of "problematic situation" or "problem." To begin with, Dewey's view cannot tell what is the exact *contents* of the problem in a given situation. To be more precise, since Dewey denies any absolute standard of completeness, it is impossible to specify what or how much is lacking in a given situation. Let us give some examples to make the point clearer. (a) Some primitive people might not care for any artificial tooth, believing the falling away of aged men's teeth quite natural. Suppose a member of this primitive society lost a couple of teeth when his age had approached to fifty. Now, is something lacking with this man's alveoli? Does he have the "problem" of having artificial teeth? (b) Nancy is not very rich, but she is very eager for beautiful looks; she wants to go to the beauty-shop everyday, and she wants to have the largest diamond in her society. Mary, on the other hand, cares little about her appearance; she does not think it worthwhile to bother herself with a lipstick in spite of her mother's frequent advice; she affirms that she is little interested in boys. Now, what and how much are needed for each of these two girls to solve their "make-up" problems? (c) Suppose there is a certain island in the South Pacific. The inhabitants are quite satisfied with their primitive lives; they are happy especially because they know little about "civilization," which raises many problems. They have no schools and accordingly no troublesome problems of school-education — "troublesome" because it involves competition. (Naturally they suffer from sickness and death, but the optimistic people are not so serious as ordinary civilized people about these "natural phenomena.") Now, is it advisable for a missionary organization to establish a school in this island? Can knowledge be one of the cardinal virtues for these islanders; or is the proverb, "Ignorance is bliss," quite true for them? It seems clear that the three illustrations just mentioned suggest two general questions of importance: i) What are the conditions which determine the contents of the problem involved in a human situation; are they physical or psychological, objective or subjective? ii) Is it good to introduce or create new problems for further activities? We do not see any satisfactory answer which can be given to the first question from Dewey's position. This difficulty might be called the "ambiguity of the problem." As for the second question, to answer it negatively does not seem to be in accord with Dewey's basic viewpoint. For Dewey finds the real ideal of human beings not in the state of problemlessness or the Stoic *apatheia*, but in intellectual growth or progress, and by "intellectual growth" he means "constant expansion of horizons and consequent formation of new purposes and new responses."[67] Dewey plainly declares that "the worst thing about stubbornness of mind ⋯ is that [it arrests] development" by shutting "the mind off from new stimuli." But Dewey's affirmative answer does not follow from his fundamental assumption that problems should be solved. He is simply introducing another assumption. Dewey could justify the first assumption by arguing that human nature *necessarily* seeks for solution of problems; but can he justify the new assumption in the same way? Evidently he cannot. For to say that human nature *necessarily* seeks for new problems or new stimuli implies that even the state of problemlessness involves a problem, which is apparently absurd.

Problems are not simply given from outside. The contents of our problems are more or less modified by the ideals we entertain. It seems that human beings play a somewhat active role even in the formation of their problems. In some aspects of our experience men seems to be endeavoring to resolve those problems which are given by themselves. If this is the case, the first question of normative ethics must be, "What ideal should we entertain?" This is, however, a problem which is left inadequately studied behind Dewey's theory of valuation.

Again, not only actual deficiency but also *possible* deficiency can constitute a problem. For example, when I participate in a health and accident insurance program nothing is actually lacking at present. (Of course a sense of security might be lacking, but this psychological fact is not the primary reason for my participation in an insurance program.) I decide to participate in the program simply to make preparation for some future problem which I wish not to happen. This kind of future problem might be confronted, but it is by no means certain. This *uncertainty of problems* is worth noticing because it may constitute a factor for the *uncertainty of normative ethics*.

Next, there are cases where one and the same situation involves two, or more than two, problems the solutions to which conflict with each other. Jean-Paul Sartre gives a nice example of this kind.[68] A young Frenchman wants to stay at home in order to help his mother, who is living alone with him and whose only consolation is in this young man. At the same time, however, he desires to serve his country and avenge his brother by joining the Free French Forces. If he stays near his mother he would certainly aid her to live, but this is to commit himself to "the morality of sympathy, of personal devotion." To join the French Forces is to choose a morality of wider scope, but its effect is quite uncertain because his actions "might vanish like water into sand and serve no purpose." Now it is a matter of everyday life that we are obliged to choose between contradicting causes. One of the most fundamental problems of normative ethics is, "Which cause should we choose when we are confronted with a *complex problem* containing contradictory factors?" But Dewey's doctrine does not present any adequate principle with which to solve this problem. If our problem is to choose between some different means to satisfy one and the same desire, as is the case when we ask ourselves, like the hero of Stendhal's *The Red and The Black*, in what kind of vocation we should employ ourselves in order to achieve fame and power, the problem might be treated under the light of "scientific" knowledge because the problem is *simple* in the sense that it originated in a single desire. But when our problem has its roots in two, or more than two, contradicting desires, as that of Peter Abelard when he hesitated between love and fame, the power of science seems not to be fully available. Dewey might argue that we can evaluate the value of each desire by predicting what sort of result the pursuit of the desire will bring forth. However, this kind of evaluation would not always work. Abelard might have been intelligent enough to have foreseen what would respectively happen in case when he attached himself to Heloise, and in case when he gave her up. But he chose a course which Dewey might *not* approve. The point is that our desires, being conbined with emotions, are often too stubborn and too obstinate to be so easily controlled by rational thinking as Dewey's over–intellectualism would have us believe.

Moreover, there are human problems which, by the nature of the case, cannot be solved. Most people are confronted with this kind of problem when they more or less seriously wish everlasting youthfulness or immortality and the like. As a more specific case we might refer to Sir Chatterley's tragedy if what he really wanted was his own child. Since the knowledge that certain desires cannot be, as a rule, satisfied does not always result in the extinction of those desires, the insolubility of these problems inevitably fosters the dark side of normative ethics.

B) The second difficulty in Dewey's ethical theory centers about his interpretation of the meaning of the ethical utterance. According to Dewey the essential meaning of an ethical utterance was predictive. Besides the predictive meaning, as we have seen, he recognized some descriptive information in every ethical statement. These two kinds of meanings, predictive and descriptive, are all that are involved, for Dewey, in ethical utterances. Though Dewey's emphasis on the predictive function of ethical utterances contains highly commendable penetration, his analysis is not quite adequate. A thoughtful criticism on this point has already been presented by Stevenson. The main theses in his criticism, with which we may agree, are: a) Dewey did not pay sufficient attention to the emotive meaning of ethical utterances. b) Ethical utterances are *not always* predictive. c) Even when an ethical utterance implies some prediction the contents of the prediction is not always so clear as to offer unmistakable criteria for its verification. d) One and the same ethical expression might predict different things.[69]

a') Even if the Emotivist position is not wholly acceptable, that an ethical utterance usually contains *some* imperative (or quasi-imperative) force or *some* emotional expression should be admitted. Dewey does not seem to have entirely overlooked the fact of emotive meaning. As Stevenson suggests, by employing the notion of "prediction" in a wider sense Dewey tacitly absorbed emotive meaning into predictive suggestion.[9] Even though this procedure might not be harmful from a practical point of view, a theoretical analysis of the meaning of ethical language would be inadequate unless it clearly distinguishes between predictive and emotive meanings. A detailed discussion concerning the significance of this distinction will be given later. What we should notice here in passing is that, as Stevenson suggested,[70] in the background of Dewey's neglect of emotive meaning we might perceive his through intellectualism — his implicit assumption that all disagreement in attitude is based upon disagreement in belief, an assumption far from being an established fact.

b') When a teleological moralist like Dewey says, "Lord Nelson was wrong (or right) when he fell in love with Lady Hamilton," perhaps he may be predicting something. But when a deontologist like Kant utters the same words it seems quite difficult to imagine what he is predicting. The depth of the unconscious mind of the deontologist is hard to fathom, but the plain fact that he explicitly denies any predictive meaning in his judgment is not to be neglected. Anyhow it is

---

9 For example: In *The Quest for Certainty* we find the following passages:
To call an object a value is to assert that it satisfies or fulfills certain conditions. ⋯ It is, in effect, a judgment that the thing "will do." It involves a prediction: it contemplates a future in which the thing *will* continue to serve; it will do. It asserts a consequence the thing will actively institute; it will *do.* ⋯ [It] is⋯ an estimate, an appraisal. It denotes an attitude *to be* taken. (Unwin Brothers' Edition, pp.247–248)
A Judgment about what is *to be* desired and enjoyed is⋯ a claim on future action; it possesses *de jure* and not merely *de facto* quality. (p.250)
In these passages we see that Dewey is emphasizing both predictive and prescriptive (or hortatory) functions of a value judgment. But the two kinds of functions are not clearly distinguished from each other, as is shown by his somewhat ambiguous use of the phrase "to be." (Cf. also Stevenson's *Ethics and Language*, pp.256–259)

neither impossible nor unnatural to condemn a married man's love with another's wife without any consideration about the future consequences of it. If Dewey is willing to argue that an ethical statement *should* be uttered with some predictive consideration which can be the "reason" for the judgment, he is introducing a quite different problem. As a matter of moral *facts* it is indisputable that some moral opinions are uttered without predicting anything. Thus, if Dewey established a method for scientific treatment of moral judgments it cannot be applied to *all* kinds of moral utterances.

c') Even when a teleologist expresses a moral opinion its predictive aspect might be very often quite ambiguous. Suppose an Aristotelian says, "We ought to be brave." By this saying he might mean, "Without acting bravely we cannot be truly happy," or "If you act bravely your happiness will be promoted." Doubtless this is a kind of prediction. But since the concept of "happiness" is not so clear and concrete as that of "ice-cream," the Aristotelian himself does not know the contents of his prediction, and consequently he has no distinct idea what observations are required for the verification of his judgment. This point is closely related to what I have called the "ambiguity of the problem." To say that our problem is ambiguous is nothing but to say that we cannot give an objectively justifiable clear and concrete picture of our ideal, or of the "complete" state. Unless we can present this concrete picture we have no concrete criteria by which to judge our valuations.

d') When the prediction implied in a value judgment is concrete, people are often found to be predicting different things by the same value expression. For instance: When mother and son oppose each other on the son's marriage problem, the mother arguing, "You should not marry such an ill-bred girl as Boonee,"[10] and the son insisting that he should marry her, they might not necessarily be predicting contradictory or contrary things.[11] The mother and son may completely agree with each other's prediction, but they might still judge differently about the *value* of the marriage. This divergency of predictions would mean a serious difficulty for the scientific treatment of morals unless we can safely assume that complete agreement in belief results in, in the long run at least, complete agreement in attitude.

C) Our third criticism concerns Dewey's denial of the distinction between intrinsic and instrumental values. Dewey seems right as far as he holds that things which are usually regarded as "intrinsically valuable" turn out to be conditions which serve as the means for future values; he is also right when he asserts that, as a psychological fact, the consideration about means decisively modifies our ends-in-view.

---

10 "Boonee" is one of the popular names for "country girls" in Korea, where the marriage problem was decided almost entirely by parents in former days. Now the practices are changing there, so they have often troubles between the old and the young, as is usual in a transition period.

11 The mother, on the one hand, might be predicting: "If you marry Boonee she will not cook well for you," "You will lose the chance to be Sir Park's son-in-law," ets.; while the son, on the other hand, might be predicting: "If I marry her she will love me for life," "If I don't marry her my heart and hers will be broken," etc.

But this does not entitle Dewey to reject the logical distinction between instrumental and intrinsic values, between means and ends—in—itself. Generosity, for instance, serves indeed as means for many other goods; but a man might desire generosity even if it did not cause any further goods. It is quite possible, without any logical contradiction, that one and the same object can have *both* intrinsic *and* extrinsic values. Furthermore, Dewey himself seems to recognize that "problem solving," "progress" or "growth" are valuable, but he does not tell *for what* they are valuable. We should retain the logical distinction between intrinsic and instrumental values because this distinction might prove helpful when we consider some theoretical problems of morality.

D) Our fourth criticism concerns the problem whether the attitudes which are called prizing, liking, enjoying or interest are sufficient conditions for the existence of values, or whether another condition, namely *reflection* or *appraisal*, must also participate. As we have seen in the first section of this chapter, Dewey holds that liking or enjoying, or the like, is a necessary, but not the sufficient, condition for the occurrence of values. But the present writer is rather inclined to agree with Stephen C. Pepper who regards "conation or affection apart from any judgment element as a 'sufficient condition for the existence of values'."[71] Of course this is somewhat a verbal question; for Dewey does not deny the existence of *immediately experienced good* or esthetic goods. He would not object to calling what is simply liked or an immediate enjoyment a "good" if this "good" means an *immediate* good.

But he does object to calling the immediate good by the name of "value,"
An immediate good is, for Dewey, a candidate for value, and it becomes
a real value when it is approved by the intellectual act of "valuation."

The arguments which seem to support Dewey's position insisting
upon the neccesity of the reflective elements in value–experiences
were mentioned in the first section of the present chapter. But now we
see that none of the arguments is decisive. Firstly, the unmistakable
distinction between "desired" and "desirable," "satisfying" and
"satisfactory," etc. does not seem to show that all values necessarily
contain some intellectual element. What Dewey has shown by the first
argument is simply that *comparative value* or what is called "standard
value" necessarily contains some element of a judgment. When I say,
for example, "I should like to see the movie this evening, but that is not
desirable," I am not completely denying the value of enjoying the
movie. What I do mean by saying "that is not desirable" is that to see
the movie I must sacrifice another value which I deem more important
— to study Dewey's ethical theory, for instance. To say, "Her
performance of the piano solo was not satisfactory though some
seemed to have been satisfied," does not mean that the performance
had no value at all; what is meant is that her piano solo did not reach
the standard the critic had in mind.

Nor does the second argument of Dewey's necessitate the conclusion
Dewey wanted to defend. It may be true, to be sure, that human
appreciation or enjoyed contemplation by an adult usually includes
some reflective factor; but, to my knowledge, no experiment has

established that every appreciation implies an intellectual element. Furthermore we do not see any plausible reason why we should assert that a baby enjoying his candy is experiencing *no* value.

Nor does the third argument we mentioned seem to be fit for Dewey's purpose. Dewey's point was, we remember, that the view which regards a mere enjoyment, or an object of simple liking, as a value in itself makes it impossible to find any guiding principle in practical life. Dewey's objection seems to imply that no motor–affective theories can present any criteria by which we may compare two, or more than two, values. Indeed it would be very difficult to offer any objectively established criteria for comparative values. But in fact many defenders of motor–affective positions have attempted to find some criteria for value comparison, and evidently it would be going too far if we claim that all of their attempts are not only unsatisfactory but "futile,"[12] Moreover, Dewey himself holds that desires can be evaluated by means of observing the results which the pursuing of each desire might bring.[72] This criterion of Dewey's may be available even when a desire (as such) includes *no* reflective element.

If the above–mentioned considerations are not sufficient, we have a few more positive reasons for disagreeing with Dewey's position:

---

12 Perry's criteria for comparative values we have studied in the last chapter. Dewitt H. Parker, another defender of a motor–affective theory, suggests "attainment (or perfection), influence, and rank" as the criteria as issue. Cf. R. Leplay(ed.), *Value*, Columbia University Press, 1949, p.230ff.

i) Since Dewey holds that a valuation–judgment is a necessary condition for the existence of value, the relation between value and valuation is not quite clear in his theory. What does he *mean* by saying that a valuation is a necessary condition for the occurrence of a value? He must mean by this that *objects* of valuations are values. Evidently, however, objects of *wrong* valuations cannot be real values. It is only objects of *valid* valuations that can be properly regarded as values. But how can we judge the validity of a valuation? Dewey's answer must be that the validity is decided by observing whether the object of the valuation, namely the end–in–view, actually brings what is lacking in the situation concerned. Here Dewey is doutless assuming that the consummation of an incomplete situation is valuable in and of itself. If so, the validity of a valuation is dependent, after all, upon an ultimate value — the solution of a problem. This seems to me a sort of circular argument.

ii) Dewey assumes that "progress" or "growth" is a value. But it seems impossible to justify this assumption by any reflective reasoning. This might mean that the assumption under consideration is not a conclusion derived from any appraisal or valuation–judgment. This assumption must have been either *intuited* or *willed* by what might be called Self, or by the person's life itself. In any case it is not the product of intellect as the principle of "science."

iii) Lastly, to allow the name "value" even to what are simply liked, or immediately enjoyed, is more in accordance with the ordinary usage of our language.

Chapter Ⅳ.
STEVENSON: VALUE AND ATTITUDE

1.

Charles L. Stevenson, the last of our three writers, finds the final objective of his meta-ethics in characterizing the general methods by which ethical judgments can be proved or supported, or, to be more precise, in ascertaining how and to what extent ethical disagreements can be settled. But he strongly believes that the first step to this objective is to make the meaning of ethical expressions clear. Ethical questions which arise typically in the form of "Is so and so good?" are especially difficult "partly because we don't know what we are seeking."[1] It would be extremely difficult to investigate whether there is a needle in a haystack if we do not even know what a needle is. Hence the first thing to do is to clarify the meaning of ethical terms.

Of course Stevenson is not the first thinker who has noticed the importance of defining (or of finding some substitute of defining) ethical terms. The most clear-cut definition of the word "good" or "value" was given by those who held the positions which can be conveniently called "psychological value theories." (Stevenson prefers to name them "interest theories.") Unfortunately, however, the definitions of value expressions in terms of psychological attitudes have been strongly attacked by two groups of formidable thinkers, intuitionists and logical positivists. Stevenson admits that the criticisms of both of these groups contain partial truth, but he does not think that the definitions of "interest theories" are quite irrelevant. He agrees neither with the view that "good" is an unanalyzable simple quality, nor with the theory that ethical utterances cannot be either true or false at all. He believes that the senses of ethical terms can *be approached* "by a *kind* of interest theory."[2] An eclectic character is remarkable throughout his theory, but this fact does not prevent it from being original and challenging.

The defects of traditional "interest theories," or psychological value theories, Stevenson holds, lie in the fact that "such theories neglect the very sense of 'good' which is most vital."[3] There are three requirements with which, according to Stevenson, any acceptable definition of ethical terms is expected to comply, namely: i) A definition of an ethical term, if it is to be acceptable, must enable us to account for disagreement in ethics; ii) the definiens must be as "magnetic" as the definiendum; iii) "goodness" must not be verifiable solely through the scientific procedures.[4] But none of the traditional "interest theories" satisfies all of these three requirements. The fundamental reason why they fail to satisfy the requirements is, Stevenson affirms, the fact that they interpret ethical statements as mere descriptions of the existing state of interests (feelings, desires, and so on). It would be idle to deny that some descriptive meaning is implied in ethical judgments; but description or information of some facts is by no means the whole which an ethical judgment *means*. Indication of facts is not even the major use of ethical statements. What is peculiar to the meaning of ethical terms is to be found in their "emotive" aspect. In short, the basic shortcoming of traditional interest theories consists in the fact that they overlook the "emotive meaning" involved in ethical utterances. What exactly, however, does Stevenson mean respectively by "emotive" and "descriptive" meaning? And what is his own approach to the definition of ethical terms?

2.

A sensible start for the proper approach to the definition of "emotive meaning" and "descriptive meaning" would be to single out the *generic* sense of "meaning" which is suitable as the genus of which the two terms are species. The most conventional sense of "meaning," in which the object *to which* people *refer* when they use a sign constitutes the "meaning," of the sign, is rejected by Stevenson as "unsuitable" for his purpose. For he wants to recognize one kind of meaning even in some of those words which have no referent. The sense of "meaning" which Stevenson chooses as "serviceable" is "meaning in the psychological sense."[5] By "the psychological sense of meaning" he refers to the psychological reactions of the people using the sign.

People's reactions to a sign, however, embarassingly vary according to both situations and individuals. Therefore psychological reactions as such cannot be regarded as the proper meaning of signs unless we want to say that one and the same word has different meaning every time it is used. Thus, Stevenson finds it necessary to make some modification or restriction. Observing the fact that the psychological reactions toward a word, though markedly subject to change, show a relatively constant aspect of *tendency*, Stevenson finds his required sense of "meaning" in this aspect of psychological fact. "Instead of identifying meaning with *all* the psychological causes and effects that attend a word's utterance," he says, "we must identify it with those that it has a *tendency* ⋯ to be connected with."[6] In other words, the meaning of a sign in the psychological sense of Stevenson's consists in a "dispositional property" or "causal power" which *belongs to the sign.*

Stevenson compares the "dispositional property" of a sign with the unchanging aspect of the stimulating power of coffee.[7] The degree of the actual stimulations which accompany the situations of drinking coffee might be various depending upon many changing factors such as "the absorptive state of his stomach," "the initial state of a man's fatigue," and so forth. But if we can manage to make all the changing factors retain some constant state, we might find that the same amount of coffee causes relatively constant responses in the drinker, during some interval at least. If this is the case we may recognize an unchanging correlation between some unit of coffee and its stimulating power, even if actual responses to drinking coffee might remarkably vary according to the situations concerned. This unchanging tendency potential in coffee may be properly called the "dispositional property" of it. Similarly with a sign. A variation in the response to a word can be accounted for, so Stevenson believes, by a variation in the attendant circumstances, such as the tone of the utterer's voice, the mood or temperament of the hearer, the general situation, and so on. If we control the attendant conditions in some way we may find a certain unchanging correlation between a sign and the responses it causes. This unchanging causal property of a sign is that which is to be identified with the "dispositional property" that is roughly equivalent to the "meaning" of the sign in Stevenson's sense. Thus Stevenson reaches his desired conclusion that a sign's meaning, in the dispositional sense of "meaning" he has chosen, is more constant than the sign's psychological effects.[8]

But Stevenson does not hold that every kind of disposition of a sign can be called a "meaning;" for we may ascribe some disposition even to nonsense syllables, and to the ordinary "nonlinguistic" signs such as a cough or a sneeze. Hence he places once again a limitation, and declares that a sign's disposition to cause psychological responses is to be called a 'meaning' "only if it has been caused by, and would not have developed without, an elaborate process of conditioning which has attended the sign's use in co communication."[9]

Having thus singled out the "suitable" meaning of "meaning" in the generic sense, Stevenson proceeds to define "emotive meaning" and "descriptive meaning." Since the required genus has been clarified, the task of defining its species must be concentrated on their differentiae; and since the genus was defined in terms of psychological reactions, the species must be accordingly distinguished by the *kind* of psychological processes involved. Roughly speaking, Stevenson's point seems to consist in maintaining that a meaning is "emotive" when the psychological process concerned is "affective" or "emotional," while it is "descriptive" when the psychological process is "cognitive." But let us follow his view a little more in detail.

To begin with "emotive meaning," we read his formal definition of this term as follows:

> Emotive meaning is a meaning in which the response (from the hearer's point of view) or the stimulus (from the speaker's point of view) is a range of emotions. [10]

By "emotion" Stevenson designates here either "feeling" or "attitude." [1] The tendency of a certain word to arouse a feeling or an attitude, Stevenson holds, clings to the word so "tenaciously" that we

---

1 Stevenson does not bother himself to reach a precise definition of these terms. "Feeling" is an affective state which everybody experiences through "immediate introspection;" "attitude" is a generic term designating what are ordinarily called "desire," "wish," "disapproval," and so forth. [11]

find it often difficult to utter the word without producing the particular affective response.[2] For example, the utterance of "nigger" is usually accompanied by a particular kind of feeling while that of "negro" is not. As far as what is referred to is concerned "nigger" and "negro" indicate the same object, but from the point of view of psychological effects the former has a disposition which is not shared by the latter. This disposition peculiar to the former constitutes the "emotive meaning" of that word.[3]

Next, as for "descriptive meaning" it seems to be already clear, from what has been so far studied, that for Stevenson a sign's descriptive meaning is its disposition to produce *cognitive* mental process. It seems necessary, however, to clarify two more respects if we are to reach a little more precise definition: i) What is the nature of

---

2 Stevenson admits that the utterance of a word charged with an emotive meaning does *not always* actually arouse the affective responses concerned. But he emphasizes that to use the appropriate word is a necessary condition to produce the particular feeling or attitude. "Without the appropriate circumstances," he says, "the word will be unavailing; but without the appropriate word, the circumstances may amount to nothing." (*Ethics and Language*, p.61) In short, for Stevenson "meaning" is a kind of potential power which is "realized" when the circumstances are suitable. (Cf. also Ibid. p.49)

3 Stevenson distinguishes two kinds of emotive meaning, "first-order" and "second-order" emotive meaning. This distinction is based on the conception of "orders of dispositions" indicated by Broad. A property is a first-order disposition when, for its full manifestation, only one condition is required to be fulfilled, as is the case with "magnetism;" a second-order disposition when two conditions are needed to be fulfilled, as is the case with "the disposition of a metal to *acquire* magnetism." A term's emotive meaning is "first-order" to the extent that it shows the tendency to evoke a feeling; "second-order" to the extent that it tends to produce an attitude. (Cf. *Ethics and Language*, p.53, p.60)

"cognition;" or what kind of characteristics makes a psychological reaction "cognitive?" ii) Does whatever disposition of a sign to affect cognition constitute the descriptive meaning of the sign? Let us follow, in turn, Stevenson's own considerations on these questions.

i') Stevenson rejects, first of all, the view which identifies a "cognitive" reaction with a "flat piece of experience" the nature of which can be fully grasped through immediate introspection. As the alternative to supplement that purely introspective definition he holds the view that cognition is (in part) a "disposition to actions."[12] But of course *not all* dispositions to actions are to be considered cognitive. What *kind* of disposition to actions, then, is to be regarded as "cognitive?"

Unfortunately, however, Stevenson finds the question he asked himself, "What are the differentiae which distinguish 'cognition' from other dispositions to actions?", is too difficult to be adequately answered. He only asserts that "cognition" is to be conceived "as a disposition whose response is modified by that of many other dispositions."[13] This assertion of Stevenson's is based on the observation that a concrete action is not related exclusively to one, simple belief, but to *many* beliefs and attitudes. For instance: when an explorer in Africa carries a hunting gun this action is not exclusively caused by the belief that he might meet some wild animals in the jungle; some other beliefs such as that a sword is not powerful enough, or that a machine-gun is too heavy, as well as his attitudes of hating to be hurt, wishing to increase knowledge, and so on, are closely related to his action of carrying a hunting gun. As for the question *how* several dispositional properties work together to determine an action, Stevenson suggests that their way of acting might be analogous to that of electromagnets surrounding a small ball of iron when they influence each other to determine the motion of the iron ball.[14)]

ii') Stevenson finds that there are cases where a sign's disposition to arouse a cognitive reaction cannot properly be called the "descriptive meaning" of the sign. Consider, for example, the proposition, "Susan is an actress." This might have the tendency to make us imagine that Susan is young and beautiful. But we should not say that the term "actress" strictly means something about youthfulness and beauty, for linguistic rules do not connect that concept with these qualities. In such a case, Stevenson proposes, we should say, in order to distinguish what a sign *means* from what it *vaguely allude to*, that "actress" *suggests* "beauty," "youthfulness," and so forth. A disposition of a sign can be regarded as its meaning only when the disposition is, in some measure, rendered fixed through linguistic rules. Thus, placing the restriction required by the last consideration, Stevenson reaches his full definition of "descriptive meaning" as follows:

> The "descriptive meaning" of a sign is its disposition to affect cognition, provided that the disposition is caused by an elaborate process of conditioning that has attended the sign's use in communication, and provided that the disposition is rendered fixed,

at least to a considerable degree, by linguistic rules.[15] [4]

We have so far seen Stevenson's distinction between emotive and descriptive meaning. Now it would be advisable to add a few lines by way of noticing that Stevenson does not hold that these two kinds of meaning are entirely isolated from each other. It is admitted that one and the same word may have both kinds of meaning. And emotive and descriptive disposition of a sign, both in their origin and operation, "stand in extremely close relationship."[16] In most cases the emotive meaning of a word is more or less dependent upon the descriptive meaning of the word, the former changing in accordance with the latter. But, on the other hand, the two aspects of a sign's meaning do not always grow or decline in a parallel way. In other words, it is not always the case that one of the two kinds of meaning is strictly a function of the other. By virtue of the "inertia" of meaning, one kind of a sign's meaning might survive a change in the other kind of meaning. The inertia of emotive meaning, according to Stevenson, is worth special attention from the point of view of an ethical study. Thus he

---

4 In one of his later articles, Stevenson defines "descriptive meaning" by a different route, saying:
S has a descriptive meaning, for A, that is about X, will analytically imply the statement:
S *tends* to strictly evoke, in A, a thought about X.
("Meaning: Descriptive and Emotive", *The Philosophical Review*, Vol. LVII, 1948, p.131)

finds it important to introduce a new terminology; "independent emotive meaning" and "dependent emotive meaning." We are told: "To whatever extent emotive meaning is *not* a function of descriptive meaning, but either persists without the latter or survives changes in it," it is to be said "independent," while "to whatever extent emotive meaning is a function of descriptive meaning, changing with it after only a brief 'lag'," it is to be modified by the adjective "dependent."[17]

3.

We could now directly proceed to Stevenson's conception of the meaning of ethical terms. Yet, before approaching that central problem, it would prove convenient to let ourselves a digression to survey his discussion of the "kinds of agreement and disagreement," for he makes frequent use of this discussion in his analysis concerning the problem of defining ethical terms. And this survey will turn out to be even more helpful when we study the methodology of Stevenson who declares, "My methodological conclusions center less on my conception of meaning than on my conceptions of agreement and disagreement."[18]

There are, according to Stevenson, two kinds of disagreement (or of agreement) which must be sharply distinguished if we are to properly understand the nature of ethical problems. The first type of disagreement[5] is called "disagreement in belief." Cases of this kind of disagreement are often experienced when we talk about scientific problems, historical facts, probable future events, and so on. Dissent on the nature of sleep, on the author of the *Iliad*, and on the probability of rain tomorrow, are concrete examples of this type of dispute. Disagreements in belief, as a rule, are settled by means of appealing to actual observations, or to some relevant basic propositions the truth of which is not questioned.

There is, however, another kind of disagreement. When, for instance, a wife insists on buying a new car, and her husband considers it "unnecessary" or "extravagant," the dispute is not primarily concerned with *facts*, though some *latent* disagreements in belief may be involved in it. The same sort of disagreement occurs whenever a dispute involves an opposition, not of opinion on facts, but of liking preferring, desiring, approving, etc. Stevenson refers to this type of disagreement as "disagreements in attitude."[19] [6] When two men have opposed attitudes to the same object each usually has a motive for altering or calling into question the attitude of his opponent. But disagreement in attitude is not necessarily an occasion for forensic rivalry. "It may be," says Stevenson, "an occasion for an interchange of aims, with a reciprocal influence that both parties find to be beneficial."[20]

---

5 For the sake of expository economy, we shall hereafter pay attention chiefly to "disagreement," leaving its logical contrary, "agreement," to be understood by implication.

6 In one of his earlier papers, "The Emotive Meaning of Ethical Terms" (1937), Stevenson names the second type "disagreement in interest." (Cf. Op. Cit. p.426)

What then is the relation between the two kinds of disagreement? It is obvious that there is some reciprocal relationship between belief and attitude.[7] Our attitudes often affect our beliefs and, conversely, they are often modified through our beliefs. There must be, consequently, an intimate relation between the two kinds of disagreement under consideration. In some cases the disagreement in attitude may be hinged decidedly upon the disagreement in belief. When this is the case, the former sort of disagreement will be settled if the latter sort of disagreement is somehow removed.

But we should not regard the relation between the two kinds of disagreement as a logical one; it is always factual. From the purely logical point of view, one type of disagreement may occur without the other. Hence Stevenson asserts that we "must appeal to experience to determine which of the possibilities, in any given case or class of cases, is in fact realized."[21]

The reasons why Stevenson deems his conceptions of two kinds of disagreement so important seem to be: i) Ethical issues, in principle, may involve both disagreement in beliefs and disagreement in attitudes, and consequently without full consideration of both of these factors an analysis of ethical problems cannot be adequate. ii) "The central problem of ethical analysis" is to clarify the precise relation

---

7 Cautiously enough Stevenson admits that the strict distinction between beliefs and attitudes can be sensibly questioned. But he insists that the distinction can be soundly made for practical purposes at least. (Cf. *Ethics and Language*, pp.7–8)

between beliefs and attitudes. These points would receive fuller illumination on our way to further study. Let us now return to the problem of the meaning of ethical terms.

4.

We have seen that, according to Stevenson, the fundamental defect of the traditional "interest theories" in their attempt to define ethical terms, was in their failure to grasp the "emotive" meaning involved in value expressions. And we have also seen that Stevenson rejected the hard-boiled logical positivists' position which denies any descriptive meaning in ethical utterances. In short, this much has already become clear: for Stevenson ethical terms have *both* descriptive and emotive meaning. Therefore what is required hereafter is to trace his specification of the descriptive and emotive meanings involved.

What Stevenson discovers at the outset of his approach to the definition of ethical terms is that, strictly speaking, ethical terms are indefinable. They are indefinable mainly because of two reasons:

The first reason comes from the well-known fact of "linguistic flexibility." As we have already seen in the study of Perry's theory, no ethical term is used always in the same sense in common discourse. For instance: the term "good" is used sometimes in the sense of "effective," and other times in the sense of "in accordance with the custom of the times." It might be used even to indicate the act of "going faithfully to church on Sundays." To put it in a general way, the descriptive meaning of an ethical term can be made, to some extent, either "rich or poor" according to the user of the term, without violating "the elastic requirement of 'natural English usage'."[22] Consequently it is impossible to single out, or to determine, *the* descriptive meaning of any given ethical term.

The second reason of the indefinability under consideration comes from the *subtlety* of the emotive meaning of ethical terms. The emotive meaning of an ethical expression is so unique and subtle that it cannot be exactly translated into any other expressions. In other words, the customary emotive meaning of an ethical term "has *no* exact emotive equivalent."[23] Therefore a given ethical expression cannot be replaced by some other expression without changing its emotive subtlety.

If adequate definition is impossible some substitute must be sought for. Thus Stevenson finds that a convenient way to clarify the meaning of ethical terms is to approach it through "working models."

Now Stevenson finds two remarkable features in connection with the meaning of ethical terms. Firstly, most ethical utterances contain, in their descriptive aspect, some information *about* the utterers' attitudes or interests towards the objects referred to. Secondly, the emotive meaning of ethical expressions and the function of "ordinary imperatives" have the following similarities: i) "Both imperative and ethical sentences are used more for encouraging, altering, or redirecting people's aims and conduct than for simply describing them." ii) "Both differ in this respect from the sentences of science."[24]

Making use of these two features as the clue to his approach Stevenson devises a set of "working models" as follows:

1) "This is wrong" means "I disapprove of this; do so as well."
2) "He ought to do this" means "I disapprove of his leaving this undone; do so as well."
3) "This is good" means "I approve of this; do so as well."[25]

The conditions which Stevenson considered here to be the central requirement for a serviceable working model seem to be these: i) A working model must retain, approximately at least, the emotive meaning of the original expression; ii) a working model must be able to provide for agreement or disagreement in attitude. The reasons why Stevenson emphasized these two points instead of accentuating the aspect of descriptive meaning, or that of disagreement (or agreement) in belief would be: (a) The basic defect of traditional definitions consists in their overlooking the emotive meaning of value terms.[8] (b) "If the model had accentuated beliefs at the expense of attitudes, the emphasis could not easily have been corrected by subsequent remarks; ··· but when the model accentuate attitudes at the expense of beliefs, the correct emphasis can easily be reestablished."[26]

8　This reason (a), unlike the other one (b), is not explicitly mentioned by Stevenson himself; but his strong intention to profit by the follies of the "naturalistic fallacy" seems to be indisputable.

Stevenson's working models introduced above, he claims, satisfy the two requirements just mentioned. First, the imperative part of the definiens, "do so as well," may have a function which is similar to that of an emotive meaning, the tendency of chaning or intensifying the attitudes of the hearer. Second, that the working models suggested can provide for disagreement (or agreement) in attitude might be shown by taking an example. Suppose A and B disagree concerning the value of X, respectively asserting:

A: X is good.

B: No, it is bad.

If we translate this according to the model 3), it will become:

A: I approve of X; do so as well.

B: No, I disapprove of it; do so as well.

Here the declarative parts of the translated sentences clearly show the disagreement of A and B in their attitudes; and the imperative parts show, in addition, that each man is suggesting the other to change his attitude.

Stevenson, however, fully admits that his models are too crude to be adequate. The first inadequacy lies in the "bluntness" of the imperative component. The psychological effects caused by an explicit command is not exactly the same with those of an ethical term. Moreover utterers of ethical judgments, as a rule, are more ready to redirect their own attitudes than those who simply command. The second inadequacy is connected with the declarative component of the models. The declarative component is too simple to represent the whole descriptive meaning which ethical terms might have. Furthermore, the flexibility of common language is not reflected here. Thus, the next thing for Stevenson to do is to correct or somehow supplement these inadequacies.

Since strict definition of ethical terms is impossible for Stevenson, he endeavors to accomplish the supplement required by means of "characterization" of the terms to be defined. The way of his "characterization" seems to be based mainly on these principles: i) To analyse the emotive meaning of ethical terms *in close connection with* the "attendant circumstances;" ii) to complement the "descriptive meaning" through another pattern of analysis, a clue to which might be found in a consideration of the "supporting reasons" that might attend ethical judgments; iii) to pay keen attention to the "flexibility of language."[27] Let us study his procedure a little more precisely by taking "good" as an example.

5.

Stevenson's approach to a more precise meaning of "good" by means of supplementing the working model begins with his attempt to "characterize" the emotive aspects of that term. The main points which Stevenson suggests in this connection seem to be: i) The emotive meaning of "good" varies with the attendant circumstances. Sometimes it is strongly hortatory, but at other times it may be very weakly so. There are even cases where "good" is used practically without any emotive effects.[9] ii) The emotive meaning of "good" is different from the function of any sheer imperative in (a) that it does not appeal to self-conscious efforts, but influences the hearer through a subtle mechanism of *suggestion*, and (b) that it readily permits a *mutual* influence. iii) The emotive meaning of "good" is independent *only in part*. A great part of it may be *dependent* (or *quasi-dependent*) on the descriptive meaning of the term. In other words, not all of the emotional effects of "good" are exclusively a matter of mere emotion. A great part of it may suggest the close relationship between belief and attitude.

The next step for Stevenson to take is to clarify the descriptive aspect of "good." We have already seen that Stevenson repeatedly emphasizes the flexibility of language. If the "One-And-Only-One-True-Meaning" is a mere "superstition" evidently it is impossible to decide the "true" contents of the descriptive meaning involved in "good." We have difficulty even in distinguishing what "good" actually *means* from what it simply *suggests*. There is no predestinated descriptive meaning of "good," or of other ethical concepts, to be *discovered*; the meaning is rather "in the course of *becoming* what the analyst makes of it."[28] But this does not mean that an analyst may properly interpret the descriptive aspect in accord with his caprice.

---

9 Stevenson does *not* say that ethical terms are sometimes devoid of any emotive *meaning* because he holds that emotive meaning is simply *potential* in such cases.

There are some linguistic rules which must be taken into consideration, and there are broadly limited purposes for which any ethical term is ordinarily used.

Now, in the already introduced "working models" of Stevenson's, and in his so-called "first pattern of analysis" as an extension of those models, the descriptive meaning of "good," as well as that of other terms, has been taken to be exclusively about the speaker's attitudes. Of course information about the speaker's attitudes is only a small part of the whole descriptive meaning an ethical judgment might possibly have. To reach a fuller sense of an ethical term, the remaining part of its descriptive meaning must be more or less clarified. But as far as an ethical utterance, for example, "X is good," as such is concerned, the remaining part is not explicit. We see, however, that some suggestion about a more amplified meaning of the term presents itself when the utterer begins to offer some "reasons" to support his judgment. Consider, for instance, the following conversation:

A: John is a good boy.

B: Why?

A: He is honest, kind, and brave.

B: ⋯

It seems evident from this that there is, at least for A, some relation between a man's "goodness" and the qualities of being "honest," "kind," and "brave." But before we can I conclude that honesty, kindness and courage are components of the descriptive meaning of "good," a general question must be answered. The question is this: Are *all* supporting reasons suggested by the utterer of an ethical statement parts of the descriptive meaning of the utterance? The reason why this question is necessary might be shown by the following considerations among others:

i) The disputant might give supporting reasons which he had *not* in mind *at the moment when he uttered the judgment.* For instance: A girl might say that John is a good boy simply because they like each other. But when she is questioned, "Why?" she might notice that their liking each other is not quite suitable as the reason to be openly given. Then she may answer, "He is honest, kind, and brave."

This illustration might suggest at least two things. (a) A supporting reason may not have been included in the descriptive meaning of the statement *when the latter was uttered.* (b) There might be cases where supporting reasons are, strictly speaking, the reasons why the utterer likes (dislikes) or approves (disapproves) the object judged, rather than the reasons why it is "good" or "bad."

ii) Supporting reasons suggested by the utterer will not be always accepted by the opponent as "appropriate." At times, even the utterer himself might admit later that his supporting reasons were not tenable. This fact seems to suggest that people deem some qualities or relations to be acceptable as the components of a value-term's descriptive meaning, but others unacceptable.

From the above considerations, we may safely conclude that the mere fact that certain qualities or relations were suggested in the "supporting reasons" is not sufficient to qualify the qualities or relations to be the components of the descriptive meaning of the term concerned. Here the question suggests itself, "What kinds of qualities or relations are qualified to be the legitimate components of 'good' (or of any other ethical term)?" This fundamental and controversial problem leads us to the study of Stevenson's "second pattern of analysis."

If we designate whatever qualities or relations which properly, or "naturally," constitute parts of the descriptive meaning of "good" by X, Y, Z⋯, the meaning of "good" may be translated into the general form of the following schema:

> "This is good" has the meaning of "This has qualities or relations X, Y, Z⋯" except that "good" has as well a laudatory emotive meaning which permits it to express the speaker's approval, and tends to evoke the approval of the hearer.[29)]

Now what constants can properly replace the variables X, Y, Z⋯ in the schema? Manifestly, not all substitutions are to be admitted. Our linguistic rules would reject some descriptive meanings as "unnatural." Thus, if Stevenson's "schema for the second pattern" is to be complete, some limiting remarks concerning X, Y, Z⋯ must be added. Stevenson, however, does not attempt to specify the boundaries within which the descriptive meaning of "good" is to be allowed to fluctuate. His main purpose here is not to enumerate various possible definitions of "good," but to clarify the *nature of language* which enables various definitions of one and the same word to be equally permissible. "The importance of the second pattern," we are told, "lies not in revealing new ethical 'content', but rather in revealing new complexities of language⋯."[30]

If we consult a big dictionary to study the sense of "good," we will find many definitions having different descriptive meanings. And so long as we remain persistently pure analysts we would see no reason to adopt any special definition as the "true" one rejecting others as "false;" all of the definitions would seem admittable as far as none of them are violating linguistic rules. This remains the case even if we limit ourselves to the *moral* sense of "good." Some writers define "morally good" in terms of "the greatest happiness of the greatest number," and some others in terms of "universal love." The same concept may be defined in still other ways; to have the meaning of "self-realization," or of "survival,"or of "pleasure," and so forth. From a purely analytic or linguistic point of view, all of these definitions must be recognized to be acceptable. But the usual *moralist* would *not* actually admit that they are all equally good definitions. He would choose *one* definition and would claim that it is *the right* one.

Now what is the nature of a moralist's assertion that only his definition is "true?" Is he simply informing about some *facts?* To this question Stevenson gives a definitely negative answer. The moralist is pleading a cause; he is revealing his attitude. "To choose a definition," says Stevenson, "is to plead a cause, so long as the word defined is strongly emotive."[31] When two writers are contending about definition of an ethical term this dispute most likely includes their disagreement in attitude. To put it in another way, when a writer insists that *only* certain specified constant terms can legitimately replace the variables (X, Y, Z···) of the schema for the second pattern, he is "persuading!"

When a writer persuades through his definition, he is giving, according to Stevenson's naming, a "persuasive definition." Since the conception of "pursuasive definition" is of central importance in Stevenson's view, it would be worthwhile to pay further attention to his analysis of this conception.

6.

Stevenson's definition of "persuasive definition" reads as follows:

> A "persuasive" definition is one which gives a new conceptual meaning to a familiar word without substantially changing its emotive meaning, and which is used with the conscious or unconscious purpose of changing, by this means, the direction of people's interests.[32]

Not only philosophical controversies but political disputes and even everyday conversations are abundant in examples of this type of definitions. When rightists and leftists dispute about the "true democracy," or when sophisticated guests of a tea-house argue on "culture" or on "freedom," or when women's gossip has reached the topic whether Mr. Smith is a "real gentleman," there we find almost surely instances of persuasive definitions. In short, whenever a vague concept is connected with value and charged with emotive meaning, the possibility of persuasive definitions is open.

To illustrate what an important role persuasive definitions have played in the history of ethics, Stevenson refers to Plato's *Republic* where Socrates endeavors to reach the "true" definition of "justice." In the first book of the *Republic* Socrates, instead of directly setting about defining justice, concerns himself in considering "whether justice is virtue and wisdom, or evil and folly." (354, Jowett) This procedure, according to Stevenson's interpretation, has the important function of making sure that the laudatory emotive meaning of "justice" is well established. In the fourth book, after redirecting the hearer's attitudes through the two intervening books where a moving description of the ideal state is presented, Socrates finally finds the definition: "Justice of the state consists of each of the three classes doing the work of its own class." (*Republic*, 441, Jowett) "The persuasive character of this definition," Stevenson confidently affirms, "can scarcely be denied"[33] Plato himself would not admit that his definition is persuasive, insisting that it was fashioned after the eternal Idea of "justice." But Stevenson asks, how did Plato determine whether his "recollection" of the Idea was correct? Nothing else. He considered it correct "when he reached a conception which satisfied his deepest, inmost aspiration,"[34] And the problem of what kind of aspiration we entertain, is at bottom a matter of attitude.

Plato, we are told, is only one of a great number of philosophers who presented persuasive definitions. Stevenson finds the same persuasive character also in Bentham's definition that "justice" is an "imaginary personage, feigned for the convenience of discourse, whose dictates are the dictates of utility, applied to certain particular cases."[35] Even in Sidgwick's definition of "justice," which is much more careful and analytic, Stevenson does not fail to find a touch of persuasive character.[36]

To sum up: All writers who pretend to offer *the true* definition of any ethical term such as "good" or "justice" are pleading a moral cause. Many writers have correctly noticed the inadequacy of variously suggested traditional definitions of ethical terms, and they dimly perceived the element of persuasion involved in them. Thus they endeavored to give the truly decisive definitions which are free from all sorts of irrational factors. However, "ironically enough," none of these "decisive" definition was really exceptional. Each of them simply added *another* persuasive definition![10]

Stevenson's objection, we should notice, is not against the fact of persuasiveness, or that of "pleading a cause," as such. His point is that we should not (and that we often do) confuse *persuasion* with *analysis*. He repeatedly emphasizes the distinction between *meta*-ethics, the concern of pure analysts, and *normative* ethics, the business of

---

10   We have seen an instance of this in Perry's theory of value.

moralists or reformers.

Stevenson does not deny the possibility of successfully combining the two aspects of ethical philosophy. He even explicitly admits that analysis and evaluation must be ultimately "brought together."[37] But he steadfastly warns that, if this combination is prematurely attempted without paying adequate attention to the essential difference between analysis (which is a "narrow, specialized undertaking, requiring only close distinctions, careful attentions to logic, and a sensitivity to the ways of language")[38] and evaluation (which is a broader undertaking requiring something beyond mere logical training and linguistic knowledge), a serious confusion will be inescapable. A remarkable instance of this type of confusion Stevenson finds in Sidgwick. Sidgwick endeavored, more or less, to make a distinction between the analytic and evaluative aspects of ethics. Yet, Stevenson affirms, since he finally attempted to combine the functions of analyst and moralist without sufficient caution, he was not completely free from the "confusions that are most prevalent and central."[39]

We have so far studied Stevenson's analysis of the meaning of ethical term. (Though we have done this mainly through considerations of "good," it would not be questioned that similar considerations can generally be applied to other ethical concepts.) But Stevenson's ways of analysis were embarrassingly roundabout. And consequently, our exposition of his view, trying to follow his thoughts closely, could not be entirely free from the same sort of shortcoming. Thus it would not be superfluous to sum up his main ideas, before we proceed to his methodology which constitutes the second central part of his theory. Steverson's central ideas are:

i) Ethical terms imply both descriptive and emotive meanings, when "meaning" is interpreted in the sense of "dispositional property."

ii) Descriptive meaning of an ethical utterance implies, at least, some information about the utterer's attitude, which can be generally expressed in the form of either "I approve of…," or "I disapprove of…." Emotive meaning of an ethical statement is somewhat analogous to the function of an imperative, though they are not exactly the same. Therefore we may roughly translate the meaning of any ethical judgment into a sentence which is composed of two parts; the declarative component which informs the attitude of the utterer, and the imperative component which would stand proxy for the emotive function of the ethical statement. Thus, "X is good" may be translated into the model of "I approve of this; do so as well."

iii) But the "working models" in the form of "I approve (or disapprove) of…; do so as well," are too crude to be regarded as "definitions" of ethical terms. Therefore we must add some supplementary analysis if we are to approach more closely the sense of ethical expressions. This supplement must be accomplished through two patterns of analysis. The first pattern of analysis chiefly concerns itself with closer characterization of the emotive aspect of ethical terms; the second pattern with extended considerations of the descriptive aspect of them.

iv) Besides information about the utterer's attitude, the descriptive meaning of an ethical expression may include designation of several other qualities or relations. Yet we cannot precisely define these qualities or relations with constant terms. The flexibility or vagueness of language permits us to define one and the same term in various ways, though the range within which descriptive meaning of an ethical term may fluctuate is confined in some measure by rules of common language. When a writer insists that a certain specified definition is *the true* one he is giving a "persuasive definition." And as soon as a writer dares to give a persuasive definition he, leaving the position of a pure analyst, begins to be a moralist.

7.

As can be expected Stevenson developes his methodological conceptions on the basis of his analysis of the meaning of ethical terms. Accordingly, his methodological analysis also includes two main parts: the "first pattern" and the "second pattern." Let us begin with his first pattern.

The central point upon which almost all of Stevenson's methodological conclusions are hinged, is his observation that the way of settling in disagreements in attitudes is fundamentally different from that of settling disagreements in beliefs. Disagreement in attitudes, as we have seen, cannot be *logically* solved by means of appealing to observations or to any established principles. There are cases, to be sure, in which disagreements in attitudes can be, *as a matter of fact*, resolved by means of changing the opponents' beliefs on facts. But this kind of situation can occur only when the disagreement in attitudes to be settled is based upon the disputers' disagreement in beliefs. And since the relation between a certain attitude and a certain belief is not logical but only factual or causal, the method of changing opponents' beliefs is not guaranteed in its effects. Thus, the fundamental difference between the way of settling disagreements in attitudes and that of settling disagreements in beliefs remains all the same.

Since ethical utterances express not only beliefs but also attitudes, when people dispute on an ethical matter ordinarily their controversy involves disagreement in attitudes. And consequently ethical disputes cannot always be resolved by the same methods which have been recognized to be reliable in the field of the "natural sciences." We may illustrate this point by making use of one of his working models.

According to the working models, "This is good" is roughly equivalent to saying "I approve of this; do so as well." The declarative component of the latter sentence is an ordinary psychological statement, and is open to empirical verification. But the imperative component, like any other imperative, can be, strictly speaking, neither proved nor disproved. Furthermore the declarative component represents only a small part of the meaning of the ethical judgment. Consequently, to prove an ethical statement seems, in a sense, basically impossible.

Yet, Stevenson holds, there might be "some substitute for a proof in ethics ⋯ which will be equally serviceable in removing the hesitations that usually prompt people to ask for proof."[40] In fact, both imperatives and ethical statements, if they are objected to, usually are followed by some reasons or arguments to "support," if not to "prove," them. And Stevenson's methodological analysis, we are told, has its object in *characterizing* the general methods by which ethical judgments can be supported. Here we must notice that Stevenson's aim in his methodology is not to establish any "valid" method by which ethical judgments *should be* supported or rejected. In other words, what Stevenson is primarily concerned with is not *evaluation* but *description* of methods that are, as a matter of fact, presented to support ethical judgments. Stevenson does not deny the "unquestionable importance" of the normative problem of evaluating ethical methods, yet he wants to leave normative problems outside the limits of his "metanormative but nonnormative inquiry."[41] It might be questioned if a *purely* non-normative theory of ethics is possible, and whether Stevenson himself is perfectly consistent in his with-holding of all normative problems. This question does not seem quite negligible, but it would be preferable to reserve it until we finish surveying his whole discussions. Let us then study how he "describes" the general methods of ethical agreements.

The supporting arguments for the settlement of *interpersonal* disputes on ethical matters are classified by Stevenson into four groups:[42]

I) The first group arguments markedly resemble factual ones in their ways of settling disagreements. They are exceptional to the general rule of Stevenson's that "ethical judgments are supported or attacked by reasons related to them psychologically, rather than logically."[43] For example:[11]

A: It is a good thing to give money to poor men.

B: But remember; you agreed the other day that "laziness" is one of the most serious vices. And nothing is more likely to promote a man's laziness than giving money without any reason but his being poor.

II) Supporting arguments belonging to the second group are those which endeavor to alter the attitudes, and consequently the ethical judgments, of opponents by pointing out the nature of the objects judged, or the consequences that would be caused by them. For instance:

A: Mr. Smith, at bottom, is a really good man.

B: How can you say that such a sullen and harsh fellow is "a really good man?"

A: But; his sullenness is caused by a heartbreaking event he experienced recently, and his harsh manner is only a pose. Whoever understands his deepest heart would agree that he is good.

---

11   This and the following examples, unless otherwise indicated, are mine,

To take another example:

    A: Breaking one's promise is wrong.

    B: But why?

    A: If everybody breaks his words no one would trust any one, and consequently social co-operation would hardly be performed.

Ⅲ) The third group is like the second one in that it presents empirically verifiable reasons which are psychologically related to an ethical judgment, but differs from the latter in that the reasons offered are remote in the sense that they explain the nature or the probable effects of the things judged only indirectly.[12] To introduce one of the illustrations given by Stevenson himself:

    A: Education is a fine thing.

    B: For some people only.

    A: The consensus of opinion is wholly against you.

There are many ways in which people attempt to alter other's attitude by means of giving "indirect" reasons. Genetic explanation of the moral opinion at issue, appeal to authority or to public opinion, or pointing out the motive of the action judged, are only some of familiar ones. Whatever way a disputer may choose, the relation between supporting reasons and supported judgments are not strictly logical; and consequently whether any supporting reason is effective or not is

---

12 We might consider the second and the third groups as essentially in the same category, though Steveson prefers to distinguish them.

a factual problem. Of course this is also the truth in the cases of the second group.

IV) In the fourth group, one of the disputers endeavors to temporarily evade the force of the opponent's argument by changing the point at issue. For instance:

A: It was wrong for you to have told a lie yesterday.

B: You are not entitled to say so. Don't you remember that you yourself told a lie the other day?

So far we have confined ourselves to situations that involve "interpersonal" disputes. If we turn our attention to the problem of settling "personal" conflicts the essential points discovered in the case of interpersonal decisions would remain the truth all the same.

A man feels the need of making up his mind about an ethical problem when he is confronted with an internal *conflict* of attitudes, which, in its essence, is much the same as an interpersonal disagreement in attitudes. And when a man feels the necessity of making a decision between two conflicting attitudes in himself, he thinks of various *reasons* which might support or reject either of the two attitudes. The conflict is resolved when he finds some reasons with sufficient power to support one of his attitudes. In this case too, the relation between the decision and its supporting reasons are not logical but psychological. In other words, a reason becomes relevant when it actually brings about a modification of any of the conflicting attitudes.

However, there is one point concerning which a little difference between personal and interpersonal decisions is to be noticed. That is, the effect of cognitive arguments, or intellectual reasonings, in bringing about desired modifications of attitude is more reliable in the case of a personal decision than in that of an interpersonal decision. For, "in making a personal decision, a man is very likely to find that his reasons, if carefully developed, will resolve his conflict to a significant degree and hence lead him to a definite judgment," but "in an interpersonal problem … the case may be different."[44]

It is in connection with the problem of "personal decison" that Stevenson most confidently emphasizes the *cognitive implications* of the emotive conception of ethics. The emotive conception of ethics is often criticized for its "depriving ethics of its thoughtful, reflective elements." But, Stevenson affirms, it is not the emotive conception of ethics, but those views which neglect emotive meaning paying attention only to descriptive one, that "underestimate the cognitive content of ethics."[45]

To illustrate the truth of this paradoxical affirmation, Stevenson asks us to consider the form of definition which holds that "X is valuable" is equal to saying "X is conducive to E." Such a definition, Stevenson claims, implies that, to evaluate X, "one need only examine its consequences upon E." But in fact one must take into consideration the consequences of X upon things unrelated to E, and he must examine the consequences of E itself. For,

a person may have *doubts* as to whether E will resolve the conflict from which the need of his evaluative decision arose. He may wonder whether his approval of E is strong enough to outweigh his disapproval of the other consequences⋯.[46]

Stevenson's point (though his reasoning is not clear enough) seems to be that the definition is inadequate because, when we employ this definition as the principle by which we settle our conflicts, we might find cases in which the definition does not *actually work* as the principle of "personal decision." Questions might be raised concerning this, but let us confine ourselves here to noting that Stevenson is eager to show that his position by no means implies making little of cognitive or reflective factors in ethics.

Even if we fully recognize the importance of reflective factors in ethical methods, Stevenson admits, it seems undeniable that there is a serious limitation as to the degree to which rational methods in ethics can approach finality. We have seen that the relation between an ethical judgment and its supporting reasons is not logical but psychological. Because of this fact it is evident that no unmistakable methods by which the possibility of settling ethical problems is guaranteed are provided. For no matter how many reasons are presented conjointly to support an ethical judgment, and no matter how completely each of the reasons is established, these might not be enough, in some cases, to convince all people, so long as "to prove the reasons is a different matter from using the reasons to prove an ethical judgment."[47]

That no unmiskable methods for ethical decision are provided does not mean that the impossibility of such methods is decisive. If an assumption proves to be true, Stevenson asserts, the possibility of reaching, by rational methods, ethical agreement in any case would be open. The assumption is: "All disagreement in attitude is rooted in disagreement in belief."[48] But this assumption can properly be doubted. What prevents us from unhesitatingly admitting it, is that some disagreements seem rooted in the inevitableness of the struggle for existence, and some others in temperamental differences. On the other hand, though the assumption is far from being established, the possibility of its being the case still remains. Hence Stevenson's conclusion about the decisiveness of rational methods in ethical problems is necessarily hypothetical. His conclusion reads:

> *If* any ethical dispute is rooted in disagreement in belief, it may be settled by reasoning and inquiry to whatever extent the beliefs may be so settled. But if any ethical dispute is *not* rooted in belief, then no *reasoned* solution of any sort is possible.[49]

The rational methods in ethics are lacking finality. Yet disputers on ethical matters do not always give up the effort to have their opponents agree with their own positions when the rational methods reach the limitation. The rational methods are not the only resource people use to change attitudes. There are other ways, which Stevenson calles "the nonrational methods of ethics."[50]

The most important of the nonrational methods, according to

Stevenson, is "persuasion." A persuasive disputer seeks to redirect the hearer's attitude not through the mediacy of changing his beliefs but by means of "the sheer, direct emotional impact of words."[51][13] Persuasive methods, of course, need not be used in separation from rational methods. In many cases rational and nonrational methods are used in close combination. Nor is the use of persuasion confined to situations that involve interpersonal disagreement. It finds its place as well in cases of "personal decision." "Self-persuasion" is a commonplace occurrence.

8.

Stevenson's "second pattern" methodological investigation does not discover anything very different from what he has already found in his "first pattern" investigation. He finds that the methods which are used to settle the second pattern arguments are, at bottom, the same methods which are used in the first pattern arguments. The only difference which must be noted is this: For the second pattern both rational and nonrational methods are employed to support persuasive *definitions*; while for the first pattern they are used to support ethical *judgments* themselves. We might make this point clear by means of an

---

13 As for the detailed technique of persuasion, see the *Ethics and Language*, pp.140–147, and pp.240–242.

illustration.[14]

Let us suppose that A and B disagree with each other on the problem of whether an object, O, is good or not, using the term "good" in some second pattern sense. Let us assume again that A's assertion that O is good has the descriptive meaning "O has qualities X and Y," and that B's claim that O is not good implies the descriptive meaning "O has not the quality Z." Then the argument between A and B would take one of the following forms:

i) A might reject B's claim by proving that O *does* have the quality Z, *or* B might reject A's assertion by establishing that O does *not* possess at least one of the qualities X and Y. In this case both A and B are using exclusively rational methods. But the agreement thus reached between A and B is only apparent. In other words, A and B agree that O is good (or is not good), but each of their judgments means different things as far as the descriptive meaning of their judgments is concerned.

ii) A might deny B's judgment by pointing out that O does contain the quality Z, *and* B might reject A's claim by eatablishing that O does *not* possess at least one of the qualities X and Y. In this case the disagreement between A and B concerning the value of O still remains,

---

14　This illustration is similar to Stevenson's own example No. 4 given in the *Ethics and Language*, p.233. My analysis is not exactly a summary of Stevenson's analysis, but I hope it is in line with his own, and is sufficient to show that ethical methods are ultimately the same whether they are based upon the first or the second pattern of definition.

though their positions are exchanged. If any agreement is to be reached between them each of them must continue to support his definition by reasons or persuasions until the other's attitude is redirected.

iii) A and B might fully agree that O possesses the qualities of X and Y, but does not Z. Yet they may still disagree as for the "goodness" of O; A saying it is good, but B saying it is not. Here A and B would endeavor to change each other's value judgment concerning O, by defending respectively their persuasive definitions. Now the methods to support a persuasive definition need not always be nonrational. Rational methods can be still employed, for "there is manifestly such a thing as giving *reasons* for accepting or rejecting a second-pattern definition."[52] For instance: A might show by rational methods that Z, which B believes a thing must include if it is to be "good," causes R which B thinks intrinsically bad; and B might redirect his attitude towards Z noticing, for the first time, its connection with R, and consequently his judgment about O's value. Thus the agreement required may be attained. But the methods used by A so far are entirely rational.

iv) A and B might present *every* reason which they believe relevant to support their definitions, but they might *still* disagree about the goodness of O because of their sticking to different definitions of "good." In this case the disputants would begin to use nonrational methods to defend their definitions, thus making the "persuasive" nature of their definitions explicit.

As is clear from the above mentioned illustration, the rational methods which are used in the first pattern arguments can be also used in the second pattern disputes. But unless disputers are entertaining the same definition of the ethical term used, the rational methods do not possess any finality because the relation between a persuasive definition and its supporting reasons, here also, are not logical but psychological. Thus Stevenson reaches again the same conclusion that "rational methods can resolve ethical disagreement if and only if it is rooted in disagreement in belief."[53] [15]

9.

So far we have studied Stevenson's "description" of ethical methods that are in fact used in common life. Some would hold that mere description of methods actually used is not adequate as a methodological investigation. They might claim that the central problem of a methodology is to find *valid* methods, or to establish the criteria by which valid methods can be distinguished from invalid methods. Hence it would be advisable to see what Stevenson says about the "validity" of the ethical methods he has described.

---

[15] Here I illustrated only a case which concerns interpersonal disagreement. So I must add that Stevenson claims that the similar parallels between the first and the second pattern arguments can be found in cases of "personal decision." (*Ethics and Language*, pp.238–239)

As has been already mentioned, Stevenson's methodology is primarily concerned with *description*, but not with *evaluation*. Hence he does not attempt to show any criteria of "valid" methods. His fundamental question in connection with "validity of methods" is not "What kind of methods are valid?" but rather "Can we properly assign 'validity' or 'invalidity' to those methods which are peculiar to ethical, or valuative, arguments?"

It is obvious that we can properly question the *validity* of an ethical argument when (a) it applies formal logic, and (b) when it is concerned with *factual* study of the truth or falsity of empirical reasons offered to support ethical judgments. But in these cases the argument, though closely connected with an ethical problem, is not in itself peculiarly "ethical." Again, from Stevenson's point of view, persuasive methods might be considered peculiar to valuative arguments. But it seems "cognitively nonsensical to speak of, 'valid' or of 'invalid' persuasion,[54] unless we use the term "valid" or "invalid" in a figurative way of speaking.

Thus there remains only one aspect of ethical arguments concerning which the assignability or the attributability of "validity" can be seriously questioned. The aspect we are referring to is nothing but that peculiar process of inferring an ethical conclusion from a factual reason. When we say, for instance, "Mutual aid is good *because* it promotes social welfare," this inference is not a mere persuasion since it is mediated by an articulate reason; nor is it, as such, any inductive or deductive procedure. Hence Stevenson's concern centers on the question whether the step of inference from a factual reason "R" to an ethical conclusion "E" can be properly evaluated as "valid" or "invalid."

Since the term "validity" is not free from ambiguity, Stevenson admits that the term can be defined in a broad sense in which inferences from R to E could be called "valid." But he suggests that to use the term in such a sense would be "impractical" and "injudicious." The reason why Stevenson rejects this broad usage of "valid" is this: In any preferable use of the term, "valid" is intimately related to "true;" but if we apply "valid" to the inference from R to E, then "the word could not have its accustomed connection with 'true'."[55] The reason why the application of "valid" to an inference from R to E deprives the term of its "accustomed connection" with "true," is that, in the step of the inference considered, "the reasons *do not establish or call into question* the truth of an ethical judgment's (descriptive) meaning."[56] [16] Thus, Stevenson concludes that it would be advisable, for the sake of clarity, *not* to apply the term "validity" to the method of inferring from factual reasons to an ethical conclusion.

However, Stevenson warns, to say that ethical methods distinct from logic and scientific methods have nothing to do with validity, is not to say that there is no ground for choice between those typically ethical

---

[16] Here Stevenson is talking about the first pattern of arguments, and his point is that the reasons supporting the ethical judgment say nothing about the truth or falsity of the judgment's descriptive meaning which refers to the utterer's attitude to the object judged.

methods. Even when a moralist cannot choose a method by a consideration of validity, there are other considerations in accordance with which he may choose between methods without being simply swayed by caprice. Suppose a man wants to have his definition of "good" accepted by one of his friends who is holding a different definition. Should he support his definition by presenting "reasons," or by methods that are predominantly persuasive? He cannot decide his methods by consideration of their validity, because there is, strictly speaking, no "valid" method to support a persuasive definition. But he may find some other grounds upon which he is to choose between available methods. For example, he might find that the situation requires a quick attainment of an agreement which could be better brought about by an eloquent persuasion. Or he might wish to build up in the friend "an inquiring habit of mind" which would help him to make all future ethical decisions "in the light of full knowledge,"[57] and then he may find it desirable to employ rational methods to make use of the present chance for that far-seeing purpose.

To say that ethical methods irrelevant to "validity" are not, as a matter of fact, chosen capriciously, but on some grounds which do not necessarily amount to the considerations of the sheer impressiveness of available methods, is not to say that there is *the* method which we *ought to* choose. According to Stevenson, there is no such absolutely authorized method. Any argument about the question "What method *ought* we to choose?" will involve disagreement in attitude. Thus the question about what methods we should choose in ethics, is itself a matter of normative ethics. Consequently, to support a certain method, we might employ all kinds of methods which can be used in ordinary ethical arguments. But here again we cannot always expect to reach, by means of these methods, finality in arguments about "the proper method;" for these arguments might also involve the inference from factual reasons to valuative conclusions as well as persuasions, of which we cannot properly raise the question of "validity." "To evaluate or recommend an ethical method (whenever validity can have no bearing on the case)," says Stevenson, "is to moralize about the ways of moralists."[58)]

10.

Stevenson, as we have seen so far, has paid little attention, in the development of his methodological conceptions, to the distinction between "intrinsic" and "extrinsic" values—a distinction which many writers consider to be of central importance in connection with methods of ethics. Actually he does not sanction any emphasis on the distinction. What grounds does he have to reject the current view which holds that a "division of labor between those who recommend ends and those who study means"[59)] is profitable? His position concerning the concepts of "intrinsic" and "extrinsic" values is remarkably close to that of Dewey.

Stevenson's view in question can be conveniently presented through a study of his criticism of the "specialist's conception." By "specialist's conception" Stevenson refers to the position of those who believe the "possibility of isolating moral and factual questions, and of making questions about intrinsic value an independent study."[60] According to the "specialist's conception," decisions about ultimate ends or intrinsic values can be made apart from any consideration on the means of obtaining them, and it is wise for philosophical moralists to confine themselves to problems of intrinsic value leaving questions of extrinsic value to other specialists such as social scientists or psychologists.

The specialist's conception, Stevenson holds, is based upon two assumptions, which make it appear plausible. The assumptions are:

Agreement on intrinsic value (i) is presupposed by, and (ii) does not itself presuppose, any other type of ethical agreement.[61]

The relation of these two assumptions to the specialist's conception of ethics seems obvious. If the first assumption is true, then agreement on intrinsic value will be an indispensable foundation for all other types of agreement, and will provide ethical philosophy a peculiar subject-matter. And if the second assumption is true, then it will be possible for ethical thinkers to limit their concern to questions of intrinsic value, leaving other questions, in accord with the principle of "division of labor," to "scientists" such as psychologists and sociologists. If, on the other hand, these assumptions prove untenable, so Stevenson maintains, the specialist's conception will lose most of its points.[62] Thus Stevenson's criticism of the specialist's conception centers on these two "tacit" assumptions.

Stevenson's criticism of the first assumption consists in asserting that there are cases in which ethical agreements may occur even without any agreement on ends of intrinsic values. Two types of these cases are conceivable:[63]

i) A may approve of X *as an end*, and B, even without recognizing its intrinsic value, may approve of it *as a means* to Y which he believes to be intrinsically good. Thus, unless some other factors enter, A and B will agree that X is "good" though they do *not* agree with each other on the *intrinsic* goodness of X.

ii) A may approve of X as a means to Y which he believes intrinsically good, and B may approve of X as a means to Z which he believes to be intrinsically good. But A may be indifferent to Z, and B may be indifferent to Y. Thus, unless some other factors enter, they will agree that X is good — good as a means to their *divergent* ends.

The above-mentioned two types of cases, according to Stevenson, are not only logically possible, but must actually occur in some situations, "if there is to be any ethical agreement at all."[64] The ground for Stevenson to affirm this, is the egoistic aspect of human nature. Stevenson maintains that it is indisputable that egoistic ends do exist. And it is commonplace that egoistic ends, though divergent in themselves, can sometimes lead to convergent attitudes. If so, Stevenson reasons, we must admit that there are cases where ethical agreements are reached even without any agreement on "ends-in-themselves."

In connection with his criticism of the first assumption Stevenson introduces two noteworthy conceptions. The first one is that of "complex agreement." In his criticism under consideration Stevenson introduced four basic types of agreements,[65] of which I have mentioned only two. And "complex agreement" can be best illustrated in terms of these basic types. For, it occurs when agreement exemplifies two or more of these basic types "simultaneously, with regard to the same object, for a *single pair* of men."[66] For example: A might approve of X *both* as an end *and* as a means to Y which he intrinsically approves of; B might approve of Y as an intrinsic good, and of X as a means to Y though he does not intrinsically approve of it. In this illustration two types of agreement are involved with regard to the same object X. i) A and B agree that X has *instrumental* value as a means to Y. (Stevenson's Type II) ii) They agree that X is "good," but, this time, their agreement is not complete in that A approves of X as *intrinsically* valuable, while B recognizes X's extrinsic value only. (Stevenson's Type III)

The conception of "complex agreement" is particulary important because it calls attention to a psychological situation which Stevenson refers to as "reinforcement." "Reinforcement" takes place

> when the same man approves of something both as an end in itself and as means to some further end, or else when he approves of it as a means to several ends.[67]

In the above-mentioned case, to use the same illustration, A's intrinsic approval of X is "reinforced" by his extrinsic approval of it; and conversely, his extrinsic approval of X is reinforced by his intrinsic approval of it. The conception of "reinforcement" calls our attention to the fact that in many cases a man values one and the same object both as an end and as a means to something else, and that there are many cases where a man's intrinsic approval and extrinsic approval cannot be profitably isolated if we are to fully understand how he actually evaluates an object in a concrete situation.

It would be rather unusual that a man has *only one* end in his mind. Generally speaking, a man may have several different ends. The plurality of ends results in the phenomenon of reinforcement as well as that of complex agreement. Few objects of desire are "ends" exclusively. Intrinsic desires may be reinforced by extrinsic ones, and extrinsic desires may reinforce each other. Consequently, in many cases ethical agreemnt may be complex. Hence Stevenson's conclusion: "No theory of ethics can be acceptable which leaves complex agreement out of account."[68]

Now let us proceed to Stevenson's criticism of the second assumption. He bases it upon the psychological fact that "what is first favored as a means may on that very account grow to be favored as an end."[69] One's intrinsic attitudes are not immutable. In other words, what we approve of as "intrinsically good" is determined not only by our hereditary dispositions to acquire certain attitudes, but also by many environmental factors. One of the factors which determines intrinsic attitudes, Stevenson holds, is "habituation." At first we may approve of X as a means to Y, but if the approval of X becomes a "habit" we might continue to approve of it even when, because of changed circumstances, X is not required any more as far as the accomplishment of Y is concerned. Consequently it may happen that a man who first agreed that X is valuable only as a means, later comes to agree that it is valuable as an end as well. Hence Stevenson concludes:

> An effort to establish commonly accepted means, even to divergent ends, can be a step that is necessary — not logically, of course, but practically — to establishing commonly accepted ends. [70)]

Stevenson's criticism of the second assumption, which is based on W. Wundt and G. W. Allport, and which reminds us Perry's conception of "mutation of interest," might seem commonplace as far as his psychological discussion is concerned. But Stevenson finds that the view that means pass into ends has remarkable significance for ethical methodology, which has not been fully realized by many writers.

If a moralist makes use of the psychological fact that means pass into ends, he might be able to resort to rational methods. For instance: Suppose A wants to have B agree that X is intrinsically good. Then he may begin with pointing out the consequences of X upon Y which B already accepted as an intrinsic good. If, in this way, A succeeds in making B accept, in the first place, the instrumental value of X, then there might be some chance for him to reach his initial aim, namely, to make B agree that X is intrinsically good; for, by virtue of Allport's principle,[71] B might later come to accept X as an intrinsic value as well.

On the other hand, however, a moralist who abides by the specialist's conception would hope to establish common ends by some procedure in which a consideration of means has no part. Then, Stevenson says, it would be very difficult for him to make use of any rational method in order to reach agreement in attitudes. For, "if intrinsic attitudes are not redirected by a knowledge of the factual situation which confronts them, they are not directed by knowledge."[72] In other words, the only method available for him would be the exclusive use of persuasion. But, Stevenson holds, few moralists would commit themselves exclusively to the method of persuasion. Moreover, the exclusive use of persuasive method is not likely to lead to permanent effects. Thus Stevenson concludes that "a study of means is wholly indispensable to ethics, if moral judgments are to have effective support."[73]

11.

Since we have studied Stevenson's main conceptions concerning the two central problems of his ethical investigation, the meaning of ethical terms and methods of ethical arguments, let us now proceed to consider what contribution or shortcomings they may involve.

One of the chief merits of Stevenson's analysis in his study of the controversial problem concerning the definition of ethical terms, seems to be that he fairly recognized all the partial truth which are implied in different theories of opposing writers. It seems to be admitted that all of the three most influential positions on the problem of the definition, namely, the positions of "psychological value" theorists like Perry, of logical positivists like Carnap, and of those who, like Moore, claim the "indefinability" of ethical terms, though they contradict each other, have clarified respectively some important aspects of the meaning of ethical terms. And we see that in Stevenson's mild version of the emotive conception of ethics the achievements of all these three different views are in some measure reflected. We should not assert that Stevenson's analysis regarding the definition of ethical terms are quite satisfactory, but it might be admitted that his careful approach has brought to light several important respects which had been overlooked by many other writers.

As one of the most important theses maintained by Stevenson we might refer, in the first place, to his recognition that ethical terms have both emotive and descriptive meaning. We have seen that Perry's definition of "value" could not explain the fact that an ethical disagreement may remain even after complete agreement on psychological facts is attained. And this difficulty would not exclusively belong to Perry; any theory which maintains that a value–judgment can be completely translated into a nonvalue–judgment, must be confronted with the same difficulty. Because of this difficulty, the so–called Naturalists were charged by Moore with the "naturalistic fallacy." Yet the inadequacy of the "naturalistic" definition does not necessarily justify Moore's realistic view that "good" is a unique unanalyzable quality. In fact, the difficulty of the "naturalistic" definition under consideration might be more neatly explained when we regard it as a result of neglecting the "emotive" or the prescriptive meaning of value terms, than when we put the blame on a logical fallacy. Now we have also seen that logical positivists' exhaustive denial of descriptive meaning in ethical utterances is untenable. (Ch. Ⅲ, Sec. 2) The descriptive meaning of an ethical statement might be only implicit. One and the same value term might be used in different senses. Nevertheless it seems ridiculous to insist that ethical utterances are entirely "nosensical." In short, the plain fact that ethical expressions are neither mere informations as to psychological situations nor mere revelations of sheer emotions, has been long overlooked by many writers who wanted to describe moral experience in accord with their favorite systems of ethics instead of adjusting their systems in accord with ethical experience. Indeed Stevenson's "working models," as Henry D. Aiken has said,[74] are "crude and even bizarre," but they contain at least a partial merit so far as they retain both descriptive and emotive or presciptive meanings in ethical expressions.

As the second significant point Stevenson has brought to light in connection with his study of the meaning of ethical expressions, we may refer to his distinction between disagreement (or agreement) in beliefs and that of attitudes. It might be properly questioned, to be sure, whether beliefs and attitudes are different *in generic nature*. Aiken affirms, by way of charging Stevenson with ignoring "the fact that 'belief' and 'attitude' are both affective–ideational process," that belief is a type of attitude because "acceptance or rejection of a proposition is an affective process ⋯ and not itself an act of cognition."[75] Yet even if Aiken's view is accepted, his argument no more nullifies Stevenson's distinction between two kinds of agreement or disagreement than the fact that "experiment" is a type of observation nullifies psychologists' distinction between methods of "experiment" and those of "observation." Even after the discovery that a human being is a kind of animal, it is often convenient to *distinguish* between "man" and "animal." Anyhow it would be admitted that Stevenson's distinction between the two kinds of agreement or disagreement is *serviceable* for the analysis of ethical expressions, as well as for the study of ethical methodology.

Another respect to be mentioned is Stevenson's emphasis on the "flexibility of language." That words, in general, are used with more or less flexibility is a so plain fact that very few would deny it. Therefore, to say simply that ethical terms are used, as a matter of fact, in different ways in different situations, involves neither any novelty nor any problems. Problems begin to appear when the flexible usage of language is considered from a normative or evaluative point of view. If there is something new in Stevenson's conceptions regarding the flexibility of ethical language, it would be found in his interpreation of the nature of the problems which present themselves when the divergent use of ethical language is considered from any evaluative point of view.

It is interesting, though paradoxical, that people, who are generally indifferent or generous concerning the flexible use of nonvalue terms, are particularly critical and faultfinding as to the use of value terms, while the flexibility of language is most remarkable in the use of valuative terms. The divergent use of value terms seems too familiar to require any illustration. Even those words that are not ordinarily considered "value terms" but can be used like value terms, show a notable tendency of flexibility in their meanings whenever they are used as indicators of (positively or negatively) valuable things. We see typical examples of this sort in the use of such terms as "art," "science," "culture," "lady," "love," "sexual," etc. As a curious example, we might suggest the fact that, when "colored people" is uttered to designate certain races which are frequently considered inferior, some colors (that are relatively close to white) are excluded from the "colors" of men. Thus, generally speaking, words which are connected with "value" are more likely to be used in diverse ways. And, paradoxically enough, the more flexibly a word is used, the more likely people incline to claim respectively that their own usage of the term is *the only true one*.

The crucial fact seems to be this: Few people doubt that, as a matter of fact, words are used with more or less flexibility, but many hold that the "true" meaning of a term cannot be found through the analysis of the common use of the term. In other words, many people seem to believe that some ways of using a term, especially when the term is directly connected with value, are *wrong* even if they do not violate any linguistic rules. Even moralists admit the fact that moral terms are used diversely within a certain range. But they believe that the very task of a moral philosopher is to establish *the standard meaning* of moral terms by which the embarrassingly various actual use of them is to be corrected.

Stevenson does not object to moralists' attempts to make their own use of ethical terms accepted by all people. What he does object to is the moralists' claim that their definitions are *the only true* ones. Many writers have maintained that the criteria through which an acceptable definition is distinguished from unacceptable ones are predetermined wholly objectively in the sense that no interest or aspiration of the user of the term defined has anything to do with the criteria. Some have believed that the true meaning of ethical terms can be discovered through the nature of "reality," and some others in the light of the *universal* nature of human beings. And various definitions have been suggested on diverse grounds as the "true definition." But no one of the definitions thus presented, whatever ground it may be based on, has been able to prove that it was exclusively the true definition. This does not mean that the definitions suggested had no reason to support themselves. They were respectively based on some more or less relevant reasons; yet unfortunately none of the reasons were *logically* related to the definition to be defended. Thus no definition could reach finality. Here Stevenson holds that the lack of finality in ethical definitions comes from the very nature of ethical definitions. According to him, we can neither prove nor disprove an ethical definition unless it violates any linguistic rule. An ethical definition reflects the ideal or the aspiration of the man who gives it. Consequently it is impossible to conclusively defend or reject an ethical definition unless we can logically establish that an ideal or an aspiration is "right" or "wrong." When a writer pretends that his definition is conclusive, Stevenson says, he is "persuading."

Stevenson's conception of "persuasive definition" does not provide any positive resolution to our normative problems. Its contribution seems merely negative, in the sense that it only suggests the impossibility of any conclusive definition of ethical terms. And this suggestion, to be sure, seems rather discouraging. Nevertheless it should be admitted that the conception clarifies some important aspects in connection with the controversial problem of ethical definitions. And it might be also admitted that the conception of persuasive definition provides a good starting point for a careful approach — an approach which is free from dogmatism and self-complacency — to the solution of normative problems of ethics.

However, in spite of several admirable merits, Stevenson's approach to the definition of ethical terms is far from being adequate. A fundamental difficulty seems to be implied already in his conception of "meaning." Stevenson's generic sense of "meaning," as we remember, was defined "in terms of the psychological reactions of those who use the sign."[76] Even if we admit that to say, "The meaning of a sign is its dispositional property to cause psychological reactions in its users," is *one of* the linguistically permissible definitions of "meaning," it is quite doubtful whether this definition is really "more serviceable" for a study of ethical methods.

The final purpose of inquiring into the meaning of an ethical expression, as far as a meta–ethical study is concerned, seems to be to judge whether and how the expression can be justified. However, if the meaning of an ethical utterance is interpreted in the psychological sense, I am not quite sure what is there to be justified. When a man tries to verify or justify a judgment he must be endeavoring to verify or justify what he *means* by the judgment. Then if the meaning of the judgment consists in the "power" or tendency of the judgment to cause certain psychological reactions, he must be defending the power or tendency. But is he really endeavoring to defend exactly the power or tendency? Psychological reactions are simply *natural* phenomena causally related to various preceding factors. If so, what is the point in affirming to "justify" the *tendency* of an expression to cause certain psychological reaction? It seems neither possible nor necessary to justify any natural tendency. In some tropical countries it is apt to rain too much during a certain season. Yet I can hardly imagine how we can "justify" this *tendency*, and how such a justification can be required, except from a teleological view of the world, to which Stevenson would not want to commit himself. To be sure, we might be able to justify such a *statement* as "It rains too much in India," or "The tendency of raining too much is undesirable." But this is quite another thing.

In fact, what disputers endeavor to justify is *not* any tendency or power involved in their utterances. It is their beliefs and attitudes as expressed through their utterances that people try to defend or attack in ethical disputes. That Stevenson himself fully admits this fact is evidently shown by his whole discussion of methods. In short, there in some kind of inconsistency between his definition of "meaning" and his methodological considerations. And the fault seems to be in the former.

Again, even if we consent to speak of tendency or power as equivalent to the meaning of a term, it is not quite convincing, as D. H. Parker pointed out,[77] that the tendency or power is located in the word itself rather than in the users of the word. Strictly speaking, what Stevenson refers to as "dispositional property" is *relational* to *both* a word and its users, and accordingly it cannot be properly called "the power *of the word*."

Another difficulty in Stevenson's approach to the definition of ethical terms, is in the inadequacy of his characterizing emotive meaning only as "imperative" or "quasi-imperative." Even if emotive meaning may be analogous to an imperative in many cases, there are cases where it is not so. Suppose, for instance, a school boy happily reports to his mother that he got the grade "A" for the other day's examination, and his mother says, "That is good!" It seems strange to interpret the mother's utterance as "I approve of it; do so as well;" for it is doubtless the case that the boy has already approved of it. In such a case, as well as when a man staying alone finds a work of art "beautiful," the emotive meaning of a value term might be better interpreted in terms of an *expression of emotion*. Or again, in some other cases the "emotive" meaning of a valuative utterance may be better characterized, in accord with J. L. Austin's suggestion, as "performative."

12.

When we remove our attention to Stevenson's methodological investigation, we again find that he has made several noteworthy contributions. It seems indisputable that as a *description* of ethical methods his study is exhaustive enough to show the various types of ways of arguments which are commonly used in moral disputes. His distinction between rational and non-rational methods, and his conception of the limit of the former, are full of suggestions. And his analysis of the means-end relationship is also admirable. Yet those who carefully study his methodology as a whole might find themselves not quite satisfied.

The first reason why Stevenson's methodology is found unsatisfactory might be the fact that one of the fundamental assumptions on which his methodology is based, is not fully convincing. The assumption is: Disagreement in belief and disagreement in attitude are wholly different in their nature.

As for the inadequacy of this assumption we have Vincent Tomas' penetrating criticism. The central points of Tomas' arguments relevant to the assumption are:

i) Disagreements in belief, no less than ethical disagreements, involve question of appraisal.

ii) Disagreements in belief, no less than ethical disagreements, are of two kinds.

iii) Disagreements in attitude, like disagreements in belief, presuppose criteria of correctness. [78]

I do not think that Tomas' criticism is sound at all its points. [17] Nor do I agree with Tomas' belief that his criticism nullifies the distinction itself Stevenson made between two kinds of disagreements. Nevertheless I am inclined to think his criticism brings to light several defects in Stevenson's analysis which are connected with the assumption under consideration and which are not negligible. First, as Tomas' first thesis suggests, Stevenson's understanding of the nature of disagreements in belief seems to be too crude. Apparently he paid too little attention to the factor of appraisal involved in beliefs. Second, Stevenson tacitly assumed that all disagreements m beliefs can be, in principle, settled, or brought near settlement, by "rational" or "scientific" investigations. But the term "rational" or "scientific" is not quite free from ambiguity. Thus if two men entertain different

---

[17] For example, Tomas' argument in defense of his third point is not convincing; for his use of Stevenson's own illustration given in the *Ethics and Language* (pp.13–14) to attack the author seems to be based on misunderstanding of the text, especially the last sentence of the first quotation. (Cf. *Mind*, Vol. 60, pp.211ff)

conceptions of "rational" or "scientific," a disagreement in belief between them could hardly be settled. Moreover, as Tomas points out in defence of his second thesis, *not all* disputants commit themselves to "scientific" methods. This would be obvious to everybody who stops to think of the existence of intuitionists, mysticists, authoritarians, and so on. Indeed it is undeniable "that disagreements in belief which are rooted in normative disagreements abound in philosophy and in the social sciences."[79] Third, Stevenson seems to have overlooked the analogy between disagreements in belief and disagreements in attitude. For example: He did not pay enough attention to the fact that to reach agreements in belief, as to reach agreements in attitude, is one thing and to reach the "truth" is another thing. Nor did he attend to the fact that "the relation between the epistemic attitude of belief and its supporting reasons is not logical, but psychological,"[80] and that, consequently, nonrational methods can be (or are) also employed in cases of disagreements in belief.

Stevenson's assumption that disagreements in belief and disagreements in attitudes are wholly different in nature, seems to be a corollary of a more basic assumption, which is: In the matter of beliefs there are objective criteria by which the correctness or incorrectness of a given belief can be finally decided, but in the matter of attitude there is *no* such criterion. I am not ready to reject this assumption entirely, yet I do not believe that this is to be taken for granted. It is true, to be sure, that it is relatively easier to settle disagreements in belief, than to settle disagreements in attitudes. And it is also undeniable that this difference comes from the fact that the problems of belief are directly concerned with what we call "empirical facts," while the problems of attitude are not directly concerned with anything which can be properly called so. But the concept of "empirical fact" itself, which seems to designate something which can be, in principle at least, commonly perceived by all men, is a product of some assumption. And unless all men share some basic assumptions concerning "knowledge," the possibility of a "rational" settlement of disagreements in belief is not guaranteed. If, on the other hand, all men share some suitable assumptions, the possibility of a "rational" settlement will be open even for disagreements in attitude. Of course, we should not neglect the fact that the remarkable development of the modern sciences, which seem to be approaching some convergent conclusions while the opposition of divergent moral principles appears to remain as notorious as ever, shows that sharing common assumptions seems to be easier in connection with matters of belief than with matters of attitudes. But this difference would not provide any final proof until we establish the necessity of agreement in factual assumptions, and that of disagreement in valuative assumptions.

Another reason why Stevenson's methodology seems unsatisfactory might be the impression that it is "opening the doors to all sorts of irrationalism," providing a justification even for "unprincipled rhetoricians with dictatorial ambitions."[81] If Stevenson answers the objection that he opens doors to all sorts of irrationalism by saying "Why not?" and if he really means that all sorts of irrational methods are permissible, that would be the end of the matter, though few would accept his theory. But, judging from the suggestions Stevenson gives in the last chapter of the *Ethics and Language*, he is not likely to answer the objection in such a way. His suggestions about the "proper use of science" and "justifiable uses of persuasion" by no means encourage any unprincipled irrationalism. [82] Yet the connection between these suggestions and the general position of his meta-ethics is too weak. In other words, it is difficult to understand why the "practical" suggestions he gives, and not others, follow from his "theoretical" view. Suppose we admit, in separation, both his practical suggestions and his theoretical view, yet we might still find his theory as a whole is lacking in something — something which would connect the two parts in a unified system.

If Stevenson, by way of rejecting such an objection, replies that meta-ethics and normative ethics are to be sharply differentiated, and that a meta-ethical study of methods should not involve *any* evaluative consideration, he would be confronted with further difficulties. The reasoning Stevenson would present to justify the reply would be something like this: The object of meta-ethics is to explicate ethical phenomena through purely logical analysis together with observation; from an analytic point of view, there is no logical ground to judge any of the methods which are in fact available for ethical arguments to be *the proper* method, or to be better than others, as far as they involve reasoning from factual premises to an ethical conclusion; therefore to defend this or that method as a good or the legitimate one is not a task of an analyst, but of a moralist. But the fact that the major premise of this reasoning is far from being quite convincing undermines the value of the whole argument. Let us see why it is so by asking two questions. i) Why a meta-ethical study must be purely analytic or non-normative? ii) Does not the so-called "pure analysis" of moral phenomena, such as Stevenson's theory, involve *any* normative implication?

i') Stevenson, who declares that his ethical study is "metanormative but nonnormative inquiry," seems to hold that it implies a sort of confusion for a meta-ethical study to involve any normative factor. But I am inclined to think that meta-ethics and normative ethics are not necessarily contradictory concepts. If a writer, to be sure, introduces normative factors into his meta-ethical study *without noticing the fact*, his study must be considered confused. Yet the concept of "meta-ethics" itself does not seem to exclude *all* normative elements.

I am tempted to regard meta-ethics as a foundation of normative ethics. It is not impossible, of course, to have a meta-ethical study for its own sake. But when we think of the deepest need of the human mind which has impelled thinkers, since ancient days, to ethical philosophy, we might find it hard to be completely satisfied with a meta-ethical theory which is indifferent to normative ethics. A meta-ethical study without important normative implications might be possible, yet its significance must be comparatively small.

I do not claim that a meta-ethical study *ought to* imply normative factors. But I do believe that a meta–ethical study with full significance must be a *connected part* of ETHICS as an integrated whole of moral thoughts. This is equivalent to saying that there must be somewhere a kind of *copula* which may mediate the normative part of ethics with its nonnormative part to make them a *connected* whole. A systematizing writer may include the mediating principle either in his meta–ethical study or in his normative study according to his convenience. But when a writer confines himself to a meta–ethical study, as is the case with Stevenson, it seems advisable for him to include in his study *some* normative principles which would integrate his theory as a foundation on which a normative system can be established.

ii') Some writers such as P. B. Rice and F. A. Olafson seem to charge Stevenson with the ignorance or ignoring of normative implications of the meta–ethical theory of emotivism. And they endeavor to show that the meta–ethical analysis may have some normative *effect*. But what they chiefly emphasize seems to be the *psychological effect* of the meta–ethical theory. Rice, for instance, indicates that if Stevenson "really does succeed, in clarifying ⋯ the meanings of such terms as 'good' and 'right,' it would seem that this would have some normative effect: that we should be able to use them better after reading his book."[83] Again, Olafson asserts that the meta–ethical theory of emotivism changes the nature of a moral judgment to make it "a kind of symbolic action that is now often called a performative utterance," and that "since the conscious agent who forms the moral judgment and embraces the meta–ethical theory is one and the same, a performatory analysis of moral statements generates a performatory moral life."[84]

I do not believe, however, that this criticism is quite to the point, for Stevenson himself does *not* seem to deny the *effect* which a meta-ethical theory will cause. The following quotations might show that the criticism involves some misunderstanding:

> The purpose of an analytic or methodological study ⋯ is always indirect. It hopes to send others to their normative tasks with clearer heads and less wasteful habits of investigation.[85]

> So let us see whether our conclusions can give normative discussions a needed discipline, and let us see whether they can serve, indirectly, to hold up certain methods as more serviceable than others.[86]

Yet it might be argued that Stevenson is partly responsible for the misunderstanding, since he seems to have emphasized the nonnormative character of his theory more than enough. It might be also asserted that Stevenson's conception about the relation between meta-ethics and normative ethics is not sufficiently clear.

At any rate, Stevenson recognized the normative implications of meta-ethics as far as the psychological effects of the latter are concerned. Yet, I like to ask, are the psychological effects the only normative implications of a meta-ethical theory? I suspect there are some others. For example: Was not Stevenson implicitly asserting that a writer *should not* pretend that his definition of an ethical term is *the only true* definition, when he claimed that there is no such thing as "the only true definition?" Was not he tacitly suggesting that a moralist, whatever methods he may use, *should not* claim that his moral principles are strictly established, when he affirmed that *no* method can be properly called "valid" so long as it involves reasoning from nonvalue premises to an ethical conclusion?

In my opinion, there *are* really normative elements in all meta-ethical theories. Stevenson's theory, naturally, is not an exception. But the normative factors in his theory are rather *negative*, and consequently they are not sufficient to integrate the whole theory as a strong foundation for a constructive normative system.

I pointed out some inadequate aspects in Stevenson's methodology. But my criticism has been rather of supplemental nature. It seems that, generally speaking, I am still on Stevenson's side when many writers tend to reject him fundamentally.

Chapter V.

CONCLUDING REMARKS

1.

We have so far studied some main aspects of the three ethical theories that are respectively held by Perry, Dewey, and Stevenson, with a view to perceiving what suggestions these distinguished empiricists make for the solution of our fundamental problem: Can ethical utterances be justified or rejected on an empirical ground? Some critical considerations as to the contributions and shortcomings of these theories have been made. Now it seems that I have come to the corner where I must leave our writers to grope for my own words by way of attempting a solution to our central problems.

I agree with Perry and Stevenson that the clarification of the meaning of ethical expression is prerequisite to a study of the methods concerning the justification of ethical utterances. Thus I should like to begin by occupying myself with the problem of defining ethical terms.

It might be profitable, however, to briefly review, at the outset, what has been rejected, as well as what has been admitted, in the course of our previous discussions of the problem we are going to tackle anew. For this will show us the general direction of approach which we must follow if we are to make proper use of our foregoing studies.

i) I have rejected, with all of our three writers, the positions of the out—and—out logical positivists. This rejection, however, did not imply any acceptance of the view that the evaluative utterance and the factual judgment are essentially the same in their logical nature. We must admit that logical positivists are right at least in their assertion that typically ethical judgments have *some* emotive meaning which cannot be adequately translated into factual expressions.

ii) I agreed with our three writers in rejecting the realistic view of values which holds that values exist absolutely independent of any attitude of any sentient being. Some reasons why I rejected this view were given when I defended Perry against Moore in the last section of the second chapter. The arguments given there, I admit, were not quite conclusive. But I hope they, together with Perry's own discussions, were enough to show that the realistic view is not wellfounded, and that the relational view which regards the existence of some sentient being's attitude as one of the necessary conditions for the occurrence of value seems more plausible. In any case, it was the initial aim of this thesis to attempt an empirical approach to certain basic problems of ethics; and this initial standing—point finds it difficult to be satisfied by the realistic position. (See the second section of the introductory chapter.)

iii) The same attempt of empirical approach which laid aside intuitional views excludes also all kinds of metaphysical views. Metaphysical views in ethics are different from intuitional ones in that the final principles upon which they rest are not ethical in themselves. Nevertheless they are far removed from any empirical viewpoint so far as their final principles refuse scientific establishment. Hence an empirical mind is entitled to defer, even without questioning the logical difficulty involved in the reasoning from a nonvalue premise to an evaluative conclusion, the acceptance of any metaphysical position until it shows a more convincing ground.

iv) I agreed with Perry in so far as he claims that an object must be of actual interest to some kind of sentient being before it can be valuable. But I did not fully agree with his definitions, mainly because of two reasons: namely, (a) Perry's definitions fail to retain the "emotive" meaning, or the prescriptive functions, of value terms; (b) Perry claims that his definitions of ethical concepts are *the true* definitions, without noticing that this claim implies a "persuasive" characteristic.

v) I approved of Stevenson's approach to the meaning of ethical terms in so far as his "working models" retain both descriptive and "emotive" meanings of the terms defined, and his second pattern of analysis explicates the flexibility of ethical language as well as the "persuasive" character of "the only true" definitions which moralists are apt to present. Yet I pointed out that his approach is inadequate because (a) his definition of the generic sense of "meaning" in terms of psychological reactions is not suitable for the clarification of ethical expressions, and (b) his characterization of the "emotive" meaning of ethical terms is not exhaustive.

Now let us attempt anew a study of the meaning of ethical terms on the basis of those critical view-points just summarized. It seems that some serious confusions have been caused by those who intermingled these two different questions, "In what sense is an ethical term *actually* used in common language?" and "In what sense *ought* an ethical term to be used?" These two questions are to be sharply distinguished as they belong to entirely different categories. And it goes without saying that our study is primarily concerned with the *facts* of moral language.

2.

One and the same ethical term is used so diversely that it is almost impossible to enumerate exhaustively all ways in which a given ethical concept is employed. Besides, as Dewey and Stevenson hold, the inmost sense of such concept as "good" or "value" cannot be adequately translated into any other expressions. Most words have something *unique* in their meaning. This is especially the truth with ethical terms, for they typically imply some prescriptive or emotive meaning which is ordinarily too subtle to be completely copied by other expressions. Judging from these two obvious facts — the flexibility and the uniqueness of ethical language — it seems, strictly speaking, impossible to find definitions of ethical terms. But there must be some ways to clarify approximately the meaning of ethical concepts. Stevenson attempted to "characterize" ethical terms through linguistic analysis; and Dewey endeavored to approach the essence of "value" by analyzing experience itself in which value occurs. Naturally these two ways of approach cannot be basically different in their nature; for the language of morals is nothing but the expression, or rather the external aspect, of moral experience. Thus it is beside the point to ask which approach is the legitimate one. But let us borrow the linguistic method first, since it seems a good start to begin with more concrete and more external aspects of the subject to be studied. And then, if necessary, let us make use of the Deweyan way of approach for a complementary step.

Let us choose "good" as one of the most typical value-terms, and examine in what sense it is used in common language.

It is admitted that one of the central points in an investigation of the meaning of value-terms is to explicate what similarities and differences there are between the meaning of value-terms and of nonvalue-terms. It seems, therefore, convenient to begin our examination of "good" by comparing its meaning with the meaning of nonvalue-terms such as "portable."

We find there are some similarities between "good" and "portable" in connection with their meanings. In the first place, both can and do convey some information of a factual character concerning the objects to which the adjectives are applied. For example: When the word "portable" is used to characterize a typewriter, it stands for several more or less specific properties, such as "light enough to be carried by one hand," or "has an attached case with a handle," etc. Thus if one of your friends tells you, "I bought a 'portable' typewriter the other day," you, provided you are familiar with typewriters, will understand something about the typewriter he bought. That "good," when it is employed concerning a typewriter, also has some *descriptive* meaning, is shown by the fact that you will understand something *more* about his typewriter if your friend adds, "But I have found that it is not a very 'good' typewriter." We must admit, however, that a couple of difficult questions arise in this connection: First, it must be asked, does "good" also stand for several more or less specific properties; in other words, is "good" an epithet for a compound quality analysable into simpler qualities? Second, is what is true about a "good *typewriter*" also true about a "good *man*" or a "good *life*?" To the first question we may answer as follows. When the criteria by which a "good" typewriter (for example) is to be distinguished from a bad one are conventionally laid down among people who talk about goodness of typewriters, "good," as it is employed to assess a typewriter, may be considered to designate some specific properties; but when there are no conventionally accepted criteria this is not the case. (When a man says that an object X is "good" he has usually some criteria of a "good" X in mind, and the hearer also ordinarily understands approximately what his criteria are. Thus, I believe, the assertion that "good" conveys some factual information is still tenable.) Our second question is closely related to the first. The difficulty comes from the fact that the criteria for a "good man" or a "good life" are much more disputable than those of a "good typewriter," or of a "good pencil." Yet, it seems, this difference does not prevent "good" from telling *something* about the object when it is applied to a man or a life. (I will treat this respect a little more fully in what follows.)

The fact that "good" designates certain specific properties when, and only when, there are commonly accepted criteria about goodness, seems to suggest that there is some intimate relationship between the meaning of "good" and the publicly accepted opinion. Something similar can be said also as to the word "portable." The original meaning of the English word seems to be "transportable" or "carriable." But we do not ordinarily apply "portable" to those classes of things every species of which is supposed to be easily carried, such as watches, hand-bags, and pencils. Nor do we apply the word to animals, saying "portable chickens" or "an unportable elephant." It may be of course possible to present some reasons why the application of the term "portable" to the classes of things just mentioned is ridiculous. But the criteria of the applicability of the term are primarily conventional rather than strictly logical. Hence a second similarity between the two words, "good" and "portable;" that is to say, in both cases the proper meaning of the term must be something which is generally accepted or *public*. And the relation between the first and the second similarities is obvious, for a word could not have the function of conveying some factual information if its meaning were not something commonly accepted.

As we have seen before, if the criteria by which a good X is distinguished from a bad X are laid down, "good" can be considered to represent some specific properties when it is used in connection with X. But in many cases the criteria under consideration are not strictly laid down. When we talk about, for example, goodness of apples, the criteria of evaluation may be disputed about, so long as people's tastes concerning apples are diverse, and their purposes in eating them are different depending upon their physical conditions. This uncertainty of criteria directly leads us to the flexible use of value terms. But the flexibility of language becomes more remarkable when a term is applied to different classes of things. When we judge an apple to be "good" the goodness usually implies sweetness, freshness, ripeness etc., but the same word designates quite different qualities when it is applied to a typewriter. Now the flexibility of language is by no means limited to value-terms. It is not impossible for makers to produce typewriters or televisions which might embarrass those who want to decide whether the products are to be called "portable" or not. Here again, the flexibility becomes more remarkable when the term is applied to different classes of object. For instance: The "portability" of a radio implies, among others things, "operatable with a battery;" but this is not the case with a "portable" typewriter. For another example: many "portable" televisions are *larger* and *heavier* than many "non-portable" radios. Thus we reach a third kind of similarity between "good" and "portable," namely: both terms are used implying different descriptive meanings in different situations.

Next, let us proceed to see what logical *differences* there are between the two terms under consideration. As Stevenson holds, when "good" is used in ordinary contexts it always expresses a certain attitude of the utterer. In other words, when I say "X is good," this utterance implies at least the descriptive meaning of "I like X," or "I approve of X." But, generally speaking, this is not the case with the word "portable." When "portable" is used as a purely nonvalue-term the statement "X is portable" informs nothing about the utterer's attitude towards X. What is most important in this connection is not the bare fact of the difference existing between the two terms, but the fact that whenever "good" is employed as an evaluative word it *always* expresses a certain attitude of the utterer towards the object evaluated. This fact is of importance because i) it might suggest some intimate relationship between goodness and attitude, and ii) it will enable us to find certain *constant* descriptive meaning in the term "good."

Another difference between the two terms is that "good," unlike "portable," has some extra meaning which cannot be translated into descriptive terms, and has been called by Stevenson "emotive." That "good," as well as other value-terms, possesses some "emotive" or prescriptive meaning, besides a descriptive one, has already been shown repeatedly. Accordingly let us here confine ourselves to the characterization of what has been called "emotive" meaning.

Stevenson characterized the "emotive" meaning of ethical terms as "imperative" or "quasi-imperative." But the prescriptive function of "good" is much subtler and milder than that of an imperative sentence. Therefore it seems that R. M. Hare's terminology "commending"[1] is preferable as an adjective to characterize the prescriptive aspect of good. The English word "commend" means both "to recommend" and "to praise." "Commending" in the sense of "recommending" might be better to describe the only *subtly* and *mildly* "imperative" function of the term under consideration. Besides, "commending" in the sense of "praising" may cover another aspect of the "emotive" meaning which I briefly refered to in the last chapter (Section 11), namely, the "emotion-expressive" or "emotion-evoking" aspect; for an utterance of praise is usually accompanied by a certain emotion either of the utterer or of the hearer, or of both. (I am not sure that Hare used "commending" to imply both "recommending" and "praisng," yet I believe the term can be employed in the broad sense suggested above.)

I am not asserting that Stevenson neglected the emotion-expressive or emotion-evoking aspect of ethical terms. In fact he fully recognized this aspect. According to him, we remember, "X is good" is roughly similar to "I approve of X; do so as well." Thus the emotion-*expressive* aspect of "good" is retained in the declarative component; and the emotion-*evoking* aspect of the term is emphasized in the imperative component, since the imperative component is requiring the hearer *to approve* of X, which necessarily involves some emotion. What I am arguing is that Stevenson's interpretation of the "emotive" aspect under consideration is inadequate in some points. Let me enter a little further into detail.

According to Stevenson, the utterance "X is good," i) always informs the hearer of the utterer's attitude towards X — the attitude of "approving;" ii) it expresses the utterer's emotion as far as the act of "approving" involves some emotion; iii) it *always* commands (in a roundabout way) the hearer *to approve of* X; iv) it accordingly commands (in a roundabout way) the hearer to evoke in himself a certain kind of *emotion* or *feeling* as far as the act of approving is conmonly supposed to involve that kind of emotion or feeling. The first and the second points just mentioned seem to be acceptable if we take the words "approve" and "emotion" in a rather broad sense. But about the third and, accordingly, the fourth points I have some doubts.

In the first place, it is not convincing that the utterance *always* commands (or suggests) the hearer to approve of X. Suppose A says, "This is a good picture," and B answers, "Yes, it's really good." In this case it seems strange to assert that B is commanding (or suggesting) A to "continue" approving of the picture. The strangeness becomes manifest if we suppose that A is an expert in arts while B is an outsider. Naturally B's utterance involves some "emotive" meaning, but its "emotive" meaning cannot be adequately characterized in terms of an "imperative." B is rather *praising* the picture, and he is expressing his feeling about it as far as the act of "praising" involves some feeling.

Second, the assertion that "X is good" commands (or suggests) the hearer *to approve of* X, is doubtful. Suppose I want to buy a typewriter and ask you, "What do you think is the best typewriter for a student?";

and suppose you say, "I think the Royal–Wood Model 33, is the best." In this case you are not primarily suggesting me *to approve of* the Royal–Wood Model 33, but rather *recommending the typewriter itself.* Or again, when you say, "Telling the truth is good, " you are not primarily commanding or suggesting the hearer *to approve of* telling the truth. If you are "commanding" or suggesting something at all, you must be rather commanding or suggesting the act of *telling the truth itself.* It is absurd to attempt to have a man approve of an object, or to make him evoke certain emotion in himself, by means of an imperative, because "to approve of" or "to entertain certain emotion" is not a voluntary act.

The difficulties mentioned above might be overcome if we characterize the prescriptive aspect of "good" as "commending" — "commending" in the sense of both "recommending" and "praising." This point may be well illustrated by using again the example of the boy who got an "A" mark in his examination. The case was as follows:

> A school booy happily reports his mother saying, "Mamma, I've got an A for the other day's exam:" and the mother says, "Oh, it's good!" (Cf. Sec. II of the last chapter.)

It was pointed out that it is strange to interpret the mother's utterance as "I approve of your getting an A mark; *approve* of it as well." But it will sound quite natural if we interpret the utterance as *praising* the boy's getting an A mark, and *recommending* that he gets 'A's in future as well. Or again, when you say to yourself, "This is a good picture," you are not telling yourself *to approve of* the picture; but you are praising, or recommending to yourself, *the picture*.

There seem to be cases, however, in which to characterize the prescriptive meaning of "good" as "commending" is inadequate, though it is by no means irrelevant. The most typical example of such cases is encountered when "*the* definition" of "good" is given by a moralist. Suppose a writer declares that the highest good is "the greatest happiness of the greatest number." It is true, to be sure, that the statement "'Good' is the greatest happiness of the greatest number" implies, as a part of its prescriptive meaning, recommendation and praise of "the greatest happiness of the greatest number." But the prescriptive or "emotive" meaning of the sentence seems to have a more essential aspect. That is to say, through the definition under consideration the moralist is committing himself to a cause of life. He is *choosing* a basic principle of morals. To borrow J. L. Austin's terminology, he is engaging himself to a certain course of "performance."

Such utterances as "Good is the greatest happiness," "The highest good is eudaimonia," "Good is Self-realization," and so forth do not *primarily* intend to convey any information. Nor can they be translated without awkwardness into the imperative mood. And we can explicate them only inadequately as an act of "commending." It seems there is a fundamental difference between the two forms of utterances, "X is good" and "Good is A, B, C,⋯."[1] When we say, "X is good," we are applying the term "good" to an individual object, X, taking the meaning of the term to be understood. It is X, in this case, that is elucidated or characterized; and since "good" has the function of commending, X is accordingly praised or recommended. But when we say, "Good is A, B, C, …," the contents of "good" itself are questioned. It is not A, B, C, … but "good" which is elucidated or explained in this case. Accordingly we cannot adequately characterize our utterance as "praising" or "recommending." Thus it seems obvious that we cannot properly assert that the prescriptive function of *all* ethical statements is "imperative," or "commending."

When the concept of "good" is employed in a *moral* context[2] the concept seems usually to involve the meaning of "ought." Among those who use the term "good" in ordinary moral contexts, it is customary assumed that "good" is "something we ought to seek after." And this assumption is based upon another assumption which is more

---

1 When I use the model "X is good," X is an object of a judgment and "good" is a predicate to characterize the object, while whenever I use the model "Good is A, B, C, …," "Good" is the noun and the whole sentence is a proposed definition of the term "good," or of goodness.

2 Here I use the term "moral" in a rather narrow sense. Indeed every problem concerning the value of conduct or of a character can be considered a concern of morality in a broad sense. But when "moral" is interpreted in a narrow sense, "X is good" is a "moral" utterance only when it implies, implicitly at least, that the performance of X is worthy of *social* approval while the default or neglect of X deserves censure. For example, "It is good to hear some light music when you are tired," is not ordinarily a "moral" judgment in the narrow sense, while "It is good to keep your promise," is usually a "moral" statement even in the narrow sense. (I shall refer to "morally good" again in the end of the present section.)

fundamental, namely: there are things which we ought to do. Thus when a moralist uses "good" as a *subject* of a moral statement, he frequently uses the word as a generic term to represent all sorts of things which we ought to seek after. And those claims expressed in the form of "Good is A, B, C,…" are primarily attempting to specify what the "something" we ought to seek after is composed of. It seems that this attempt contains something more significant than mere recommending or praising. Stevenson characterized the definition in the form of "Good is A, B, C,…" as persuasive. Indeed it will gain the property of persuasiveness when it becomes a subject of dispute, but its primary characteristic might be better elucidated when we understand the utterer as *choosing* a cause, or engaging himself to a certain course of "performance" as he declares that the definition is the most proper one. The problem whether or how this kind of "choosing" or "performative" statements can be justified, is naturally a methodological problem. So let us leave this problem for later discussion.

We have seen that if the criteria of "good" typewriters, "good" apples etc. are laid down, "good," when it is employed to evaluate a typewriter, an apple etc., designates certain specific properties. We have also seen, however, that the criteria in question are not always fixed, and that the term "good" may consequently be used by different speakers to designate different qualities. This must be also the case with a good *life* or a good *man*. Besides, since we cannot convincingly tell any universal purpose for which a life or a man is supposed to serve, it is much more difficult to reach any generally accepted criteria for a "good" life or a "good" man than in the case of typewriters, or of apples. Thus it is no wonder that "good" *as a generic ethical concept* is used very easily to designate different things by different writers, for "good" as a generic ethical concept can mean nothing but the goodness of "life" as a whole. As it is possible to present reasons on the basis of reflections to support proposed criteria for good typewriters, it must be also possible to give reasons on the basis of reflections to support proposed criteria for good life. But it may be significantly questioned whether criteria for a good life can be rationally justified to the same degree as criteria for good typewriters can be rationally justified.

From the analysis so far it seems clear that the meaning of "good" can be divided into two parts, constant and flexible parts. Whether I say, "X is good," or "Good is A, B, C, ⋯" the statement implies that "I approve of (or like) X (or A, B, C, ⋯)." Whenever I utter "X is good" in an ordinary evaluative contexts, my utterance involves some emotive, or rather prescriptive, meaning which can be characterized as "commending" using the term "commending" in a broad sense to include both "praising" and "recommending." The commending function of "good," to be sure, might be changeable *in its strength*, but the basic characteristics of the emotive or prescriptive meaning of "X is good" are almost constant. When I say, on the other hand, "Good is A, B, C, ⋯" with a view to giving *the* definition of "good," my utterance, besides its commending function, has a special function which can be conveniently characterized as "choosing a cause" or, borrowing

Austin's terminology, as "performative." But the "performative" function is not peculiar to the "Good is A, B, C, ⋯" type of utterances. In some contexts, the same function can be found also in utterances in the form of "X is good," as would be the case when a governmental leader says in a public speech, "I believe, democracy is the best policy!"; or again, when you say, "This is good music," intending ostensively to set up the standard of "good" music. In short, "commending" and "choosing" are so intimately related that any attempt to differentiate them too sharply would not be profitable.

The larger part of the descriptive meaning of "good" is more or less flexible according to contexts and utterers. The flexibility corresponds to the fact that the standards of "goodness" of things are not generally fixed, or to the fact that different people define "good" in different ways. Some might be tempted to limit the "meaning" of value-terms to its constant part only so that they may have more precise definition of terms without being bothered by the flexibility of language. But I am inclined to interpret "meaning" in a broad sense to include the changeable part as well because of two reasons. In the first place, in many cases the utterer, by saying that an object is "good," does mean, implicitly at least, that the object has such and such qualities. When you say, for instance, "This is a good watch," I understand that you *mean*, among other things, that the watch keeps good time. In the second place, the most fundamental problems of meta-ethics seem to be connected with the methodological problems of justifying moral judgments; and the problems of ethical justification are significantly related to the flexible part of the "meaning" of value–terms, for the questions which arise in connection with the flexible part are nothing but the questions of the criteria of values.

We have not paid, so far, much attention to the commonly held distinction between "intrinsic" and "instrumental" goods. It seems that the distinction has little to do with our theses, i) " 'Good' implies the descriptive meaning of 'I approve of' or 'I like'," ii) " 'Good' has some prescriptive (commendatory or performative) meaning. In other words, it seems that if these theses hold good in connection with either of the two kinds of "good" it must hold also in connection with the other. But when we come to think of another of our theses — " 'Good' conveys some information *about the object* to which it is applied" — we are tempted to entertain some doubts. Obviously "X is good" tells something about X, if "good" is used in the *instrumental* sense in the utterance. But is it equally clear that "X is *intrinsically* good" also gives some information about X? Indeed such a statement, if our first thesis is correct, does imply that the utterer approves of X and desires it for its own sake and not as a means only. But what does the statement say *about the object* X? For example, suppose a man says, "To take a walk on a sunny day is good even apart from all of the effects it may cause." What kind of descriptive meaning can his statement have (except that he likes to take a walk on a sunny day)? When a man says, "This is a good typewriter," the best way to elucidate what he means by "good" in this context seems to be by asking, "Why do you say it is good?" This process might work in cases where "good" is used in the intrinsic sense. So let us ask him why it is good to take a walk on a sunny day. His answer might be, for instance, "Because it is , pleasant," or "It is delightful." In this case we may interpret his reasoning as follows: All things that are pleasant, are intrinsically good; Taking a walk on a sunny day is a case of pleasant things; Therefore taking a walk on a sunny day is intrinsically good. Now let us press him a step further by asking, "But why is a pleasant thing intrinsically good?" Perhaps he will find it hard to present adequate reason for calling pleasant things "good." If he could offer any reason we may press him again by asking another similar question. In any case we will sooner or later come to the corner where he must say something not much different from saying, "It is good because it is good," or "It is evident that it is good," or "It is good because I cannot help believing it good." Whatever answer he may give for his last words, an obvious fact is this: When "X is intrinsically good" is uttered as the *final* principle of valuation, the utterance has *no* "descriptive" meaning *except* that which concerns the utterer's own attitude, such as "I believe X is good," "I like X," "I approve of X," or the like.

There is another distinction to which I have not paid sufficient attention, namely, the distinction between "good" in a generic sense and "morally good." But I don't believe that this distinction requires so much emphasis as some writers seem to deem necessary. "Morally good" designates nothing but "goodness of man." The term may be used, indeed, in a broader sense to include "goodness of society" or even "goodness of life." Yet in any case it is directly or indirectly concerns virtues of *man*. And what has been said about "good typewriters," or "good apples" and so forth, can be also held about "good men." When I say, "James is a good man," this utterance implies at least that I approve of James. It also implies the function of praising or recommending James. And it may give some information as to James' characteristics or virtues, according to what criteria of "good men" I am holding. Or again, when you say, "Good men are such and such," you are attempting to lay down the criteria of good men, just as your statement, "Good typewriters are such and such," is an attempt for laying down criteria for good typewriters.

Of course "moral goodness" may have its own peculiarity and its own problems. But these aspects might conveniently be left until we later study the nature of morality.

In order to prevent a conceivable misinterpretation, it seems advisable to refer briefly before closing our discussion of the meaning of "good," to what Maurice Mandelbaum terms "the principle of universality." I have said that the prescriptive aspect of the moral judgment can be characterized as "commendatory" or "performative." This assertion, to be sure, implies that the moral judgment, as far as its prescriptive aspect is concerned, is to be considered "subjective" in a sense. But the assertion does not negate the psychological fact that the utterer of a moral statement, if it is an authentic moral statement, *means* to affirm an *objective* truth and the statement *purports* to be such. It is evident that anyone who passes a moral judgment, at the time he passes it, "is attempting to assert something which he regards as true."[2] In other words, the utterer of a moral judgment claims the *universal validity* of his judgment. And obviously this claim is based on his belief (or tacit assumption) that his judgment refers to a certain quality which "truly belongs to that of which it is predicated" — another psychological fact which leads Mandelbaum to his another principle, namely, "the principle of the primacy of the facts."[3] But, as Mandelbaum warns, the psychological fact of claiming a judgment's universal validity is one thing, and the logical justification of the claim is quite another. It seems true that my characterizing the prescriptive meaning of moral terms as "commendatory" or "performative" implies a sort of doubt on the claim made by those who make moral judgments. But it by no means denies the fact those judgments purport to be objective.

3.

We have so far studied the meaning of "good." But our interest has not been limited to "good;" our primary concern has been rather to clarify the *general* nature of ethical statements. So it seems necessary to study some other value–terms in order to see whether the logical characteristics of those statements which are expressed in the form of

---

3 As for the definition and the detailed explanation of "the principle of universality" and of "the principle of the primacy of the facts," see M. Mandelbaum, *The Phenomenology of Moral Experience*, The Free Press, 1955, pp.243–277.

"X is good," or of "Good is A, B, C, ···" can be considered to be the *general* nature of all sorts of ethical statements. But it does not seem necessary to analyze all kinds of ethical terms. It would be enough to study two more major ethical terms, "ought" and "right." Nor is it necessary to detail the distinction between "good" and "ought" and "right." Yet it may be profitable to exmine what kinds of relationship can be found between these three basic terms, for if an ethical term can be defined in terms of another ethical term we may well dispense with the separate consideration of the fomer in the following studies.

That "good" and "ought" are seldom used to express exactly the same idea is well understood. "It will be very good for you to read this book," and "You ought to read this book," might be uttered to convey remarkably similar opinions of the utterer. Yet their meanings are not exactly the same. That there are essential differences between "good" and "ought" is obvious also from the fact that we can say, "It will be very good if you send him a note of thanks, but it is not necessary," while it is ridiculous to say, "You ought to send him a note of thanks, but it is not necessary."

Similar things can be said about the distinctions between "good" and "right." There are occasions, indeed, when "good" and "right" are used almost interchangeably. For instance, when a correct answer is given by a student, his teacher may approve of it by saying either "Good!" or "Right!" But that the two words are not used in exactly the same sense even in this context is manifest from the fact that the teacher may say, "Very good," but he is not apt to say, "Very right." Moreover, there are cases where "good" and "right" can *not* be used interchangeably. Thus we cannot say "Have a right time" instead of "Have a good time;" nor can we say "the good man in the good place" *instead of* "the right man in the right place."

Nevertheless, we find that, as far as major logical characteristics are concerned, what is true about ethical statements containing the term "good," is also true as to statements containing "right" or "ought."

In the first place, ethical statements in the form of "X is right," or "A ought to do X," as well inform the hearer of a certain kind of attitude of the utterer toward the object judged. In other words, they imply the descriptive meaning of "I approve of X," or of "I desire A's doing X."

In the second place, "right" and "ought" are used also with some extent of flexibility. Many writers hold that the essential meaning of "right" is equivalent to "fit." But since the term "fit" itself is quite ambiguous what is implied concretely in the descriptive meaning of "right" might be different according to different contexts. For instance: By saying "It is right to help the poor and the old," the utterer may be refering to the fact that most people in his society believe that the helpless should be protected, or to the fact that helping the poor and the old is in accord with the teachings of Jesus Christ, or to something else. A school child often says, "That isn't right!" having in his mind what his teacher said the other day. Again, by saying "Borrowed money ought to be paid back," the utterer may refer to certain articles in the civil law of his country, or to the fact that paying back of borrowed money is requisite for mutual trust in a society, or to some other facts. In short, "right" and "ought," like "good," may have different descriptive meanings according to the contexts in which they are uttered and to the criteria the utterer holds as to the rightness or oughtness of the objects judged. And it goes without saying that when, and only when, there are commonly accepted criteria about rightness or oughtness, "X is right" or "X ought to be done" conveys a certain specific, or fixed, information.

If we shift our attention to the emotive or prescriptive aspect of "right" and "ought," we also find notable similarity between these words and "good." There are occasions, to be sure, in which "right" is used almost entirely for a descriptive purpose, as is the case when we say "the right hand," "the right side of cloth," or "Few students could give right answers to all of the questions." But as far as moral contexts are concerned we may safely assert that "right" always carries some emotive or prescriptive function. The statement, for instance, "It is right to punish the troublemaker," apparently prescribes what to do with the troublemarker, as well as it shows some kind of emotional attitude of the utterer. In short, it is *commending* the punishment of the troublemaker. Whatever example we may take the similar function can be generally found. In some instances the prescriptive aspect is very obscure being overwhelmed by the emotion–expressive aspect, as might be the case when we say, "What you have done is, in my opinion, absolutely right!"; and in other instances the opposite is the truth, as is the case when we say, "The right time to transplant the young–plants of rice in this district is mid June." But in any case the "commending" characteristic of the utterance is retained.

When a man says in a particular situation, "It is right to punish the troublemaker," he is not, generally speaking, refering *only* to the particular troublemaker of that occasion; his utterance usually implies also that *any* troublemaker is to be punished. In other words, implicitly he is laying down, whether consciously or unconsciously, a standard for punishment. As far as his utterance implies the attempt to lay down a standard, it contains in some measure the aspect of "choosing a cause," or the "performative" aspect. We may make this clearer by supposing what kind of answers he would give if we go on to ask him the reasons why the troublemker is to be punished.

Let us suppose that his answer to the question why it is right to punish troublemakers is this: "Because troublemakers disturb the public peace." This implies that it is right to prevent people from disturbing the public peace. Then let us ask him again why it is right to prevent people from disturbing the public peace. Here he might answer, "Because the public peace is necessary for the greatest happiness of the greatest number," or "Because most people desire the public peace," or in some other ways. But we can continue to ask him the similar kind of questions until he cannot present any more "reason." In other words, if we continuously ask him to justify the reasons of reasons of reasons of reasons⋯, he will at last come to the point where he has to say, "It is evident that it is right," or "It is right because it is right," or something of similar nature. When a man insists that X is right even without being able to offer any reason to support his assertion, he is declaring his decision of attitude, or he is committing himself to a cause of life. And any attempt to lay down a standard shares this aspect of committing oneself to a cause, namely, the aspect of choosing a principle of conduct, in so far as the attempt is based upon the fundamental attitude of the attempter.

The prescriptive aspect of "ought" is even more manifest than that of "good," or of "right." It seem that to characterize moral expressions as "imperative" is more plausible in cases of "ought"–statements than in cases of moral statements implying "good" or "right." Compare, for example, the following four sentences, and you will find that the ethical statement with "ought" is closest to the sentence of imperative mood.

i) It is good to keep your promise even if the promise turns out to be disadvantageous to you.

ii) It is right to keep your promise even if the promise turns out to be disadvantageous to you.

iii) You ought to keep your promise even if the promise turns out to be disadvantageous to you.

iv) Keep your promise even if it turns out to be disadvantageous to you.

There are, of course, occasions when "ought" is used with little prescriptive or emotive meaning, as is the case when we say, "I was still in the bus when I ought to have reached the classroom." But with such occasions our present study is not much concerned, for they happen only when "ought" is used in primarily *descriptive* judgments.

Yet however analogous an "ought"-statement and an imperative utterance may be, the former cannot be completly translated into the latter. The most fundamental distinction between the two forms of utterances seems to be that an ought-statement in a moral context involves implicit referring to some *standard* of conduct, while an imperative utterance as such prescribes simply what to do in the particular occasion. That this is so may be most manifestly shown by the fact that imperatives, in ordinary contexts, can be used only in the form of the second person concerning present and future actions, while ought-statements can be employed in connection with any person, and indeed can be used in connection with past actions. Such a statement as "I ought to have followed your advice," cannot be properly translated into any imperative form. Thus, as it was the case with "good" and "right," "commending" seems to be a better word than "imperative" for the purpose of characterizing the "ought"-statement.

Naturally "ought" can also be used to express one's choice of a moral cause. Accordingly, when "X ought to be done," is declared as a *final* principle, the utterance may be better characterized as "choosing" or as "performative."

4.

Let us now proceed to see what relations there are between "good" and "right" and "ought." Some writers hold that among moral concepts only one is absolutely fundamental, others being rather derivative, and that some moral concepts accordingly can be defined in terms of other moral concept which is more basic. For instance: G. E. Moore, though he definitely rejects any attempt to define value-terms by means of nonvalue-terms, seems to believe that "right" can be somehow defined in terms of "good" when he says, "To assert that a certain line of conduct is, at a given time, absolutely right or obligatory, is obviously to assert that more good or less evil will exist in the world, if it be adopted than if anything else be done instead."[3] Again, we have already seen that Perry, following the traditional teleological interpretation, maintains that " 'right' means conduciveness to moral good," and that "ought" stands in a dependent relation against "good." (Cf. Ch. II, Sec. 6) However, that the type of views under consideration is untenable as long as the defenders of the views regard their definition of "right" as the only legitimate one, seems to be evident, as W. D. Ross suggests, from the fact that "when a plain man says 'it is right to fufil promises' he is not necessarily thinking of the total consequences of such an act."[4] The misconception involved in the views at issue may be also indicated by mentioning the plain fact that the statement "It is right to act so as to produce the greatest possible amount of good," or "It is right to act so as to realize the moral good of a given situation," is *not* quite tautological.

Indeed moralists can and do assert that the term "right" *should* be used in the sense of "conducive to the greatest happiness," or in the sense of "conducive to moral goodness." But in this case they are not describing the actual usage of "right" in common language. It is by no means against linguistic rules to use "right" in the sense of, for instance, "in accord with the teaching of The Ten Commandments." Whenever a moralist insists that his definition of "right" is *the only* legitimate one, he is, as in the case of defining "good", choosing or persuading a cause of morals.

Nor can "ought" be adequately defined in terms of "good." In other words, "obligation" can not be properly reduced to something other than itself. If "ought" could be defined in terms of "good," "Such and such act ought to be done" must mean "Such and such act is conducive to the greatest possible amount of good," for it would be absurd to say "You ought to act to produce such and such amount of goodness though it is possible for you to act so as to bring forth more goodness." But, as a matter of fact, when a plain man says, for example, "You ought to return the same amount of money as you borrowed from him," he does not necessarily have in mind what would be the total consequences of returning the borrowed money. Again, the clear fact that to say "We ought to act so as to produce the greatest possible amount of good," or "Good ought to be realized," is not tautological seems to suggest something conclusive for our discussion.

Nor does the contrary attempt to define "good" in terms of "ought" seem to be promising. The plain fact that people do *not always* believe that *all* sorts of good ought to be performed might be enough to thwart this attempt. Many people believe that it is good to drop some money into a charity pot in the Christmas season, but they do not necessarily think they *ought* to contribute some. Again, as far as common language is concerned, it is not contradictory to say, "It would be very good if you do this, but I don't mean that you ought to do it." (In this case the utterer does not necessarily referring to the fact that the adressed might be able to do something instead which is more valuable.) But if "good" were to be defined in terms of "ought," all sort of good must imply oughtness.

The similarity between "right" and "ought" seems greater than the similarity between "good" and "right," or between "good" and "ought." In many cases "it is right to do X," and "X ought to be done," are used almost interchangeably. But the meaning of "right" is not quite the same as that of "ought." To show that "right" and "ought" (or "obligatory") are not identical in their meaning, brief mention of Ross' argument would be appropriate. Ross asserts that there are at least two points of difference between the two terms. In the first place, *not all* "right" acts are "obligatory." To be more precise, people do not necessarily regard what they judge to be right as obligatory. When "any one of two or more acts would completely satisfy the requirements of a given situation, or would satisfy them to an equal extent and to the greatest extent possible," *any* of the two or more acts are considered. to be "right," but none of them is regarded as "obligatory." What is obligatory, or what is usually considered obligatory, is "to do one or other of them."[5]

The second point of difference which Ross claims to exist between "right" and "ought" is based upon the observation that it seems ridiculous to include certain emotions among those which are obligatory because they are not in our power, while it sounds quite natural to call a certain emotion "right" provided it fits to the situation in which it is felt.[6)]

Though this second point does not seem convincing,[4] Ross' first point may be acceptable as a good argument to show that "right" and "ought" have some differences in their meaning. Even in those cases where one and the same act X is judged to be both "right" and "obligatory," to say "X is right," and to say "X ought to be done," do not mean exactly the same thing. For example, the following sentence is not repeating one and the same idea: "It is *right* for you to fulfil your promise of yesterday; you *ought to* fulfil it." Again, you may believe that it is right to require your friend to return the book which he borrowed from you last year, but might not necessarily think you *ought to* do so provided you are not in a hurry with the book.

To say that "good," "right," and "ought" have different meanings does not imply that there are no relations between them. We have already seen that the three words in question, belonging to the same

---

4 This second point is not quite convincing, because i) people *actually* say such things as "You ought to feel sorrow," or "They ought to have felt sympathy for their unfortunate friend," ii) emotions are *not* entirely uncontrollable. (If you believe that the James–Lange Theory is wholly mistaken, kneel before the crucifix in a Catholic cathedral, then say softly "Oh God!" and you will feel something you have never felt otherwise. Again, sons in Korea, when they are in the period of mourning, ought to and can cry whenever a new guest comes to mourn. In old China professional "criers" were employed in funeral ceremonies.)

genus, value–term, have several common characteristics. One of the essential characteristics they have in common was that all of them are conditioned by human attitude. Let us consider this point a little further to see how each of the three concepts and human attitude are related.

It might be admitted that the human attitude with which "good" is fundamentally related is what we usually call "desire," the most basic of human attitudes. Whatever we deem "good," unless some other factors are introduced, is an object which we desire. Nothing we do not desire at all is considered to be good. Whether we desire an object because it is good, or it is deemed good because we desire it, it is beyond doubt that all things a man believes good are desired by him after all.

All things considered "right" are also desired unless some other factors are brought in. But simple desiring of a given object does not make us judge the object to be right. When we judge an act right we naturally like the act, but bare liking of an act does not lead us to judge it right. An act must be considered *fit* in the situation concerned before it can be judged right. Fitness seems to be a necessary condition of rightness.[5] It seems that "right," in its origin, was a descriptive term to mean "straight," "direct," "upright," "fit," etc. "Fit" also might have been originally a descriptive term to be used in such expressions as "This coat does not fit me." But since every normal person prefers at any situation a fit thing to an unfit one unless some other factors are taken into consideration, some evaluative meaning must have been attached easily to the term "fit," just in the same way as "great" has become to be used as an evaluative term. Now there are many cases in which *objective* criteria for judging fitness or unfitness of an object can hardly be established. That is to say, in many cases the judge's subjective attitude is necessarily woven into the criteria by which *he* judges the fitness or unfitness of a thing. For instance, the criteria for judging whether your marriage with Nancy fits the present situation or not cannot be so objective as the criteria of judging whether a fountainpen-cap is fit for a fountainpen-holder. The fundamental point is this: In the case of a marriage the problem of fitness is inseparably connected with a number of human attitudes which often contradict each other. If your marriage with Nancy were to be *completely* fit for the present situation, it must satisfy all desires of all people connected. But to satisfy all desires of all related people is usually impossible. Thus, you might find in Nancy something different from your "ideal" bride; Nancy's mother might not want you as a son-in-law; another boy may be seriously in love with Nancy; some Catholic churches might object to the marriage; and so forth. Since, as

---

5　The idea that "right" implies "fit" of course is not new. For instance, we find in Richard Price's *Review of Morals*(1757) the following passage: "*Fitness* and *unfitness* most frequently denote the congruity and incongruity ⋯ of any means to accomplish an end. But when applied to actions, they generally signify the same with *right* and *wrong*." (Raphael's edition, p.104) And it is well-known that W. D. Ross and C. D. Broad are following the same tradition established by Clark and Price.

far as present human intellect is concerned, no objective scale by means of which you can precisely weigh the comparative significance of conflicting interests is provided, your subjective attitude must be introduced as one of the factors in accord with which the final decision as to the *fitness* of your marrying Nancy should be made. For your decision should not be postponed infinitely, and nothing but your own determination can afford the final decision. It is important here to notice that the fact that your marrying Nancy will necessarily sacrifice some interests is not the sufficient reason to judge the marriage to be "unfit." If your giving up the marriage requires a greater sacrifice, the marriage must be considered fit. "Fit" or "unfit" is a relative concept. "Fit" means nothing but "less unfit."

The plain fact that we *must* choose a course of an act at every reflective moment seems essentially related to the existence of "ought" as an ethical term. You ought either to marry or not to marry her. You ought to do this or that. Doing *nothing* is not allowed. Thus it is understood that human conduct has an aspect of inevitableness, and that "ought" accordingly implies a descriptive meaning which is synonymous with "inevitable" or "necessary." But the necessity in human acts is not quite the same with the necessity in simply physical changes. When, for instance, billiard-balls move around on their table, it is commonly held that they are behaving in accord with certain universal physical laws. Of course the balls' own nature is one of the important determinants of their behavior; but this fact does not make it sound natural to call the balls, which are conscious of nothing, "active" or "free" agents. In the case of human conduct, on the other hand, though it involves some sort of inevitableness, it is not determined wholly passively. As a conscious agent a man *actively* participates in the determination of his own actions. We need not be involved here in that partly verbal problem of "free will." At any rate, as far as his consciousness is concerned, a man has a *choice* between some possible acts. What is inevitable for him is not to act in this or that specific way, but to choose among some possible ways. If moral laws were as decisive and as objective as physical laws there would be certainly no room by virtue of which attitude can thrust itself in the court of moral decisions. Yet as far as the present human intellect is concerned, no such absolute moral laws are known. If there are no objectively given laws which are powerful enough to lead us to certain decisions, while the decisions are to be made inevitably at the spot, some subjective factors must necessarily be introduced to perform what objective factors cannot do by themselves. And theses subjective factors are nothing but the attitude of the agent himself. Thus whenever a final decision, "X ought to be done," is actually given, this decision necessarily involves as one of the determinant factors someone's attitude.

There is another aspect of the relation between "ought" and attitude. That is, whenever a man judges, "X ought to be," or "X ought to be done," X at bottom is *desired* or *liked* by the judge. For, the judge's attitude which brings forth the final decision of what ought to be done, is nothing but an act of *choosing* in its essence, and an act of choosing always involves "liking" if we may consider even "less hating" a kind of liking.

From what has been said above we notice that "good," "right," and "ought" are significantly related *in connection with their denotations*. The relations are these: i) Every thing (especially acts) which is judged "ought to be" or "ought to be done," is also judged to be "right" by the same judge; and ii) every thing (especially acts) which is judged to be "right" is also judged "good" or "less bad" by the same judge. i) is true because to choose an act as the one we ought to perform involves regarding it as the *fittest* act in the situation concerned; and ii) is evident by the fact that what is judged to be really the fittest is necessarily considered the most *desirable* among things which are possible in the given situation. In short, from the point of view of the denotation, "good" includes "right," and "right" includes "ought." Consequently one and the same thing (especially acts) can be "good" and "right" and "in accord with what ought to be" (or "duty-fulfilling"). One and the same act, for example, telling the truth in a given situation, is "good" because it is judged "desirable," is "right" because it is fit, and is "obligatory" because our moral sense judges it to be inevitable. In other words, one and the same thing, in some cases, can be "good" or "right" or "duty-fulfilling," in accordance with the point of view from which it is estimated.

5.

After studying the meaning of major ethical terms, now we are ready to tackle our methodological question, whether and how moral judgments (or utterances) can be verified or justified. To begin with this problem we must first of all clarify *what aspect* or aspects of the meaning of the statement are required to be verified or justified when verification or justification of an ethical statement is required.

When you require me to verify or justify my statement is "S is P," of course you are requiring me to verify or justify what I *mean* by the statement. However, we have taken the meaning of "meaning" in a quite broad sense. The meaning of "meaning" has been taken in a so broad sense that it does not seem to be the case that, when verification or justification of a statement is required, everything "meant" by the statement is required to be verified or justified. According to our interpretation, to say, for instance, "John is a good boy," involves the "meaning" of "I like John" or "I approve of John." But when you ask me to verify or justify my statement that John is a good boy, you are *not* ordinarily asking me to verify that I like, or approve of, John. If you really doubt that I approve of John perhaps you will not feel like asking me to justify my statement that John is a good boy, for to say "John is a good boy" without really approving of John, is nothing but cheating or joking. Thus the *constant descriptive* meaning which concerns the utterer's psychological state is irrelevant to the problem of verifying or justifying moral statements.

What about, then, the flexible descriptive meaning of ethical terms? By saying "John is a good boy," different speakers might allude to different facts as to John's character. A's saying "John is a good boy," may imply implicitly that John is *honest, generous, and benevolent.* The same utterance of B's may imply implicitly that John is *intelligent, courageous, temperate, and honest.* And C might imply still something different. Now this flexible part of the descriptive meaning of the ethical utterance does not seem to be quite irrelevant to the problem of verification, or of justification. Suppose my saying "John is a good boy" implies that "John is honest and generous." And suppose again that you prove that John is honest and generous *only apparently* and that the deepest recesses of his mind shows a quite different aspect. Then your disproof will be sufficient to overthrow my assertion. What if, however, I prove, on the contrary, that John is truly honest and generous? Is my assertion about John's goodness proved, or indisputably justified? Evidently not. You are still entitled to argue against me asking why being honest and generous makes a man "good," for from the factual judgment, "John is honest and generous," the evaluative judgment, "John is good," does not follow immediately. In short, to establish the flexible part of the descriptive meaning of an ethical statement in a necessary, but not a sufficient, condition to establish or justify the statement. That is to say, when I say, "John is a good boy," implying that he has the properties of X, Y, Z, ···, and am required to verify or justify my statement. I must, besides establishing that John really has the properties of X, Y, Z, ···, show why John's possessing X, Y, Z, ⋯, can be a sufficient *reason* for me to "commend" him. Thus it is clear that the necessary and sufficient conditions for the verifications or justification of an evaluative utterance is i) to verify the descriptive implication to which the utterance allude *concerning the object evaluated*, ii) to justify the prescriptive or "emotive" meaning of the utterance.

It seems indisputable that the descriptive aspects of an evaluative utterance can be proved, or disproved, by means of the same methods which "scientists" employ when they deal with factual problems. It is possible, in principle, to "scientifically" investigate whether John is honest, generous, intelligent, and so on; whether telling the truth in a given situation helps solving the problem involved in the situation; whether stealing generally disturbs the public peace. Hence it is clear that the most important and controversial problem in meta-ethics, "Can ethical utterances be justified?", primarily concerns the justification of the prescriptive meaning in ethical expressions.

6.

If the criteria or of goodness, or of any other value, are once laid down undeniably concerning a class of things, acceptability or unacceptability of value-judgments as to any particular individuals belonging to the class, would doubtless be determined through ordinary methods of "scientific" investigation, observation and experiment. If you are provided with fixed criteria of good motor-cars, scientific examinations of your car will be all that are necessary to judge whether your car is good or bad. If you are provided with undeniable criteria of good men, or of good life, you will certainly be able to investigate "scientifically" whether John is a good man; whether John's ways of living are good. Thus the methodological problems which are peculiar to studies of "value" are problems of establishing, or justifying, *standards* of values.

Can standards of values be established or justified? As a clue to approaching this controversial problem, it would be profitable to study how people *actually* attempt to establish or justify standards they hold. However, to support a proposed standard of ethical valuation as *the* standard is nothing but to support a proposed definition of an ethical term as *the* definition. As for methods actually employed in support of "persuasive definitions," we have already surveyed Stevenson's painstaking analysis. So it may suffice here to confine ourselves to inquiring into the logical nature of the supporting process.

Suppose we ask a utilitarian to show the reason why "the greatest happiness of the greatest number" is the highest good. And let us assume that he, answering our question, suggests the following two reasons: i) Everybody necessarily seeks for his happiness. ii) Everyone prefers a greater happiness to a smaller one. Let us suppose again that we admit his first reason to be corresponding to the fact of human psychology (interpreting satisfaction of a man's altruistic desires as an important part of *his* happiness), but disagree with the second reason on the ground that some individuals might prefer a smaller happiness *of their own* to a greater happiness *of others*. If our objection against the second reason is acceptable, clearly our utilitarian's attempt to justify his definition of "the highest good" fails to be successful so long as the utilitarian sticks to his second reason. Then the utilitarian, provided he himself admits our objection, must do one of these two things: i) He presents some other reason (or reasons) instead of the second of his initial reasons. ii) He gives up or modifies this definition of "the highest good."

Our utilitarian might argue, for instance, that everyone *should* prefer a greater happiness to a smaller one, no matter to whom the happiness in question might belong. In this case he, unless he could offer plausible reasons why we should prefer a greater happiness, is *not reasoning* but simply insisting or "persuading." He might, of course, endeavor to suggest reasons why a man *should* prefer a greater happiness of other to his own smaller happiness, if he believes he can do so without contradicting his other thesis that everybody necessarily seeks his own happiness. But let us stop our consideration of this case at this point since we may meet the same logical situation later again.

If he gives up his definition, that would be the end of the matter. But he may want to keep some of his basic position alive by partly modifying his original definition. Suppose he suggests his modified definition as this: The highest good is the greatest satisfaction of *harmoniously integrated* desires of the greatest number. And let us assume that he presents the following reasons to support his revised definition: i) Everybody necessarily seeks satisfaction of his desires. ii) Our love of logical consistency, together with the moral sense of "justice," requires us to esteem equally the same kind of desires of different individuals. iii) Everyone prefers a greater satisfaction of given desires to a smaller satisfaction of *the same* desires. To investigate whether these three propositions as such are psychologically sound or not, is not an object of our present interest, since we have already seen that disproof of any supporting reason invalidates the attempt of justification for the sake of which the reason has been given. Our concern is to consider whether the attempted justification or verification is entitled to be deemed acceptable when all of the suggested supporting reasons turn out to be the truth.

As pointed out by many writers, there is an unsurmountable gulf between factual judgments and evaluative judgments, and accordingly no evaluative conclusion logically follows from factual premises. Therefore, however many supporting reasons you may present, and however indisputable the judgments constituting the reasons, as such, may be, your attempt to support your definition of a value–concept cannot be logically complete so long as all of your supporting reasons are composed of factual judgments. Thus it seems obvious that a definition of a value–concept, or a standard of valuation, *cannot* be "verified" in principle if "to verify" means to support a judgment by means of other established judgments *of facts*. What if, however, a writer or a moralist presents a fundamental practical principle which you cannot *actually* reject. For example: Suppose the reasons given by the above–imagined utilitarian to support his revised definition of the highest good are all, as such, acceptable. And let us assume again, for convenience sake, that, as a matter of psychological fact, we cannot actually reject his revised definition, "The highest good is the greatest satisfaction of harmoniously integrated desires of the greatest number," after admitting that all of his supporting reasons, as such, are correct, though we may verbally argue against him by questioning "Why is it so?" Then it might not be strange to claim that our utilitarian has, in a sense, "justified" his definition, though we cannot properly say that he has "verified" the definition. (Reasons will be given later to show why it is not strange to use the term "justify" in this sense.)

After reaching a negative conclusion as to the question whether a definition of a moral–concept, or a standard of moral valuation, can be *verified*, we may now confine our methodological considerations to the question whether a definition of a moral concept, or a standard of moral valuation, can be *justified* — "justified" in the sense just mentioned. And, from what I have mentioned in the last paragraph, it may be clear that our considerations of the remaining methodological problem must be concentrated on this question: Is it possible to present a fundamental practical principle (or principles) which all (or most) reflective minds, as a matter of fact, cannot reject? To the extent that this question is answered affirmatively or negatively, our answer to the remaining methodological problem might turn out to be affirmative or negative. By "fundamental *practical* principle," however,

I do not refer to any simply *formal* principle or "begging the question" type of principle. A moral principle cannot be really *practical* unless it is concrete enough to give unmistakable prescriptions. For example: "We ought to choose as our common ideal such an end–in–view as the human reflective mind recognizes to be most suitable for human efforts," can be fully practical only when it is made clear *what* "the human reflective mind" recognizes to be most suitable for human efforts. Or, "Act in accordance with the conscience's commands," cannot be adequate unless it is precisely shown *what* "the conscience's commands" are. And it is commonplace that a simply "formal" principle, such as Kant's first "categorical imperative," cannot be practical enough.

7.

To live necessarily involves to desire, and to desire inevitably causes actions. The plain fact that desires conflict with each other, both within a person and between persons, obliges men to choose between desires and, accordingly, between actions. The categorical condition that a man must choose, naturally raises the question, "*What* is to be chosen?" But, as Dewey said following James, a man is not allowed to choose between doing something and doing nothing. He is obliged to *do something* as long as he is alive. The fact that man must incessantly do something passing through the process of choosing, and the fact that he is gifted with "intellect," which necessitates him to ask "What is to be chosen?", make it inevitable that every normal person seeks after "what is wiser" or "what is better." The human beings have become "valuative animals." That human beings are valuative animals implies not only that they prefer somethings to others, but also that they have principles of choice. (Even a dog prefers a bone to a piece of wood.) Everybody finds his instincts and caprice are not enough to guide him satisfactorily in human situations which force him to choose. As a so-called "rational being," as an animal with strong memory and extraordinary foresight, a man does not want his choices to be principleless. Almost every mature mind thinks, at times at least, of his career as a whole, and consequently he entertains some kind of "ideal," though he may not be clearly conscious of it, or the ideal might not be quite distinct in its outlines. To entertain an ideal implies having a practical principle; and the more definite a man's ideal is, the more definite his principle or principles become. There is another factor which forces a man to have some practical principles, namely, the fact that he must choose a course of acts *without taking too much time*. If a man, whose instincts or innate tendencies are not efficient enough to guide him well, had no principles of conduct, his nerves would have to be exhausted in mid course of hesitations, and he would not be able to adjust himself to his everchanging environment.

From what has been said in the last paragraph, it seems undeniable that every mature mind necessarily has some kind of practical principles. Indeed, someone might not be fully conscious of the principle upon which he is acting; his principles might be nothing but products of his habits or routine; and he might not be quite consistent in the principles to which he commits himself on different occasions. But at any rate we may safely assert that every normal adult must and does act on some kind of practical principles, if we are allowed to employ the term "principle" in a broad sense.

Now the question with which we are at present concerned is whether it is possible to offer a fundamental practical principle (or principles) which all (or most) reflective minds cannot, as a matter of fact, reject. And we have just seen that every normal adult is obliged to have *some* practical principle (or principles). In other words, we have choice among principles, but we have no liberty to choose between "having" and "not having" principles. We have no choice but to have *some* principle (or principles). Some one might pretend that he does not admit any kind of principle of conduct, and sometimes we actually hear this kind of pretention from a "tea-room existentialist." But his intentional rejection of all sorts of principles itself is nothing but an act of choosing a principle; he is choosing the maxim, "Live without any principles." If it is clear that everybody with a mature reflective mind (and I believe everyone who discusses moral problems at all can be said to be provided with a mature reflective mind) is obliged to have some principle of conduct, the answer to our present question must hinge on whether there are any *common factors* which condition the determination of men's choice of practical principles, namely, whether there is any *generally* working force by which all or most human minds are necessarily controlled when they *reflectively*[6] choose between suggested practical principles. If everybody's *peculiar* traits are the principal source by which his principles are determined, it would be almost impossible for a moralist to suggest any principle which has a strong appeal to all or most reflective minds. But if, on the contrary, some *common* nature which is universal in, or generally shared by, all normal people is the principal cause by which the basic attitudes of all normal people are determined, a moralist might have a chance to conceive of a principle which has so strong an appeal to everybody's heart that no one can reject it reflectively.

I can think of no other clue to the solution of the problem whether the principal determinants of a man's basic attitude toward human life are located in the man's peculiar individual traits or rather in what is commonly called "human nature" which supposedly everybody shares with other fellows, than the psychological–sociological facts of moral phenomena. If we could study exhaustively all types of moral convictions, and if we could tell precisely what are the causes of them, then we would reach a perfect solution of our problem. But, unfortunately, I haven't heard of any such excellent studies of human beings. I do not have in my hand even such data as perhaps can be obtained from achievements of psychologists, sociologists and other

---

6   We may legitimately confine ourselves only to cases of *reflective* choice, because the moral problem "What ought we to choose?" itself is a reflective question to be answered reflectively. Moral problems are problems of reflective acts, and the ethical discussion is primarily conversation between reflective minds.

students. Accordingly what I can attempt here is only some rough and tentative intimations.

It is understood that what a man aspires to or the ideal a man entertains is conditioned by both his personality and his environment; and it is admitted that a man's personality is determined by his hereditary elements and his environmental conditions. What we can safely tell from these admitted facts is this, namely: Ideals or aspirations entertained *in the concrete* by different persons cannot be either completely homogeneous or entirely heterogeneous. For few writers would doubt i) that every two men's environments contain both homogeneous and heterogeneous aspects, ii) that any two men's hereditary elements involve both homogeneous and heterogeneous (except for identical twins) factors. However, the individual differences in concretely pictured ideals or aspirations should not be identified hastily with differences in *moral* convictions. When two men, each taking into consideration his peculiar environmental conditions and individual personality, formulate different ideals of life, they are not necessarily committing themselves to different *moral* principles. Moral differences occur only when two men (or two groups of men) pass different evaluative judgments on *the same* situation or problem. To say, "Ancient kings' keeping mistresses was permissible, but to-day's presidents should not have any concubine," is not necessarily self-contradictory. In short, a moral difference occurs when differences in attitude are based not on the *consideration* of the environmental and personal differences, but on the environmental and personal differences themselves.

Even in the above-mentioned strict sense, the existence of diversity in morals cannot be denied. Hence our question is not to ask, as defenders and opponents of "absolute conscience" theories did, whether there are differences in moral convictions, but to ask whether moral disagreements can be, *in principle*, removed *by reasoning or by persuasion*. The answer to this question must hinge on whether, or to what extent, the elements in which moral disagreements are rooted can be removed.

As the by far most important cause of moral disagreements we may reckon, with Stevenson, disagreements in factual belief. Is it, then, possible, in principle, to remove all sorts of disagreement in belief? Stevenson seems to assume tacitly that it is possible. Yet, as far as known facts are concerned, nothing ensures that *all* reflective minds will reach sooner or later complete agreements on *all* matters of facts. Nevertheless, judging from what human understanding has achieved in the course of human history, we seem to have reasons to expect that human minds will approach step by step to the ideal of sharing "the common knowledge." Consequently we may also hope that disagreements in morals can be lessened, at least to some extent.

Here we have to meet Stevenson's great puzzle: Are *all* disagreements in attitude rooted in disagreements in belief? To answer this question in the affirmative implies asserting that all individual differences in other elements of personality than intellectual elements, and all environmental differences are essentially irrelevant to moral disagreements. I am not provided with any conclusive psychological data to disprove this assertion. But we may think of some simple facts which will make the assertion at issue look rather implausible. For instance, the notorious disagreements in sexual morals do not seem to be rooted exclusivily in disagreement in factual belief. I do not believe that you can *always* be successful in persuading conservative fathers to agree to your proposal to enroll their daughters in your Experimental Marriage Club, if you can make them completely agree with your "enlightened" beliefs on sexual *facts*. Nor do environmental and cultural differences seem quite irrelevant to moral differences. For instance: Morality and custom, one of the chief factors which constitute the social environment of human beings, are intimately related as writers such as W. G. Sumner or John Dewey have made clear, while it is plain that two countries which are not remarkably different in their scientific levels, often observe some quite different customs. Again, it is commonplace that different political–economical situations are apt to bring forth different moral convictions. I can hardly believe that all moral differences between, for example, Americans and Russians have come from their different "sciences." We cannot reduce all sorts of differences in ideology just to differences in factual belief.

It may be possible to approach, to some extent at least, a unified system of moral convictions by means of modifying people's personalities, their environments, and their cultural patterns. But this is a quite different point; what we are asking is whether and to what extent disagreements in moral opinions can be removed *directly* by reasoning or by persuasion.

However, the diversity of morals should not be emphasized excessively. If different elements between persons, between environments, and between cultures (strictly speaking, cultural differences melt into personal and environmental differences) necessarily modify people's moral ideas, identical factors shared in common by human creatures also must condition the formation of moral convictions.

A traveller in foreign countries, provided he is a good observer, will be deeply impressed more often by similarities of human minds than by their differences. Under the surface of apparent differences in modes of life he will find something more basic which is shared in common by the "family of man." Accounts of travels, perhaps conditioned more or less by readers' curiosity as well as by the writers' own, seldom tell the whole story.

Almost everyone believes love is better than hatred, peace is better than war, wealth is better than poverty, and so on. Few believe it good, from the bottom of their hearts, to neglect every other person's interests for egoistic purposes. Few sincerely condemn "benevolence," "generosity," "justice," "gratitude," "veracity," "knowledge," "freedom," "satisfaction," and so forth, at least when these are considered without reference to any other things. Almost all populations would judge at bottom that if there is a way to make the whole world happy the way ought to be chosen.

There are so many examples of commonly held moral convictions that it seems almost impossible to enumerate them exhaustively. Yet this does not necessarily justify the ethical realism, or the absolute objectivism in ethics. For we may explain this fact as well from other sources, namely, from those biological, psychological, and sociological factors which most people share in common. As a matter of psychological fact, different aspects among individuals, or among societies, invite our attention much more easily than universal elements of human beings or common conditions of human societies. Nevertheless that the universal elements and the common conditions are incomparably overwhelming will become clear even to high school girls, if they think of the whole biological world and compare "men" with another kind of "higher" living things, for example, with "frogs." And it seems to me that these overwhelming universal elements and common conditions are sufficient to be the source of the common convictions in morals.

Can we say, then, that such statements as "Generosity as such is good," "Justice as such is good," and so on, are justified, if it is shown that no one (of few) can *actually* reject them? In a sense, in a sense of "justified" which is not much different from that of the German word "gelten," I should answer this question, "Yes!" But the fact that these statements are justified or justifiable in the sense just mentioned, is not of much practical value. In other words, to recognize that, e. g., "justice," "benevolence," "freedom," and "happiness," as such, are good, is not very helpful for the solution of disagreements in *actual* moral problems. This is so because: i) disagreements in actual moral problems seldom concern whether justice, freedom etc. are, as such, good or not, but they occur when a situation forces people to choose between freedom and life, between veracity and physical pleasure, and so forth; ii) "justice," "freedom" etc. are not free from ambiguity, and controversies take place concerning "the real freedom," "the real happiness" etc. Thus if an ethical study is to be profitable for the solution of practical problems, it must be provided with some principle by which the *comparative* weight of conflicting values can be scaled. In other words, what I called before "the fundamental practical principle (or principles)" is needed. But, to my knowledge, no one has offered any universally accepted measure which directly shows the comparative importance of diverse values, in such a way as "Justice is prior to generosity, and happeness is prior to justice, and…." I suspect it might in principle be impossible to present any such measure which all reflective minds would inevitably accept, unless the present differences in personalities and in environments were perfectly removed.

One way of presenting a fundamental practical principle which, if accepted, can serve as a principle for choice between conflicting values, is to suggest "the final aim" or "the highest good" for the realization of which the whole human race ought to endeavor. Once such a teleological principle were laid down clearly and concretely, all moral problems would become problems of *means* for the final end, and consequently could be dealt with "scientifically." But the difficulties involved in this attempt have been already pointed out by Dewey and others. Perhaps it might be possible to suggest, *in a quite abstract way*, a universal ideal of the human race which most people, or rather most reflective minds, will accept in practice. For example, such a dictum as "The final aim of the human race is the greatest satisfaction of harmoniously intergrated desires of the greatest number," or "The highest good is the greatest *eudaimonia* of the greatest number," might be accepted actually by most people, provided everbody is allowed to interpret "harmoniously integrated" or "eudaimonia" as he likes. But obviously even after such an agreement difficult problems will still remain, for the agreement, partly at least, is verbal. One of the most important results entailed by this kind of agreement will be to remove the focus of issue to a new value term, "harmonious integration," or "eudaimonia."

Another way of giving a fundamental practical principle required is to suggest a "supreme imperative" which, if accepted, might serve as the major premise for all prescriptions of human acts. But I doubt that any supreme imperative which is so "reasonable" that most people cannot help accepting it can be so concrete and clear as to make everybody understand precisely what it is commanding. It is conceivable that, for example, the following maxim could be accepted, as a matter of fact, by most reflective minds: Act so as to conform yourself to what your deepest heart commands you. Yet this maxim, though it is by no means of no significance, does not tell precisely what to do in a given situation, for the trouble in a moral indecision is frequenly the fact that the very "deepest heart" itself is hesitating on the horns of a dilemma. Again, let us consider another form of maxim: Act in such a way that every reflective mind approve of your conduct. This dictum as such might not be objectionable. But it tells you very little unless you are informed of what people's "reflective minds" would approve of with one voice. Furthermore, we have seen that there are individual differences in personality as well as cultural differences which might prevent "reflective minds" from reaching unanimous agreements on moral problems. As another example of probably unobjectionable principles we may refer to Kant's fundamental imperative: Act on a maxim which thou canst will to be law universal. This imperative as such can be hardly refused, because ethical discussions, since they are "conversation between reflective minds," presuppose *logical consistency*. But Kant's "formal" principle tells little *in the concrete* about what we should do, for, before anything, *both* of a pair of contradictory maxims, e. g., "Everyone should pay back money which was lent to him on promise of repayment," and "Everybody need not pay back money which was lent to him on the promise of repayment," can satisfy Kant's principle as far as we consider the principle from the purely formal point of view, though Kant himself believes otherwise.[7] Moreover, two groups of people might actually will

---

7 As one of the good criticisms of Kant's position at issue we might regard C. D. Broad's in his *Five Types of Ethical Theory*. (Cf. London, 1930, pp.129–131)

respectively each of two contradictory maxims "to be law universal;" for example: "Boys and girls should preserve their chastity until they marry," and "Boys and girls need not preserve their chastity until they marry;" or "Birth should be controlled," and "Birth should not be controlled," etc.

To sum up: Everybody is obliged to hold some kind of practical principles, and what kind of principles a man actually holds, seems to be determined both by his nature and his environmental conditions. Since a man's personality and his environment involve both unique and common aspects, the practical principles he holds also possess two aspects, the aspect which is peculiar to him and the aspect he shares in common with his fellow creatures.

There are things which, as such, almost everyone believes to be good, for example, life, health, pleasure, knowledge, friendship, benevolence, generosity, and so forth. Consequently, such judgments as "Health is good," "Knowledge is good," "Benevolence is good," etc. are justified by the plain fact that they are *actually* accepted at bottom by almost everybody. The existence of those "commonly recognized goods" constitutes an important part of the foundation which makes morals a common property of the human race.

Another part of the foundation for common morality is laid by the human intellect which inevitably seeks after logical consistency. Like all other investigations the ethical investigation also presupposes the respect for logical consistency. Without this presupposition no moral discussion would be possible. Accordingly all sorts of moral thoughts that involve logical inconsistency, are to be rejected for that very reason.

On the basis of the requirement of logical consistency we might formulate, as Kant admirably did, some basic, but formal, principle of conduct which may claim properly general acceptance. Again, by combining the requirement of logical consistency and certain universal psychological principles, we might reasonably arrive at some *less formal* principles of morality that are generally acceptable. Thus, on the ground of the facts i) that everyone's every desire requires to be satisfied, and ii) that we have no logical reason why one desire should be entirely sacrificed for the sake of another, one might reach a practical principle which is more or less similar to Perry's principle of the "inclusive harmonious integration of interests." Or again, on the bais of the facts i) that everybody seeks for the realization of some end-in-view, and ii) that it is, in a sense, self-contradictory not to act so as most aptly to realize one's reflectively chosen end-in-view, you might suggest the following as a generally binding principle: Act so as to make your conduct fit your end-in-view.[8]

The above-mentioned elements which constitute the foundation for common morality, elements originated from commonly held evaluative

---

[8] I am not attempting here to lay down any "moral principles" in my own person. I am simply indicating some kind of possibility. Perhaps better examples might be given by professional moralists.

attitudes of simple nature, or what we might call "the common moral sense," and elements connected with the requirement of logical consistency, though they provide morality with some general rules, are by no means sufficient as the conditions to establish a complete system of universal morals. As the main conditions which prevent us from having a complete system of universal morals, I have mentioned these two: i) There is no commonly accepted scale for comparison of values. ii) General principles which can be obtained on the ground of the general human nature and the requirement of logical consistency, do not precisely tell what to do when we are in a dilemma. And it seems clear that these unfavorable conditions against universal morals are rooted in the different factors which exist both between personalities and between environments.

Since "the common moral sense" and the requirement of logical consistency do not provide a man with a concrete moral code of practical use, he must give himself what is not given otherwise. In other words, he must choose, or commit himself to, a cause of life. Naturally he should not choose capriciously, if he wants his choice to be "justified" in the sense mentioned before. To begin with, he must conform his choice to the general tendency of "human nature," or to "the common moral sense." And second, his chosen cause of life must be free from any self–contradiction. But these two things are only necessary conditions. Besides them, it seems, there are some other conditions to be fulfilled by a "justifiable" moral choice.

In the first place, a justifiable moral choice must entail *practicable* moral prescriptions. If the primary purpose of choosing moral principles is to guide human life in practice, there is no point in choosing an unrealizable aim, or to command an act which is beyond human power, however desirable the aim or the act as such might look in appearance. Of course this is no more than to say that the choice of an end should not be isolated from the consideration of means.

In the second place, a justifiable moral choice must meet the requirements of the times and places in which it is to be justified. Between universal (or semi-universal) human nature and individual peculiarity there are certain tendencies which are commonly called "the spirit of the times" or "the national traits." Moral principles which are inconsonant with these tendencies, can not be accepted, and accordingly are "unjustifiable," as far as the particular places and times are concerned. For instance, "Everybody should try to live the most easy-going life possible," is not a maxim which goes against any *universal* human nature, nor does it involve any logical contradiction, nor is it unpracticable. But this principle cannot be justified in some societies, e. g., in twentieth century Korea. Of course a moralist who is not accepted in his own days and in his own country might be approved of in future or in other countries. This fact implies that the criticism or evaluation by an age, or by a nation, is itself a new object for criticism or evaluation. Thus it seems clear that my assertion does *not* imply that the acceptability of a moral principle is decided by the simple principle of "majority vote." What I do mean is this: Propriety of a moral principle is affected by *facts of history*.

8.

Value–judgments, as nonvalue–judgments, are based on some assumptions. The fundamental assumptions on which all sorts of moral judgments are grounded are themselves a kind of moral judgments. They do not primarily intend to convey any information. They express the basic attitude of those who embrace them. Some of the fundamental moral assumptions are rooted wholly, or rathar mostly, in what is called "the general human nature," while some others are rooted partly in characteristics peculiar to the individuals, the times, or the societies that advocate them. Since they do not primarily intend to convey some information they cannot be supported by means of showing some empirical facts which *correspond* to what they announce or predict. They can be "justified" only by the fact that they possess, *in practice*, irresistible appeal to human hearts. These are the "peculiar nature" of the ethical assumption I mentioned at the beginning of this thesis. And it seems plain that the justification of those judgments which are founded on an ethical assumption must be accordingly conditioned by the peculiar nature of the assumption.

Some might be inclined to object to the present view by arguing that the view at bottom denies the *true* difference between "justifiable" and "unjustifiable" moral judgments. They may assert that the bare fact of being generally accepted does not make a moral judgment justifiable, that the term "justifiable" or "justify" cannot be used properly in my sense.

To meet this objection I should like to point out a sort of analogy between morals and language, between moral laws and grammar.[9]

Ordinary adults believe in the distinction between the "correct" and "incorrect" uses of language; for them this distinction is a "real" one. There are "good" pronunciation, the "correct" word-order, "wrong" spelling, etc. You meet foreigners who write "good" English, and recall some of your friends whose style is "terrible." But what ground do we have to make these distinctions at all? Why is it unacceptable to say, "I *is* going to buy a good*er pant* than the one I buy*ed* two months *before*?" Why should we not apply the grammar of the Korean, or of the Japanese, word-order to English and say, "She 1917 in Clifford Chatterley a month for leave on home (at) was when, he (with) married," instead of saying, "She married Clifford Chatterley in 1917, when he was home for a month on leave?"

I myself do not doubt that some ways of using words are acceptable while others are unacceptable, but I cannot think of any other grounds for making this distinction than the historical fact that some ways are accepted *in practice* while others are rejected. But this does not make

---

9   Morals and language, it seems, have several similar aspects. But I am not going to study all of these aspects here. I shall confine myself to the aspect which is seen from the point of view of "justifiability." Dewey, from whom I have got the hint for the present comparison, has explicated another aspect of analogy between morality and language, namely, from the point of view of their origins and vicissitudes. (Cf. Dewey's *Human Nature and Conduct*, Modern Library Press, pp.79-80)

it ridiculous to approve of some expressions as "good," "correct," "acceptable," "justifiable," etc, while condemning others as "bad." "incorrect," "unacceptable," "unjustifiable," etc. And the same with morals.

Both in morals and in language, established practice is seldom perfect, and, in both fields, change of conditions which influence the establishment of practice frequently requires a new type of practice. Hence new morals and new language for new ages. Here again we find a kind of analogy between the two fields in connection with the transition from the old to the new. In both fields the *public agreement*, whether conscious or unconscious, is a necessary condition for rendering a new practice "right" or "legitimate." Usually, in both fields, some influential individuals play the leading part in the introduction of new practice, and typical relationship between the leading individuals and the public in the case of one of these two fields is remarkably similar to the corresponding relationship found in the case of the other field. In other words, we find notable analogies between the part played by great writers in the formation of new expressions and the part played by great moralists in social reformations.

That rules of language are not entirely subjective is proved by the fact that you cannot coin a word capriciously. Indeed you may employ your own peculiar expressions to talk only with yourself, but the expressions will never become "language" in any proper sense, unless others follow your practice. "Language" is, in nature, a *public* phenomenon. Likewise, that morals are not wholly subjective becomes clear through the fact that you cannot make any new moral law at your pleasure. You might make perhaps a set of strange regulations for your own practice, but the regulations will never become "moral" unless others come on your heels. "Morality" is in its essence, concerns of *people*, but not of a single man.[10]

Here we see, however, that the force of *social compulsion* works even more strongly in the case of morals than in that of language. People ordinarily are rather generous when you use "wrong" words. This is especially remarkable when you employ a foreign language. But when you behave "wrongly" in a moral situation, people will not be so generous even if you happen to be a foreigner in the place concerned. Your attempt to coin new words, when it does not please the people around you, may not cause anything beyond their ignoring your new words. But your ambition to be a reformer is likely to cause more serious enmity around you. Even apart from objections of an egoistic nature, to found a new standard of morals would be generally difficult. This means that there are many conditions which a "justifiable" moral principle must satisfy. And these conditions, whether they are rooted

---

10 The Korean word "yoon-lee," which is equivalent to "morality," originally meant "the grain (or reason or logic or rules) *between* men." Another word for "morals" is "dou-teok." "Dou" means "way" or "path," which, at first, came to existence perhaps naturally through repeated passage of many people; a man's footprints cannot open a way. While "teok" means "what is *gained* (in personality through practice or habits)" or "virtue."

in the general "human nature" or in the particular requirements of the time and place concerned, are something which can be called in a sense "objective."

The "objective" requirements which every kind of morals must satisfy are not the same in all ages and all countries. Thus it is quite natural that different moral codes are accepted in different societies, as is the case with language. As we cannot say that any particular language is *the only* right language, we cannot call morals of any particular society "the only right morals." If two societies are completely separated from each other, the "justifiable" morals might be remarkably different in these two societies, though all morals must satisfy the common conditions rooted in the common human nature. But the historical fact that all people on the earth are more or less related with each other raises the problem of "common morals."

The restriction of the "objective" conditions which every "justifiable" moral judgment must satisfy, is not always so tight as to allow *only one* "right" action in each case. Consequently it is possible that two or more to some extent different moral judgments are all justifiable, just as two or more different expressions can sometimes be all correct. For example: when you happen to get some unexpected money, you might have more than one "right" ways of spending it. Or, when you are invited to a party, your situation might be such that either accepting or refusing the invitation is quite all right. Again, perhaps you ought to have *some* vocation, but you might have *no duty* to choose a *particular* one.

From what has been said so far we may conclude that morality is a "creative process." I have said that a justifiable moral principle or moral judgment must conform itself to certain "objective" conditions. But these conditions, though they can be called "objective" in a sense, are not absolutely fixed; nor are they given altogether from outside. The so-called human nature has not been finally cast once and for all. It is in the process of development. And what is more important is that moral agents themselves play an active part in the making process of human nature. Men's environments of course change more remarkably. And here also moral agents are by no means simply passive; they are the most vital factors among the causes of changes in human environments. In short, moral judgments must accord with some conditions, but these conditions are given partly by those who pass the judgments.

If i) the conditions to which moral judgments must conform themselves are given partly by moral agents themselves, while ii) the restriction of the conditions is not always strict and tight, and individuals have chances to choose between some range of "justifiable" actions, it might be affirmed safely that to be "morally good" does not exactly mean to be "merely obedient" to certain given laws or rules. Moral agents are lawgivers as well. They are "free" in this sense. But since they give laws to themselves they are doubly responsible for the self-given laws.

To recognize moral agents as lawgivers is to grant them the prerogative of the "creator." A creator may make what he likes. But his creations must be publicly approved of, if they are to be justifiable. If his creations are to be publicly approved of, he must either conform to the public conditions or make, through his own influence, the public conditions conform to his own standard. If you are a really great moralist, the public will follow you some day; if not, perhaps you will be obliged to follow the public sooner or later unless you are to be satisfied with bare self-righteousness.

I am inclined to liken a system of moral thoughts to a work of art, a moralist to an artist. Or rather, I am tempted to deem a good life itself good works of *art*.

NOTES

Chapter Ⅰ. The Problems

1) J. S. Mill, *Utilitarianism*, The Liberal Arts Press, 1957, p.44.
2) R. B. Perry, *General Theory of Value*(Hereafter to be referred to as *G. Theory*), Harvard Press, 1965, p.17.

Chapter Ⅱ. Perry: Value and Interest

1) *G. Theory*, pp.136–137.
2) R. B. Perry, "The Definition of Value," *Journal of Philosophy, Psychology, and the Scientific Method*, Vol. 11(1914), p.143.
3) Ibid. p.143.
4) Ibid., p.144. and *G. Theory*, p.35.
5) *G. Theory*, pp.36–37.
6) R. B. Perry, *Realms of Value* (Hereafter to be referred to as *Realms*), Harvard Press, 1954, pp.1–2.
7) Ibid., p.2.
8) *G. Theory*, pp.17–18.
9) *Realms*, p.2.
10) *G. Theory*, p.27ff, 52ff, 81ff, 115ff.
11) Ibid, pp.28–45, and *Realms*, pp.145–148.
12) *G. Theory*, p.30.
13) Ibid., p.30.
14) Ibid., p.31.
15) *Realms*, pp.146–147, p.129, and see also *G. Theory*, pp.44–48.
16) Perry, "The Definition of Value," pp.145–146, see also *G. Theory*, p.40ff.
17) *G. Theory*, p.53ff.
18) Ibid., p.56.
19) Ibid., pp.69–70.

20) *G. Theory*, p.71.

21) Ibid., pp.71–77.

22) Ibid., pp.77–80.

23) Ibid., pp.81–82.

24) Perry, "The Definition of Value," pp.157–158, and *G. Theory*, pp.82–108.

25) Perry, "The Definition of Value," p.158; Italic is mine.

26) Ibid., p.157.

27) Ibid., p.159.

28) *G. Theory*, p.124. See also his *The Moral Economy*, New York, 1909, p.11, his *Realms*, pp.2–3, and "The Definition of Value," p.153.

29) *G. Theory*, p.116

30) *Realms*, p.3.

31) *G. Theory*, p.115.

32) *Realms*, p.6.

33) Ibid., p.7.

34) Ibid., p.2.

35) Ibid., p.3.

36) Ibid., pp.3–7.

37) Ibid., pp.13.

38) *G. Theory*, p.125.

39) *Realms*, pp.8–9.

40) Ibid., p.9.

41) Ibid., p.11.

42) Ibid., pp.11–12.

43) Ibid., p.13.

44) *G. Theory*, p.137.

45) Ibid., p.611.

46) Ibid., p.183.

47) Ibid., p.183.

48) *Realms*, p.41; *G. Theory*, p.182, also p.176ff.

49) *G. Theory*, p.349.

50) Ibid., p.612.

51) Ibid., p.362.

52) Ibid., p.613.

53) Ibid., pp.612–614.

54) Ibid., p.630.

55) *Realms*, p.53.

56) Ibid., p.60.

57) *G. Theory*, p.616.

58) Ibid., p.657.

59) Ibid., p.644, p.653, and p.657.

60) Ibid., p.658.

61) Perry, *The Moral Economy*, p.10.

62) Ibid., p.13.

63) Perry, "The Conception of Moral Goodness", *Philosophical Review*, Vol. 16(1907), p.153.

64) *Realms*, p.88.

65) Ibid., pp.89–90.

66) Ibid., p.9.

67) Ibid., p.92.

68) Ibid., p.93.

69) Ibid., p.94.

70) Ibid., pp.94–95.

71) Ibid., p.100.

72) Ibid., p.101. A similer definition apperars also in *The Moral Economy*, pp.15–16.

73) *Realms*, p.104.

74) Ibid., p.106.

75) *G. Theory*, pp.686–687.

76) *Realms*, p.106.

77) Ibid., p.107.

78) Ibid., pp.107–108.

79) Ibid., p.69.

80) Ibid., p.109.

81) Perry, "The Question of Moral Obligation", *International Journal of Ethics*, Vol. 21(1911), p.288.

82) Ibid., p.293.

83) *Realms*, p.110.

84) Perry, "The Question of Moral Obligation," p.288.

85) Ibid., p.294ff. and *Realms*, p.110.

86) *Realms*, p.87.

87) Ibid., p.122.

88) Ibid., p.123.

89) Ibid., p.132.

90) Ibid., p.132.

91) Ibid., pp.134-135.

92) Ibid., p.133.

93) Ibid., pp.135-136.

94) Ibid., p.136.

95) G. E. Moore, *Ethics*, Oxford Press, 1955(Reprinted), pp.100-102.

96) Thomas E. Hill, *Contemporary Ethical Theories*, New York, 1957, p.240.

97) C. L. Stevenson, *Ethics and Language*, New Haven, 1953, p.271.

98) *G. Theory*, pp.657-658.

99) *Realms*, pp.132-136. See also Ch. II, Sec. 7 of the present thesis.

Chapter III. Dewey: Value and Problematic Situation

1) Morton White, *The Age of Analysis*, The Mentor Press, 1955, p.176.

2) J. Dewey, "Values, Liking, and Thought," *Journal of Philosophy*, Vol. 20(1923), p.620. (Italic is mine.)

3) J. Dewey, "The Logic of Judgments of Practice," *Journal of Philosophy*, Vol. 12(1915), p.512.

4) J. Dewey, *The Quest for Certainty*, London, Unwin Brothers Press, 1930, p.213.

5) George R. Geiger, *John Dewey in Perspective*, New York, 1958, p.46. Cf. also J. Dewey, *Theory of Valuation*, p.4ff.

6) D. W. Prall, "Value and Thought-Process," *Journal of Philosophy*, Vol. 21(1924), p.122.

7) D. W. Prall, "In Defense of a *Worthless* Theory of Value," *Journal of Philosophy*, Vol. 20, pp.131-132.

8) J. Dewey, "*Values, Liking, and Thought,*" pp.617-618. See also, "The Meaning of Value," *Journal of Philosophy*, Vol. 22, p.120.

9) J. Dewey, "*Values, Liking, and Thought,*" p.618.

10) J. Dewey, *The Quest for Certainty*, p.246.

11) Ibid, pp.247–248.

12) J. Dewey, "*The Logic of Judgments of Practice,*" p.520.

13) J. Dewey, "*Values, Liking, and Thought,*" p.622.

14) J. Dewey, *Experience and Nature*, Dover Press, 1958, p.401.

15) Dewey & Tufts, *Ethics*, Revised Edition, New York. 1932, p.202.

16) *The Quest for Certainty*, p.251.

17) Ibid., pp.271–272.

18) J. Dewey, "*The Logic of Judgments of Practice,*" p.520. See also Dewey's *Theory of Valuation*, p.5.

19) J. Dewey, *Theory of Valuation*, The University of Chicago Press, 1939, p.11.

20) Ibid., p.13.

21) J. Dewey, *Reconstruction in Philosophy*, New York, 1937, p.173.

22) Adams & Montague, eds., *Contemporary American Philosophy*, New York, 1930, p.23(Quoted by Feldman in *The Philosophy of John Dewey*, p.91).

23) J. Dewey. "Logical Conditions of a Scientific Treatment Of Morality"(1903), Reprinted in the *Problems of Men*, New York, 1946, p.215.

24) Ibid., p.217.

25) Ibid., p.225.

26) Ibid., p.216.

27) *Theory of Valuation*, p.19.

28) J. Dewey, "*The Logic of Judgments of Practice,*" p.505.

29) Ibid., p.506.

30) Ibid., p.506.

31) Ibid., pp.509–510.

32) Ibid., p.510.

33) *Theory of Valuation*, p.22.

34) J. Dewey, "*The Logic of Judgments of Practice,*" p.514.

35) *Theory of Valuation*, p.23.

36) J. Dewey, *Human Nature and Conduct*, Modern Library Press, 1922, p.224.

37) Ibid., p.225.

38) Ibid., p.234. Cf. also Dewey's *Theory of Valuation*, p.35.

39) *Theory of Valuation*, p.26.

40) Ibid., p.49.

41) *The Quest for Certainty*, p. 266., Cf. also *Theory of Valuation*, p.27, p.29.

42) *Theory of Valuation*, p.27.

43) Ibid., p.25.

44) Ibid., pp.27-28.

45) Ibid., p.33.

46) *Human Nature and Conduct*, p.225.

47) Ibid., p.227.

48) *Theory of Valuation*, p.49.

49) Ibid., p.53.

50) Ibid., p.58.

51) J. Dewey, *"The Logic of Judgments of Practice,"* p.519.

52) Dewey & Tufts, *Ethics*, p.343.

53) *Human Nature and Conduct*, p.283.

54) *Theory of Valuation*, p.42.

55) G. R. Geiger, *John Dewey in Perspective*, p.48.

56) *Problems of Men*, p.212

57) Ibid., p.218.

58) *Human Nature and Conduct*, p.211.

59) *Reconstruction in Philosophy*, pp.169-170.

60) Cf. *Human Nature and Conduct*, Pt. 1. Sec. V

61) Dewey & Tufts, *Ethics*, p.237.

62) From Dewey's article "Anthropology and Ethics" included in *The Social Sciences and their Interrelations*(ed. by Ogburn and Goldenweiser), Boston, 1927, p.34.

63) *Theory of Valuation*, p.59.

64) Ibid., p.60.

65) Ibid., pp.60-61.

66) Ibid., p.62.

67) J. Dewey, *Democracy and Education*, New York, 1916, p.206. Cf. also Kingsley Price's article, "Some Doctrines of John Dewey," in the *1957 Year Book of Education*, Cross Currents, 1957.

68) Jean-Paul Sartre, *Existentialism and Humanism*(Translation by P. Mairet), London, 1948, pp.35-36.

69) C. L. Stevenson, *Ethics and Language*, New Haven, 1944, pp.256–264.

70) Cf. Ibid., p.259.

71) Ray Lepley, ed., *Value*, New York, 1949, p.260.

72) Cf. *Theory of Valuation*, p.52.

Chapter IV. Stevenson: Value and Attitude

1) C. L. Stevenson, "The Emotive Meaning of Ethical Terms," reprinted in the *Reading in Ethical Theory*(Edited by Sellars and Hospers), New York, 1952, p.415.

2) Ibid., p.419.

3) Ibid., pp.416–417.

4) Ibid., pp.417–418.

5) C. L. Stevenson, *Ethics and Language*, New Haven, 1944, p.42.

6) *Readings in Ethical Theory*, p.422.

7) *Ethics and Language*, p.46ff.

8) Ibid., pp.54–55.

9) Ibid., p.57.

10) Ibid., p.59.

11) Cf. Ibid., p.60.

12) Ibid., pp.62–63.

13) Ibid., p.66.

14) Ibid., p.65.

15) Ibid., p.70.

16) Ibid., p.76.

17) Ibid., pp.72–73.

18) C. L. Stevenson, "Meaning: Descriptive and Emotive," *Philosophical Review*, Vol. 57(1948), p.142.

19) *Ethics and Language*, p.3.

20) Ibid., p.4.

21) Ibid., p.7.

22) Ibid., p.36.

23) Ibid., p.82.

24) Ibid., p.21.

25) Ibid., p.21. Cf. also *Readings in Ethical Theory*, p.425.

26) *Ethics and Language*, p.23.

27) Cf. Ibid., pp.32–36, and pp.82–83.

28) Ibid., p.87.

29) Ibid., p.207.

30) Ibid., p.210.

31) Ibid., p.210.

32) C. L. Stevenson, "Persuasive Definition," *Mind*, Vol. 47(1938), p.331.

33) Ibid., p.342. See also *Ethics and Language*, p.224ff.

34) Ibid., p.342, and *Ethics and Language*, p.225.

35) Ibid., p.343, and *Ethics and Language*, p.219.

36) *Ethics and Language*, p.219ff.

37) Ibid., p.222.

38) Ibid., p.222.

39) Ibid., p.219.

40) Ibid., p.27.

41) C. L. Stevenson, "Brandt's Questions about Emotive Ethics," *The Philosophical Review*, Vol. 59(1950), pp.528–529.

42) *Ethics and Language*, pp.115–129.

43) Ibid., p.115.

44) C. L. Stevenson, "The Emotive Conception of Ethics and its Cognitive Implication," *The Philosophical Review*, Vol. 59(1950), p.303.

45) Ibid., p.296.

46) Ibid., p.297.

47) *Ethics and Language*, pp.135–136.

48) Ibid., p.136.

49) Ibid., p.138.

50) Ibid., p.139.

51) Ibid., p.139.

52) *Ethics and Language*, p.235.

53) Ibid., p.237.

54) Ibid., p.152.

55) Ibid., p.154.

56) Ibid., p.154.

57) Ibid., p.157.

58) Ibid., p.158.

59) Ibid., p.177.

60) Ibid., p.175.

61) Ibid., p.179.

62) Ibid., p.180.

63) Cf. Ibid., p.180ff.

64) Ibid., p.184.

65) Ibid., pp.180–181.

66) Ibid., p.187.

67) Ibid., p.188.

68) Ibid., p.191.

69) Ibid., p.193.

70) Ibid., p.193.

71) Cf. Ibid., pp.195–197.

72) Ibid., pp.199–200.

73) Ibid., p.201.

74) Henry D. Aiken's "Review of Stevenson: *Ethics and Language*," *The Journal of Philosophy*, Vol. 42(1945), p.467.

75) Ibid., p.461.

76) *Ethics and Language*, p.42.

77) Cf. D. H. Parker's "Review of Stevenson: *Ethics and Language*," *The Philosophical Review*, 1946, p.707.

78) Vincent Tomas. "Ethical Disagreement and the Emotive Theory of Values." *Mind*, Vol. 60(1951), pp.209–211.

79) Ibid., p.211.

80) Ibid., p.214.

81) Philip B. Rice, *On the Knowledge of Good and Evil*, New York, 1955, p.68.

82) Cf. *Ethics and Language*, pp.328–335.

83) Philip B. Rice, *On the Knowledge of Good and Evil*, p.68.

84) Frederick A. Olafson, "Meta–ethics and the Moral Life," *The Philosophical Review*, 1956, p.174, p.175.

85) *Ethics and Language*, p.1.

86) Ibid., p.319.

Chapter V. Concluding Remarks

1) R. M. Hare, *The Language of Morals*, Oxford, 1952, Ch.5.
2) Maurice Mandelbaum, *The Phenomenology of Moral Experience*, The Free Press, 1955, p.258.
3) G. E. Moore, *Principia Ethica*, p.25.
4) W. D. Ross. *Foundations of Ethics*, Oxford, 1939, p.42.
5) Ibid., p.43.
6) Ibid., p.45ff.

BIBLIOGRAPHY

I enumerate here only those books and articles that have been actually consulted in the present dissertation. An almost complete bibliography of John Dewey up to 1939 can be found in M. H. Thomas, *A Bibliography of John Dewey, 1882–1939*, Columbia University Press, 1939. R. B. Perry's writings up to 1941 are catalogued in the *Who's Who in Philosophy*, New York: Philosophical Library, 1942, pp.208–210. As for general references by other writers. see M. L. Munitz, ed., *A Modern Introduction to Ethics*, The Free Press, 1958, pp.631–632 and p.639.

I. Selected works by Ralph Barton Perry

A. Books (In chronological order)
The Moral Economy, New York, Scribner's, 1909.

General Theory of Value, New York, Longmans Green, 1926(A recent edition is published by Harvard Press, 1954).

Realms of Value, Cambridge, Harvard Press, 1954.

B. Articles (In chronological order)
"The Conception of Moral Goodness," *Philosophical Review*, Vol. 16(1907), pp.144–153.

"The Question of Moral Obligation," *International Journal of Ethics*, Vol. 21(1911) pp. 282–298.

"The Definition of Value," *Journal of Philosophy, Psychology and the Scientific Method*, Vol. 11(1914), pp.141–162.

"Dewey and Urban on Value Judgments," *Journal of Philosophy, Psychology and the Scientific Method*, Vol. 14(1917), pp.168–181.

"A Behavioristic View of Purpose," *Journal of Philosophy*, Vol. 15(1921), pp.85–105.

"Value as an Objective Predicate," *Journal of Philosophy*, Vol. 28(1931), pp.477–484.

"Value as Election and Satisfaction," *International Journal of Ethics*, Vol. 41(1931), pp.429–442.

"Value and its Moving Appeal," *The Philosophical Review*, Vol. 41(1932), pp.337–350.

"The Moral Norm of Social Science," *Journal of Social Philosophy*, Vol. 5(1939), pp.16–28.

II. Selected works by John Dewey

A. Books (In chronological order)

Outlines of a Critical Theory of Ethics, Ann Arbor, 1891(Reprinted by Hillary House, 1957).

Democracy and Education, New York, Macmillan, 1916.

Essays in Experimental Logic, Chicago, 1916.

Human Nature and Conduct, New York, Henry Holt, 1922.

Experience and Nature(2nd edition), New York, Norton, 1929.

The Quest for Certainty, New York, 1929(London, Unwin Brother's, 1930).

Ethics(In collaboration with James Tufts), 2nd edition, New York. Henry Holt, 1932.

Theory of Valuation, The University of Chicago Press, 1939.

Problems of Men, New York, Philosophical Library, 1946.

B. Articles (In chronological order)

"Logical Conditions of a Scientific Treatment of Morality," The University of Chicago Press, 1903(Reprinted also in the *Problems of Men*, New York, 1946).

"The Logic of Judgments of Practice," *Journal of Philosophy*, Vol. 12(1915), pp.505–523 and pp.533–543.

"The Objects of Valuation," *Journal of Philosophy*, Vol. 15(1918), pp.253–258.

"Valuation and Experimental Knowledge," *Philosophical Review*, Vol. 31(1922), pp.351–361.

"Values, Liking, and Thought," *Journal of Philosophy*, Vol. 20(1923), pp.617–622.

"The Meaning of Value," *Journal of Philosophy*, Vol. 22(1925), pp.126–133.
"Value, Objective Reference, and Criticism," *Philosophical Review*, Vol. 34(1925), pp.313–332.
"Anthropology and Ethics," *The Social Sciences and Their Interrelations*, edited by Ogburn and Goldenweiser, Boston, 1927, pp.24–36.

III. Selected works by Charles L. Stevenson

A. Books
Ethics and Language, New Haven, Yale University Press, 1944.

B. Articles (In chronological order)
"The Emotive Meaning of Ethical Terms," *Mind*, Vol. 46(1937), pp.14–31.
"Avoidability," *Mind*, Vol. 47(1938), pp.45–57.
"Persuasive Definitions," *Mind*, Vol. 47(1938), pp.331–350.
"Moore's Arguments Against Certain Forms of Ethical Naturalism," *The Philosophy of G. E. Moore* (edited by Schilpp), Chicago, 1942, pp.71–90.
"Meaning: Descriptive and Emotive," *Philosophical Review*, Vol. 57(1948), pp.127–144.
"The Emotive Conception of Ethics and its Cognitive Implication," *Philosophical Review*, Vol. 59(1950), pp.291–304.
"Brandt's Questions about Emotive Ethics," *Philosophical Review*, Vol. 59(1950), pp.528–534.
"Determinism and Freedom" (Unpublished).
"John Dewey's Ethics" (Unpublished).

IV. Selected works by other writers

A. Books

1. Classical works
Aristotle, *Nicomachean Ethics*.
Bentham, J., *An Introduction to the Principles of Morals and Legislation*.
Hume, D., *Enquiry Concerning the Principles of Morals*.

Kant, I., *Fundamental Principles of the Metaphysics of Morals*.

Mill, J. S., *Utilitarianism*.

Plato, *Republic*.

Price, R., *A Review of the Principal Questions in Morals*.

Sidgwick, H., *The Methods of Ethics*.

Spinoza, B., *Ethics*.

2. Contemporary writings

Ayer, A. J., *Language, Truth and Logic*, 2nd edition, London, 1946.

Broad, C. D., *Five Types of Ethical Theory*, New York, 1930.

Feldman, W. T., *The Philosophy of John Dewey*, Baltimore, Hopkins Press, 1934.

Geiger, G. R., *John Dewey in Perspective*, New York, 1958.

Hare, R. M., *The Language of Morals*, Oxford, 1954.

Hill, Thomas E., *Contemporary Ethical Theories*, Macmillan, 1950.

Lepley. R., ed., *Value*, New York. 1949.

Mandelbaum. M., *The Phenomenology of Moral Experience*, The Free Press, 1955.

Mead, M., *Sex and Temperament*, New York, Mentor, 1935.

Moore, G. E., *Principia Ethica*, Cambridge University Press, 1903.

Moore, G. E., *Ethics*, Oxford, 1912.

Pell, O. A. H., *Value–Theory and Criticism*, New York, 1930.

Prall, D. W., *A Study in the Theory of Value*, Berkley, 1921.

Rice, Philip B., *On the Knowledge of Good and Evil*, New York, 1955.

Ross, W. D., *Foundations of Ethics*, Oxford, 1939.

Russell, B., *Human Society in Ethics and Politics*, New York, 1955.

Sartre, J.-P., *Existentialism and Humanism*(translated by P. Mairet), London, 1948.

White, M., *The Age of Analysis*, Mentor Press(paper back), 1955.

Wolstein, B., *Experience and Valuation: A Study in John Dewey's Naturalism*, New York, 1949.

B. Articles

Aiken, H. D., "Review of Stevenson's *Ethics and Language*," *Journal of Philosophy*, Vol. 42(1945), pp.455–470.

Austin, J. L., "Other Minds," *Logic and Language*, 2nd Series, edited by Flew, 1951, New York, pp. 123–158.

Olafson, F. A., "Meta–ethics and the Moral Life," *Philosophical Review*, 1956, pp.159–178.

Parker, D. H., "Review of Stevenson's *Ethics and Language*," *Philosophical Review*, 1946, pp.704–707.

Prall, D. W., "In Defence of a Worthless Theory of Value," *Journal of Philosophy*, Vol. 20(1924), pp.117–125.

Price, Kingsley, "Some Doctrines of John Dewey," *1957 Year Book of Education*, Evans Brothers, 1957, pp.335–344.

Stuart, H. W., "Dewey's Ethical Theory," *The Philosophy of John Dewey*(edited by Schillp), Evanston, 1939, pp.191–333.

Tomas, V., "Ethical Disagreement and the Emotive Theory of Values," *Mind*, Vol. 60(1951). pp.205–222.

요지

이 논문의 주요 목표는 현대 윤리학의 기본 문제의 하나인 다음 물음에 대한 해답의 실마리를 찾아보려는 데 있다. "윤리적 판단의 옳고 그름을 경험적인 논거 위에서 밝힐 수 있는가? 있다면 어떠한 방법으로 어느 정도까지 그것이 가능한가?" 그러나 이 문제에 대한 접근에 앞서는 윤리적인 언표(言表)의 의미의 분석이 요구되므로, 필자는 평가적 언어의 의미에 관한 연구에 상당한 지면을 나누지 않을 수 없었다.

선택된 문제가 본래 어려움을 고려하여, 필자 스스로의 견해를 곧장 모색하기 전에 같은 문제에 대한 몇몇 위대한 사상가들의 업적을 조심성 있게 검토함이 마땅하리라는 생각이 앞섰다. 현대의 저명한 윤리학자들 가운데서, 페리(R. B. Perry), 듀이(J. Dewey) 그리고 스티븐슨(C. L. Stevenson)의 세 사람이 선택되었다. 사실은 이 세 사람의 학설에 관한 연구가 이 논문의 3분의 2 이상의 지면을 차지하고 있다. 그러한 점으로 볼 때 이 논문은 예비적인 시론(試論)의 단계를 벗어나지 못하였다.

세 사람의 학설 하나하나에 대한 정확한 파악이 먼저 시도되었고, 다음에 각자에 있어서 동의할 수 있는 점과 그렇지 못한 점을 비판적인 각도에서 찾아보았다. 마지막 장에 있어서, 세 학설에 대한 비판을 토대로 삼고 필자 자신의 잠정적인 견해의 윤곽을 그려 보았다. 그러나 그것마저 '나의 견해'라고 떳떳이 내놓을 처지는 못 된다. 마지막 장도 그 정초(定礎)는 이미 세 학자를 비롯한 여러 선철(先哲)들의 현저한 영향 밑에서 이루어졌기 때문이다.

평가적 언어의 의미에 관한 한, 이 논문의 마지막 장이 옹호한 견해는 스티븐슨의 견지에 가깝다. 그러나 몇몇 중요한 문제에 관하여 스티븐슨과 견해를 달리한 점이 있다. 스티븐슨의 견해를 떠난 각 지점에 있어서 필자의 사고는 헤어(R. M. Hare), 오스틴(J. L. Austin) 같은 영국 학자들의 시사(示唆)에 영향된 바 적지 않다. 그러나 필자는 견지를 달리하는 몇몇 학설을 단순히 결합하거나 적당히 절충해 보려는 동기에 지배된 기억은 없다. 필자 자신이 앞의 여러 장(章)에서 도달한 비판이 결론적인 하나의 장을 위한 당연한 토대가 돼야 한다는 생각을 잊지 않았다.

평가적 언명의 정당화에 관한 방법론에 이르러서는, 다른 어느 학자에 의해서보다도 듀이에 의하여 영향을 입은 바가 크다 하겠다. 방법론에 관한 논술 가운데서 마지막 여러 절은 필자 자신의 미숙하나마 독립된 사고를 표시했다고 생각한다.

마지막 한 장을 엮는 동안 필자를 지배한 것은 "더 나은 생각이 떠오를 때는 서슴지 않고 뜯어고치려는 마음의 준비만 있다면, 학도는 잠정적으로나마 일단 제 자신의 견지를 가져 보는 것이 좋다."는 신념이었다. 따라서 이 논문에서 도달된 사고에 "Concluding Remarks"라는 이름을 붙인 것은 그리 적절한 표현이 아닐지도 모른다. 이 논문의 끝을 일단 마무르기 위한 잠정적인 결론에 지나지 않기 때문이다.

편　　집 : 우송 김태길 전집 간행위원회

간행위원 : 이명현(위원장), 고봉진, 길희성, 김광수, 김도식,
　　　　　 김상배, 김영진, 박영식, 손봉호, 송상용, 신영무,
　　　　　 엄정식, 오병남, 이삼열, 이영호, 이태수, 이한구,
　　　　　 정대현, 황경식

우송 김태길 전집

윤리학 개설
Naturalism and Emotivism

지은이　　김태길

1판 1쇄 인쇄　　2010년 5월 20일
1판 1쇄 발행　　2010년 5월 25일

발행처　　철학과현실사
발행인　　전춘호

등록번호　　제1-583호
등록일자　　1987년 12월 15일

서울특별시 종로구 동숭동 1-45
전화번호 579-5908
팩시밀리 572-2830

ISBN 978-89-7775-711-0　94100
　　　 978-89-7775-706-6　(전15권)
값 20,000원

●잘못된 책은 교환해 드립니다.